J. A. Rogers

J. A. ROGERS

Selected Writings

Edited by Louis J. Parascandola

THE UNIVERSITY
OF TENNESSEE PRESS
Knoxville

First Edition.

LIBRARY OF CONGRESS CATALOGING-IN-PUBLICATION DATA
Names: Rogers, J. A. (Joel Augustus), 1880–1966. | Parascandola, Louis J., 1952– editor.
Title: J. A. Rogers : selected writings / edited by Louis J. Parascandola.
Description: [First edition.] | Knoxville : The University of Tennessee Press, [2023] | Includes bibliographical references and index. |
Summary: "Largely self-educated, Joel Augustus Rogers spoke several languages and researched archives throughout the world in search of Black history. He was known as the 'people's historian,' devoting his life, alongside his supporters Marcus Garvey and Arturo Schomburg, to chronicling Black life to counter the negative stereotypes prevalent in the first half of the twentieth century. His numerous newspaper columns exhibited a gift for speaking to the average person yet were well-researched enough to earn praise from his more formally trained contemporaries, including W. E. B. Du Bois and Hubert H. Harrison. Surprisingly, Rogers's works, with the notable exception of the two-volume *World's Great Men of Color*, have not been published by mainstream presses and are only available in unannotated electronic editions"—Provided by publisher.
Identifiers: LCCN 2023013321 (print) | LCCN 2023013322 (ebook) | ISBN 9781621907725 (hardcover) | ISBN 9781621907732 (pdf)
Subjects: LCSH: Rogers, J. A. (Joel Augustus), 1880–1966. | African Americans—History. | United States—Race relations—20th century. | Pan-Africanism. | BISAC: LITERARY COLLECTIONS / American / African American & Black | HISTORY / African American & Black
Classification: LCC E185.61 .R726 2023 (print) | LCC E185.61 (ebook) | DDC 305.896/073—dc23/eng/20230425

LC record available at https://lccn.loc.gov/2023013321
LC ebook record available at https://lccn.loc.gov/2023013322

Contents

Acknowledgments

This project has been finished, in fits and starts, over a decade. During those years, there were many people whose encouragement and support allowed for its completion. I would like to thank some of those people below:

My undergraduate and graduate classes at Long Island University, Brooklyn, where I taught about Rogers in several courses on West Indians in the Harlem Renaissance. Whenever he was introduced, the interest and enthusiasm of the students demonstrated to me the need to make his writings more easily available.

Several of my graduate students, some research assistants, aided me, particularly Rajul Punjabi, Yani Perez, Alex Dermody, Willie Perdomo, and Malik Crumpler. Tiani Kennedy especially stands out for reading and commenting on much of the manuscript. You guys were often my teachers (and friends) as well as my students.

I thank my colleagues at LIU, especially my chairs, Vidhya Swaminathan and Leah Dilworth, for their support. In addition, I thank LIU for providing some needed travel funds and for granting a sabbatical which made much of the writing possible.

Many scholars have encouraged my work on early Caribbean American writers including Barbara Bair, Robert Bone, Louis Chude-Sokei, James Davis, Rhonda D. Frederick, Heather Hathaway, Gary Edward Holcomb, George Hutchinson, Winston James, Michael Niblett, Carl Pedersen, Kenneth Ramchand, Amritjit Singh, Michelle A. Stephens, and especially Carl A. Wade.

My thanks to pioneering Rogers' researchers including Linda Ray Peters, Valerie Sandoval, Malik Simba, Joyce Moore Turner, W. Burghardt Turner, and particularly Thabiti Asukile.

My editor, Thomas G. Wells, had unfailing faith in this project. I would also like to thank editorial assistant Jonathan Boggs, designer

Kelly Gray, and the rest of the staff at the University of Tennessee Press for their help and support. In addition, I thank the anonymous reviewers of the manuscript whose suggestions, and sometimes criticisms, helped make this a better book.

Thanks to Suzanna Tamminen, editor in chief at Wesleyan University Press, for allowing me to reprint several of Rogers's works.

Thanks to Balsa for indexing.

Many libraries provided access to necessary resources. Two in particular stand out: Fisk University, where Rogers' papers are housed, and the Schomburg Library, part of New York Public Library. Pre-Covid-19 I made several trips to Nashville to utilize the Rogers Papers in the Special Collections of the John Hope and Aurelia E. Franklin Library at Fisk University. There, librarian DeLisa M. Harris aided me and allowed me permission (through Helga Rogers' donation of her husband's papers to Fisk) to publish certain Rogers' material. Since Covid-19, with Fisk's library unavailable to visitors, Brynna Farris has been an invaluable source, sending me material, including two wonderful photos of Rogers. Closer to home, the Schomburg Library has, as always, proven to be a seminal source for my research. It is a blessing to have it in my backyard and to have such knowledgeable and helpful staff to assist researchers. Hillary Lindsay and Maira Liriano have gone above and beyond their job requirements helping me locate material, maneuver cranky microfilm to get the best images, and to even make suggestions on interpreting sometimes difficult-to-read passages.

On a more personal level, I wish to thank my ever reliable family members. John, my "younger" older brother, has been a great source of support and encouragement, reading parts of the manuscript and offering helpful suggestions. The Nero family again has provided sustenance and support. They remain my in-house advisors on all things Caribbean.

My greatest debt goes to the two women to whom this book is dedicated: One I barely know while the other is one who knows me better than anyone else. I had the briefest of correspondence with Helga

Rogers Andrews many years ago, yet even then, I could see her devotion to spreading the message of her late husband. She made his books available for years. And she made sure that his work would be preserved before her passing by donating his papers to Fisk, thereby making them accessible to interested parties. My wife, Shondel Nero, continues to be my greatest source of strength. My work would be much less rich without her and my life even less so. I thank her again for always being there for me to lean on, to provide advice and encouragement, and to share the good times. I look forward to more life, love, and adventures together.

Introduction

> Expression of ourselves must come from ourselves.
> And before we can feelingly do so, we have much to unlearn.
>
> —J. A. ROGERS, *As Nature Leads*, 1919

> I felt I have looked into books and dug up buried knowledge that many college professors or doctors of philosophy do not know exist, because just as there is a life in the deeper depths of the ocean of which the average fisherman knows nothing so there are depths in the ocean of research of which some of the most learned have never dreamed.
>
> —J. A. ROGERS, *Sex and Race*, 1944

As scholar Henry Louis Gates, Jr. contends, Joel Augustus (J. A.) Rogers was a major—in many cases the only—source for the ordinary Black person to learn of their history from the 1920s through the '70s (Gates 3–7). They certainly did not get it in their schools and universities or find out about it in mainstream newspapers and books. The vast majority of historians had largely ignored or distorted it, questioning whether there even was such a thing as Black history. Rogers brought the idea of Black history to the fore, maintaining that the conventional scholars had a blind spot about the legacy of the African Diaspora, and he attempted to provide a corrective lens through which to see what had been omitted or falsely presented in the dominant narrative. In this way Black people and their history and culture could be understood in a proper, unbiased light by both Blacks and whites. He does this largely by using biography, grounded in solid research and facts, to instruct the reader and to dispel myths. The findings that this anti-racist was able to uncover are nothing short of remarkable in presenting little-known Black achievements in history while simultaneously pointing out the absurdity of any biological notion of "race."

To understand how Rogers came to his findings, one must start by learning something about the man himself. This is especially important for someone who is not a well-studied figure and for someone who himself so heavily valued the importance of biography. Much of Rogers's early life is somewhat sketchy. What we do know often comes from his wife, Helga Biesenthal Rogers Andrews, a German government translator whom he married in 1957 (Helga Martha [Rogers] Andrews "Obituary") and a couple of his essays containing bits of autobiographical material.[1] Rogers was born in Negril, Jamaica, on September 6, 1880 (some sources say 1883). His father Samuel was a schoolteacher and a Methodist minister, and his mother Emily (Johnstone) bore four children before her death in 1886. Although Rogers's father was a teacher, he was never able to provide more than "a good basic education" (Helga Rogers qtd. in J. A. Rogers *One Hundred Amazing Facts* 7) for his children. However, the limited schooling Rogers had helped to bring about his lifelong interest in Black history, although probably not in the way his teachers desired: "I think it really began in my early childhood when it was firmly impressed on me by the ruling classes that black people were inherently inferior." He goes on to elaborate, "My Sunday School teacher, an almost unmixed Negro, told us that black people were cursed by God and doomed to eternal servitude to white people because Ham had laughed at his drunken father, Noah. To clinch his argument, he read to us from the Bible, which we were taught was infallible" ("How and Why This Book Was Written" 1). These offhand comments from a teacher, remarkably similar to ones his friend Arturo Schomburg had also heard as a youngster, were seared into his memory, and helped to shape his future (Sinnette 13). Unable to accept what he had heard, especially coming from someone who looked like him, he decided to devote his life to challenging this assumption of Black inferiority in any manner he could.

After finishing primary school, Rogers advanced his learning by reading from his uncle's extensive library. He attempted unsuccessfully to gain a scholarship to continue his education. The inability to afford a better education wounded Rogers deeply. He enlisted in the British army, serving with the Royal Garrison Artillery for four years until a heart murmur was discovered, ending his military career. With limited educational and career opportunities in Jamaica, Rogers decided to emigrate to the United States in 1906, during the period defined by historian Rayford Logan as the Nadir (1877–1914), a time marked by white backlash to the Black gains made during Reconstruction (74–96). The Ku Klux Klan was revived during this period and lynchings were on the rise. White historians such as John Burgess (*Reconstruction and the Constitution* 1902) and William Dunning (*Reconstruction Political and Economic* 1907) were redefining recent history through a racist lens that matched the mood of the period (Simba 47–52). This is the America into which Rogers had emigrated.

Upon his arrival in the United States, Rogers stayed briefly in New York City and Boston before settling in Chicago in 1908. He had hoped to study at the University of Chicago but could not gain admittance since he lacked a high school diploma. So, instead, he studied commercial art at the Chicago Art Institute while working as a Pullman porter from 1909–19. Rogers used his time on the railroad to read, to study human nature, and to indulge his love of travel (Rogers "Young Novelist" 3). However, during these years, he witnessed and endured himself many demeaning experiences. Being a Pullman porter was a much-sought-after position, given that it was a steady, decent paying job, one that put him on the path to the Black Middle Class; nevertheless, it was also challenging employment, one where Blacks often had to endure torturous insults from white passengers determined to humiliate them at every opportunity. Despite these demeaning experiences and unlike the vast majority of early Caribbean immigrants who generally chose not to become naturalized, Rogers became an American citizen in 1917.

After his stint with the railroad, Rogers decided to use his pen to earn a living, beginning as a reporter with the Chicago *Enterprise*. Feeling there were better journalistic opportunities in New York City, he relocated there in 1921. His first job was as an assistant editor for the *Daily Negro Times*, published by Marcus Garvey, whom Rogers had known briefly while both were living in Jamaica. After that publication soon folded, he began writing for several Negro newspapers including Garvey's *Negro World* and the socialist *Messenger* before starting long-running columns with the New York *Amsterdam News* and the Pittsburgh *Courier*. He would go on to write for many other disparate journals, both white and Black owned, popular, and more scholarly, including Du Bois' National Association of the Advancement of Colored People (N.A.A.C.P.), *The Crisis*, H. L. Mencken's *American Mercury*, the National Urban League's *Opportunity*, the Civil Rights era *Freedomways*, the academic *Review of Nations*, and the humanistic *International Review*. His reporting was based both on events in the United States and the global scene. He worked for the *Courier* as an international correspondent, frequently based in Paris, where he lived for several years. While working with the *Courier*, he was assigned to cover the Italo-Ethiopian War (1935–37), becoming the first Black foreign war correspondent. Rogers's journalistic career, often undervalued in discussions of him, formed one of the "major contributions to black print culture in the 20th century" (Asukile "Black International Journalism" 323).

Whether in journalistic pieces or his larger book-length works, Rogers's writing is steeped in Black history and culture. He has often been described as writing "vindicationist history." Such historians are said to maintain that certain groups have been undervalued and vindicationalists attempt to correct this (Drake 4). However, as Edward Bryan Cooper Owens points out, Rogers's work was more than this. Writers such as Rogers "constructed a parallel historiography and structure for African history" and cultural diffusion that was in opposition to Western history" (Owens 54). Rogers is unconventional in many ways; he was a historian not formally trained, one of a small cadre of what Earl Thorpe describes as "historians without portfolio" (143–53). Although he lacked the "portfolio," the academic pedigree normally expected of the serious researcher, he did not lack the skills of even a "W. E. B. Du Bois and Carter G. Woodson" (Gates 4). In fact, Du Bois said that despite his lack of academic credentials, "no man living has revealed so many important facts about the Negro race as has Rogers" (Du Bois *World and Africa* 185). Rogers himself said, "I go to as great pains as any of the most conscientious of these experts to get my facts straight, checking and re-checking, and travelling hither and yon to see with my own eyes whenever possible what I am writing about; and quoting only from the original sources and from those I have reason to believe are the most reliable. One can do no more" (Rogers "Remarks on the First Two Volumes of *Sex and Race*"). Yet as an uncredentialed researcher and as a Black man, Rogers was often dismissed by mainstream academic historians. He had no team of researchers, no foundations, no academic institutions to support him. He did his research on his own while supporting himself by working demanding day jobs and, when he could find time, giving talks about his findings. All his books were initially self-published, in part because Black people in his writings were not presented as "clown or victims," their usual image in published works (Rogers, Pittsburgh *Courier* December 1, 1945). Despite these obstacles, Rogers taught himself four languages—French, Spanish, German, and Portuguese—and managed to utilize many of the great libraries in Europe and America. Rogers also used unconventional sources in his research, going "off the beaten track of the college curriculum" and thus finding unexpected answers which were not always accepted by the scholars ("Remarks"). On the other hand, Rogers's unusual background with respect to academic training allowed him to appeal to a more popular audience, "advancing what he considers 'commonsense' explanations of discrimination and segregation" (Drake 99). The thoroughness of his research is apparent in the many notebooks he kept, available in the Rogers papers at Fisk University.

Rogers did this research because he considered that "history was . . . an essential tool in counteracting racism" (Moore Turner 68). He was a firm believer that if Blacks learned of their past achievements, which had been omitted by most historians, they would look at themselves with pride, and if whites learned about these achievements, they would not treat Blacks in an inferior manner. This was a similar concept as that posited by such Black leaders of the time as sociologist Charles S. Johnson, editor of *Opportunity*, and Howard University professor Alain Locke, who maintained that overall advancement for the race could be made through cultural and artistic success and an understanding of Black history. Education about Black achievements by both whites and Blacks was key for these events to occur. Rogers wrote for Blacks "to provide sources they could turn to when arguing about racism. For whites his strategy was to impress on their minds the many great contributions and accomplishments the Black man has presented to world culture, which in itself refutes a number of justifications given for racism" (Peters 13).

Rogers attempted this process of education via two avenues: biography and race-mixing/ intermarriage (Turner 36; Willis 342). The best examples of his biographical work, documenting the achievements of Blacks, are his books *One Hundred Amazing Facts about the Negro with Proof* (1934); *Your History* (1940), thumbnail illustrated sketches of famous Black people; and the two-volume *The World's Great People of Color 3000 B.C. to 1946 A. D.* (1946–47), 200 short biographies. Rogers felt that biography, which shows the best and worst of people, "will ever be the highest and most civilizing form of literature" ("How and Why This Book Was Written"). His essays are "principally success stories, chiefly for Negro youth" ("How"). We see an example of the power of such education in the fictionalized conversation between a Black Pullman porter and a racist senator in *From Superman to Man* (1917). That such a hard-core racist as the senator can finally recognize his own biases through the porter's teachings and do something about it shows that, for Rogers, change is possible. Since he maintained that racism was something learned, not innate, it could also be unlearned.

A core belief of Rogers, then, was that education was central to disproving the dubious concept of racial categorization. When Rogers began writing in the 1910s and '20s, scientific racism, buttressed by "evidence" utilizing anthropology, biology, and other developing sciences and pseudo-sciences, was being employed to depict Black people as inferior or even a different species entirely than whites. Eugenicists often embraced the long-discredited theory of polygenesis, the concept that there were multiple origins for humanity. Rogers challenged these ideas, arguing that racism could only be combated by disproving that there are "pure" racial groups with some being better than others, and instead advocating that we are all of one race, humans. This is evident in the essay "Is Black Ever White?" in which Rogers disputes the whole notion of race: "I see but one American people, speaking a common language, and at bottom having a common ideal, shading in color by imperceptible degrees from white or black, or black to white, as you will." Several of Rogers's works including *As Nature Leads* (1919), the three-volume *Sex and Race* (1941–44), and *Nature Knows No Color-Line* (1952) speak of the futility of attempting to stop racial mixing and even arguing for the possible benefits such mixtures could bring. In these works, Rogers "contends that it is inevitable that black and white will have the urge to mix, and always will do so, despite the most virulent opposition and stringent regulation" (Sandoval 6).

Rogers's belief in the necessity for whites and Blacks to work together to combat racism caused him to reject Black Nationalist groups such as Marcus Garvey's Universal Negro Improvement Association (U. N. I. A.). However, his optimism about the inevitability of the races coming together did not mean that he turned a blind eye to the problems of such a possible occurrence. Although he felt like-minded whites and Blacks would have to join forces to change the situation, he was suspicious that whites would try to manipulate Blacks in any organizations; therefore, he questioned radical socialist and communist groups that stressed class rather than race, viewing them as often ignoring the unique challenges faced by Blacks. He was equally suspicious of groups favoring assimilation like the N. A. A. C. P. and the National

Urban League, which he feared were ruled by their white members and financiers. He had a firm belief that Blacks needed to have control over and a powerful voice in whatever organization they belonged to that was having a say about their conditions in America.

Rogers also was aware of the extent of racial prejudice. This is apparent in his interview with Earnest Sevier Cox and John Powell, two leaders of the Anglo-Saxon Clubs of America, a well-heeled national white-power group in 1926. It is also evident in his powerful pamphlet on the *Ku Klux Klan Spirit* in 1923, published during the height of the resurgence of the terrorist group. His militancy in resisting supposed white superiority is evident in his essay "Who Is the New Negro, and Why?" (1927), where he praised the courage and pride of the New Negro, tracing this fighting spirit back to the leaders of slave rebellions, Nat Turner and Denmark Vesey. This New Negro is unafraid of being labeled "rebel, atheist, pagan, infidel, Socialist, Red, heathen, radical . . . [.] He will be anything but a sheep."

Rogers is not only concerned with historical and political issues. He posits that the image of Blacks is also expressed through art and culture as well. This is demonstrated in interviews with key Black performers such as Josephine Baker and in his seminal essay "Jazz at Home," published first in *Survey Graphic* and then in the groundbreaking anthology *The New Negro* (1925). In this essay he maintains that jazz is a quintessential Negro form that is a contribution to America as well as the world. It is a "tonic" to soothe a society maddened by technology. As Thabiti Asukile states, the article is a significant piece on the history of jazz ("'Jazz at Home'" 23).

Like such race leaders as Du Bois and Garvey, Rogers believes in the credo of racial uplift through art, that the creative work should present realistic, ordinary Black people and not stereotypes that pander to white audiences. In his own fictional writings such as *From Superman to Man*, *As Nature Leads*, *Blood-Money*, and *She Walks in Beauty*, there are no racial stereotypes. The works provide what he would call "aspiration" and supply positive models and lessons for his readers much in the same manner as his essays. To Rogers, the reader should come away from a work of literature feeling he or she has learned something, ideally something that will make the reader feel proud about himself/herself and the race. In that way the race will advance.

Rogers judges other artists' works by the same high standards that he holds for his own writings. The arts should, according to Rogers, advance the race in the same manner as social and political forces. His reviews of literary works, written by Blacks or whites, show his concern about the image of the Negro. He dislikes Claude McKay's *Home to Harlem*, the first African American novel to top the New York *Times*' best-seller list, because of its depiction of the unsavory side of Black life. His review of white novelist Margaret Mitchell's blockbuster *Gone with the Wind* criticizes the author for romanticizing the South during slavery and the Civil War; therefore, she is perpetuating rather than correcting the historical myth around the Lost Cause. On the other hand, he praises Richard Wright's autobiography *Black Boy* because its gritty but realistic portrayal of urban life is presented "clearly and vividly." It is a book that he thinks "can do an immense amount of good."

Of course, many of Rogers's unconventional positions met with stiff resistance. His views on literature, for example, would be challenged by some of the younger Black writers such as Langston Hughes, Eric Walrond, and Claude Mc Kay who felt his ideas of racial uplift were too conservative and overly concerned with how whites view the Negro. As Hughes stated in his artistic manifesto "The Negro Artist and the Racial Mountain": "We younger Negro artists who create now intend to express our individual dark-skinned selves without fear or shame. If white people are pleased we are glad, If they are not, it doesn't matter" (qtd. in Levering Lewis 95). The debate between "art and propaganda" was one that was widely argued through the Harlem Renaissance years, and Rogers with his writings and through his forum as a well-known journalist would be at the center of it. As scholar Joyce Turner Moore states, "he contributed to the outpouring of essays that spawned the Harlem Renaissance" (68).

Some of Rogers's hypotheses on racial matters were even more controversial and continue to be today, in part because they challenge some still prevailing ideas. His claiming of Black ancestry for a number of notable people normally thought of as white met with harsh reaction from many people who wanted to think of their heroes as being from their race. Sometimes this was because of race prejudice, but sometimes because they, including Black people, simply did not want "the present knowledge in their brains disturbed" (Rogers "Remarks"). However, we must recall one of Rogers's core contentions: that the idea of race is preposterous, so to him speaking of Black achievements is no different than praising white achievements. We are all simply humans. The difference is that whites looked down on Blacks and sometimes did not even credit them for their successes.

This brings us to what, as Wilson Moses rightly points out, is the central paradox in Rogers's work: that he is both celebrating the contributions that Blacks have made to civilization, while at the same time claiming that there are no separate races, Black, white, or anything else. As Moses states, "The bitter joke that underlies all of J. A. Rogers's work is his thorough commitment to the idea that race is a meaningless concept" (43). However, Rogers was also aware that although there was no biological support for the concept of race, there certainly was a social construction of it, one that has been used for centuries to create a hierarchy with Europeans on the top and Africans on the bottom. It was an insidiously developed system perpetuated by whites to the detriment of people of color. This was particularly the case in the late 19th century and first-half of the 20th century when fields such as anthropology and biology were often marshaled in the cause of white superiority. So, pointing out that people who have been thought of as being white had some Black blood, enough to classify them in many states as Negroes, disrupted how both Blacks and whites could think about themselves.

The idea of race-mixing, of course, destroys white myths of racial purity. For Rogers, nothing is more ridiculous than the idea that any "race" is pure; it simply flies in the face of scientific evidence. If anyone's history can be traced back far enough, none of us is composed of all one race or ethnicity. Today, a simple swab of saliva can quickly dispel anyone's notions that all his or her DNA is from one group; however, Rogers was not blessed with such scientific evidence, so he had to do the back-breaking work of checking sources, finding evidence, and using illustrations to confirm his findings. What he uncovers in books such as *Sex and Race* and *Nature Knows No Color-Line* is disturbing to many readers, especially ones who maintain that 1/16th, or even 1/32nd part of one's blood is enough to determine one's "race." Thus, whites' own racial formula is preventing many people they would like to claim from being considered "white." For those in the South simply looking around them showed how much racial-mixing existed. It must have been terrifying for whites to be wondering what generations of their ancestors they had never even known might have been doing over a hundred years ago and when that dark secret might emerge and show their own hidden racial identity. As Henry Louis Gates, Jr. states, "There are a *lot* of white people with 'hidden African ancestry,' and they don't have to look too far back in time to find it" (284). It was often too painful for them to accept as in Rogers's novel "Blood-Money" where one wealthy white character pays a fortune in blackmail to prevent her alleged Black blood from being revealed.

Rogers's belief that Egyptians were Black was also a frightening thought for many whites, particularly when one considers how much the ancient Greeks and Romans, the major source of Western Civilization, owed to the Egyptians as well as the Ethiopians. He writes on this in such essays as "Ethiopia and Egypt Made Nordic Civilization Possible," Pittsburgh *Courier* (April 30, 1927) and "Roman Ideas of Life Come from Ethiopia," Pittsburgh *Courier* (May 28, 1927). Of course, books can (and have) been written about the melanin level of the ancient Egyptians, but that is not my purpose here. One must also remember that Rogers based his views on the research available to him, not recent DNA tests that suggest ancient Egyptians were genetically closer to those of the Middle East than modern-day Egyptians (Watson). The debate over whether the Egyptians were Black or not goes back to Classical Greece when historians such as Strabo, Diodorus, and Herodotus spoke about the dark complexions of Egyptians. Rogers was a strong supporter of the theory that the ancient Egyptians were Black and that from them have sprung the origins of Western civilization. He maintained that "Egypt had a profound influence on Greece and not the other way around, that the White man's civilization was only a continuation of African civilizations of antiquity" (Helga Rogers, qtd. in J. A. Rogers *100 Amazing Facts* 9). Whatever our views on the matter, Rogers's contentions about the ancient Egyptians did help to usher in further scientific and historical inquiry on the subject. His findings encouraged a group of scholars often better armed to conduct their research than he was. These include John Henrik Clarke (*African People in World History*), Chancellor Williams (*The Destruction of Black Civilization*), Martin Bernal (*Black Athena*), Basil Davidson (*Africa in History*), Frank Snowden (*Blacks in Antiquity*), and Cheikh Anta Diop (*The African Origin of Civilization*) among others. A scholar like Martha Hodes "follows trails taken by Rogers, trails to sources once considered suspect, too subjective, for real historiography" (Pinckney 51). Many of the findings of these academics encounter the same lively challenges as Rogers faced from modern scholars such as Mary Lefkowitz (*Not Out of Africa* and *Black Athena Revisited*) and Stephen Howe (*Afrocentrism: Mythical Pasts and Imagined Homes*). Lefkowitz, in fact, was highly critical of Rogers' findings (*Not Out of Africa* 30–42).

The real value of reading Rogers today, however, is not necessarily to find definitive answers to the problematic questions he often raises. One reads him for what other historians have often either inadvertently or deliberately omitted. As historian Lerone Bennett states, Rogers's most important contribution may be "the carrying of the history of black people to the masses long before it was popular" ("Scholars Mourn," 27). In the words of Henry Louis Gates Jr., because of Rogers, "the field of black history has never been stronger" (7). He challenges our more conventional thinking and makes us question our own, sometimes racist, assumptions. His subject matter remains topical on many contentious matters. For example, his 1963 article "Civil War Centennial, Myth and Reality" examines a subject much in the news today, the treatment of the Confederate flag and monuments honoring the Civil War. The argument is almost identical to the one that still rages.

African novelist Chimamanda Ngozie Adichie astutely speaks of the danger of having only one story (TED Talks). Rogers provides another narrative that has too long been ignored. As he himself said, he is not attempting to write world history: he is writing "the bran of history," the part that has been bleached out by "white imperialist propaganda." As he also said, "Those who will forget their orthodoxy for a while and read my books might not find them so fantastic after all. And even should they reject them they might still profit to the extent of knowing the arguments on the other side and thus be able to refute them, not by denunciation, but in a manner more compatible with common sense" ("Remarks").

Rogers offers a unique platform for scholars of Black history and other interested parties to wrestle with some of the complex questions around the psychological, structural, and material consequences of racism and identity that we still, often uncomfortably, struggle with today. His work can provide a starting point for this necessary conversation, particularly in the classroom. As Wilson Moses observes, "The best way for a sophisticated college teacher to approach Rogers is not to oppose him but to show students that he was an absolute antiracist" (43). Rogers makes us question what we consider sources for knowledge. Do they always have to come from the standardized methods and materials and from the so-called experts that we often use to measure facts, or can our knowledge also be derived from lesser studied venues, from oral and visual material as well as the written, which is often privileged, and can they even come from people outside the academy? Whether one agrees or not with all his conclusions, Rogers provides a much-needed forum to reflect on and possibly even rethink things we always took for granted that we knew. In the words of George Schuyler, "We all owe a tremendous debt to people like . . . J. A. Rogers . . . who have chronicled our past and thus strengthened our pride and resolution to prepare in the present for a brighter future."

Rogers would never give up the task of writing and educating. During his lifetime, he had been honored to be a member of the Paris Society for Anthropology, the International Congress of Anthropology, the American Geographical Society, and the American Academy of Political Science. He held his post as a columnist for the *Courier* until his death on March 26, 1966, at St. Clare's Hospital in New York. He is buried in Ferncliff Cemetery and Mausoleum in Hartsdale, New York. Even on the day he had the stroke that hastened his death, Rogers had been visiting a museum in Washington D.C. to do research for one of his projects. This dedication to his work typifies Rogers's life. As John Henrik Clarke said of him: "In the books of J. A. Rogers an attempt has been made to locate Africa's proper place on the maps of human geography. That is what his life and research were about" (1:xi). However, his many articles and books, most of which went through numerous editions and are still widely available today, are his real legacy, kept alive by the demands of the common reader to whom his work was always addressed.

Notes on the Selections and the Text

CHOOSING THE PIECES for an anthology on an author as prolific and as topical as J. A. Rogers can be challenging. The guide, to me, was to provide a representative sample of work spanning his almost fifty-year career from 1917 to 1963. Thus, I chose writings which exemplify his major interests such as Black heritage, identity and self-identification, anti-racism, social justice, racial construction, and racial mixing. To get a sense of the development of his ideology over the years, it seemed best to organize the works chronologically. As Rogers's reading and research increased, in large part through his extensive travels, his thinking deepened, and his writing tended to become more like the traditional scholar with such apparatus as footnotes and illustrations to buttress his argument; however, his writings remained lucent and understandable to the common reader in a way most such works are not. Even when the books went into later editions, he added this new information, but never altered his basic premise.

Although the situations that drove Rogers's writings changed over the years, his essential beliefs tended to stay remarkably consistent as is reflected in the constancy of themes. Virtually all of his writings are eerily prescient and what we would call today anti-racist. His first work included here, for example, the conversation between a Black Pullman porter and a racist politician in *From Superman to Man*, is innovative for its time in its blend of fiction and non-fiction and in its subject matter, that the notion of race is socially constructed, and not based on biology. His last piece included, the powerful essay, "Civil War Centennial,

Myth and Reality," published in the important Civil Rights journal *Freedomways*, criticizes the celebration of the flag of the Confederacy and monuments to its heroes and, more importantly, the racism that these powerful symbols continue to manifest. That the issues Rogers discussed remain frighteningly modern shows how intractable they remain. They also show how Rogers is simultaneously a product of his time and often ahead of it. Despite Rogers's vast knowledge of the uphill battle he was fighting to correct historical blind spots, he remained optimistic about his undertaking, maintaining a lifelong belief that the only way things can ultimately be changed is through education. People need to be told of history truthfully without the filter of racial prejudice. This was the unchanging core of Rogers's philosophy.

The selections in this anthology provide some tantalizing chunks from the several books he wrote, including samples from all four of his published works of fiction (there is also a manuscript for another novel *Golden Galleons* in Rogers's papers at Fisk University). I have been unable to locate another fictional work, *The Golden Door*, which is listed in some sources as being from 1927. In addition to his fictional works, there are complete biographical sketches and anthropological essays from the works he may be best known for today: *World's Great Men of Color* and *Sex and Race*. Also included are essays published in such important journals as W. E. B. Du Bois' *Crisis* , the iconoclastic H. L. Mencken's *American Mercury*, Charles S. Johnson's *Opportunity*, Marcus Garvey's *Negro World*, and A. Philip Randolph and Chandler Owen's socialist *Messenger*. Rogers is likely one of the few authors to be published in so many disparate venues often with conflicting editorial policies, which speaks to how widely respected he was. In the words of Richard B. Moore, "Rogers had the capacity to get along with people even when he saw things from the opposite point of view" (quoted in Turner Moore 68). Finally, there are articles from his long-running columns for the important Black newspapers, the New York *Amsterdam News* and the Pittsburgh *Courier*. These range from interviews with such notables as Emperor Haile Selassie, Black Nationalist Marcus Garvey, writer Claude Mc Kay, and performer Josephine Baker. He also writes articles on his travels throughout Europe and the Jim-Crow South, focusing on what he felt was the systemic racism embedded in the societal structures of the United States and Great Britain as compared to France and the rest of Europe.

I have tried to present works in their entirety if possible; thus, the bulk of the over forty pieces included are complete. However, some works are too long, and some are too dense and would need extensive notes for many modern readers. In the instances where omissions are necessary, they are indicated by a type ornament (❧). It is hoped that when excerpts are utilized, the pieces will spur the reader on to examine them in their entirety.

Although the writings are from a variety of publications with different editorial standards and with different manners of copyediting, I have attempted to be faithful to the original sources as much as possible. Rogers had an unconventional sense of punctuation and often employed the British spellings of his youth (e.g., colour, travelled), and I have kept those as is. Errors of places and names of people are also kept as is in the text, but are emended in my end notes. I have silently corrected a few obvious typographical errors.

Rogers was incredibly well-read, and he makes extensive use of what he has learned. I have provided end notes (numbered sequentially restarting after each selection) for references that may be unfamiliar to the modern reader. Rogers also sometimes utilized his own notes. Those are marked by asterisks (*) and are located at the end of each piece in which they appear.

Rogers' works were published privately, the early editions in fairly small numbers. It is virtually impossible to find copies of some of these editions, but I have used the earliest texts that were available to me. In most cases, these were first editions, providing an opportunity for readers to see Rogers's writings as he originally intended them. This is particularly important in cases such as *World's Great Men of Color*, later republished by Simon and Schuster, which made many changes from the original text, sometimes omitting entire sentences. It surely would have irritated Rogers to see a term like Jim Crow used instead of his preferred jim-crow.

Excerpt: *From Superman to Man* (1917)

Rogers worked as a Pullman porter[1] from 1909 to 1919, when his earnings helped defray the cost of his studies at the Chicago Art Institute. Rogers utilized his experience as a porter in *From Superman to Man*. He employed a combination of partially fictionalized autobiography and "[h]istory, sociology, anthropology, psychology, economics and politics—even theology" (Harrison 300). It is a form that Darryl Pinckney calls a "discussion novel" (13). The narrator, Dixon, was a thinly veiled mouthpiece for Rogers to address race relations in America. Using the narrative device of an extended series of conversations between an Ivy-league educated Black porter, forced to work at a job beneath him, and an ignorant but powerful white politician, was a brilliant choice by Rogers. Much like Chaucer utilized a pilgrimage in *The Canterbury Tales* to bring together many people who would not intermingle in normal social situations, the train trip from Chicago to the West Coast allowed a more natural setting to unite two people from very different social classes. Rogers himself stated that the job as a porter allowed "the first hand opportunity to study human nature as few people have" (Pittsburgh *Courier* May 10, 1924). Dixon (ironically named after Thomas Dixon[2]) bravely and very cleverly refutes all the racist politician's arguments about Black inferiority. By the end of the three-day journey, the flummoxed politician must admit defeat at the hands of the lowly porter whose argument has been ably augmented by a massive amount of factual information largely taken from white sources. Thus, Rogers dismantles white privilege and shows "the stupidity of racism" (Turner 34). In this manner, the white "superman"

has been reduced to a mere mortal, and the story serves as, in the words of a Brooklyn *Daily Eagle* reviewer, "a vindication of the American Negro" (cited in Turner 35). That even such a hard-core racist as the senator can finally recognize his own ignorance demonstrates one of Rogers's fundamental beliefs, that racial prejudice is not an inherent trait but one that can be eradicated through education. The hybrid novel went through several editions, each adding more material. It has remained one of Rogers's most important writings, one that W. E. B. Du Bois urged people to "buy, read and recommend" ("An Array of Books"). For an excellent discussion of the book, see Thabiti Asukile, "Joel Augustus Rogers's Race Vindication: A Chicago Pullman Porter & the Making of the [*sic*] *From Superman to Man* (1917)," *The Western Journal of Black Studies* 35.4 (2011): 281–93; see also the two reviews of the book by Hubert H. Harrison, Rogers's contemporary, reprinted in *A Hubert Harrison Reader*, pp. 299–305. This excerpt is taken from the second edition of 1917 (Goodspeed Press).

FROM SUPERMAN TO MAN

First Day.

The limited was speeding to California over the snow-blanketed prairies of Iowa. On car Bulwer, the passengers had all retired, and Dixon, the porter, his duties finished, sought the more comfortable warmth of the smoker, where he intended to resume the reading of the book he had brought with him—Finot's "Race Prejudice."[3]

When the train started again Dixon returned to the smoker and resumed his reading. But too tired to concentrate his thoughts on the scientific matter he closed the volume, placed it behind him in the hollow formed by his back and the angle of the seat and began to reflect on the passage he had just read: "The doctrine of inequality is emphatically a science of white peoples, it is they who have invented it." This recalled to him some of the many falsities, current about his people. He thought of how in nearly all the large libraries of the United States in which he had been permitted to enter, he had found books advancing all sorts of theories to prove his people were inferior. Some of these theories even denied them human origin. He went on to reflect on the discussions he had heard on the cars and other places from time to time, and of what he called, the heirloom ideas that many persons had concerning the different varieties of the human race. These discussions he went on to reflect had been the means of his acquiring a fund of knowledge as he would note any opinion that he thought incorrect and look it up in the works of the standard authors. These facts once ascertained, he would keep in the same notebook.

"Your book, George?"[4]

"Yes, sir."

"What is it about?"

"Oh, only a scientific work," said the other, carelessly, not wishing to broach the subject of racial differences that the title of the book suggested.

Dixon's very evident desire to evade a direct answer seemed to sharpen the other's curiosity, for he suggested off-handedly, but with ill-concealed eagerness: "Pretty deep stuff, eh?" Then in the same manner, he inquired, "Who's the author?"

Dixon noted his curiosity, and deciding to gratify it, handed him the book, which he took with feigned indifference. He opened it near the beginning, and moistening his fore-finger, began turning over the leaves. Now and then he would stop to read a marked passage, each time muttering half-audibly, "Nonsense, ridiculous!"

After glancing through the book, the passenger[5] turned back to the frontispiece in a search for the author's name. When he found it, he blurted out with ill-concealed disgust, "Just as I thought! Written by a Frenchman," then, before he could recollect to whom he was talking—

so full was he of what he regarded the absurdity of Finot's view—he again blurted out, "Do you believe all these impossible views about the equality of the races?"

Now Dixon's policy was to carefully avoid any topic that would be likely to produce a difference of opinion with a passenger, provided that the avoidance did not entail any sacrifice of his self-respect. In this instance, he regarded his questioner as one to be humored, rather than vexed, for just then the following remark, made by this same man that afternoon, recurred to him.

"The Jew, the Frenchman, the Dago,[6] and the Spaniards are all 'niggers' to a greater or less extent. The only white people are the Anglo-Saxons, Teutons and Scandinavians." This, Dixon surmised, accounted for the remark the other had made about Finot's adopted nationality, and it amused him.

Dixon pondered his question for a few moments, then there occurred to him a method by which he could retain his own opinion, even while in apparent accord with the views of the other. He responded accordingly:

"No, sir, I do not believe in the equality of the races. As you say, it is impossible."

The passenger looked up from the book as if he had not been expecting a response, but seemingly pleased with Dixon's acquiescence continued.

"Writers of this type don't know what they are talking about. They write from mere theory. If they had to live among 'niggers,' they would sing an entirely different tune."

Dixon felt that he ought not to let this remark go unchallenged. He protested courteously: "Yet, sir, M. Finot has admirably proved his arguments. I am sure if you were to read his book you would agree with him, too."

"Didn't you just say you differed with the views in this book?" questioned the other sharply.

"I fear you misunderstand me, sir."

"Didn't you say you did not believe in the equality of races?"

"Yes, sir."

"Then, why?"

"Because as you said, sir, it is impossible."

"Why? Why?"

"Because there is but one race—the human race."

The train stopped and Dixon went out to open the trap-door. During his absence the passenger was again diligently revolving in his mind all the conventional points of Negro[7] inferiority. At last he found one—a trait which he felt sure the whites had never possessed. Now, certain of victory, he waited for Dixon's return. Seeing him pass, he hailed him. Dixon, however, had to put some newly-arrived passengers to bed and it was some time before he could return. When he did return the passenger said impressively: "I have a point here which conclusively proves Negro inferiority. The Negro, and the Negro alone, is guilty of the most repulsive, the most debasing practice known to humanity—the eating of human flesh. Negroes are still cannibals. Even in this country you can find Negroes whose parents were cannibals, since it was not until 1830[8] that the importation of Africans to these shores ceased. And these, who are here, would be cannibals yet if we had not dragged them away. The Caucasian has never been guilty of cannibalism,[9] not so far as we can trace our history, thank God."

Dixon seemed unimpressed. He said, quietly, "It is true that cannibalism still exists in parts of Africa and I understand among certain Indian tribes in the wilds of Brazil, but these savages do not view this practice in the light we do. I wonder if I may read you what Finot has to say on this subject?"

The passenger did not reply; however, Dixon found the place and began: "If a mother passes through a village with her little one, a traveller tells us, all the others will go to her and take the child, hold it in their arms and make it jump. A cannibal who had just enjoyed a piece of human flesh is quite as capable of doing this as the most sensitive of our civilized folk. Cannibalism itself does not there present to these people the repulsive aspects that affect us, and to which we object so strenuously."

Dixon closed the book and continued: "Contrary to your assertion, however, sir, branches of the white variety of mankind have been cannibals. Herodotus[10] tells us that the Scythian[11] soldier, vampire-like, used to suck out the blood of the first enemy he killed in battle. The Issedonians,[12] he also says, used to eat their dead, and the Padaeans[13] would kill and eat those of their numbers who were sick or approached senility. The Huns used to drink human blood out of the skulls of the enemies they killed in battle. But more, I think I have a quotation here from St. Jerome.[14] Yes. Here it is. He says, 'When I was a boy in Gaul I beheld the Scots, a people living in Britain, eating human flesh, and although there were plenty of cattle and sheep at their disposal, they would prefer a ham of the herdsman or a slice of female breast.' So you see, sir, cannibalism among black and white is rather a matter of time than people or place. But the men who steadily grind out the lives of their fellows in sweat shops and live on the proceeds are, to my thinking, less merciful than the African who eats the flesh of his enemy slain in battle."

Shortly afterward the passenger retired, but the thought of his defeat forbade sleep. He was in a blind rage. Why had he started to argue with this menial? The idea of a Negro, a common porter, belonging to a race he so heartily contemned, possessing enough knowledge to beat him in an argument! His anger increased as he remembered the calm and polished bearing of his opponent as contrasted with his rude manner, he, a Caucasian and a state senator. And, worst of all, too, he had to acknowledge even to himself the logic of the porter's argument. As he kept revolving some of the points in his mind, his hatred for the whole

Negro race welled up in his heart stronger than ever. Ah! but after all, there was some consolation! This man was only a Negro porter, and no matter how much knowledge he possessed, he, as a Caucasian, was a better man. Everybody recognized him as such. He had better advantages and could enter places where this Negro dared not. But deep in his heart was an involuntary admiration for his opponent.

Second Day.

[During the rest of the trip, Dixon has consistently been outwitting the passenger, who is slowly being won over by the porter's arguments].

The passenger got up excitedly. This lecturing, he thought, this presumption on the part of the Negro, was a little more than he could stand. He started for the doorway, but when half way changed his mind. No, it would never do for him, a white man, to run away and leave the Negro master of the field. He began pacing the room, reflecting in the meanwhile, his body swaying with the motion of the train. Why should he be angry? First, it was he who had invited the discussion, then the other, even though frank, had been respectful. Indeed, he was struck by the courteous bearing of the man. Second, this man was telling the truth. What was his reason for being angry at hearing the truth told? In the analysis of this question many points between right and policy in the treatment of the Negro dawned upon him for the first time. The latter course he had begun to see was wrong. In this thoughtful vein, he reseated himself, lit another cigarette and relapsed into thought.

Third Day.

Dixon now consulted his watch and informed the other that they would arrive at the next station in fifteen minutes and would stay there ten minutes. Remembering that he would probably not have another chance to speak with this man, he decided to summarize his argument, and as the other did not speak, he continued:

"Looking back on the conversation we have had, sir, and supported by a mass of other information gathered from various sources, I am confident that every argument brought forward to prove Negro inferiority, of which I have heard, is wrong; that there is no bad trait possessed by the Negro which cannot be paralleled by the white man. In short, 'that black is not so very black, nor white so very white'; that the Negro is disliked, not so much for his features, his criminality and his imputed bad traits, as for the color of his skin and the nature of his hair.

"But is that the real reason?" he continued, in a spirit of raillery. "For instance, if a Negro has money, he will find any number of whites to kowtow to him. Foreign Negroes, too, or any Negro who can pass off as Spanish, French—in short, anything else but United States citizens, are better treated though these persons are of the same mixture of black and white. Many of the most prejudiced whites, too, have Negro intimates. Really, this prejudice, habit, affectation, whim or whatever it is, is so ridiculous, so utterly opposed to everything bordering on intelligence, that it is a wonder these persons never happen to see themselves in their true light and have a hearty laugh at their own expense."

"What do you think would offer a solution to the problem?" asked the passenger earnestly.

"A sense of humor."

"Something easier than that."

"Then I should like to see the formation of a national commission for an inquiry into the subject and to ascertain the best means of adjusting the relationship between these two bodies of our citizens. There are also three measures which I have always thought would help a great deal: first, text-books in the public schools, teaching in a simple manner the latest scientific findings in this matter, without making any special reference to the situation here in America; second, the establishment of federal schools in those parts of the South where the Negroes abound; and third, a non-political provision for a certain number of Negro congressmen. I consider the matter sufficiently serious to be taken in hand by the federal government, and the stoppage of the evil might—indeed, I am sure it would—save future generations a great deal of trouble."

Fourth Day.

> "The strongest is never strong enough to be always master unless he transforms his strength into right and obedience to duty."
>
> —J. J. ROUSSEAU[15]

The next day, before arriving at his destination, the passenger, calling Dixon to his seat, invited him to sit down, and with an air of frankness and earnestness that greatly gratified him, said: "I want to thank you for enabling me to see the other side of the story. I never did realize before the vast injustice that is being done to certain American citizens, and also the vast amount of ignorance we, Caucasians, have to combat in our own people. Hitherto I have prided myself on my broad humanity, but I now see how narrow it has been. I think every true American should do his best to end this great wrong, and I am going to do mine. As a legislator, I promise you to see that the truth is more fully disseminated. And more, yesterday you spoke of Ira Aldridge,[16] the famous Shakespearean actor. Now, I have been thinking that since a Negro could win such high dramatic honors, it would be quite possible to find Negro talent for our best dramas. The connection is this: I have interests in a large motion picture concern (here he handed Dixon a card) and I have been thinking that in order to create a better understanding of the Negro, and as an offset to the caricatures so often made of him, that I would get Negro actors for such plays as call forth the best expressions of the soul. I will begin with a few and hope to popularize the venture. In the meantime, you shall hear from me. Call to see me any time within the next two months, and I will show you how motion pictures are made. Glad indeed to have met you." And the two men shook hands cordially.

"Thank you, sir," said Dixon, in a voice vibrant with gratitude. "And I must say that I note many signs pointing to an amicable solution of this vexing question of race. Among them are these: The salt of the intellectual world, as represented by Abdul-Baha,[17] Liebknecht,[18] Shaw and others, seems determined to disseminate truth in spite of the barriers of nation, race or creed; a growing desire on the part of all peoples to probe for truth, despite emotional influences; and so far as we of America are concerned, the earnest and untiring effort of a very large number of our citizens to make of our beloved country a real Republic."

From *As Nature Leads: An Informal Discussion of the Reason Why Negroes and Caucasians Are Mixing in Spite of Opposition* (1919)

Rogers repeats, with some variation, the same formula utilized in *From Superman to Man* in his second book, *As Nature Leads*. Again, the work is a blend of fiction and facts, another type of "discussion novel." However, instead of using the fictionalized conversation between the porter and the passenger as in the former book, in *As Nature Leads*, much of the story is told in an epistolary style, a series of letters. In the book, as early reviewer Hodge Kirnon[1] notes, "Even though Mr. Rogers deals with deep subjects, they are easy to comprehend, inasmuch as his method of presentation is conversational, a similar method to that of Plato and George Berkeley, the [Anglo-Irish] metaphysician" (qtd. in Martin 56).

The frame of the book revolves around a dispute between three Black friends—James Trent, a university student, Walter Perry, an artist, and Robert Hamilton, a postal worker—after attending an anti-race-mixing lecture where the white speaker condemned Blacks as being inferior. As is indicated in the novel, anti-miscegenation laws were being passed in a number of states as part of a larger anti-Black movement which resulted in the bloody race riots/massacres of the "Red Summer" of 1919. The three men take different positions on the speech and the subjects it addresses. Trent wants to lash out angrily against racism, but Hamilton maintains that the best strategy is to "Squelch your opponent with a shower of facts." The lecture and subsequent conversations with his friends, along with seeing an article critical of miscegenation written by one of Trent's white professors, prompts Hamilton to compose a number of letters to his friend challenging these racist views. Hamilton goes on to dispute the racist theories expressed in the professor's essay, demonstrating not only that whites benefit more than Blacks through the intermingling of the races, but that it is whites, including white women, who generally initiate the social contact. Such an assertion backed up by evidence from multiple sources, completely disarms the white professor, whose only flimsy arguments against Hamilton appear in snippets contained within Hamilton's own letters. Again, Rogers co-opts the white strategy, allowing for a dominant voice in the narrative, but in this case, as in *From Superman to Man*, the Black speaker controls the conversation. The argument Rogers raises in this highly controversial work is that it is natural that many people from different races will choose to intermingle sexually. Laws cannot prevent the course of human nature. This is another of Rogers's central issues. This theme would be explored further in the three-volume *Sex and Race* (1941–44) and *Nature Knows No Color-Line* (1952) . The text used here was printed by M. A. Donohue & Co., 1919. It was reprinted by Black Classic Press (1987).

AS NATURE LEADS

From Rogers's Preface

This volume is the expansion of a single thought, expressed in "From Superman to Man." The thought, which was expressed for the first time in philosophy, as far as I know, is as follows:

Inasmuch as every civilization the world has known, has gone down or out and that even as the present ones have their rise and adolescence like the others it is safe to assume that they too will decay; therefore it would no more be desirable to have the whole world civilized at one and the same time than it would be to have all the land under cultivation or all the ore in use. Hence, undeveloped peoples should not be despised.

The thought, as I say, may or may not be original, but one thing seems sure: few of the wisest of that most developed variety of the human race sense this fact even subconsciously, or how to explain that race's great disdain for primitive people and the tendency to regard their undevelopment as guilt?

Another fact regarding the volume:

Remembering how books on sex are barred from the mails in the United States—the most cultivated persons will talk sex facts in an indelicate manner but will be quite shocked to see these same facts presented in the coldest manner in print—I thought it wise economy to omit certain data which I had spent a great deal of time and effort in securing and which would have given stronger point to my theory of racial intermixture.

My sole aim has been to express "the truth as Nature leads." In planning the volume I had in mind the old Roman engineers who laid out their roads in a straight line, cutting through all obstacles. Truth is light, and perhaps the second most remarkable quality of light is the directness of its rays. There are always two theories of every subject, one of which contains more truth than the other, and my aim has been merely to glean from both, using as my guide experience and an open mind. As everything that is, is truth, so by truth I mean that principle which at every present moment upholds the right of the honest individual to life, liberty, and the pursuit of happiness regardless of "race" or religious beliefs.

The reading of "From Superman to Man" is essential to a better understanding of this volume; indeed it would best precede it.

J.A. ROGERS
4700 State St.
Chicago, Ill.

From the Prologue

Washington, D.C., 1913.

A wave of Jim-crow bills was sweeping the United States. In the legislatures of Wisconsin, Iowa, New York, Minnesota, New Jersey, Michigan, Illinois and Indiana—states hitherto regarded friendly to citizens of African descent—had been introduced anti-marriage bills, and now in the national legislature had been introduced a national bill to prevent mixed marriages.

This eruption of ill-will was due, it was averred, to the marriage of a stenographer of European origin to a noted pugilist of African descent,[2] in spite of the tearful pleadings of her widowed mother, and the hostile rumble of public opinion. This irritation, following sharply the crushing defeat of the white champion by the black one and the consequent heavy financial loss in the defeat of the favorite, it was said, was too much for the whites, and they had urged their representatives, civic, state, and national, through press, letter and telegram, to the introduction of these bills.

The bill had excited a feverish interest at the capital, and for days past had been the leading topic. Numbers of visitors had come from adjacent southern states to hear the debate and to lend their support, and every available seat in the balconies was occupied.

A Southern Congressman, with one eye,[3] but whose burning brilliancy compensated for the loss of the other,—a man of commanding height and a voice that dominated the hall—had taken the floor, and with gesticulation of arms and a terrific smiting of palms was pounding in his convictions with dynamic vigor and intensity.

Gentlemen, he was saying, never since the day that the white man superseded the Indian, never since the day the decision was made that civilization and not barbarism should rule this Western Hemisphere, have we been called to decide a question of graver import. Think well upon what I am going to say. Do you realize what a fearful danger threatens the culture of the western world? Do you realize how the venomous, diseased, jungle blood of Africa like a slow and deadly poison is creeping over your civilization and mine, turning its lily purity into blackness. Forty-two years ago when as a boy I trod the streets of this proud and beautiful city Africans were the color they ought to be, but now you see them of all shades from black to white. As white and as blue-eyed as you and I. But white and blue-eyed only on the outside. Inwards they are as black as midnight in the depths of their native jungles. A man may be as white as the drifted snow on the inaccessible mountain peak, his eye the blue of the skies of sunny Italy, his hair of the finest silk from the loom of the Creator, his nose as perfect as the ravished dream of a sculptor of old Greece, but if one single drop of African blood pulses in his veins he is pure African. No scientist needs determine it. It will be unmistakably evident in the depravity of his morals and that lack of respect for law and order, that utter lack of virtue and chastity so markedly characteristic of the colored race. (Applause, followed by hisses).

Gentlemen, the danger lies greatest in that they look like you and me and all the rest of us. But nothing is further from the truth. They are no more like us than midnight is like mid-day. Take a lump of coal, put a beautiful coat of white enamel over it, does it not remain a lump of coal? So it is with the white Negro. The Ethiopian can change his skin but he cannot change his heart. Deck a hog in silk and he will return to wallow in the mire. Two hundred years of civilization and look! They are no higher in virtue and morality than their brothers in the jungles. They have no conception of virtue (applause and hisses). Gentlemen, do not misunderstand me. I have no prejudice against the African. No man is a better friend to those Africans who will stay in the place for which an all-wise Creator intended them, hewers of wood and drawers of water[4] for our race—the superior race. I speak from a sense of duty, the duty I owe my race, the peerless all-conquering Anglo-Saxon. Consider the majestic morality of the white race, its glorious traditions, the inheritance of six thousand years of the greatest civilization the world has ever known and then barbarous, benighted, cannibalistic Africa who, in the same long span, has accomplished nothing, nothing, absolutely nothing. I most emphatically insist that the Ethiopian is a menace to Anglo-Saxon culture. They have not hesitated to mix shamelessly with the white race and to glory in their bastardy. They are proud of the blood so shamefully acquired. Let not sentiment deter you any thought of personal liberty. It is only the worst of the two races that mixes. The white man who will stoop to consort with an African woman is already of a low type of beast. The white man who will mate with a black woman, who will so far debase his body, the temple of the living God, merits the penalty of this bill. You owe it to your wives, your daughters, your sons, to support this bill to protect them from this menace. Anyone of these white-skinned blue-eyed Africans, God perish the thought, may mate with your son, your beloved, your cherished daughter, your beautiful white daughter, the pride and darling of your life-long dreams, and produce Oh, horrors of horrors, a child of purest Africa, coal-black, flat feet, blubber lips, nauseating odor, and woolly detestable hair. How would you fathers—and you mothers too, sitting up there—feel to see your daughter standing at the altar of matrimony beside a black nigger? How would you feel? How would you feel? The black nigger is nothing but a brute, he is beneath a dog. Think of it and support this bill. This bill should receive the support of every member of this historic hall, and any white man who has not sufficient love for his race and honor for its glorious deathless traditions to support it, is unworthy of the love of his people, the wife of his bosom, the children of his loins, his country and the people who honored him with their votes. He is a traitor, a double-dyed traitor to his race."

Among the large number of visitors in the balconies were the three friends: James Trent, a university student; Robert Hamilton, postoffice clerk-laborer, on a visit to the capital city, and Walter Perry, an artist. Keenly interested in everything that concerned the welfare of their people, they had come to hear the debate on the bill.

[The three friends have different reactions to the speech, but the most disturbed by it is **Hamilton, who speaks with his friends** below:]

"The more I think," resumed Hamilton, with conviction, "the surer I am, that if we are to have effective representation, we must make strenuous endeavors to have congressmen of our own people. However good and just a white man may be, I doubt his capability to represent us. He is far more likely than not to lack the experience—our peculiar experience—and so will never be able to uphold our cause as effectively as one of us. Every heart must know best its own troubles. We need colored representatives of a type bold, unafraid, sensible—men who have come in touch with life, men who have studied the situation from all angles and are not afraid to stand up to an audience were its members Olympians and each Olympian no less than the terrible Zeus himself, and tell them the plain, unflinching truth to their faces."

"You already know how deeply I feel on that subject," said Perry, "how heartily I agree with you."

"And not in politics only but in every other field—in literature, art, music," agreed Trent. "Take a book like—that is attracting such a deal of attention just now. For a Caucasian author, it is of unusual fairness and knowledge of our living conditions, and while I have no other than gratitude and commendation for authors like these who have been so good as to interest themselves in us, yet I do feel and I regret to say it, there is a something lacking in their portrayal of our people—the nobler sort, I mean—some interpretation that seems to miss them entirely."

"Lack of experience," said Hamilton. "Anyone who attempts to portray the life of a people in a manner to satisfy its thinking element must live and suffer with it, must experience all its longing and discontent, must feel the chafings of the ambitious man who rages at the injustice which bars him from reaching the place he feels is his, as a newly-caged lion at the bars between him and his native liberty, must experience that profound depression arising from hurts unjustly inflicted, a condition he is impotent to relieve in spite of all the good he may do, must experience that indignation which so boils in his breast, that on hearing of some new injustice, however gentle he may be, he feels like Caligula[5] when he wished that all his enemies had one neck, so that he could by one swish of the sword be rid of them forever. To write of a people one must see them on the heights and in the depths, must feel as they feel, must live their lives as they live it, in short, must envisage all the circumstances peculiar to the situation. Expression of ourselves must come from ourselves. And before we can fittingly do so, we have much to unlearn. We must learn to shun the deadly mechanical and frigid civilization of the white man as we would a prison—a civilization, whose members conspire to make of one another boxes, and not human beings—a civilization that would reduce humanity with its soul-moving variety of tint, color, and shades of feeling to its own cold, white and sorrowing pattern."

[From Letter XIV, **Hamilton to his friend Trent**, regarding color prejudice]

For color prejudice is really crudity—paucity of world variety in the mind. To show its infantile nature. Once in a tropic clime, I saw some children playing. One little girl picked some berries and stained her face and hands a reddish brown. Her three year old brother upon seeing her thus changed, ran away, yelling lustily, but as soon as the stain had been washed off he was no more frightened at his sister before she stained her face or after she had washed it, that it was not the intrinsic human quality, but only the color to which he objected, due to a change his infantile intellect could not comprehend. It is evident that the attitude of this child, the untutored African who shuns a white skin and the Caucasian of reputed refinement who shuns a cultured man because of color, are all the same. The untutored African seeing the nearly uncolored skin and not realizing the fundamental unity of the human race is frightened until he sees that it entails no fundamental difference. Stanley[6] says that while he was wondering whether the Uhombo[7] were human, they too were doing the same. Similarly certain whites not grasping the truth of the oneness of the human race imagine that the possessor of the black skin is fundamentally different from them. What is called instinctive repugnance is a second nature due to fear of competition. That it is not instinctive is proved by the fact that were some great calamity to happen to the South, some strong invaders perhaps, see how quickly they would want to make common cause with the black man, just as the so-called instinctive dislike for horse-flesh vanishes in time of famine or the yellow dogs of Eastern Europe that are kicked and buffeted around in times of peace, become in war times a very dear friend, in the pot. In the presence of the German enemy white American soldiers quite forgot a life time of dislike for the black man.

R.H.

Letter XXXI.

The function of sex is first variation, second, reproduction. To produce variety is pre-eminently the first function of sex. Even the casual observer of the aspect of nature cannot but be struck by the infinite multiplicity of form and color. No two races alike, no two nations, no twins, no two sides of one's face, no two voices, no two handwritings, no two trees, no two blades of grass. Variety is undoubtedly the first characteristic of Nature, a strict necessity of her continuance.

To better understand the workings of sexual selection let us consider man, where it is best observable. Think of the great scrupulosity with which the man regards the woman, and she in turn regards him. If reproduction and not variation was Nature's chief aim would this have been so? Would not a man mate with any woman? But everyone has a quite special choice. The unconscious determination of the child to be produced influences this choice—of course I speak of normal love. The case of the soldier's standing in line to get into the house of prostitution was a perversion of Nature arising out of civilization. Prostitution is one of the products of civilization.

From Letter XXXIII, Hamilton to Trent

To briefly summarize:

Beginning with crude matter, forms of life, in their ascending scale, prey on other forms. Higher forms of nature eat the lower forms, therefore, intellect, the highest form of Nature, preys upon and consumes the body of man, the next highest form.

Civilization, or intellectual development, then is digestion. It is to animate Nature at large what digestion is the individual. Just as the individual puts food into his stomach so does that omnipotent Force we call nature places man into its stomach and digests him.

Just as the food in the stomach of the individual changes, the essence going to the nourishment of the body, the rest being expelled, so it is with the digestion of Nature.

The essence or chyle[8] from this digestion is intellectual development, as we see it in our skyscrapers, railways, works of art, and other products of the brain.

The dead or decayed races, nations, individuals are merely the excrement.

Civilized people are the food in the stomach today. Even as the food once placed in the mouth will normally pass through the alimentary canal in the form of chyle and waste, they too will pass.

Primitive peoples are the food of tomorrow. Some of these are peoples who have been through the process and are again ascending toward it, even as the dead body immediately again begins its ascent toward life.

The mixing of the races is the variety in food.

The mixing of Negro with Caucasian is nature's getting at her reserve food. Food, rich with the accumulated sunshine and cheeriness of the ages, is being put into a pale, starving, intellectual body.

Racial intermixture is to the benefit of the Caucasian, and to the detriment of the Negro, even as the animal that is being eaten by another is the sufferer.

Another proof that racial intermixture is to the benefit of the Caucasian is that that race as we saw is more strongly attracted to the Negro than is the Negro to it.

The intellectual development of the Caucasian and its relation to the Negro is what a stimulant is to the stomach—not always wise to take.

How admirable, if cruel, is then the provision of nature in regulating her food supply!

And how blurred the vision of those who disdain "races" not civilized like theirs!

Greedy, improvident fools! What, would you eat all at once?
R.H.

[Hamilton's conclusion]

At present the Africans of America do not know themselves, do not realise the incisive quality of their latent power. They cater to the white man, they look at themselves through his eyes, their sunny, forgiving natures permit them to be deceived, but some day they are really going to think for themselves, and when they do, they are going to rise to a point where they will be stronger and more aggressive than if they had been fairly treated. Misfortune crushes the weak man, the strong man deliberately seizes it and therewith builds a ladder rising transcendent above his fellows. It is the nature of the Negro to progress, even as it is that of hydrogen to rise above the surrounding atmosphere. Today, in many a university, many a position, the Negro youth has outstripped his white fellows simply because he felt it incumbent to do something to offset the stigma placed on his color.

The good name and all the democratic pretensions of the United States are quite at stake in this matter of Negro treatment, for as long as a cultured and refined man who is "colored" is restrained by law from coming and going with the freedom of an ex-convict, who is "white," then our pretensions to democracy is a brutal and barefaced humbug; as long as color distinctions continue the upholders of the dignified Constitution of the United States are confederates of the miserable Jim-Crow laws of the Southern States; as long as human beings continue to be burnt alive on the altar of the God, Racial Superiority, so long will the statue of Liberty, torch in hand, be peculiarly reminiscent of the lyncher, and as long as talent, refinement, and education are depreciated in citizens because of color, so long will the Caucasians of the United States be not unlike that other portion of their race—the uncouth, purblind, illiterate, much to be pitied, Bolsheviki of Russia.

While every group has a perfect right to keep itself to itself, to entirely control its own affairs, to say where it will and where it will not marry, yet the instant it enters the life of another group, so surely does it forfeit that right, and the other group has now a right to reciprocally interfere. It is clear that in the beginning the black man wished no association with the white, and that the white has all along forced his company upon him. If the white man will not leave the Negro alone, but wishes to mix with him, the Negro has a perfect right, that is, if justice is to prevail, to say under what conditions that mixing shall take place.

It is evident that the irritation proceeds rather from the Caucasian, therefore, it is his duty to take the forward steps in adjustment, in short, it would be well to bear in mind that we have not so much a Negro problem as a Caucasian one.

For my part, I earnestly desire a kindly and unqualified justice for every citizen regardless of color or sex. The trend of events points to the welding into one of this heterogeneous mass, we call America, and it is the bounden duty of every lover of his country to see that that process be accomplished with the least rancor, and the greatest degree of high-mindedness.

The color line bestializes. It forces human beings to meet on a plane where the barriers of decency are already broken down.

A developed Negro means a richer United States.

An oppressed Negro means not only a weaker United States but a weaker Caucasian race.

The unvarnished truth is that in this treatment of the Negro, the whites, and I have in mind the majority of most of the cultivated classes, are not observing the first principles of politeness, of that good breeding and courtesy to all, which the wisest, best and noblest of their race for the past three thousand years have unweariedly taught.

Does our cause, be it racial, religious or political, render us inconsiderate of the rights of others? Then it is wrong and sure to fail.

Every Caucasian who stands against Negro development is an enemy of his country, and the principles for which it stands.

"The Thrilling Story of the Maroons," *Negro World*, March 18, 1922

Rogers states that the term *maroon* is derived from the Spanish word *cimarrón*, a variation from the Taino word for "fugitive." He was proud of the fighting spirit of the Maroons, who resisted their enslavement, and wrote three articles on them in 1922 in Marcus Garvey's publication *Negro World* during the time Rogers's friend Hubert H. Harrison[1] was the editor. Rogers categorizes two types of Maroons (individual or small groups of escaped slaves, *petit maroonage*, and entire semi-autonomous communities, *grand maroonage*). There are examples of Maroons throughout the Americas, but perhaps the most famous Maroon settlements existed in Jamaica, where they lived in a harsh, inaccessible environment making it difficult for them to be recaptured. The success of the Maroons helped undermine the plantation system. In Jamaica, the English were forced to recognize the independence of the community in exchange for promises to not raid colonial settlements and to help the colonizers to capture other escaped slaves. The best known of the Jamaican Maroons was Cudjoe, who led a group of about 500 slaves from Clarendon parish to their freedom in 1690. He terrorized the English colonists for almost fifty years until a treaty was signed in 1739, giving the Maroons full freedom and more than 1,500 acres of land

"THE THRILLING STORY OF THE MAROONS"

Band of Heroic Negroes Defied the British Government for One Hundred and Fifty-one Years and Finally Forced It to Come to Terms; Maintained Their Independence with Arms and Ammunition Captured from the Oppressors.

The African, in spite of his great reputation for docility, did not everywhere submit calmly to slavery. In Cuba, Haiti, Porto Rico, Brazil, and even in the United States, where he was hopelessly outnumbered, he would revolt from time to time. Then he would wreak terrible vengeance on his oppressors, slaying right and left like an enraged demon. In 1791 at Cape Francia,[2] Haiti, the slaves revolted under Oge and wiped out the entire white colony, slaughtering men, women and children, and burning plantations with a ferocity paralleled only by the attacks of the Jews on the Canaanites or of the mob on the nobility during the stirring time of the French Revolution. This phase of Haitian history has been graphically told by Victor Hugo in his powerful story, "Bug-Jargal."[3]

The most refractory of all slaves, by far, were those on the Island of Jamaica. This, no doubt, was due to the fact that slaves always outnumbered the whites and near-whites by at least eight to one. The history of that island from its occupation by the British in 1655 to the Emancipation in 1838 is one long record of the attempts of those hot-headed blacks to gain their liberty. A large number of the Jamaican slaves were descendants of the Coromantin[4] [one of the] most warlike tribes of the West African coast. The Coromantins refused to accept the religion of their masters, worshipping instead the terrible Obi.[5] Even after they were set free the Jamaican blacks revolted against unjust taxation. At Morant Bay in 1865[6] they attacked the officials in a court house, set fire to the building and gave the occupants the alternative of coming out to be shot or of being burned alive. Hundreds of blacks were wantonly killed in reprisal and their towns and villages destroyed wholesale, but the oppressors were taught a lesson. The almost total absence of racial friction on the island is due, perhaps, wholly to the determined stand the Jamaican black has always taken against unjust treatment.

Foremost of the insurrectionists were the Maroons, or hog-hunters. These blacks, whose name is still a by-word of dread, maintained an almost unbroken guerrilla warfare against the slaveholders for one hundred and forty-one years (1655–1796).[7] When the African gets the recognition that is his in the history of the New World these primitive, untaught blacks in whose bosoms burned the inextinguishable fire of liberty, will be worshipped. They will be worshipped for their daring, their arduous feats, and the great privations they suffered in the cause of liberty. The Spartans, the Swiss mountaineers, the Scotch Highlanders, the American Colonists and the Belgians are today the leading idols of Western civilization. But these black men were the greater heroes, for while the American Colonists and all the others were on their own soil and free, these black men were not only escaped slaves, thousands of miles from their native land, but maintained their freedom solely by the arms and ammunition they took from their oppressors.

Origin of the Maroons

When the English captured Jamaica in 1655 from the Spaniards, the latter fled to Cuba, ninety miles away. In the flight they had to abandon the greater part of their slaves. Several hundreds of these took to the mountains, carrying with them food and clothing, arms and ammunition. Here they were joined from time to time by other runaways, where they became a perpetual thorn in the side of the English—the drop of gall in the enjoyment of this most beautiful and bountiful island. Jamaica is called "the black man's paradise." Its inhabitants are 85 per cent. black. That this is so is due largely to the terror inspired in the hearts of perspective white settlers by the Maroons at the time when it was easiest for the white settlers to get on.

At first the Maroons roved in bands. Whenever they needed food, arms and clothing they would descend on the white settlers, and after plundering and killing in true Scotch Highlander fashion, would escape to their mountain fortresses. The island, though arable throughout, is very mountainous. Tradition says that Columbus, its discoverer, when asked by Ferdinand and Isabella for a description of it, took up a piece of paper, crumpled it in his hand and threw it on the table, saying "There it is."

Chief among the tormentors of the English at this period was a chief named St. Juan de Bolas.[8] For eight years he ceaselessly harassed the whites, massacring settlement after settlement and preventing the advance of the planters. It must be remembered also that these blacks had been living on the island for more than a century and were fighting not only to prevent enslavement, but in defense of what they regarded their native land. At last, worn out by age and fatigue, St. Juan de Bolas surrendered on a promise of freedom and land for himself and his followers.

The bands of the Maroons, however, refused to consider any terms. They continued their depredations being the terror of the slaveholders. It was almost impossible for the residents of the plantations to escape their attacks, as they would learn all their movements from the slaves, with whom they would mingle in the markets and other public places. Thus they knew the favorable moment to strike. Descending on a plantation they spared no white person or faithful slave. Toward the latter they were especially vindictive. After liberating the slaves, they took all the arms and the food, set fire to the plantation and retreated to the mountains.

After repeated attempts to defeat them had failed, the governor now resorted to conciliation. To each Maroon that would surrender he offered a sum of money and twenty acres of land. But the Maroons were already free and in possession of thousands of acres of the richest land and spurned his offers. At last, their old leader, St. Juan de Bolas, was persuaded to lead an expedition against them. He met with some success for a while, breaking up several bands, but at last he fell into a trap. His forces were cut to pieces and himself slain.

For the next ten years the Maroons continued their raids successfully preventing the spread of the white settlement in the interior of the island.

But soon a crisis came. The slaves in one of the parishes named Clavendon[9] rebelled. Killing all their masters they took arms and ammunitions, including four field pieces, and joined the Maroons. At that time there were 8,000 whites, 80,000 slaves and a number of Indians on the island. The Maroons numbered about 900—men, women and children.

Their numbers augmented [,] the Maroons became more daring and destructive than ever. The administration provoked beyond endurance decided to make war on them—resistance hitherto had been left to the planters themselves. A large expedition was assembled. Soldiers led by Indians and faithful slaves now succeeded in penetrating the retreats of many Maroon bands, killing and dispersing them.

The Maroons, up to this period, had been roving in bands. They now saw that safety lay in union, and concentrated their forces under one of the most daring and resourceful of their chiefs, a Coromantin, named Cudjoe.[10] Cudjoe appointed his two brothers, Johnny and Accompong, lieutenants, and made preparations for yet bolder attacks on the whites. In the words of Dallas,[11] an Englishman, and a writer of those days, they began "a regular and connected system of warfare, and in their frequent skirmishes with the troops sent against them, acquired an art of attack and defense in the difficult and inaccessible fortresses of the interior of the island, which has since so often foiled the best exertions of disciplined bravery." In nearly every encounter Cudjoe was victorious and there is good reason to believe, that had he been better armed, he might, with the aid of the slaves, have eventually succeeded in driving out the English as a similar untaught Negro[12] had forced the French from the neighboring island of Haiti.

Description of the Maroons

"In their person and carriage," says Dallas, in his "History of the Maroons," "the Maroons were erect and lofty, indicating a consciousness of superiority vigor, appeared upon their muscles and their motions displayed agility. Their eyes were quick, wild and fiery, the white of them appearing a little red owing, perhaps, to the greenness of the wood they burned. They possessed most, if not all, of the senses in a superior degree. They were accustomed from habit to discover in the woods objects which white people of the best sight could not distinguish, and their hearing was so wonderfully quick that it enabled them to elude their most active pursuers. In character, language and manners they apparently resembled those Negroes on the estates of the planters that were descended from the same race of Africans, but on closer inspection displayed a striking distinction in their personal appearance, being blacker, taller and in every respect handsomer.

"They were seldom surprised. They communicated with one another by means of horns, and when these could scarcely be heard by other people they distinguished the order the sounds conveyed. It is very remarkable that the Maroons had a particular call upon the horn for each individual by which he was summoned from a distance as easily as he would have been spoken to had he been near."

Cudjoe Wins Decisive Victory

At last, in 1730, the government, in despair, decided to attack them at all costs, and began to build forts and outposts near their resorts. Mosquito[13] Indians were imported from Central America to track them down, and a force of 500 white and black soldiers under Captain de Lemelia advanced against Cudjoe. The latter, who had learned all the details of the expedition through his spies, laid plans to outwit his foes. Causing to be conveyed to Captain de Lemelia a false tale of the Maroon location, he then advanced several miles down the mountain. Here he took his position in a spot the attacking force would have to pass—a narrow [illegible word] flanked on both sides by precipices. Cudjoe now divided his band into four parts and placed them such at each point of the compass on the rocks overlooking the pass. This done he lay quietly down to wait the approach of the foe.

From "The West Indies: Their Political, Social, and Economic Condition," *The Messenger*, September–December 1922

At the time Rogers was writing this long piece (spread over four issues), the West Indian immigrant population in the United States, particularly in New York City, was exploding. Between 1900 and 1930, a series of events, including chronic overcrowding in the islands, high unemployment rates, natural disasters, and limited educational opportunities caused West Indians, taught from birth to look outward, to migrate. For example, the foreign-born Black population, mostly West Indians, in New York City grew from 3,552 in 1900 to almost 60,000 in 1930 (Holder 9). As a result, interest in Caribbean issues was extremely topical in New York and around the nation. Rogers's comprehensive essay published in A. Philip Randolph and Chandler Owen's socialist- leaning periodical *The Messenger*, covered a range of topics. It is significant that Rogers was able to have such a lengthy piece in the periodical, which was often seen as being anti-West Indian because of its strong stance for deporting Marcus Garvey.

This essay informed Caribbean immigrants of the conditions back in their homelands and also told native-born Americans of the forces driving West Indians to come to America, including the exploitation the islanders faced at the hands of their British colonizers. The essay itself is one of the most substantial sources to be written on the subject by a West Indian-born person contemporary to the period. The increased number of immigrants from the Caribbean and other locales such as Southern Europe would soon lead to the Immigration Act[1] (also known as the Johnson-Reed Act) of 1924, drastically reducing the number of new immigrants allowed to enter the country. For more on contemporary reactions to Caribbean migration to the United States in this period, see Ira De Augustine Reid, *The Negro Immigrant: His Background, Characteristics and Social Adjustment, 1899–1937* (1939).

"THE WEST INDIES"

September 1922

Considerable light will be thrown on the present political, social and economic status of the British West Indies, at the outset by pointing out the following: first the purpose of the earliest Europeans who visited them; second, that Negro slavery existed in all of the islands; and third, that present conditions are very likely to be an evolution of the above-named facts.

Purpose of the Earliest Europeans

In the colonization of the New World there was a distinct difference between the type of European who came to the region north of the Rio Grande and the one that went to all that region south of it. The former came to settle; he was the victim of religious and political persecution; the latter came to plunder. Like burglars, the sole aim of the Europeans of the second type, was to get all the wealth they could lay their hands on in the shortest time and scuttle home to live at ease. The result was that the natives were ruthlessly butchered, and their civilization quickly swept out of existence. The planting of crops was out of the question with these Europeans.

Negro Slavery

To replace the Indians, who were nearly all exterminated, Negroes were introduced. Slavery began in the West Indies more than a century earlier than in the United States and was abolished in the British Islands in 1838, twenty-seven years earlier than in the United States.

Population

The population of the British West Indies including British Guiana is approximately two million, three hundred and fifty thousand, about half a million less than that of Cuba. Of the forty-five islands or so that comprise the group, Jamaica with 4,209 square miles and a population of 858,118 is the largest. Trinidad, next in size, is 1,863 square miles and has 312,803 inhabitants. The vast bulk of the population are full-blooded Negroes; from twenty to twenty-five per cent are mulattoes, while the whites number about 40,000 or less than two per cent. A third of the population of Trinidad, and nearly half of that of British Guiana, are Hindus. Jamaica has about five thousand Chinese, eighteen thousand Hindus, and a sprinkling of Syrians. Antigua and St. Kitts have a considerable number of Portuguese. Dominica and St. Vincent still have a hundred and fifty of the aboriginal Indians. In short almost every race and nationality under the sun can be found in the British West Indies.

Politics

All of the islands, except the Bahamas and Bermuda, which have a measure of self-government, are Crown colonies, that is to say, the control of affairs that are really vital lies in the hands of the Secretary of State for the Colonies, who sends officials from Downing Street as governors. Jamaica is said to have representative government but this will be found to be merely a euphuism, as in really vital matters the representatives of the people have no real power. The chief legislative body of that island is composed of fifteen government officials and fourteen members elected by the people, with the governor as president of the Council. The fifteen officials are directly and indirectly appointed by the Crown, and vote always as directed by the Governor. These officials, except in rarest instances, are all white and from the British Isles. The elected representatives, as will be seen, are always outvoted by a permanent majority of one. To defeat or to pass any measure the Governor has but to declare it "a matter of paramount importance," and bring up his battery of officials. He, himself, has a casting vote.

In Barbados[2] the government consists of a Governor, a legislative council of nine members appointed by the Crown, and a house assembly elected annually by less than two thousand voters. The executive council consists of the governor and any number of officials the Governor thinks fit, together with one member of the legislative council and four members of the assembly named by the Governor. The latter body introduces all money votes, prepares the estimates, and initiates all government measures. Barbados is empowered to refuse a Governor it would not like, but, as with Jamaica, the Crown controls in vital affairs. Trinidad is a Crown Colony pure and simple, the people having almost no voice in the control of their own affairs.

Unlike Martinique, which sends representatives to the French Chamber of Deputies and the Senate, no British West Indian goes to the British Parliament. The West Indian, with all his patriotism, thus has no means of influencing British imperial policy. His only method of redress is by petition or memorial. For the first time in the history of Jamaica, a dark mulatto, Rev. A. A. Barclay,[3] has been appointed a member of the local privy council.

In minor domestic affairs there are lesser houses, like the State legislatures in the United States. In these the peoples of nearly all the islands are permitted their own way. The Governor, however, is permitted to dissolve them when he sees fit and appoint a Commission to administer affairs.

The Vote

In the West Indies there is no manhood suffrage as in the United States. To vote one must pay taxes. In Jamaica one must have or hold property on which he pays not less than ten shillings (normally two dollars and a half) a year; or must have a personal property on which he pays seven dollars and a half a year; or must receive a salary of not less than two hundred and fifty dollars a year. The result is to disqualify the greater part of those of voting age. Many of the peasantry own their land, but the land tax is twenty-five cents on every fifty dollars' worth. Many also rent land for which they pay five dollars an acre per annum. Most of the taxation, as will be shown later, is indirect.

The high financial qualifications for eligibility to the Legislative Council, and other assemblies, effectively bar black men from these places.

The salary qualification would seem absurdly low, but the low wages, as will also be shown later, makes it excessive. In 1921 there were only 42,267 Jamaicans qualified to vote, about one in every 200. In Barbados matters are even worse. Barbados is a sugar country, and like most sugar countries the land is in the hands of a few. Barbados presents, possibly, the most perfect example of a landless proletariat anywhere in the world. There are less than two thousand voters in Barbados. The census of 1913 give 1886. In Trinidad, where Hindus constitute a third of the population the percentage of voters is even less. As in parts of Mississippi and North Carolina, where Negroes are not permitted to vote, the total polling strength for the election of important offices does not exceed twenty in many districts in the West Indies.

Very little interest is taken in elections, except in the larger towns like Bridgetown and Kingston. Elections are usually uncontested. When contested the numbers of voters at the polls rarely exceed one-sixth of the voting strength. In short, the black population is pretty thoroughly disfranchised. The difference between the disfranchisement in the Southern States and that in the West Indies is solely that in the latter place the process is more politic. The government of the British West Indies, like other British Colonies where colored peoples predominate, may accurately be called a Caucasian oligarchy.[4]

Social Conditions

As was said, the first Europeans who went to the West Indies were adventurers. Having thoroughly plundered the Indians, many of them next started to exploit the soil. Establishing sugar and tobacco plantations, they then left them to overseers, and returned home to live on the monies from them. Because of this there was at all times a great preponderance of first, Indians, and then Negroes, over the whites. Massacres of the whites in all the islands, British, French, Spanish, or Dutch, were numerous. The Maroons, or runaway Negroes, of Haiti, Cuba, Guiana and Jamaica, wiped out settlement after settlement. Slave revolts were common. The whites now resorted to strategy to make their position safe. A mixed population had grown up in the islands. These, the whites erected into a superior caste over the blacks to serve as a buffer between them and the blacks with the result that throughout the West Indies there exists at the present time an officially and unofficially recognized color line between the mulattoes and the full-blooded blacks.

Everyone in the West Indies, except Asiatics, belongs to one of three divisions. The first in importance is the whites, which includes the near whites, or white-by-law, as they are called. Many classed as Negroes in the United States would be counted as white in the West Indies. The second is the colored, or those whose white blood exceeds the black. The lowest in the scale are those with a preponderance of Negro blood. How the distinction between colored and black is determined it is difficult to tell. By some subtle process of judging, now of hair, now of color, one is immediately placed in his proper group at sight. The census reports of the different islands all give populations as belonging to one of three groups. The Asiatics are generally regarded by the blacks as being inferior to them.

As W. P Livingston, author of '"Black Jamaica"[5] puts it, society in the West Indies is like a pyramid; "the whites constitute the apex; the colored, the middle courses; and the masses, or Negroes, the broad base." In other words, the whites are seated on the shoulders of the colored, who in turn are seated on those of the blacks.

Many visitors to the West Indies, like the late Ella Wheeler Wilcox,[6] Prof. Royce,[7] W. E. B. Du Bois,[8] and Robert R. Moton,[9] give the impression that there is no color line there. Such also is the proud boast of many West Indians in the United States. This view is very superficial, and far from being correct.

The difference between the United States and the West Indies as regards color differences is merely the difference between an active volcano and an inactive one, or between a visible disease and a secret one, which, while leaving the victim in apparent good health is undermining his constitution, just as effectively.

The color question is little agitated because the black peasantry, as a mass, are extraordinarily, almost preternaturally, good natured. Intensely religious and patriotic, they accept their inferior position and regard the mulattoes as superior. They voluntarily segregate themselves as in street cars and urban churches. The mixed bloods, in their turn, having a left-handed association with the whites, are content with their superior position over the blacks. They also look up to the whites, and permit them, with their vastly inferior numbers to stay at the top. The color question will then be seen to be merely dormant and as having all the potentialities it manifests in the United States. But let the mass of struggling blacks be once aroused to a sense of their great injustice, let them once feel that they are the equal of the mixed-bloods, and there would be the devil to pay. Now and then one may catch fierce glimpses of the revolt that slumbers deep in the sub-conscious minds of the blacks, when pushed too far, they raise the cry of "color for color."

Again, let the number of whites be suddenly increased, as in Cuba and the West Indian whites would no longer be forced to maintain their left-handed alliance with the mulattoes. They would very likely declare, as in the U.S. and Cuba, that one drop of Negro blood makes a Negro. In that event the mulattoes would then throw in their lot with the blacks in the U.S. Patriotic West Indians will assert that race discrimination as it exists in the United States would not be permitted on British soil. One has, however, but to point to South Africa.

In 1865 the blacks in a corner of the island of Jamaica revolted because of oppressive taxation and injustice in the courts under Paul Bogle and a mulatto named George William Gordon. They killed twenty-one whites and near-whites. The blacks were punished with such ferocity and brutality that they have been intimidated ever since. Four hundred and thirty-nine were killed, six hundred men, women and children were scourged, and over a thousand of their homes burnt to the ground.

"We shot the niggers like the blackbirds off the trees," said an English soldier in a letter.

There is no color question in the West Indies simply and solely because the black peasantry accepts exploitation passively.

Two other factors that aid in keeping the color question dormant are education and emigration. These will be dealt with later.

OCTOBER 1922

No Jim-Crow Laws

There are, of course, no jim-crow laws,[10] written or unwritten in the West Indies, except in Bermuda, where because of the objections of American tourists, persons of Negro blood are barred from the hotels and segregated in the churches, schools and theatres. One may generally go to any public place in the West Indies. It takes money, however, and the blacks of the West Indies, unlike those of the Northern United States, are wretchedly poor. Thus they are automatically barred.

Black men of wealth and education, unlike in the United States, are generally accepted in the outer, and sometimes even the inner circles, of white society. Some of them hold high governmental and even high private positions, but these are the rare exceptions. The whites usually have the plum of the positions and next the colored, of whom the merchant and legislative classes are chiefly composed. There is good cause to believe that were the masses of the blacks more aspiring, the lines would be more sharply drawn as in the United States where color friction increases as the Negroes advance. In 1905, competitive Civil Service was abolished in Jamaica, and appointments left to a selection committee. The popular reason for this change was that it was done to keep out the blacks, too many of whom were winning high positions.

Black men and women experience great difficulty in getting those private positions that are regarded as respectable. The colored get the preference, precisely as in the United States. Negro business men give the preference to mulatto girls. Black clerks are employed in rare instances. They are rigidly excluded from the larger business establishments. Most of the clubs are formed on the basis of color. Cricket is a popular game, but even here black men are usually barred from the exclusive cricket clubs.

Marriage Relations

It is in the marriage relation, however, that the color line or lines are most evident. Unlike the American girl of the same color, the West Indian light-colored girl will generally shun marriage with a black man. She is as emphatic on this as a Southerner in the U.S. would be to a marriage with her. These girls will mate generally only with men of their own complexion, or with white men, preferably the latter. The relation between the colored males and the black women is usually one of concubinage precisely as in the case of the white men and Negro women in the United States. Colored persons who marry blacks, unless wealthy, are usually ostracized by the colored and the whites.

There are no laws against intermarriage. A black man and a white woman may appear in the streets or at any public place, and unlike in the United States, attract not the least attention. Some of the leading black lawyers and doctors have studied in England, and have brought back white wives with them. Some foreign whites have black wives. A former white mayor of Kingston, the principal West Indian city, had a black wife. Marriages between the mulattoes and near whites are frequent. Unions of colored with the whites are not infrequent. In short with money and social position one may marry any color one pleases and be received anywhere. The manner in which the whites are willing to compromise with the colored in the West Indies in order to hold their place does seem to prove that the race question is almost solely an economic one.

Blacks Gaining Over Whites and Colored

In spite of their superior position, however, both the white and the colored are steadily giving way to the blacks, and the whites to the colored. The 1911 census of Jamaica showed 15,605 whites; the 1921, 14,476 a decrease of 1,129. The colored in 1911 were 163,201. In 1921, 157,223, a decrease of 5,978. On the other hand the blacks had 630,181 and 660,420 in 1911 and 1921, respectively, a gain of 30,239. The blacks in Jamaica have been steadily gaining since 1791. In 1834 the whites numbered 30,000, twice as many as at present.

The same is true of Barbados, the stronghold of the whites. The 1891 census of Barbados gives 15,613 whites; the 1911, gives 12,603, a decrease of 3,013. This decline of the whites holds true of all the other islands. The blacks will in all probability absorb the white and colored in time, even as in Cuba and the United States the whites will perhaps absorb the blacks. Jamaica seems an ideal place for black colonization. If the assertion is true that black men will get their rights only in those places where they dominate, then the full-blooded Jamaican black might be the first of the oppressed to get his rights.

Economic

Industrial depression and poverty is the normal state of the British West Indies. Bryan Edwards,[11] writing as far back as the 18th century, described it as "a progressive degeneracy."

Three causes may be given for this: It is the policy of the British government to discourage manufacturing in its colored colonies. The raw material must be sent to the British Isles to provide work for the people there, and then shipped back at a high duty; second, the nature of the education, and third, the strangle hold the English banks had on the islands until within recent years. Two other minor causes are the almost annual destruction of certain crops by hurricanes; and praedial larceny.[12]

Excepting a few of the Bahama islets all of the West India islands and British Guiana are of unbelievable fertility. The farmer, as the saying goes, has but to tickle the soil and it laughs with a harvest.[13] He has not a twentieth part of the trouble of the American farmer. The planting of corn, for instance, is a simple process. The bush is cut down and burnt. Women then go over the ground and with a single stroke of the hoe make holes at regular intervals. Boys follow with baskets of corn, throw in four grains, and kick the soil over them with their feet. A few weeks later the weeds are removed. There is no more trouble until the harvest. A similar process is followed with many other crops, as bananas and peas. Another thing greatly in favor of the West Indian is that most of the valuable crops are perennial. Bananas, cocoa-nuts, cocoa, cotton, kola-nut, coffee, sugar cane, pimento, pineapples and many other products, once planted, will thrive generation after generation with little care. Again there are dozens of fruits as mangoes, avocado pears, guavas, apples of a dozen diverse kinds, guineps,[14] papaws,[15] cherimoyas,[16] naseberries,[17] and plums,[18] as well as such edibles as jack-fruit, bread-fruit, and varieties of nuts growing in a wild or almost wild state, all in the most lavish profusion. From April to September, mangoes are a veritable plague in many of the islands. They fall from the trees in heaps to breed great swarms of flies; man, bird, and beast being tired of them long before the season ends. And in spite of all this large quantities of jam are imported from England. Fruit that would bring a fortune to the American canners goes to absolute waste. There are no jam factories worthy of the name. Mr. Gladstone[19] once suggested the establishment of such factories but beyond making a pun about "making Jamaica into a successful jam maker," he did nothing more about it.

Again, hogs thrive on these fruits. Yet ham, bacon and salt pork in vast quantities are imported. With an abundance of grass and some of the finest pastures in the world, cattle are easily reared. Sheep and goats can also be reared with little trouble. Yet vast quantities of pickled beef, and condensed milk are imported. Almost all of the butter comes from abroad. The seas teem with fish, yet thousands of tons of salted codfish and herring are brought in annually. The islands could produce all their flour (banana flour)[,] rice, cornmeal, corn, white potatoes and peas they need. Yet the peasant relies to a considerable extent on the imported variety of these articles for his daily food. In a case of war with the United States the islands would be hard pressed for food. Most of the food used in the Bahamas and Barbados come from America.

Although timber is abundant, lumber is imported. Raw sugar is exported and then imported in a refined state. The only manufactures of any importance are cigars, cigarettes, certain essential oils, dyewood extracts, biscuit making, and hat-making, the last by hand.

Why is all this so, when the British islands, like Cuba and Porto Rico, could grow most of their own food? Simply, as was said, because of the policy of the British government to discourage manufacture in the colored colonies. Again, the tariff is framed for two reasons, first to make revenue for the islands. As was said, most of the taxation is indirect and comes from a high ad valorem duty[20]—even as high as 16 2–3 per cent—and second to give preference to British products, many of which such as bricks, bridges, carts, locomotives and machinery are duty free.

More than half of the revenue of Jamaica comes from the ad valorem. With the exception of Trinidad the imports of all the islands considerably exceed the exports.

Why?

The explanation will be found in what was pointed out at the beginning of these articles [,] namely that the earliest Europeans came to exploit and not to settle, and that that policy has remained unchanged. In a country where the bulk of the population wears little and inexpensive clothing, go barefooted the year round, and live in small dwellings, shacks, and mud-huts, exploitation through food is the only hope of the trader. The peasant must be made to pay and to pay high for his daily salt-fish, herrings and cornmeal. In return he gets little for his agricultural products. The government, it seems, deliberately discourages the preservation of the surplus food stuffs,—which are highly perishable—at the time they are in season, in order to bleed the peasantry through high import duties on food. This policy, of course, makes the revenue sure, as one must eat. Sir David Barbour[21] who headed a royal commission to the West Indies some years ago, declared that the Jamaican tariff was "the most brutal in existence and worse than that of Egypt."

One explanation of the necessity for the high tariff is the enormous salaries paid to officials, who are nearly always English. For instance the governor of Barbados gets $12,500 a year; the Governor of the State of New York gets $10,000. Yet place Barbados in the middle of New York State, and one would have to travel nearly a whole day on a fast train to reach it. New York has 10,000,000 population. Barbados 170,000. The same with Trinidad, whose Governor gets $25,000 in salary and allowances. The Governor of Jamaica gets $35,000 in salary and allowances. The President of the United States gets $75,000. Yet Jamaica is smaller than Connecticut and has a half a million less population. Secretary of State Hughes[22] gets $12,000 a year; the Colonial Secretary of Jamaica gets $10,000; the Chief Justice of the United States gets $15,000; that of Jamaica gets $10,000. And so on with a host of other officials. Then there is the enormous pension list, and the honorariums that are sometimes voted.

Merchants and others of the exploiting class in power also make huge profits from the foodstuffs, and it is, of course, to their interest to see that the old order holds—that imports shall exceed exports, that the islands shall continue to be unable to feed themselves. In 1920–21, the imports of Jamaica were $51,568,410; the exports $35,730,050. The island had to pay $16,000,000 to the outside world for the privilege of existence.

NOVEMBER 1922

Education

The nature of West Indian education was given as one of the causes for the chronic economic depression. Education in all of the islands and British Guiana is of a metaphysical and most impractical nature. The objective is purely classical.

The first stress is laid on loyalty to the king, who is worshipped in an equal breath with God. Titles are regarded with bated breath. A Sir So-and-So or a Lord That is worshipped as the savage worships his lesser gods. With the West Indian patriotism is a fetish, a fact that undisguised race prejudice in the United States serves to strengthen.

The second defect is that most of the schools are denominational, that is, each religious body, as the Anglicans, Baptists, Methodists, Presbyterians and Roman Catholics who generally predominate in the order named, maintains its own schools. In Barbados the Anglican Church is endowed by the government. Great stress is laid on religion in the schools. A great part of the time is used in studying the exploits and achievements of the ancient Jews. The subjects taught have little relation to life as lived there. Most of it is pro-British propaganda. And of course, as in all oppressed countries great stress is laid on the ethical in the instruction of the peasant.

The Under-Secretary of State for the Colonies, Major Wood, recently made a tour of the islands, with a view to bettering conditions. His report to Parliament was published in the Jamaica *Daily Gleaner*, July 4, 1922, and following dates. He has suggested that Handwork, Agriculture, Domestic Economy, Hygiene and Practical Nature Study be taught in the elementary grades, which is the stage at which West Indian education usually stops. The teachers also complained to Major Wood about the denominational system and "of the employment of the clergy who had often no educational experience as sub-inspectors of schools."

Prior to emancipation there was no education of any sort for the blacks. Later there was introduced a system of school fees of from six to twelve cents a week. Most of the peasantry were too poor to pay this. All of the islands now have free schools and education is compulsory on some of them as Jamaica and Trinidad. Purely elementary subjects are taught. All education beyond that is expensive, and beyond the reach of the lower middle classes. There are no free high schools, as in the United States. The West Indian has perhaps not a hundredth part of the educational opportunity of the Northern Negro in the United States. Something less than one in 20,000 West Indians are college graduates. The following from the report of the Under-Secretary, already mentioned, will throw some light on the situation: "As in England, so in the West Indies, the elementary school curriculum shows a tendency to be too elaborate. . . . A good deal was said in the various colonies about compulsory education. . . . Compulsory education cannot be extended to areas more than two or three miles from a school and of such areas there are many. It must be remembered in this connection that in most of the colonies—more than half in some colonies over 70 per cent of the children are illegitimate and that parental control and parental responsibility are unenforceable. In Trinidad, which is about the best colony as regards attendance, 56 per cent of the total number of children are at school.

"As regards curriculum and text books, dependence upon English models and English publications, is the rule. There is so much local history, so much of interest in the local natural history that it should be easy to produce a 'West Indian Reader.'"

Nearly all of the teachers of the elementary schools are colored and black males. Their salary is very small ranging from three hundred to seven hundred dollars a year, the latter amount in rare instances. This salary depends upon the average attendance. In Grenada the teacher is paid according to the marks his school made at the last inspection. The teachers of Trinidad are the best paid.

Schools are examined annually by inspectors, who formerly were all white men from the British Isles. Within recent years a few colored and black inspectors have been appointed.

There are a few scholarships to universities in the British Isles and to local colleges. The principal colleges are Queens College[23] in Trinidad, Mico College Barbados.[24] George Washington received a part of his education in Jamaica and Harrison[25] and Codrington College[26] in education in Barbados.

Emigration

As was pointed out emigration is one of the causes for the inactivity of the color question. Every year large numbers of the most progressive and educated spirits leave for Panama, Costa Rica, Guatemala, Cuba, Nicaragua, South America, the United States and Canada, because of inability to find work. The islands being agricultural and with no scientific agriculture to engage their higher talents, they must either do laborer's work at an absurdly low wage and loss of caste or join the scramble for the few clerical positions. The departure of these discontented spirits acts in the nature of a safety valve or there would probably be a revolt worse than that of 1865.

There are about 50,000 British West Indians in Cuba, 28,000 in Costa Rica; 65,000 in Panama, and 60,000 in the United States.

It has been asserted that many West Indians leave because they object to manual labor. Abroad, as in the United States, there is hardly any other field open to them. The difference is that abroad they receive many times more pay than they would get at home. How emigration affects the social progress of the islands will clearly be seen.

Result of Emigration

One result of emigration is that the population of nearly all the islands is decreasing. According to the 1891 census, Barbados had a population of 182,306. In 1911 it had 171,893, a loss of 10,423. In 1919 the deaths exceeded the births by 675, a phenomenal case in any country, but easily explained when one understands the severe struggle for existence. The land as was said is in the hands of the few.

Barbados is perhaps the most thickly populated integral spot on earth. In 1891 it had 1096 people to the square mile; in 1914, 1033. Prewar Belgium comes next with 600. Grenada and Nevis are also thickly populated, having 500 and 400, respectively, to the square mile.

In Jamaica, while the increase of births over deaths in the years between 1911 and 1921 was approximately 125,000 the census for 1921 showed an increase of only 27,735 in the same period.

West Indian laborers have contributed greatly to the development of Costa Rica and Panama. They built up the banana industry in Central America, the railroad in Ecuador, and built the Panama Canal. Many of the leading doctors, lawyers, preachers, writers, and educators among Negroes in the United States are from the West Indies. The first

Negro to publish a newspaper in the United States was John Brown Russworm,[27] a native of Jamaica. Alexander Hamilton, who laid the foundation for the financial greatness of the United States was a West Indian.

Wages

Previous to the war, the West Indian laborer received from twenty-five to thirty-six cents a day.[28] Women got from eighteen to twenty cents. This has been the rate since emancipation 76 years before.

Work is irregular and laborers leave in large numbers for Cuba and Central America under contract which in many instances is little short of slavery. In those countries they get from a dollar to a dollar and a half a day, returning when work is exhausted.

The pay of housemaids is from thirty-six cents to a dollar a week without board. Cooks get from a dollar and a half to two dollars a week. None but the menials are content to do this work. The term "servant" is one of opprobrium, and so is the word bium [*sic*].

Clerical work is also poorly paid in comparison with the United States. Fifteen dollars a week is considered a very good salary. Wages are higher in Trinidad than in any of the other islands.

Industrial Conditions

Industries, as was said, are chiefly agricultural. Jamaica produces bananas—about a quarter of the bananas used in the U. S. and England come from Jamaica—sugar, cocoa, cocoanuts, ginger, dyewoods. A valuable by-product of the sugar industry is the well-known Jamaica rum. Prohibition[29] in the United States and the war with Germany caused the islands to lose two of its best customers. During the last few years the demand for rum in Great Britain has fallen off 1,295,433 gallons. Stocks in bond have reached the enormous figure of 11,689,000 proof gallons with no business in sight.

DECEMBER 1922

Local Race Problems

Both Jamaica and Trinidad have local race problems. The former with the Chinese and the Hindus; the latter with the Hindus.

After emancipation the slaveholders seeking the cheapest possible labor, imported East Indians. They were indentured for five years and paid twenty-four cents a nine-hour day. The Jamaican laborer got 36 cents. These East Indians were virtually slaves. The indenture system has ceased.

The question of the Chinese is more aggravated. About 5,000 in number, they have cornered the small retail grocery trade in pretty much the same way the Jews and the Greeks have cornered Negro business in the United States. With their superior trading instincts the Chinese merchants are driving out the Jamaican ones. They grow fat where others fail. The governor in Council, July 5, 1922, said: "The Government was fully resolute that the time had come when the Chinese settlement should not be allowed to increase in size." A literacy test will be used in an endeavor to keep them out. Emigrants to the island will be called upon to read and explain any fifty given words in the English language.

In Trinidad and British Guiana, East Indians constitute 33 and 42 per cent of the population, respectively. They are the backbone of agriculture. According to the report of Major Wood they complain of discrimination in the schools, and of having no voice in political affairs.

In Antigua and St. Kitts, the Portuguese have cornered the retail business, as the Chinese in Jamaica.

Annexation to the United States

This is a topic that provokes great bitterness in the West Indies. The mere thought of annexation is regarded with horror. In 1860, when during a period of unusual depression, it was seriously suggested that the islands be given over to the United States, the people were near the point of rebellion. In 1907, when an American admiral landed in Kingston to relieve the earthquake sufferers, he was very coldly received, and in the sharp diplomatic correspondence that ensued the governor was recalled. American visitors are well received with that courtesy native to all classes in the islands, particularly as the former have money to spend. But annexation they do not want.

The case of Cuba and Haiti has but served to aggravate this decision. In Cuba before the war of 1898, Negroes had equal rights. Intermarriage was common. They took an equal part in the war of liberation. Many of the most famous leaders, as Antonio Maceo, were Negroes. American intervention awoke color prejudice. This resulted in a rising of the Cuban Army of Liberation, in which Estenoz[30] and over five thousand of his followers were slain. Race prejudice is an American disease and like the Wandering Jew,[31] the American spreads it wherever he goes. Annexation would mean an influx of Americans, who would at once side with the native whites and establish an aggressive white despotism. The near-whites, colored, and blacks would then be thrown together, and violence would undoubtedly result. The question as it stands is: Which is preferable? Peaceful exploitation of the blacks by the whites, near-whites and colored, or violent exploitation of the near-white, colored and blacks by the whites?

On the other hand the economic condition of the islands would be undoubtedly improved by annexation, something like that of the West Indian immigrant to the United States who, although he suffers more sharply from color prejudice, lives much better than at home.

Cuba and Porto Rico have benefitted enormously from American intervention. In 1899 the total exports of Porto Rico was $10,156,541. Under American rule it leaped in 1919 to $150,841,449. During the same period imports have increased from nine to ninety million dollars. Cuba has shown a similar phenomenal increase. In both Cuba and Porto Rico exports now exceed imports; while in the British West Indies the opposite is true except in Trinidad. Both these countries have the advantage of American capital and they have enjoyed the greatest prosperity of their entire history under American control.

Proximity makes the United States the logical market for West Indian goods, and the logical protector of the islands.

Political Attitude of British West Indians in U.S.

The census of 1920 gives 73,803 foreign-born Negroes in the United States. The majority, say about 60,000, are British West Indians, the most of whom live in New York City.

Comparatively few West Indians become American citizens. Coming to the United States with a strong British bias and hatred of American color prejudice, they see the Negro Americans possessing few rights that they, the West Indians, cannot get. Indeed, a certain preference is given them particularly outside of New York, the more so if they have a smattering of French or Spanish. They see that even a newly landed immigrant, who is white, is accorded privileges that are withheld from the Negro America[n], and that late enemies in the last war, though they had each slain a thousand Americans, and made a thousand widows and orphans, have opportunities that are denied a Negro American veteran though he had saved an army division from destruction. Consequently they are inclined to look down upon the value of American citizenship, while their pride takes refuge in their British birth. But it is precisely because of this that the West Indian should draw closer to the American Negro, it is precisely because of this that a feeling of common humanity should prompt him to aid the American Negro in his long fight for liberty.

The facts to be taken into consideration are that the West Indians came here almost solely because of the pressure of conditions at home, and they have found relief; that as long as they are here they are virtually American Negroes, being indistinguishable from them except by their accent; and that they will in all probability stay here for the remainder of their lives.

At the present time the Negro in New York is greatly handicapped in the fight for his rights because of the large percentage of West Indians who cannot vote. New York has the largest Negro population in the United States, yet in political strength it is behind Chicago with nearly forty thousand less Negroes.

The destiny of the West Indian Negro and the American brother, as is also that of the white American, appears to be firmly linked. To the far-visioned and humane it will seem no different whether the battle against color hate and economic injustice be fought in the West Indies or in the United States.

From *Blood-Money*, New York *Amsterdam News* (begins April 11, 1923)

Rogers was primarily a non-fiction prose writer, but occasionally he tried his hand at fiction. *From Superman to Man* and *As Nature Leads* are often classed as novels, but they also mix in long stretches that seem more like non-fiction. In these early pieces, Rogers was experimenting with form as he tried to find the best vehicle to voice his beliefs. *Blood-Money* is a more traditional work of fiction; it is a novella that was published in serial form. Fiction written serially, going back to the time of Dickens, needs to follow certain conventions, chief among them that the author end each section with enough suspense to make the reader come back for the next installment. Rogers does keep the reader's attention with a lively narrative. The opening sets the tone as we have to wait to find out what is in the letter the narrator so anxiously receives. Rogers keeps the reader in suspense throughout the story, providing some dramatic action in the first half with an encounter with the Klan. However, the story gains real momentum after the protagonist, John Walton, is falsely accused of the murder of his white professor's wife. Then the story is largely left in the hands of John's girlfriend and amateur sleuth, Lucille Page. We know John will ultimately be saved, but how that happens is quite unexpected. Despite its sometimes wooden dialogue, its improbable events, and its lack of real character development, the novella is overall a satisfying read if not great literature. Though it is largely a pot-boiler, Rogers's interest in racial issues is also present throughout the story.

BLOOD-MONEY

Chapter I

"Hey, John. Here's your letter," shouted the postman, jovially, as he stopped his horse, dismounted from the wagon, and advanced toward the vine-covered fence surrounding a little cabin in the small town of Salem, Ga.

John Walton was intently hoeing his corn and had not heard the rumble of the approaching wheels. At the words, "Your letter," he started, his heart beating violently. He had been expecting a certain letter every day for the last six weeks—a letter on which his very destiny seemed to hang. Now the postman's accent on the "your" told him that this letter had come at last. Dropping his hoe he advanced to meet the mailman.

Taking the missive, his hands trembling with excitement, he feverishly scanned the return address. Yes, it was the letter!

With the long expected bit of mail in his hands at last John Walton stood hypnotized with doubt. Would the simple words within announce that he had won his seven years of grueling, up-hill fight, did they signify that he was going to take the first step toward his life's fondest dream? Or did they mean that he was going to remain in the dull, flat, soul-benumbing environment of this sleepy, dusty village until God knows when? He dreaded to take the plunge that would decide his fate[1] once for all.

"What's the matter, John? Scared to open your mail?" chaffed the postman, noticing his agitation. The postman knew everyone's affairs intimately, and was himself eager to know what the letter contained.

The remark woke John Walton from his reverie. He rapidly tore the envelope apart [,] unfolded the sheet within and began to scan it nervously. A look of doubt clouded his strong, manly features, but as he read on he uttered a loud yell, waved the sheet of paper high in the air and did a war dance to the detriment of several roots of corn.

"I've won! I've won! Ma!" he shouted jubilantly. He started wildly to run indoors. The postman grabbed at his sleeve and held him back.

"Let me see it," he said. John thrust the letter into his hands.

An elderly woman in a loose cotton gown emerged from the low doorway, followed by an old man toddling with the aid of a stick.

John ran to meet the woman shouting, "I've got it, ma! I've got it!" He grasped her about the shoulders, kissing her impetuously.

"That ain't no news to me," she replied dryly, hiding her emotion as best she could. "Didn't I tell you so all along?"

The old man had taken the letter from the postman and was looking at it, pretending to understand what it was all about.

"Sho is a clevah boy. Sho' is clevah," he said with deep satisfaction.

A group of ragged children crowded around.

John took the letter from his grandfather and read aloud.

Dale University

Nortonville, Conn.

Mr. John B. Walton,

Salem, Ga.

Dear Sir:

With reference to the Arnold Scholarship for which you competed August 5th of this year, we take great pleasure in informing you that you are the winner. Under its terms you are entitled to free tuition at this University for three years and the sum of $300 annually.

The Autumn Session begins October 4th. May we hope to hear from you at your earliest convenience.

Yours sincerely,

Walter Pringle,

Registrar.

A shout of joy went up from the little audience. The old man placed his hand on John's head and made an oration praising him as a great hero. Tears of joy came into his eyes. This grandson of his he felt was going to be all that he had longed to be but had never had the chance.

Mrs. Walton was happy, happy. But suddenly a grave look swept over her face. How would certain of her white neighbors take the story of her boy's success? With a mother's ever watchful eye for possible harm to her offspring, she instinctively sensed trouble ahead. There were the two Parkers,[2] for instance, bullies of the town, who were always teasing her son about his studious habits. Vividly there flashed through her mind the terrible fate that had overtaken her husband in a neighboring county many years ago because of his industrious habits. Silence about her boy's success she hurriedly decided was the best course.

"Sh-h. Don't-don't tell anybody" she said cautiously. "They might—." She suddenly remembered the postman. "Run, Bert, run. No. John, you go and tell Bill not to say nothing about it."

John dashed through the gate and hurried up the dusty lane as fast as his legs could take him. On rounding the corner he saw the postman talking with Dick Parker, an elderly white farmer and father of the two ne-er-do-wells, the objects of Mrs. Walton's fear. He was telling Parker about the scholarship.

"Good afternoon, Mr. Parker," said John, approaching.

"Howdy, John. I guess yo' all will be goin' North to be a professah, a doctah or somethin'," sneered Parker by way of congratulation.

"Say, Bill" said John when Parker had gone inside to give the news. "I forgot to ask you not to tell anyone. You know how it is."

"And I spilled the beans!" said the other regretfully. "I won't tell another soul."

John started thoughtfully back. Suddenly he heard something whiz by his ear and strike the earth with a dull thud, raising a little cloud of dust at his feet. It was a large stone! Ducking his head he looked hurriedly back but saw no one.

"Jim Parker, I bet," he said indignantly.

The postman's promise to keep silent was of no avail. The mischief had already been done. In this little town, as in similar communities, the least bit of news or gossip is as much an event as a letter to a man in prison. Everyone talks about everyone else's private affairs. Before the day was over John Walton's success was on the lips of everyone in Salem.

[John has several adventures in the following chapters including a brush with the Ku Klux Klan. Most of the story deals with his time in Connecticut where he meets his bride-to-be, Lucille Page. He also encounters a deadly rival from home, his half-brother Philip Breckenridge, a "white" man competing with John for a prestigious scholarship. John is accused of killing Mrs. Bruce, wife of his college professor, while it is said he is in her house looking for the exam questions for the scholarship. John is found guilty of murder and sentenced to death.]

Chapter 23

The Westham Evening News carried that day a strange story about the affair in the death chamber. "Walton," it said, "was strapped to the chair, awaiting the fatal bolt. The electrician had started the switch whose contact with the socket less than two inches away would send 20,000 volts instantly through the murderer's body; when, as if by magic, every light in the prison suddenly went out. The power had vanished in less than the second or so it would have taken to complete the circuit.

"Prison authorities at once got in touch with the Nortonville power house and were informed by Chief Engineer Walters that just a few seconds before 10 o'clock every fuse in the Westham current was blown. Some hours later the lineman found the wire, burnt and fallen apart, in Conover Woods, about two miles from the power house.

"Investigations are being made as to why the wire should suddenly have been burnt at the critical moment. Gov. Scofield, it is learnt, has said that he will commute Walton's sentence to life imprisonment unless collusion can be proved."

"The next step," said Lucille grimly, when she read this welcome bit of news, "is to find the guilty one, and, by the God above, I am not going to rest until I find him."

A few days later she read a most astonishing item in the Herald. Prof. Bruce, it said, had suddenly inherited a large fortune—five million dollars. This money had been left [to] his wife's mother, Mrs. Inglis, by a rich uncle in the South. Mrs. Inglis had died shortly after her daughter and Prof. Bruce had come into the fortune as heir of his wife.

Lucille's brain, working with feverish rapidity, recalled that John had said that Mrs. Bruce had begun her unfinished story with the words, "My mother." Just then the entrance of Prof. Bruce had cut the tale short, John had said.

As in a lightning flash Lucille saw the motive for the murder. "He hired someone to kill her in order to get her money," she said aloud. "That same person was to rob the papers for Breckenridge. I knew it. I knew it, all along!"

She added as her suspicions increased: "He was possibly scheming to marry another woman. . . . But I'm going to make him confess before this day is over. He's going to Europe, is he? Not while I'm alive."

Calling up the beauty parlor, she asked to be excused for the day, and started for Prof. Bruce's home. Arriving there the valet told her that he was out, but would return shortly. Feverishly she waited outside for his return. After what seemed an endless period, she finally saw a car stop in front of the house, the professor dismount and start up the walk. She watched him disappear through the door, then, with tigerish resolution, started after him. Something within her told her to be calm, and she suppressed her feelings as best she could. One thing she was fully determined in: She was going to make him talk. At the door once more she was invited into the parlor by the valet.

Prof. Bruce entered.

"Good morning, Miss Page," he began cordially. "I'm glad that Walton's life was so miraculously saved."

She felt like springing at him and hissing: "You ought to be glad, you murderer." But reason told her to be calm. She said aloud: "Thank you, professor, and let me congratulate you on your inheritance."

"I'd give it all back and more to have my dear wife back," he said sadly.

"The hypocrite," she said to herself, then aloud calmly: "Still it is nice to get so much money—money from the death of your wife—blood-money!"

The insinuation in her tone provoked him. He was silent for several seconds. "Miss Page," he finally said with a note of rising temper in his dignified voice, "please state the object of your visit. My time is limited."

"The object of my visit," she retorted acidly, "is to find out what you know of the murder of your wife."

"I have told you that already," he replied coldly after another pause.

"Prof. Bruce," she continued in a steely voice. "I am a desperate woman. I am here today to find out what you know. I'm going to make you talk."

She thrust her right hand into her beaded bag, agitated it ominously within, and kept it there.

"Are you threatening me?" demanded Prof. Bruce turning pale, and starting to rise.

"Keep your seat, professor," she warned in a deadly tone, lifting her hand slightly from the recesses of the bag.

He sank back into his seat. She continued: "As I said I'm a desperate woman. Come on, tell me who killed your wife and be quick about it."

"I swear before God that I know no more of my wife's death than you or anyone else," he replied nervously, frightened by her wild, staring eyes.

"You lie. Both you and Breckenridge know of this murder. I felt—everybody felt—that day in the court house that you were shielding him."

"Miss Page," he replied uneasily, "I admire your faith in Walton. It is wonderful. I wish I could share it, but try as I may, I haven't been able to up to now. I liked Walton immensely. He was a fine fellow—a brilliant young man. I am a friend of your people and have always been—"

"A friend! And yet you made that atrocious insinuation about John's not being able to resist the temptation to steal because of his race when as a man of learning you know full well that your own people were bigger thieves," she interrupted with a sneer.

"I was crazed over the loss of my wife," he replied apologetically, "and one is likely to say or do anything then."

"You mean you were trying to cover your tracks or—or you were off your guard and your dirty color prejudice cropped out."

"Now, Miss Page, that's not—

She cut him short. "I'm not here to argue that. What I want to find out is are you or are you not going to say who killed your wife."

He replied with evident sincerity:

"I repeat I don't know. I'd give ten thousand—a hundred thousand dollars to anyone who could prove that it wasn't Walton that did it. I couldn't say anything more though you question me for the next thousand years."

"But why are you shielding Breckenridge? I have strong reasons to believe that you are."

He hesitated for almost a minute, apparently in deep thought, then said suddenly: "I am not conscious of having shielded Breckenridge. What I did know was this—" Lucille leaned eagerly forward to catch his words. "The morning after my wife's death I found a pencil belonging to Breckenridge on my desk."

"A pencil! Breckinridge's pencil!" she cried springing to her feet. "And what did he say?"

"He explained it in this way: He said that when I left him and Mrs. Bruce in this room while I went to get the car that she borrowed it from him to write something at the desk, and forgot to return it."

"He lies. Why did he act so queerly then when Mrs. Walton and I called at his apartment?"

"I'm saying only what I know, since his explanation was so logical I accepted it and said nothing more. I thought it unfair to drag his name into the trial, particularly as the evidence against Walton was so strong.

"Why didn't you tell me this before?"

"For the same reason."

Lucille pondered a moment. Was he telling the truth? She would see.

"Are you willing to call Breckenridge here and let him verify this statement while I hide behind that curtain?" she demanded, looking at him fiercely.

"I'd be glad to, but he and Leigh[3] left for New York half an hour ago, bound for California."

"For California?" she echoed in a daze. "It can't be true."

As the full import of his words dawned on her she sank slowly to the floor. She felt all her determined powers of resistance forsake her.

He helped her to her feet. "I'm sorry I can't help you," he said sympathetically. He added: "Perhaps—I—I may be able to help you in a financial way."

"No, thank you. I must go." She started for the door, he following. On the threshold she turned and faced him.

"Have you the pencil—Breckenridge's pencil?" she asked. She had suddenly resolved to follow Breckenridge to California and wring a confession from him.

Chapter 24

The parlor of the Montgomery home was the social salon of the better class of colored people in Nortonville.

Among the most frequent visitors was Jerry Carlton, guard and doorman at the Nortonville Bank. Jerry was not only one of the institutions of the bank, but of the town. Everyone, young and old, loved and respected him.

After forty-one years at the single bank in the town, he knew the financial affairs of almost every regular resident.

On the evening of that same day in which Lucille had left Prof. Bruce's home almost in despair Jerry had dropped in at the Montgomerys. After placing a record on the Victrola he had come and sat down by Lucille.

"I see that Breckenridge won the Stanton prize after all," he remarked.

"Ye-es," answered Lucille mechanically, preoccupied with the thoughts that mention of the prize had evoked. His next remark caused her to sit up, however.

Jerry continued: "And he paid it all out to one man. He—"

"Paid it all to one man?" interrupted Lucille curiously. "Who is the man?"

"Prof. McLean."

"Prof. McLean?" she echoed, all her suspicions immediately awake. McLean, she remembered, was the one who had testified that he had entered the Bruces' home with Prof. Bruce, to find Mrs. Bruce dead.

"Yes, Prof. McLean," repeated Jerry, "he cashed the $1,500 prize check at the bank today. The check was indorsed by Breckenridge. Prof. McLean hasn't an account with us, so the cashier asked him how he came to get it and—"

"And what did he say?" demanded Lucille eagerly.

"He said that he had received it for services rendered to Breckenridge. I was standing by the wicket[4] at the time."

"Didn't he say what he had done for Breckenridge?"

"No. But it was Breckenridge's signature all right and he got the cash."

"That's queer," ruminated Lucille, ever on the alert for some new clue. Why should Breckenridge have paid him all the prize money? she asked herself. She remembered having seen McLean and Breckenridge together many times. McLean, she also recalled, had been very nervous on the stand. He had said that it was his first time on a witness stand, but had he not been a professor at the university and accustomed to addressing large audiences?

"Jerry," she said aloud, "please don't mention this to any one else. I have a reason."

She rose, put on her hat, and started for Breckenridge's apartment. Arriving there she saw the colored doorman standing on the steps.

"Is Mr. Breckenridge upstairs?" she asked.

The doorman eyed her suspiciously from head to foot.

"No," he replied tartly. "He's gone away."

Lucille ignored his attitude. "I wanted some information," she said with dignity. "Would you mind obliging me?"

After some trouble she finally learned from him that McLean used to help Breckenridge with his studies. "He used to come here four evenings a week," explained the man.

Lucille returned home, her brain in a whirl.

Early next morning she called on Lieut. Childs and told him her suspicions.

"I happen to know Prof. McLean well," said the lieutenant. "I don't think he knows any more than what he said on the stand. Mr. Breckenridge is rich and I don't see anything suspicious about his giving all the prize to him. I don't see anything wrong, do you?"

"But, lieutenant," pleaded Lucille. "As I told you, Mr. Breckenridge acted so suspiciously the day Mrs. Walton and I called on him. Then, there's the matter of the pencil found on Prof. Bruce's desk. Please—"

Lieut. Childs laughed: "I think, Miss Page, you'll be suspecting me of the murder next. I was on the scene, too, you remember."

"I'm not suspecting Prof. McLean," replied Lucille earnestly; "but I do suspect Breckenridge and the two used to be together very much. Please, won't you question him about it? Perhaps you may get something out of him."

"All right, I'll see if Prof. McLean knows anything about it. I'll ask him to come here," said the lieutenant, rather wearily.

He called him on the phone. A feminine voice said that McLean was gone to Boston and would return on the 6.15 train.

"Suppose we meet him at the station?" suggested Lucille.

"All right," agreed the lieutenant.

When the 6:15 arrived Lucille watched eagerly for the figure of Prof. McLean among the throng that got off the train. Presently she saw him and Prof. Bruce walking together on the platform. The two were conversing earnestly.

The sight of the two men together aroused her suspicions against Prof. Bruce and when Lieut. Childs started after McLean she detained him.

"Let's watch them awhile," [she] said.

Both men got into the same cab. "Let's follow them," suggested Lucille. She and the lieutenant got into another cab, and gave the driver orders to follow.

The first cab stopped at Prof. Bruce's home. Here the two men dismounted and proceeded up the walk still conversing intently. Lucille and the lieutenant followed. At the door they were admitted by the valet and ushered into the parlor.

Prof. Bruce and McLean were talking in the library. Lucille heard the former say:

"Now, McLean, you know that $200,000 is an impossible figure."

"But," objected the other with decision, "what of the agreement?"

"Did you hear that?" whispered Lucille eagerly to the lieutenant.

Lieut. Childs laughed, "Miss Page," he said aloud, "you ought to make a fine police officer. You're so suspicious of everybody and everything."

Lucille was listening eagerly for the remainder of the conversation between the two men, but it was interrupted by the knock of the valet, who had gone to announce the visitors.

Prof. Bruce entered. Through the open door McLean was visible.

"How d'ye do, Miss Page? How d'ye do, lieutenant?" said Prof. Bruce cordially.

The three chatted for a few moments about Prof. Bruce's approaching departure for Europe. McLean entered. "Good evening lieutenant" he said; then to Prof. Bruce: "Think over what we have been talking about. I'll call you up later. So long."

He started to leave the room.

"By the way, Prof. McLean," said the lieutenant in a cordial tone, "I'm glad I saw you here. There's a little matter I've been wanting to ask you about for some time."

McLean's face had suddenly blanched. He was visibly much affected. He tried to speak, but the words apparently failed him.

"In fact," continued the lieutenant in the same level tone, looking steadily at McLean, "I followed you here. You know why, don't you?"

"I—I—" mumbled McLean with quivering lips.

The lieutenant took Breckenridge's pencil from Lucille and held it out to him. "Do you happen to know this pencil?" he demanded sharply.

The other hesitated.

"Take it! Look at it!"

McLean took it gingerly. "I've never—." He did not finish the sentence. He fell in a dead faint to the floor.

Prof. Bruce telephoned for the doctor.

Fifteen minutes later, while McLean was lying on a couch, Lieut. Childs said to Prof. Bruce and Lucille, in an adjoining room:

"Why, I'm beginning to believe that he knows something. Why, I was only bluffing him to satisfy Miss Page."

"A guilty conscience," declared Lucille.

Prof. Bruce started.

"Wait," he said significantly, "I'll show you something."

Entering the room where the doctor was bending over the stricken McLean, he took a paper from McLean's pocket and brought it back to the lieutenant.

"What do you make of this?" he demanded in a strange voice.

The lieutenant read the document.

"Whew!" he exclaimed after a pause; "that's queer."

"He wanted me to pay it without saying for what," explained Prof. Bruce.

"I should say it needs some explanation."

It was a promissory note for $200,000, bearing Mrs. Bruce's signature. The sum, the paper, said, was in settlement of inestimable services and was to be paid on presentation without any questions asked. It bore the seal of a notary public.

An hour later McLean had revived sufficiently to be able to walk about.

Lieut. Childs faced him with the pencil and the promissory note. "Come on, professor," he urged. "I'd advise you to tell all you know, or under the circumstances I'll have to take you to the station."

McLean hesitated for a full minute. "Will you let me go home if I tell all?" he finally pleaded.

"I can't promise. It all depends. All that I can say is that I give you my word to do the best for you if you make a voluntary and truthful statement.

"Well," said McLean with a sigh, "I'll confess all. I've been wanting to ever since that fatal night."

Lucille listened breathlessly for his next words.

"It was all an accident," he began eagerly. "That—that paper will prove that I'm telling the truth."

He went on:

"When I resigned from the university because of a nervous breakdown I became a professional genealogist. Once while tracing the ancestry of a client in a large city in South Carolina I ran across several baptismal and marriage records that had been hidden away in an attic of the courthouse during the Civil War. On looking at the records I noticed the letters f. f. c. and f. m. c. against the ancestors of some of the most prominent men and women of the city. Puzzled to learn what these letters stood for I at last found out they meant "free female of color," and "free male of color," that is to say these citizens, many of whom held high office or were social leaders, were of Negro ancestry. The discovery created consternation, and the city council voted to burn the records unread. This they did, but not before I had saved one of them. Many of those whose ancestors were in the documents gave me sums of money to be silent."

McLean continued in an even voice. His nervousness was all gone now:

"Then I returned to Nortonville to discover that the Cobbetts, Mrs. Bruce's ancestors, were mentioned in the old record I had saved.

"A year ago last February James Cobbett, Mrs. Bruce's grand-uncle, died leaving his entire fortune to charity instead of to Mrs. Inglis, the legitimate heiress. Mrs. Inglis contested the will, as you know, and won. An appeal was made, but I felt sure she would win again.

"Then an idea came to me. Remembering the money that I had received for suppressing those ancestries down South, I decided to impose on Mrs. Bruce, who I know would finally inherit the Cobbett millions.

"Taking the old record I forged an f. f. c. before the name of Lucy Eastbourne, Mrs. Bruce's grandmother. I then showed it to Mrs. Bruce and told her that she was of Negro ancestry. For keeping the matter silent, I demanded $200,000 on that promissory note. That note will prove to you that I didn't want her to die, as you will see that I could then have collected the money easily.

"God," he continued reminiscently, while his auditors listened in amazement, "how I tortured her. To make her believe me I told her that if she had any children they were likely to be born coal-black and with kinky hair. Twice she would have been a mother, but through fear that the child would be born black she—"

Prof. Bruce, his face livid with rage, sprang at him.

"You brute! You devil in the shape of a man," he shrieked, choking him.

The doctor and the lieutenant pried him away.

"I shall tell all," continued McLean piteously. "How I tortured her to make her sign this paper. I needed money. I am getting old."

The doctor gave him some brandy. He went on: "Then I went to help Breckenridge with his studies. He promised to give me all the prize money if I pulled him through. Walton was in the way. Then that Saturday evening Breckenridge told me that the examination papers were here. I wanted to make sure that he would win and—and I decided to come here and get them. I had been here before—I'm the one that Walton heard in Mrs. Bruce's room that night—I was trying to make her sign the paper then.

"After I had opened the papers and was copying down the questions I heard a sound, and, looking up, saw Mrs. Bruce, who crept in. She ordered me away, and when I refused she took a revolver from the drawer and threatened me. I had made up my mind to get the questions, however, and tried to take the revolver from her. In the struggle it went off and killed her. That's the truth, as God is my judge."

"Why did you return?" asked the lieutenant.

"I forgot my note-book on the desk. As I was coming back I saw Prof. Bruce rushing in. We came to see Walton running away. While Prof. Bruce ran to his wife I rushed to the table and got the note-book, but forgot the pencil."

"How did the hair get in Mrs. Bruce's fingers?" demanded Lucille.

"As Walton was rushing out he stumbled against me nearly knocking me over. My outstretched hand grasped at his hair, pulling out some. When I discovered the strands in my hand I placed them in her fingers to avert suspicion from myself. I meant to save Walton later, but was always afraid of incriminating myself."

"Does Breckenridge know of this?" demanded Prof. Bruce.

McLean was silent.

"Come on," urged the lieutenant. "You promised to tell all."

"Yes, he knew. When you asked him about the pencil, he asked me and I had to tell him. He had left the pencil on the table in the apartment when he left for the theatre."

"How was it you left no fingerprints?" asked Lieut. Childs?

"I wore gloves."

"Oh, no! Well, professor, I'll have to take you to the station. You'll have to tell your story to the magistrate in the morning and let him decide."

Lieut. Childs took his prisoner away. Lucille stayed behind. Turning to Prof. Bruce, she said: "I beg to apologize most humbly for having suspected you."

"Not at all, Miss Page, not at all. I desire to join in the lieutenant's praise of you. It is a very good thing that you did suspect me, or I'd never have told you of the pencil.

"I also want to thank you for bringing my race prejudice into the open. I had hitherto deluded myself into the fact that I hadn't any. Race prejudice is a mean and contemptible thing."

Two days later John was a free man. Lucille and Mrs. Walton went to meet him at the prison.

"Oh, you wonderful, wonderful girl!" said John, repeatedly embracing Lucille again and again.

"I feel like a new man," he said, bubbling like a child as they sped home on the street car. "What a wonderful thing it is to be free! How good the people, the trees, and everything looks. Whey! but I had a narrow shave.

"Lucille," he went on, you promised to tell us how that current happened to give out at the last moment."

"I will if you promise not to tell. I learned that, if an iron bar were thrown against the wire, the wire would immediately cross-circuit and burn in two: so I climbed a tree in Conover's Woods and threw one at it. I made several misses but, thank God, I hit it in time."

That night was a night of joy at the Montgomerys. Scores of visitors, some of them among the most prominent residents of the town, came to see John and to felicitate him on his narrow escape. He received many offers of help. Someone promised to finance him during the remainder of his time at the university.

The next morning Lucille received a letter from Prof. Bruce. It bore the New York postmark. When she opened it, she grasped [*sic*] with astonishment. Taking out an enclosed slip she handed it to John. He, too, started.

"We're rich," he yelled. The slip was a check for $20,000, payable to Mr. and Mrs. John B. Walton.

"Tell John Walton," the letter said, "that I say he's the luckiest man in the world to have a girl like you."

The household crowded around in congratulation.

Presently Lucille said seriously, "Mr. and Mrs. John B. Walton. What does he mean?"

"He means that we must be married in order the get the dough," laughed John.

"But I've changed my mind about marrying," said Lucille in the same serious tone.

"You should have left me in the electric chair, then," said John, hugging her.

"Right and justice always win out," said Mrs. Walton fervently.

"True, mother," effervesced John, "but they both came mighty near slipping up this time."

A week later the Nortonville Herald announced that Mr. and Mrs. John B. Walton had left for Europe on their honeymoon.

From *The Ku Klux Spirit: A Brief Outline of the History of the Ku Klux Klan Past and Present* (1923)

In this piece, also published serially in *The Messenger* under the title "The Ku Klux Klan: A Menace or a Promise?" March–October 1923, Rogers details the history and growth of the Ku Klux Klan, the racist group that from its beginnings has always inspired fear in African Americans. Rogers traces the group's founding as a fraternal organization established by six former Confederate veterans. Its inception was marked more by its bizarre costumes and rituals than by violence against Blacks. Soon, however, with white anger bubbling over because of Reconstruction (1865–1877), which vastly improved opportunities for Blacks in the South, the Klan morphed into a much more virulent organization. It installed ruthless former Confederate general Nathan Bedford Forrest as its Grand Wizard in 1867. The group terrorized African Americans with its violent actions including lynchings. The loosely organized group petered out by the early 1870s, but a second, even more vicious, iteration of the organization roared back to life about 1915. The Klan expanded its space beyond its traditional base in the South and its terrorism extended beyond just African Americans to Catholics, Jews, and immigrants. Lynchings increased so quickly that W. E. B. Du Bois' periodical *Crisis* kept a running total. Rogers estimated at the time this article was written that there were anywhere "from a half a million to five million klansmen." As he states, "Because of the abundance of hates of various sorts in America, the Invisible Empire[1] has a profitable field for its activities." This text is taken from the Messenger Publishing Co. (1923). Later reprinted by Black Classic Press (1980).

THE KU KLUX SPIRIT

Origin of the Ku Klux Klan Proper

One evening in May, 1865, six young men, veterans of the late war, met, according to their daily custom, in a lawyer's office in Pulaski [Tennessee]. After the excitement of war they were being consumed by boredom in the sleepy little town. On this evening, one of them suggested, as a way out of the monotony, the formation of a secret society, on the model of his college fraternity. The others welcomed the idea, and the Greek word "kukloi" (circle) was suggested as a name. "Call it 'Ku Klux'" said another. "Why not Ku Klux Klan," suggested a third. The alliteration and the mysterious affect made an instant impression and the last name was immediately adopted. Officers were elected and the ritual and the oath of secrecy were composed. The main idea was to create a society, different from those in vogue—one whose aim was solely fun and frolic. Because of the prevailing belief in ghosts, it was decided that the greatest fun could be had by playing upon the superstitions of the townsfolk.

J. C. Lester and D. L. Wilson, two of the original six, in their book, "The Ku Klux Klan,"[2] say "Each member was required to provide himself with the following outfit: a white mask for the face with orifices for the eyes and nose, a tall fantastic cardboard hat so constructed as to increase the wearer's apparent height; a gown or robe of sufficient length to cover the entire person. Each individual was left free to choose his own color and cut and each endeavored to make his robe as fantastic as possible."

The greater part of the fun, it was expected would be furnished by the initiation ceremony and that was made as ridiculous as possible. Strange names were used in order to add to the air of mystery.

On Independence Day, the citizens of many of the leading towns of the South awoke to find the sidewalks littered with slips of paper with the words: "The Ku Klux Klan will parade to-night." The Klan, says Lester, had been avoiding publicity, now it had decided to get all it could.

That night the people of Pulaski thronged the streets in the hope of learning at last something of this mysterious association. The klansmen met by signal in the woods and rode through the town in soldierly formation and perfect discipline. Their hideous costumes, the flaming torches, the terrifying appearance of their draped horses, and the uncanny silence of their movements created but greater mystery and terror. Scrutinize, as the bystanders would, they could not recognize a single man or horse. For more than two hours the hooded horsemen rode in deathly silence. They numbered only four hundred, but arriving at a lonely spot they would wheel and march back, giving the impression that they were tens of thousands.

The ex-soldiers of the Confederacy rushed to join the Klan. In 1869 its membership was estimated at 550,000. The members in all the societies totalled over a million. By 1870 almost the whole Confederacy was again in arms, this time unseen—The Invisible Empire.

General Nathaniel B. Forrest, an ex-slave broker, was chose as head. Forrest was the Confederate leader responsible for the massacre at Fort Pillow,[3] where hundreds of captured Northern soldiers were shot down in cold blood. J.B. Gordon,[4] G.W. Gordon[5], A.H. Colquit[6] and other Confederate generals held high commands.

Tactics of the Klan When Ghosts Ceased to Frighten

The Klan began its intimidation by mummery. But "ghosts" do not frighten for long. Seen often enough they soon become normal to the most timid. Negroes would now and then shoot a ghost to learn its identity. Northerners also had to be reckoned with.

The next step was threat and then force. Members of the Grand Army, white Republican leaders, and Negroes were found mysteriously slain. Negro school-houses were an especial object of attack. Members of the Klan were found as mysteriously slain. Southern loyalists, or scalawags, as they were called, aligned themselves with the Negroes and then re-commenced a series of disorders that convulsed the South for the next three years. The Civil War had broken out afresh on a smaller but a more vindictive scale.

Negro leaders, Grand Army men, Republicans (then called Radicals), white teachers of Negro schools, and Southerners who had accepted the new amendments[7] were regarded as enemies by the Invisible Empire. All were grouped under the term "abolitionists" which in the parlance of the "Empire" meant "one who favors and seeks to promote Negro equality, miscegenation, rape, arson and anarchy."

In the reign of terror that followed, white Unionists and Negroes were lynched by the thousands, white women teachers were murdered, whipped and raped; women, black and white, were outraged; and pregnant women ripped open. There has probably existed, in no other nation, such lawlessness as that which then existed under the Invisible Empire.

In judging the character of the klansmen, it is necessary to remember that the majority of its members were ex-soldiers, men inured to cruelty for four years of war, and likely to stop at no excess.

It was almost impossible to punish such of these midnight assassins as were caught. Judge, jury and sheriff were likely to be klansmen. Witnesses were intimidated. All that was necessary to acquit a murderer was a sign. When the crime was so bad as to compel attention the verdict usually rendered was that death had been inflicted by the deceased himself or by Negroes.

Continued Activities of the Klan

To return to the Klan. The devil that had been aroused would not be downed so easily. The Klan had now swollen to enormous proportions, perhaps over a million in number. This most formidable aggregation of cutthroats, thieves and rapists in the history of western civilization, could not be dissipated by a few words. This great menagerie of midnight rattlesnakes and human tigers grew more unmanageable than ever, and began to attack their former comrades. Starting with the goal of white supremacy the Klan soon passed it. Now the objective was "klan-nish-ness." White men, regardless of racial or other bonds, have always had differences one with another, and when an outsider, regardless of color, offended a klansman, he was regarded as having offended all klansmen. As in the case of the Germans and the English in the late war, the bond of color was obliterated by that of klanship, or nationality. The Klan thirsted for plunder. Rich Southerners and former klansmen who refused to pay tribute were murdered or driven from the state. Their homes, in many instances, were burnt, and their wives and daughters outraged.

Most historians attempt to create a difference between the period prior to the withdrawal of Gen. Forrest and that after. It is clear, however, that one period grew out of the other as noon out of forenoon, or as the viper out of the younger. Forrest, moreover, did not withdraw until February, 1869, the same month and year that Tennessee had begun military action against his "empire," In other words, *he was a klansman, only when it was safe to be one. In this he ran true to form: masked bandits are usually less brave than unmasked ones.*

Lester and Wilson, two of the original six, who, in spite of their cautious attitude, may be regarded as champions of the Klan, say in their book already mentioned: "Nothing is more certain than that a part of the evil the Klan was combatting at his period of its history grew out of its own methods."

Aim of the Klan

The ostensible aims of the Klan were to keep Negroes in near-servitude, to oppose the new amendments to the Constitution; and to prevent

Northern whites from settling and trading in the South. Forrest, in his testimony, says: "It objects [*sic*] originally were protection against loyal leagues and the Grand Army of the Republic." It came to have a more sinister motive: it aimed to accomplish by invisible methods what the Confederacy had failed to do on the battlefield. What would have happened had the South been victorious? Slavery, without a doubt, would have been re-established in the North. Black slavery first, and then white slavery, unless England had permitted the re-opening of the slave trade. Slavery once re-established, the white race would have fought its way back to savagery.

When the Klan, which was but the Confederacy in its night-caps and night-gowns, once controlled the South, it planned to get control of the army, the navy, the Treasury, and other instruments of government. When the government, that had been so painfully and laboriously built up by the people of the nation, had once been undermined, a monarchy would have been set up, as note the absolute power that was wielded by the Grand Wizard. The Ku Klux Klan was a formidable conspiracy against the liberties of the American people. It is evident that there would have been a Klan of some sort even if the Negroes had not been given the vote.

The Klan Today

The klan of today is running true to form. Since its revival hundreds of citizens, white and black, of both sexes have been killed or outraged by it. The New York *World* has published a long list of its proven atrocities. Awaking again, in 1915, for the purpose of preventing Negro migration to the North during the war, it selected as its next task the intimidation of returned Negro soldiers, who had tasted of freedom in France. Starting, as in 1865, with the goal of "white supremacy" it has extended its activities to include not less than one-third of the white population of the North. In addition to being anti-Negro, it is now an anti-Semitic, anti-Catholic, anti-foreign-born, anti-liberal, anti-labor—one hundred per cent American organization. The Negro question furnishing too limited a field for its activities, it invaded the North and, with the shrewdness of the born trickster, so adapted itself as to take in the leading hatreds of the various sections of the country. For instance, it is anti-Catholic in the South, anti-Jew and anti-foreign-born in the North, anti-Japanese in the West, and so on. It says, in effect, be a member and be free to indulge your particular hate. At present its activities are directed mainly against white persons.

The Klan makes a great pretense—a pretense that is almost a protest, of its loyalty to the United States, precisely as the old Klan did. It is a military organization, and endeavors to entrap as many legislators, government officials, officers of the army and navy, and the police as possible. The Invisible Empire is a monarchy. The ruler is styled "emperor," is addressed as "his majesty" and holds office for life. The subjects of this invisible empire operate with masks on their faces, after the manner of burglars and highwaymen.

The Klan appears to be on the increase, particularly in the Northern States, in spite of the fight being waged against it by newspapers and liberal organizations. On July 20, 1922, at an initiation ceremony in Chicago, Ill., there were present over 4,800 novices and 25,000 klansmen from the local klan. There may be at the present time in the United States from a half a million to five million Klansmen. Because of the abundance of hates of various sorts in America, the Invisible Empire has a profitable field for its activities.

The present Klan thrives largely because many of those whom it opposes sympathize with it in its attack on certain groups. For instance, many foreign-born Protestants think the Klan does well to fight the Catholics; many Catholics think it does well to fight the radicals; the radicals that it does well to fight the Negroes and certain Negroes that it does well because it creates a division among the whites.

“Jazz at Home” *Survey Graphic*, March 1925; also *The New Negro* (1925)

Howard University professor, Alain Locke, a doyen of the Harlem Renaissance/New Negro Movement, solicited Rogers to write an article on jazz for the groundbreaking March 1925 issue of *Survey Graphic*. This volume and the book which followed, *The New Negro*, were two of the seminal works of the New Negro Movement, introducing many of the major figures of the era to white and Black readers. In “Jazz at Home,” one of Rogers’s finest essays, the author is exuberant in his encomium for jazz, quintessentially American and even more so African American. Jazz possesses so many paradoxical qualities: it is rebellious by nature, but also as Rogers claims, “a tonic,” or even a “safety valve,” to relieve anger and frustration at the “modern machine-ridden and convention-bound society” and turn it into art. Jazz combines elements of the modern age and the primitive, creating “modern man-made jungles.” Rogers delves into the history of the form, tracing it back to W.C. Handy and a more obscure Chicago musician, Jasbo Brown, from whose first name Rogers claims the term “jazz” originated. And although jazz was often scorned as an uninvited cur coming to the table of civilization, it, along with its obverse, the spirituals, encapsulates “the peculiar and unique experience of the Negro in this country.” Jazz is broad enough to also encompass the “boisterous good-nature characteristics of the American, white or black,” but its best practitioner is always the African American. Although it has moved from its humble roots to be included with the most serious music of the French modernists, particularly the Surrealists, it has never forgotten the sources from which it has sprung. At the time the article was written jazz was a controversial subject. To many, the sordid source of jazz was a threat, a pit of vice to lure the unwary into immoral, self-destructive behavior. But to others, in particular the New Negro, it represented a panacea with its joy and vitality. At its best, jazz is a powerful "leveller," having the capability "to truly democratize." Rogers points out both views, noting jazz's potential dangers, preferring the "safer" orchestral jazz to that found in the cabarets. Still, he clearly admires the power and artistry of jazz. For an insightful discussion of this article, see Thabiti Asukile, "J.A. Rogers's 'Jazz at Home': Afro-American Jazz in Paris During the Jazz Age." *Black Scholar* 40.3 (2010). See also Rogers's article "Music and Poetry—The Noblest Arts" *Music and Poetry* (January 1921) and his review of Paul Whiteman's book *Jazz* ["Is There Such a Thing as Negro Art?"] in this anthology. The text here is taken from *The New Negro* (1925).

"JAZZ AT HOME"

Jazz is a marvel of paradox: too fundamentally human, at least as modern humanity goes, to be typically racial, too international to be characteristically national, too much abroad in the world to have a special home. And yet jazz in spite of it all is one part American and three parts American Negro, and was originally the nobody's child of the levee and the city slum. Transplanted exotic—a rather hardy one, we admit—of the mundane world capitals, sport of the sophisticated, it is really at home in its humble native soil wherever the modern unsophisticated Negro feels happy and sings and dances to his mood. It follows that jazz is more at home in Harlem than in Paris, though from the look and sound of certain quarters of Paris one would hardly think so. It is just the epidemic contagiousness of jazz that makes it, like the measles, sweep the block. But somebody had to have it first: that was the Negro.

What after all is this taking new thing, that, condemned in certain quarters, enthusiastically welcomed in others, has nonchalantly gone on until it ranks with the movie and the dollar as a foremost exponent of modern Americanism? Jazz isn't music merely, it is a spirit that can express itself in almost anything. The true spirit of jazz is a joyous revolt from convention, custom, authority, boredom, even sorrow—from everything that would confine the soul of man and hinder its riding free on the air. The Negroes who invented it called their songs the "Blues," and they weren't capable of satire or deception. Jazz was their explosive attempt to cast off the blues and be happy, carefree happy, even in the midst of sordidness and sorrow. And that is why it has been such a balm for modern ennui, and has become a safety valve for modern machine-ridden and convention-bound society. It is the revolt of the emotions against repression.

The story is told of the clever group of "Jazz-specialists" who, originating dear knows in what scattered places, had found themselves and the frills of the art in New York and had been drawn to the gay Bohemias of Paris. In a little cabaret of Montmârtre[1] they had just "entertained" into the wee small hours fascinated society and royalty; and, of course, had been paid royally for it. Then, the entertainment over and the guests away, the "entertainers" entertained themselves with their very best, which is always impromptu, for the sheer joy of it. That is jazz.

In its elementals, jazz has always existed. It is in the Indian war-dance, the Highland fling, the Irish jig, the Cossack dance, the Spanish fandango, the Brazilian *maxime*,[2] the dance of the whirling dervish, the hula of the South Seas, the *danse du ventre*[3] of the Orient, the *carmagnole*[4] of the French Revolution, the strains of Gypsy music, and the ragtime of the Negro. Jazz proper, however, is something more than all these. It is a release of all the suppressed emotions at once, a blowing off of the lid, as it were. It is hilarity expressing itself through pandemonium; musical fireworks.

The direct predecessor of jazz is ragtime. That both are atavistically African there is little doubt, but to what extent it is difficult to determine. In its barbaric rhythm and exuberance there is something of the bamboula,[5] a wild, abandoned dance of the West African and the Haytian Negro, so stirringly described by the anonymous author of *Untrodden Fields of Anthropology*,[6] or of the *ganza*[7] ceremony so brilliantly depicted in Maran's *Batouala*.[8] But jazz time is faster and more complex than African music. With its cowbells, auto horns, calliopes, rattles, dinner gongs, kitchen utensils, cymbals, screams, crashes, clankings and monotonous rhythm it bears all the marks of a nerve-strung, strident, mechanized civilization. It is a thing of the jungles—modern man-made jungles.

The earliest jazz-makers were the itinerant piano players who would wander up and down the Mississippi from saloon to saloon, from dive to dive. Seated at the piano with a carefree air that a king might envy, their box-back coats[9] flowing over the stool, their Stetsons pulled well over their eyes, and cigars at an angle of forty-five degrees, they would "whip the ivories" to marvellous chords and hidden racy, joyous meanings, evoking the intense delight of their hearers who would smother them at the close with huzzas and whiskey. Often wholly illiterate, these humble troubadours knowing nothing of written music or composition, but with minds like cameras, would listen to the rude improvisations of the dock laborers and the railroad gangs and reproduce them, reflecting perfectly the sentiments and the longings of these humble folk. The improvised bands at Negro dances in the South, or the little boys with their harmonicas and jews'-harps, each one putting his own individuality into the air, played also no inconsiderable part in its evolution. "Poverty," says J. A. Jackson of the *Billboard*, "compelled improvised instruments. Bones, tambourines, make-shift string instruments, tin can and hollow wood effects, all now utilized as musical novelties, were among early Negroes the product of necessity. When these were not available 'patting juba'[10] prevailed. Present-day 'Charleston' is but a variation of this. Its early expression was the 'patting' for the buck dance."

The origin of the present jazz craze is interesting. More cities claim its birthplace than claimed Homer dead. New Orleans, San Francisco, Memphis, Chicago, all assert the honor is theirs. Jazz, as it is to-day, seems to have come into being this way, however: W.C. Handy,[11] a Negro, having digested the airs of the itinerant musicians referred to, evolved the first classic, *Memphis Blues*. Then came Jasbo Brown,[12] a reckless musician of a Negro cabaret in Chicago, who played this and other blues, blowing his own extravagant moods and risqué interpretations into them, while hilarious with gin. To give further meanings to his veiled allusions he would make the trombone "talk" by putting a derby hat and later a tin can at its mouth. The delighted patrons would shout, "More, Jasbo. More, Jas, more." And so the name originated.

As to the jazz dance itself: at this time Shelton Brooks,[13] a Negro comedian, invented a new "strut," called "Walkin' the Dog." Jasbo's anarchic airs found in this strut a soul mate. Then as a result of their union came "The Texas Tommy,"[14] the highest point of brilliant, acrobatic execution and nifty footwork so far evolved in jazz dancing. The latest of these dances is the "Charleston," which has brought something really new to the dance step. The "Charleston" calls for activity of the whole body. One characteristic is a fantastic fling of the legs from the hip downwards. The dance ends in what is known as the "camel-walk"—in reality a gorilla-like shamble—and finishes with a peculiar hop like that of the Indian war dance. Imagine one suffering from a fit of rhythmic ague and you have the effect precisely.

The cleverest "Charleston" dancers perhaps are urchins of five and six who may be seen any time on the streets of Harlem, keeping time with their hands, and surrounded by admiring crowds. But put it on a well-set stage, danced by a bobbed-hair chorus, and you have an effect that reminds you of the abandon of the Furies.[15] And so Broadway studies Harlem. Not all of the visitors of the twenty or more well-attended cabarets of Harlem are idle pleasure seekers or underworld devotees. Many are serious artists, actors and producers seeking something new, some suggestion to be taken, too often in pallid imitation, to Broadway's lights and stars.

This makes it difficult to say whether jazz is more characteristic of the Negro or of contemporary America. As was shown, it is of Negro origin plus the influence of the American environment. It is Negro-American. Jazz proper, however, is in idiom—rhythmic, musical and pantomimic—thoroughly American Negro; it is his spiritual picture on that lighter comedy side, just as the spirituals are the picture on the tragedy side. The two are poles apart, but the former is by no means to be despised and it is just as characteristically the product of the peculiar and unique expression of the Negro in this country. The African Negro hasn't it, and the Caucasian never could have invented it. Once achieved, it is common property, and jazz has absorbed the national spirit, that tremendous spirit of go, the nervousness, lack of conventionality and boisterous good-nature characteristic of the American, white or black, as compared with the more rigid formal natures of the Englishman or German.

But there still remains something elusive about jazz that few, if any of the white artists, have been able to capture. The Negro is admittedly its best expositor. That elusive something, for lack of a better name, I'll call Negro rhythm. The average Negro, particularly of the lower classes, puts rhythm into whatever he does, whether it be shining shoes or carrying a basket on the head to market as the Jamaican women do. Some years ago while wandering in Cincinnati I happened upon a Negro revival meeting at its height. The majority present were women, a goodly few of whom were white. Under the influence of the "spirit" the sisters would come forward and strut—much of jazz enters where it would be least expected. The Negro women had the perfect jazz abandon, while the white ones moved lamely and woodenly. This same lack of spontaneity is evident to a degree in the cultivated and inhibited Negro.

In its playing technique, jazz is similarly original and spontaneous. The performance of the Negro musicians is much imitated, but seldom equalled. Lieutenant Europe,[16] leader of the famous band of the "Fifteenth New York Regiment," said that the bandmaster of the Garde Republicaine, amazed at his jazz effects, could not believe without demonstration that his band had not used special instruments. Jazz has a virtuoso technique all its own: its best performers, singers and players, lift it far above the level of mere "trick" or mechanical effects. Abbie Mitchell,[17] Ethel Waters, and Florence Mills, the Blues Singers, Clara[18], Mamie,"[19] and Bessie Smith, Eubie Blake, the pianist; "Buddy" Gilmore,[20] the drummer, and "Bill" Robinson, the pantomimic dancer—to mention merely an illustrious few—are inimitable artists, with an inventive, improvising skill that defies imitation. And those who know their work most intimately trace its uniqueness without exception to the folk-roots of their artistry.

Musically jazz has a great future. It is rapidly being sublimated. In the more famous jazz orchestras like those of Will Marion Cook,[21] Paul Whiteman,[22] Sissle and Blake,[23] Sam Stewart,[24] Fletcher Henderson,[25] Vincent Lopez[26] and the Clef Club units,[27] there are none of the vulgarities and crudities of the lowly origin or the only too prevalent cheap imitations. The pioneer work in the artistic development of jazz was done by Negro artists; it was the lead of the so-called "syncopated orchestras" of Tyers[28] and Will Marion Cook, the former playing for the Castles of dancing fame,[29] and the latter touring as a concertizing orchestra in the great American centers and abroad. Because of the difficulties of financial backing, these expert combinations have had to yield ground to white orchestras of the type of the Paul Whiteman and Vincent Lopez organizations that are now demonstrating the finer possibilities of jazz music. "Jazz," says Serge Koussevitzky,[30] the new conductor of the Boston Symphony, "is an important contribution to modern musical literature. It has an epochal significance—it is not superficial, it is fundamental. Jazz comes from the soil, where all music has its beginning." And Leopold Stokowski says more extendedly of it:

> "Jazz has come to stay because it is an expression of the times, of the breathless, energetic, superactive times in which we are living, it is useless to fight against it. Already its new vigor, its new vitality is beginning to manifest itself. . . . America's contribution to the music of the past will have the same revivifying effect as the injection of new, and in the larger sense, vulgar blood into dying aristocracy. Music will then be vulgarized in the best sense of the word, and enter more and more into the daily lives of people . . . . The Negro musicians of America are playing a great part in this change. They have an open mind, and unbiased outlook. They are not hampered by conventions or traditions, and with their new ideas, their constant experiment, they are causing new blood to flow in the veins of music. The jazz players make their instruments

do entirely new things, things finished musicians are taught to avoid. They are pathfinders into new realms."

And thus it has come about that serious modernist music and musicians, most notably and avowedly in the work of the French modernists Auric,[31] Satie[32] and Darius Milhaud,[33] have become the confessed debtors of American Negro jazz. With the same nonchalance and impudence with which it left the levee and the dive to stride like an upstart conqueror, almost overnight, into the grand salon, jazz now begins its conquest of musical Parnassus.[34]

Whatever the ultimate result of the attempt to raise jazz from the mob-level upon which it originated, its true home is still its original cradle, the none too respectable cabaret. And here we have the seamy side to the story. Here we have some of the charm of Bohemia, but much more of the demoralization of vice. Its rash spirit is in Grey's popular song, *Runnin' Wild*[35]:

Runnin' wild; lost control
Runnin' wild; mighty bold,
Feelin' gay and reckless too
Carefree all the time; never blue
Always goin' I don't know where
Always showin' that I don't care
Don' love nobody, it ain't worth while
All alone; runnin' wild.

Jazz reached the height of its vogue at a time when minds were reacting from the horrors and strain of war. Humanity welcomed it because in its fresh joyousness men found a temporary forgetfulness, infinitely less harmful than drugs or alcohol. It is partly for some such reasons that it dominates the amusement life of America to-day. No one can sensibly condone its excesses or minimize its social danger if uncontrolled; all culture is built upon inhibitions and control. But it is doubtful whether the "jazz-hounds" of high and low estate would use their time to better advantage. In all probability their tastes would find some equally morbid, mischievous vent. Jazz, it is needless to say, will remain a recreation for the industrious and a dissipater of energy for the frivolous, a tonic for the strong and a poison for the weak.

For the Negro himself, jazz is both more and less dangerous than for the white—less, in that he is nervously more in tune with it; more, in that at his average level of economic development his amusement life is more open to the forces of social vice. The cabaret of better type provides a certain Bohemianism for the Negro intellectual, the artist and the well-to-do. But the average thing is too much the substitute for the saloon and the wayside inn. The tired longshoreman, the porter, the housemaid and the poor elevator boy in search of recreation, seeking in jazz the tonic for weary nerves and muscles, are only too apt to find the bootlegger, the gambler and the demi-monde who have come there for victims and to escape the eyes of the police.

Yet in spite of its present vices and vulgarizations, its sex informalities, its morally anarchic spirit, jazz has a popular mission to perform. Joy, after all, has a physical basis. Those who laugh and dance and sing are better off even in their vices than those who do not. Moreover, jazz with its mocking disregard for formality is a leveller and makes for democracy. The jazz spirit, being primitive, demands more frankness and sincerity. Just as it already has done in art and music, so eventually in human relations and social manners, it will no doubt have the effect of putting more reality in life by taking some of the needless artificiality out.... Naturalness finds the artificial in conduct ridiculous. "Cervantes smiled Spain's chivalry away," said Byron.[36] And so this new spirit of joy and spontaneity may itself play the rôle of reformer. Where at present it vulgarizes, with more wholesome growth in the future, it may on the contrary truly democratize. At all events, jazz is rejuvenation, a recharging of the batteries of civilization with primitive new vigor. It has come to stay, and they are wise, who instead of protesting against it, try to lift and divert it into nobler channels.

"J. A. Rogers Makes Comparison of French and American Customs," New York *Amsterdam News*, October 14, 1925

Rogers first visited Europe in 1925 and was immediately impressed by the better race relations in England, and particularly France, compared with the United States. For many African Americans, Paris was seen as a bastion of freedom, particularly in the years between the two world wars. Although Blacks faced much less overt racial discrimination in France than in the United States and Great Britain, the French could still be patronizing of the Blacks in their midst. Rogers could seldom see the way they often viewed Blacks through the lens of the racist concept of the "Noble Savage." As critic Tyler Stovall remarks, "Far from maintaining that blacks were equal to whites, [French society] asserted or at least implied that their lack of intelligence and civilization were virtues, not vices" (32). Rogers was one of the least willing to criticize any aspect of the French and failed to see the often condescending and paternalistic aspects of the culture. However, to be fair to him there were no lynchings, Klan groups, or Jim Crow laws in Paris, and many African American artists and writers besides Rogers have long loved France, from Josephine Baker to Richard Wright to James Baldwin.

With his loquacious personality Rogers quickly fit into the Black community in Paris, visiting jazz clubs regularly and meeting such well-known Black personalities as performer Josephine Baker, club owner/musician Bricktop, and the remarkable war pilot/drummer/night club owner Eugene Bullard. Rogers lived in Paris for several stretches between 1925 and the 1950s. By his later trips to France, Rogers, though always extremely partial to the country, began to gain a somewhat deeper understanding of the nuances of the culture. For more on African Americans in Paris, see Tyler Stoval, *Paris Noir: African Americans in the City of Light*; William A. Shack, *Harlem in Montmartre*; Michel Fabre, *From Harlem to Paris*; and Tracy Whiting, *Bricktop's Paris*.

"J. A. ROGERS MAKES COMPARISON OF FRENCH AND AMERICAN CUSTOMS"

"No Disgrace in France," He Writes, "to Be Black or Have Kinky Hair"—Hopes to Return to United States Soon

In this article I will tell of some of the French customs and how they differ from American ones.

Coming from a country where it is not legitimate to have a thirst, one of the things that has struck me most is the enormous quantity of wine that is consumed. A Frenchman takes wine with his meals as an American is supposed to take water, and in the cheaper restaurants if you do not order wine you are charged extra on your bill. Drinking with each meal is such a fixed custom in France that I fancy the foes of "the Demon Rum" will have a rather hard job trying to introduce prohibition.

One of the most difficult things to an American used to a hearty feed in the morning is the French breakfast, which consists only of rolls and coffee. It is difficult to get a substantial meal before 11:30. Unlike the American restaurants, the French restaurants are open only about three hours around noon, and about four hours in the evening. Food is about a third cheaper than in England and America, quality for quality. Many places serve an entire course, wine included, for four francs or about 10 cents. But to eat in such places one must have a rather robust stomach. Tipping is the custom in France, and if you were to forget the waiter, he'd pretty soon tell you about it.

When you go to the theatre the usher expects a tip—it is her pay—and at the hotel, one-tenth of the price of your room is added to the bill for the chambermaid.

The means of transportation in Paris are street car, auto bus, subway and taxi. The latter are even more numerous than in New York City, and ever so much cheaper. Taxis in Paris are almost as cheap as street cars and four persons can ride from one end of the city to the other for about fifty cents.

The public conveyances all have first and second class. One can ride all over the Paris subway second class for about two cents. But when you get to your station you'd better open the subway door yourself or you'll be carried by. The same holds true when you are getting on.

As was said the advocates of prohibition will find a virgin field to work in: so also will the advocates of Sunday closing as Sunday is a great business day here—many of the places close on Monday instead.

In the markets, large heaps of snails are on sale. I ate one for curiosity's sake. It was tough and rather tasteless, and I have decided that so far as snails and oysters are concerned the little dears can go on enjoying their lives.

Wine, brandy, cognac and beer are very cheap. You can get a quart of good wine for about ten cents. It is certainly not comforting to my thirsty friends in the great American Sahara to say this, but the fact is that you can get a schooner of beer (or schope, as it is called here) for three cents. Is it any wonder that almost every fifth person one meets in Paris is an American?

Omelette Without Eggs

There is never a rule without an exception. You have heard the old saying: One can't make an omelette without breaking eggs. Well, it is all wrong. The other day I stopped at a restaurant and ordered two boiled eggs. Soon the waitress returned to say something about her having no boiled eggs, but that I could have an omelette. Well, I have found that when I don't quite understand the best way out is to say: "Oui." But, when she had gone, I reflected a bit. When the omelette came my curiosity at seeing it was about as far as I got with it.

Speaking French is more than a notion. You start out to say one thing and you finish by saying another. This matter of a difference of language goes so deep that even the cats and dogs will not notice you, if you call them in the English manner.

And speaking of cats, I am reminded to say that a black cat running across your track is a lucky sign here. Thirteen is a lucky number with the French.

Another custom is that a duty is levied for merchandise brought into the city of Paris. This is reminiscent of the time when the states of the union had to pay duty on one another. A taxi-driver leaving Paris had better get a ticket for the quantity of gas taken out. And if he brings in more than he takes out he must pay the duty.

No Color Line

But to me, a Negro, the most striking thing in France is the attitude toward the Negro. Just reverse the Anglo-Saxon or cracker[1] attitude and you have it.

As I said in my last article, one finds Negroes, black Negroes, employed everywhere. I have talked with more than a score of French Negroes, principally from the French West Indies, and they tell me that the natives of those islands enjoy full equality with the Frenchman at home.

In my last article, I spoke of Benglia,[2] the magnificent Senegalese at the Folies-Bergere. I have since returned there and I have found that his contact with the white woman in his act has been cut to a minimum. One act has been entirely eliminated. I remarked on it to a Frenchman and he replied: "C'est les Americains." One hears more English than French spoken at the Folies-Bergere. At one of the side-shows I imagined that I was back in New York City.

As I write, I have before me a copy of Premiere Poincare's[3] warning to Americans to leave their color discriminations at home. Still they have money and are capable of doing a lot of mischief.

In the shop-windows on the Grand Boulevards may be seen wax-models of real Negroes, men and women, kinky hair and all, dressed with the latest clothing as advertisements. This it seems to me is a little more than even the Negro at home, with his inferiority complex would do in his shop-window. To be black is certainly no disgrace in France.

The star in Parisian shows are [*sic*] full-blooded Negroes. Some nights past I went to the Gaumont Palace,[4] one of the finest cinemas I have ever been in. After the pictures there was an acrobatic feature in which the star was a clever little black boy. The act wound up with a boxing contest between this little Negro and a white boy. As they pummeled each other, I waited breathlessly to see which would be made to win. The white boy, I said, surely. But to my astonishment the black boy not only was made to knock out the white one, but he knocked out two of the white men, then stood with one of his feet on the white boy, with arms folded as a conqueror. And the audience applauded.

In front of the Palace of the Trocadero,[5] looking toward the Eiffel Tower, among other statues, are those of two African queens, thick lips and all. I remember that the figure representing Africa in front of Buckingham Palace, London, is a white girl.

I found not a little of color discrimination in London, but so far I have been unable to find the least trace of it here, that is, so far as the French are concerned. At present, I am living in the Latin Quarter. Here one sees almost every race on earth, and all live peaceably. More than ever, am I convinced that the statement that there is a God-ordained hostility between races is one of the biggest lies ever told.

I have since had the pleasure of meeting Rene Maran, famed author of Batouala and being a guest at his home. I will say something about him in my next article.

"J. A. Rogers Gets 'First Hand' Impression of 'Blue Blood' Boosters," *Pittsburgh Courier*, March 6, 1926

One of Rogers's most intriguing interviews is with two high-ranking white supremacists: Earnest Sevier Cox and John Powell. Cox was a Methodist minister and an amateur ethnographer who wrote the once popular book *White America* (1923). Cox agreed with Marcus Garvey's plan to repatriate African Americans to Africa, and continued to advocate for segregation until he died. John Powell was a well-known composer and pianist. He was one of the drafters of the Racial Integrity Act (1924) in Virginia, banning interracial marriage and stipulating that anyone with any trace of Black blood be classified as a Negro. The act was not overturned until the famous Loving v Virginia case of 1967. Cox and Powell, along with Dr. Walter Plecker, formed the Anglo-Saxon Clubs of America, which at their peak in the 1920s had over 400 members and were a more "up-scale" version of the Ku Klux Klan. Rogers's essay shows the danger of such charismatic men, whose friendly, engaging manner frequently masked their evil.

In this chilling interview, exploring the minds of two prominent racists, Rogers reveals it is just such "upstanding" citizens who often lead the mobs to lynch, cause race riots, and commit other heinous forms of racial strife. In the interview, the reader gets a sense of a real-life scenario of Dixon and the racist politician in *From Superman to Man*. Rogers is also easily able to outwit the two "gentlemen" who clearly do not understand his frequent sarcasm in dismissing their plans for Blacks to return to Africa. In this real-life situation, however, we do not get the "happy" ending that we have in *From Superman to Man*. For further discussion of this interview, see Asukile "Marcus Garvey," 64–67.

"J. A. ROGERS GETS 'FIRST HAND' IMPRESSION OF 'BLUE BLOOD' BOOSTERS"

Says Interview With Powell and Knox [*sic*] Made Him Feel As Though He Were In Presence Of the Devil—Classifies Them As Sincere, But Dangerous.

Amazing Revelation To Be Made Next Week[1]

"I'm glad you did not find us the ogres we're said to be," said John Powell, founder of the Anglo-Saxon clubs in parting after our third meeting. "Now," he added, kindly, "if we can do anything for you be sure to let us know."

And truth to say I had not. Quite otherwise. I had found him and his co-worker, Earnest Sevier Cox, to be very fine gentlemen, indeed. Powell is earnest, sympathetic, and very kindly; Cox is jovial, mild-mannered, and quite likeable. He has travelled much, particularly in Africa, and has the free and easy manner of the globe-trotter. Had I never heard of the kind of propaganda they are engaged in I felt I could have liked them just as much as some of my excellent friends, colored and white. Both men showed, moreover, an extreme solicitude at present Negro injustices. Both seemed much moved when I told of the slaughter in the Chicago riot.[2]

BUT—

It is just here that appearances are most deceptive; it is here where so many colored folk permit themselves to be deceived for it is from just such affable sources flow the agitation which culminate in lynchings, race riot and racial discords, which is the bane in this economic paradise of America. As I listened to them my mind flew back to horrible scenes of butchery I witnessed in the Chicago riot, fomented by such pleasant gentlemen as these and I felt, indeed, as [if] I were having an interview with the Devil, himself.

Powell, particularly, strikes me as being sincere. But who knows but that the devil is quite sincere in his mischief. There are doctrines, the preaching of which stir strife, bloodshed and war; there are also doctrines which spread love and light and healing. Who doubts that an apostle of the former can be quite as sincere as the latter? If there is a Devil, you may wager, you may depend upon it he is quite an affable fellow; it is his imps who are the coarse fellows, and in this case it is the rag-tags and bobtails—the lynchers—who are the uncouth ones, and not those at the fountain head of mischief, like Messrs. Cox, Plecker and Powell.

It has been charged that both men are agitating chiefly for personal gain. Powell, it is rumored, is peeved because it is said that Nathaniel Dett[3] was chosen over him in a piano recital—but I don't think so. Both are suffering, in my opinion, particularly Powell, from swollen ego. Had they grown up in a country where there were no Negroes their excessive conceit would have found expression in dislike for members of their own so-called race: They would have been good haters of the English, French, Germans, Americans, as the case may be. Their anti-Negro feeling is only incidental.

Indeed, there ought to be nothing remarkable about this type to us, so-called Negroes, for have we not our ultra-racialists? Change the color of men like the three above mentioned—sacrilegious thought—to black, yellow, or brown, and they would bark as loudly on the other side of the fence as they are now doing on this. It is not a matter of race, but of human nature—the nature of the man who is not happy unless he is maintaining a caste or looking down upon a fellow-man.

Garvey Enthusiasts

Both are intensely interested in Garvey and are backing his movement. Powell says that Garvey is one of the greatest influences that has ever come into his life and anxiously asked me whether I thought him guilty.[4] I replied that to the best of my knowledge he had not been guilty of theft, but that false representations had undoubtedly been made to promote the sale of stock and that the law had held him, as head of the Black Star Line, responsible. Both declared that his imprisonment was a great injustice, and wanted to know if there was such a thing as justice on this earth.

After discussing the matter of Garvey's proposed release and deportation we came to the African colonization plan, which both are trying to push hard through the present session of the legislature, and which they say [they] intend to try to have introduced in all the legislatures and Congress.

"The white man," said Cox, "tore your people from Africa, robbed you of all your land and your tribal rights. He crowded you in vile ships and brought you to these shores. But he may now furnish you with ships and every comfort to take you back. We intend to see that this nation acquire African territory and divide the land among you as our government acquired the West. We pledge the white man to use his ships to carry you home, his weapons to fight your enemies, and his implements of peace to make you a wealthy people."

I thought this even fishier than the famous promise of "forty acres and a mule,"[5] and suggested that the European powers had Africa pretty well sewed up, especially so far as the American Negro was concerned. The latter, I said, was feared throughout the length and breadth of Africa because of his democratic ideals and I mentioned the complications I brought down on myself when I innocently asked for a visa to Africa. I said that the sole hope was the break-up of European domination, but Cox didn't seem to enjoy that.

"There is Liberia," replied Cox. "Liberia is capable of holding all the Negroes in America. Your only hope is colonization, for as long as the Negro remains here he will be exploited. The Chamber of Commerce wants the Negro here because they want to rob him. It is a shame."

"We stand for absolute equality of justice for both races," said Powell, "but they must be separate. Segregation which has lasted three hundred years in this state, must not be broken down. Race mixing is biologically bad."

Now I am a mixed blood and don't think I'm such a bad fellow at that, so I thought he wasn't quite complimentary. Ignoring this, however, I again suggested that from what I had learnt of the psychology of the Americo-Liberian I was led to believe that any large number of American Negroes there would be as little welcome as on British soil.

I pointed out, also, that the growth of any given population was the result of evolution, and that in the shifting of a large number of [the] population we'd have two problems instead of one on our hands—one in the place from which it was shifted and another where it was taken. However, it strikes me that deportation is one easy way to settle the Hampton Institute situation[6] and that if those gentlemen have their way I will be able to visit Africa after all.

Cox wanted to know whether Negroes would be willing to go "back" to Africa. I told him that I knew a few who were very eager to do so, but that the majority were such good Americans that when any of the number got disgusted and went to France or South America, they, like the yellow cat,[7] promptly came back.

"Tell me," flashed Powell, "have your people no pride?" Their theory is that the Negro who wants to stay here lacks pride. Cox says: "Were I commissioned to retain a part of your race in America and send the others away I would retain those who wish to go and send those who wish to remain. If I kept any it would be those who wish to build a nation of your own. If my race must lose its purity, pray God that the aliens who enter be those who value their own blood and seek to express its worth." This statement, by the way, shows that he regards amalgamation[8] as inevitable unless the Negro is taken deported. [*sic*]

Powell's question was timely. It made me wonder in [the] face of present treatment how the governments of the several states and even the federal government itself would take it if Negroes so-called showed more manly pride. One thing I felt sure that professional white men like these wouldn't find such easy sledding.

I replied to the effect that the entire training of the so-called Negro was to make him an American citizen just as the white child. That gods, heroes, and flags of both were the same; that in the matter of paying taxes and national duty such as service in time of war the so-called Negro is such a full-fledged citizen: in short, that in all those things that made for the white man's benefit the Negro was an American, but that in those things that made for his own benefit he was only a Negro.

"You and other white men," I said to Cox, two days later, "have a perfect right to keep yourselves to yourselves, and to agitate for same. You all have a right to think yourselves superior to Negroes, but no right to treat them unjustly. The Negro has at least a hard time earning his dollar as has the white man. Under segregation, however, as exists in the South, the Negro gets less for his dollar than the white man. Who gets what the Negro has lost? Segregation laws are designed expressly for the benefit of their makers."

Both men declared that they stand absolutely for equal justice to both "races" and are working hard to bring it about.

The thing I had been eagerly waiting to hear finally came up for a discussion. I wanted to know how they re-acted to the fact brought out by the discussion of the so-called race integrity bill that some twenty thousand of the leading families of Virginia were colored.

Cox brought it up, treating the whole thing as a very good joke. "What do you think of our little comedy in the legislature?" he asked laughingly. To Powell, the zealot, it was no laughing matter, however. Cox went on to tell how very mixed with Negro were some of the Indians, whom the legislature in view of the recent disclosures, wanted to class as white. These mixed Indians, he said, had the highest contempt for Negroes, who in turn disliked them.

"Stop off at West Point," they said, "and ask any Negro there what he thinks of those Indians."

Both say they are working hard to make illicit sex relations between the so-called races a crime, but that the legislators didn't seem so keen for that bill. Powell, I also learnt, has been spreading his propaganda through all the Southern legislatures, where he has given addresses. Both men are also hard at work, fostering jim-crow legislation in Northern states, particularly Ohio. They bear the inter-racialists, the N. A .A. C. P, and the Negro press no particular goodwill.

“What Are We, Negroes or Americans?,” *The Messenger*, August 1926

Rogers’s essay is somewhat of a response to fellow Jamaican writer W. A. Domingo’s earlier piece “What Are We, Negroes or Colored People” (*Messenger* June 1926). Rogers looks at the term Negro, as was his wont, first in a historical sense, tracing its origins back to the mid-15th century. Rogers points out the careful attention to detail early anthropologist Johann Blumenbach utilized when using the term unlike the racist methods employed by 20th century pseudo-scientists. Rogers particularizes the term in the context of the United States and also examines it in the sense of a national identity. He observes that Blacks have been awarded citizenship through constitutional amendments; however, the different states have never arrived at a uniform definition of the term “Negro,” rendering it almost meaningless on a national level. Rogers notes that according to the census, Blacks, unlike whites, are classified by their racial identity, and he also shows that African Americans are not treated equally with whites. Rogers rails against a Jim Crow system in which German immigrants who fought against the United States in World War I are often treated better than African Americans who defended their country. He states that the only time the United States considers Blacks as citizens is “[w]hen it comes to paying taxes, to service in the draft, to defense of the country as in case of foreign invasion.” In the face of these injustices, why should Blacks consider themselves Americans? Yet Rogers himself became an America citizen in 1917 and “was a strong supporter of ‘Americanism.’“ Rogers felt a fierce loyalty to his adopted country despite the mistreatment he faced at the hands of many Americans. He would continue to try to get white Americans to appreciate the contributions Blacks made to the country, especially in his late book, *Africa's Gift to America.*

"WHAT ARE WE, NEGROES OR AMERICANS?"

Origin

Just what is a Negro? Where and how did the term originate? Is it a term of honor or reproach? These are some of the phases [*sic*] it is necessary to discuss.

The modern use of the term, Negro, dates back to 1442, when Anton Gonsalves, lieutenant of Prince Henry the Navigator, on a trip to the coast of Guinea brought back six captive natives from that region to Spain, a step which resulted in the African slave trade.

These natives were black in color, or *negro,* in the Spanish or Portuguese languages. *Los negros* (the blacks); *los blancos* (the whites). From Spain these *negros* were taken to Cuba as slaves, and later to English-speaking America, where the word, *negro,* was used, later to replace "blackamoor" and "Ethiopian," the former English words for black men.

The whole history of the word, Negro, except for the last sixty-one years is then associated with slavery. In other words, with things, with chattels, having no rights that "the white man was bound to respect." It is important to remember this.

Scientific Use

Later, the word with a capital "N" was to find its way into scientific language, and acquire, perhaps, a slight measure of dignity. Johann Blumenbach (1752–1840), first of the great anthropologists, and perhaps, even at this late day, the greatest of them all, in founding the study of Man, as a science, divided the human race into five varieties, one of which he called, Negro. Blumenbach, it is important to note, was very careful to point out that his division was a purely arbitrary one, that there was, in reality, hundreds of varieties, which blended one into the other by "insensible and imperceptible" degrees; and, that when the last word had been said on the subject that there was but one race—*the human race*. Blumenbach did his work with the thoroughness of the German scientist, as those who will read his "Anthropological Treatise[s]," [1865] will see.

In this book he stated in no uncertain terms his opinion that the Negro, then in the very depths of enslavement in the New World, was the biological equal of the other four varieties. And Blumenbach was in a position to know as he had a whole library filled with literary, scientific, and philosophical treatises by European Negroes, many of whom had been graduated with honors from the leading universities. The European Negro has throughout received better treatment than the African or the one in the New World. Negro slavery was abolished finally in 1773, Portugal being the last place to have Negro slaves.[1]

Compare the thoroughness, the painstaking work, and the knowledge of the Negro as well as that of the other varieties, by this great master with that of the long line of quacks that have followed him as Madison Grant,[2] Lothrop Stoddard,[3] Putnam Weale,[4] Earnest Sevier Cox, R. Shufeldt,[5] Henry Fairfield Osborne,[6] and a score of others. Verily a descent from Olympus to a mud puddle! In Blumenbach's own words: "Finally I am of [the] opinion that after all these numerous instances I have brought together of Negroes of capacity, it would not be difficult to mention entire well-known provinces of Europe, from out of which you would not easily expect to obtain off hand such good authors, poets, philosophers, and correspondents of the Paris Academy; and on the other hand there is no so-called savage nation known under the sun which has so distinguished itself by such examples of perfectibility and original capacity for scientific culture, and thereby attaching itself so closely to the most civilized nations on earth, as the Negro."

Present Status

To limit now the discussion to the United States. After the black man had been a slave for two hundred and forty-four years, during which his color and physiognomy had been so changed that within his ranks almost every type under the sun could be found, and every disgrace and ignominy known to the baseness of human nature had been heaped on him, not the least of which was the white man's religion and his doctrine of superiority, at bottom the same, he was set free to become five years later a full-fledged citizen of the United States, *on the books*.

There was much opposition to this, as is known, but it was nothing singular from the standpoint of ignorance and illiteracy. The bulk of the Southern whites were in the same state that the mountaineers of Tennessee and North Carolina are now. Indeed, if the word of Olmsted, author [of] "The Slave States,"[7] and others, is to be taken, the masses of the poor whites were below the free Negroes and the slave domestics. The only asset of these poor whites was the empty honor of possessing the same color, as the top dog. Hence, if these whites could be citizens, anyone else, in common justice, could be.

Amendments to the Constitution

Citizenship and suffrage, as it ought to be well-known, were conferred by the Fourteenth and Fifteenth Amendments to the Constitution. Since it is certain that comparatively few Negroes have read them, it is well to quote them here:

Art. XIV says in part: "*All persons, born or naturalized in the United States and subject to the jurisdiction thereof, are citizens of the United States, and of the States wherein they reside. No State shall make or enforce any law which shall abridge the privileges or immunities of citizens of the United States.*"

Art. XV. "*The right of citizens of the United States shall not be denied or abridged by the United States or by any State on account of color, race, or previous condition of servitude.*"

When Is a Negro a Negro?

As the term, Negro, stands today it is fully as undefinable as electricity. A white-skinned person who is legally a white man in North Carolina can be legally a Negro in the adjoining state of Virginia; one legally white in Virginia will be classed as black in Oklahoma; the same person legally white in Oregon will be legally black in North Carolina; the whole definition for America being as uncertain and crotchety as an old maid. Each state acts according to its prejudices, or clearer yet, the exploitable possibilities of the "Negro."

Many contend that the term, Negro, is one of opprobrium. There can be no doubt that it is. It was founded on slavery and forced degradation. Further, in many of the Southern States, as in South Carolina, Louisiana, and Georgia and those states in which the population is so mixed that the imputation is likely to be true it is as libellous to call one, supposedly white, a Negro, as to call him a horse-thief, pimp, or crap-shooter. Some years ago a newspaper in South Carolina, in reporting a story, accidentally called a supposedly white man, colored. The judge in awarding him damages uttered this remarkable bit of legal wisdom: " . . . if one race be inferior to the other socially the Constitution of the United States cannot put them on the same plane." In North Carolina a man recently brought suit when called Negro.

At the mere mention of the word, Negro, particularly in white newspapers, fully ninety percent of the population of the United States, regardless of color, experience a feeling of repulsion, except in certain instances, such as when it comes to telling what the "Negro" has done for the country. Hence the just contention of those who insist the term is a debasing one. As to the word, nigger, there is really no difference, except that custom has made it so. Apart from the fact that the majority of "Negroes" refer to themselves as "niggers," that word, is only slipshod pronunciation, as "sah," for "sir." It is certain that the perverters of the word had no added insult in mind.[8]

The objectors to the word, Negro, as was said, are right, but when they suggest some other word as "colored," Ethiopian, Ethican, [*sic*] Afro-American, Race-man,[9] they but constitute themselves killers of time, and diverters from the main issue, the getting of one's rights. For it is not the name but the treatment that hurts. Anglo-Saxon, Christian, Yankee, Irish, and a host of other names were once terms of reproach. When the social, that is, the economic standing of the possessors of those names had improved, the terms also acquired dignity. With loss of economic standing names also lose their standing as Greek, Spaniard, Turk, Italian. Call the black man white, and the white man black; reverse the terms, Negro, and, Caucasian, and with treatment unchanged it will make no difference.

And the worst part of it is that the proscribed is bound to use, some time or another, the opprobrious name, given by the oppressor. For instance, in the South the "Negro" is forced by law into separate places labelled for him. In describing himself in legal documents in every state in the Union, and even in the departments conducted by the United States Government itself he is compelled to describe himself as "Negro" or "colored," as in marriage licenses, criminal proceedings, naturalization proceedings, Federal positions, census reports. Although the Constitution of the Federal Government, itself, declares that he is a citizen, yet the government goes to the length of denying this by writing him down as "Colored" or "Negro" in the census reports. It is noteworthy, in this respect that it is only those incapable of becoming citizens, who are thus enumerated separately, as Indians, Chinese, Japanese. Those of other nationalities as, Italians, Jews, Greeks, Germans, provided they are native-born are never mentioned as such. If not born here they are all classified as foreign-born whites. In short, though the Federal government calls the so-called Negro, a citizen, it classifies him as an alien, or rather something betwixt and between, that something, as I later show being still a slave, to a certain degree of the white man.

Because this is so the Supreme Court of the United States, final voice of the Federal government, always with an eye to the preservation of property rights has been notorious in its decisions as to what is justice for the black man—an old story dating from the Dred Scott[10] decision to the present segregation affair in Washington, D.C.[11]

Although forbidden by the Constitution to make or enforce any bill, based on color, these injunctions, to every state south of the Mason-Dixon line[12] and some north of it are but so many scraps of paper. "Negroes" are forced to pay the same taxes, the same railroad fare, poll-tax, bound to the same contracts, in short the same civic obligations as the white man. But when it comes to getting returns for his harder-earned dollar he gets less, anywhere from seventy-five to twenty cents, and in the matter of education sometimes as low as five cents to the dollar.

On a recent trip to the South I rode from Wilmington, N.C., to Richmond on an old wooden jim-crow car placed between a modern steel baggage car, and steel coach for the whites. In a collision the colored coach, if one can dignify it by that name, would have been crushed to tinder. Further, the conductor, the railroad employes, and the news "butcher"[13] pre-empted eight places, while passengers stood. The toilet room of the colored women happened to be nearest the baggage car, so the employes on that car, used it. Further the colored car is always placed ahead, so that in case of a head-on collision, the "Negroes" will get killed first. This, by the way, is about the only instance in the South where the black man goes first, in jim-crow street cars he rides in the rear.[14] Yet there is an impartial fare for both. This, of course, is only a very minor incident. This article is pianissimo.[15]

In all of these jim-crow states a Negro may ride in the white coach provided he is in the employ of some white person or is a prisoner. Hence, if all Negroes travelled as servants or as convicts, there would be no jim-crow cars.

Sufficient has been said in answer to the query at the head of this article to prove that in actuality, and regardless of what the Constitution may say we are not Americans, but "Negroes" or "colored" as the census reports define us. By and large we have not even the rights of the alien, even those aliens incapable of becoming citizens. With my own ears I heard the terrific fight put up, by ministers of the gospel in the Virginia senate last February to keep Chinese, Japanese and other Asiatics from being jim-crowed in conveyances and public places, and they won. A so-called race-integrity bill which passed the house ingeniously declared that the bill would not affect those persons "who by the Constitution of the United States are *ineligible* to become citizens of the United States," meaning Asiatics. Think of that! Chinese, Japanese, and Mexicans ride where they please in the South.

Then there is the Indian, a ward of the nation, and living on the reservation. He pays no taxes but when he comes among the whites, with the saloons now illegal, he may go where he pleases. No segregation for him.[16] The same holds true of any European who touches these shores. There is no segregation for a German, though he made a thousand American widows in the last war. There is segregation for the "Negro" veteran, though he saved a thousand from becoming widows, unless he is travelling as valet for the German.

The sole purpose of segregation is to preserve the status of slave and master—to so arrange it that the "Negro" will have a back-door entrance to everything.

Nor, as was said, is the Federal Government any stricter in the enforcement of the law than the states. Washington, D.C., is under the direct rule of the President and Congress, yet but for the jim-crow car one might well be in Mississippi.

But after all the Negro has been taught on the subject of citizenship, the above will sound incredible. Am I at no time a citizen, he will ask. Yes, there are times when he is not only a citizen, but he is compelled to be, and this holds true of the most barbarous of the Cracker states as of the Northern ones. When it comes to paying taxes, to service in the draft, to defense of the country as in case of foreign invasion, in short in all those things that make for the white man's benefit, he is a one hundred percent citizen. In those that makes for his own benefit, he is only a Negro. In things that make for the white man's benefit the United States is to the Negro, a nation; in things that make for his own benefit, it is a race or tribe, and he an alien in it.

In the awarding of citizenship he has received most of the bitter and little of the sweet, which makes one wonder what those who declare he shouldn't have been made a citizen, have to kick about.

The white workers sometimes call themselves wage-slaves. The Negro, by and large, is only that in all its sinister implications. There are some above this grade, yet they also are all times subject to attack by the mob and gratuitous insult by the meanest whites.

Baron d'Estournelles de Constant[17] of the French Senate made a study of the Negro in the America [*sic*] and aptly summarized it when he said the American Negro is "Freedman not a citizen." Still many Negroes fondly believe themselves citizens. These remind one of the story of the man who had a large fortune and lost it, following which he lost his mind. In this state he fancied he had got it back again, and was content as before. Many a lunatic behind bars is quite happy in the belief that he is Napoleon or Jesus Christ.

In one or two spots as New York, Boston, Minneapolis and Chicago the Negro is given a slight measure of citizenship, but compared with that accorded the French Negro it is a joke.

When is the Negro a citizen: In matters of duty. As Stephenson in "Race Distinctions in Law"[18] has demonstrated the Negro is still largely white man's property.

"Is Black Ever White?," *The Messenger*, September 1926

In this essay, "Rogers completely rejected the racial discourse initiated by white racists for their own profit and now shared by both white and black Americans" (Hutchinson 293). Rogers begins by speaking of the African American author and racial advocate Walter White (1893–1955). In addition to his work with the N. A. A. C. P., White authored two novels, *The Fire in the Flint* (1924) and *Flight* (1926). The latter novel concerns racial passing, a topic written about by numerous Harlem Renaissance authors, including James Weldon Johnson (*The Autobiography of an Ex-Colored Man* 1912), Jessie Fauset (*Plum Bun* 1928), and Nella Larson (*Passing* 1929). White himself was light-complexioned enough to possibly be able to pass if he chose to, but instead he proudly claimed his Black heritage even if it was not the dominant strain in his DNA. Rogers praises White for not disavowing this part of his identity. Rogers also was light-complexioned, enough so that some of his friends had advised him to try to pass, but he vehemently rejected these suggestions, instead delving deeper into his African heritage. To Rogers, the entire notion of "race" is biologically impossible, and thus the idea of "passing" is ludicrous. There is only one race, the human race, but if society insists on classifying people by color, it should be based on the person's appearance. Defining someone as Black because of the "one-drop" rule,[1] makes no sense to Rogers.

"IS BLACK EVER WHITE?"

Walter White, author of "The Fire in the Flint," in an interesting article on his mental reactions to criticisms of his latest book, "Flight," says among other things.

"Then there are amusing editorials like that which came to me from a Florida paper—the *Miami News*, which scored[2] me for 'drawing upon my imagination in trying to picture the experiences of a Negro who passes for white.' The writer goes on to intimate that there is no such thing as a Negro successfully passing himself off as a white person and, therefore, I wrote of things wholly foreign to my own experience. I was tempted sorely to send him a photograph—being somewhat laden with work just now prevents my paying a personal visit upon the editor in Miami—and let it convince the Florida Horace Greeley[3] that there WERE Negroes who could, if they chose to do so, might [*sic*] cross the line."

For once I find myself agreeing with a cracker. I, too, insist that you cannot find any human being of any color passing off for another color, unless he stains his face, or possesses the qualities of a chameleon, or the people he goes among are color-blind. If a man has a coloring that among human beings is known as white, he is white regardless of what his ancestry may be. He certainly isn't blue, or green, or yellow or red, not if I am to go by the color-chart, and use my own eyes, and commonsense instead of the eyes of American race prejudice.

Because of the prejudiced idea that one can be white and black in complexion at the same time, every one of known Negro ancestry has a common interest. But at the same time it is high time that we learn to use our own eyes and own judgment about things, and not to accept the biased views of others. The white man, wishes to maintain a separate exploiting caste, and when we use his phraseology—a phraseology that is two hundred and fifty years behind the time—we but help to keep the chains fastened on ourselves.

If one is dark-brown, or brown, or yellow, or white-skinned, he is that color, that's all. It is a simple fact, possessing neither honor

nor disgrace. If one is mixed Caucasian or Negro or Indian, he is that as a fact, no matter how much prejudiced whites, or blacks, who use the eyes of white men to look at themselves, may say to the contrary. No matter what others may say, I, for one, cannot see two races, or a dozen in America. I see but one American people, speaking a common language, and at bottom having a common ideal, shading in color by imperceptible degrees from white to black, or black to white, as you will—this variety of coloring being of as little moment to the real human value as the variety of hair coloring.

Yes, I agree with the writer of the *Miami News*, though I fancy he won't thank me for the endorsement, that a Negro cannot successfully pass off as a white person. A white cow or mouse; a white dog or louse hasn't to "pass off" as white: *they are white.*

One of the first things towards "solving" this so-called race problem is to learn to call things by their right name.

Mr. White's point of view is no doubt due to the fact that he is not ashamed of his ancestry—a fact, which I, for one, have ample proof. He is one of the few, regardless of complexion, who has taken up the cudgels for justice for conviction's sake rather than money's sake. He believes in the group to which, logically and biologically, he belongs least—believes in it to the extent of having in it hostages to fame and fortune, by which I mean if he were to send a photograph of his children to the editor of the *Miami News*, little as that worthy is likely to know which of his associates are white and which "colored," he would know that the children are colored.

Mr. White's attitude in this last mentioned respect is clearly a rebuke to many, obviously colored, nevertheless I, for one, do not call him a Negro. In "Flight" he speaks of his heroine, Mimi,[4] as belonging to the Negro race. There is but one race—the human race—and in so far as Mimi belonged to any variety of it, she belonged to the so-called white race. I regard any other point of view as too big a concession to the Bourbons, who insist that if one is thirty-one parts of one thing and only one of another, he belongs to the one, because of some magical, or heaven-only-knows what quality involved. Now I am not going to accept that though all the crackers in Christendom shouted it in my ear.

I recognize, moreover, that right here is the fountain-head of the so-called color line, to which I am totally and unalterably opposed particularly when there is such a large percentage of citizens of the same descent as Mr. White and either do not know or wouldn't acknowledge it.

“Talks with Garvey in Atlanta Prison: Founder of U. N. I. A. Grants Interview to Joel A. Rogers,” New York *Amsterdam News*, November 17, 1926

Marcus Garvey (1887–1940) led the largest Black organization, the Universal Negro Improvement Association and African Communities League (usually referred to as the U. N. I. A.) in the United States. Garvey’s movement swept up Blacks across the globe. His belief in self-dependence, Pan-Africanism, and setting up an African homeland attracted many followers between his arrival in New York City in 1916, and his imprisonment on trumped up charges of mail fraud in 1925 before his eventual deportation in 1927. In this important interview with Rogers, Garvey seems unbroken by his time in prison. Though he laments his betrayal at the hands of a powerful coalition of whites and Blacks of different political agendas to depose him, he still speaks passionately of regaining his leadership role once released from jail. Rogers had first met Garvey when both were children in Jamaica (Rashidi). He admires Garvey’s emphasis on Black pride and on educating the world about the achievements of Black people worldwide. He also agrees with Garvey’s emphasis on self-reliance and with his appealing to the average Black person rather than Du Bois’ more elitist Talented Tenth. Rogers would certainly agree with Garvey’s assertion that “history is the landmark by which we are directed into the true course of life” (quoted in Asukile “Marcus Garvey” 48). Nevertheless, Rogers disagrees with several important tenets of his fellow Jamaican’s agenda though he cites only one example in this article—Garvey’s decision to meet with the leader of the Ku Klux Klan in 1922 to discuss matters of race. However, he also does not like the pomp and ceremony of the Garveyite movement with its uniforms and military rigor, and he does not agree with Garvey’s separatist agenda, his qualified defense of capitalism, and his dream of an African homeland. Still, Rogers did serve as a sub-editor for Garvey's short-lived paper, the *Negro Daily Times*, and contributed to *Negro World*, the organ of the U. N. I. A. In the interview reprinted in this anthology, Rogers paints a poignant picture of the fallen leader. Rogers was one of the few journalists outside Garvey's inner circle allowed to interview him while he was imprisoned; thus, Rogers was afforded the opportunity to "act as guide for the thousands of readers of his syndicated column" (Grant 395). Rogers opines that even in prison Garvey "is the most widely discussed Negro in the world," and he concludes "that Garveyism is still very much alive." Rogers wrote a biographical sketch of Garvey in *World's Great Men of Color*. He also interviewed Garvey twice more, in 1928 and again in 1937. For more on their relationship, see Colin Grant *Negro with a Hat*, especially pages 395-396, and Thabiti Asukile's insightful article "Joel Augustus Rogers's Reflection and End of Life Admiration of Marcus Garvey in New York" *Afro-Americans in New York Life and History* July 2013.

"TALKS WITH GARVEY IN ATLANTA PRISON: FOUNDER OF U. N. I. A. GRANTS INTERVIEW TO JOEL A. ROGERS"

Convict no. 19359 Is in Good Health—Discusses N. A. A. C. P., Liberia and His Domestic Affairs

In coming to this city [Atlanta] I had among other objectives two rather itching ones: To see the home of His Majesty, the Imperial Wizard, the white king of America,[1] and to see the black king, or more correctly, the Provisional President of Africa, Marcus Garvey. Sunday last, taking the jim-crow car, I rode out six miles on Peachtree road and saw the former, an imitation White House, nestling in an oaken grove, and a few days later, piloted by two of the fine friends I have met here, Drs. C. Waymond Reeves and J. B. Brown, I motored over to the magnificent university-like building, with the beautiful sweep of lawn, that is the Federal Penitentiary, to see the latter.

Garvey Wore Red Sweater

Appearing at the barred gate under the great Doric columns we were politely ushered by the guard to a desk, where we gave our names, and after a short wait, and with much less formality than we had expected, were conducted through a heavy iron-barred door into a room where, after another short wait, we saw the stocky figure of the originator of the first world movement among Negroes enter, clad in what appeared to be the garb of any ordinary laborer hereabouts—trousers of bluish material, red sweater, and loose cap of thin dark material, nothing to indicate a prisoner in popular belief—but an unbelievable contrast to the figure in the glittering uniform, golden epaulets, plumed hat, sword and spurs on the prancing steed, which, as leader of the "400,000,000 Negroes of the World," led his followers through the streets of Harlem in 1921.

Responding to our cordial greetings with equal warmth, he took a seat facing us with the guard nearby, and opened the conversation with a remark about my recent trip to Europe. My being refused permission to visit Africa seemed a sore point with him. "Why," said he, "if there is any place a Negro ought to be allowed to go, it is Africa." He went on to speak of the world-wide attempt being made to jim-crow Negroes, and touched on the laws recently passed barring colored people from Brazil, Mexico and Panama, declaring that Negroes, particularly those of the Western World, were getting just what they deserved for their lethargy. "Soon they won't be able to travel at all, and then, perhaps, they will wake up," he said.

I went on to tell him how hundreds of persons in England and France, some of them prominent, had asked me about him; of how many Negroes in this country, some of them wealthy, who sympathized with him, and of the discussions of himself and of his movement that I knew were taking place in many of our colleges—at which he seemed quite pleased. There is much about Garveyism with which I, for one, radically disagree: as for instance his approval of the narrow radicalism of such insidious enemies of America and the Negro as Cox, Powell, and the Ku Klux Emperor, yet the simple truth remains that there is considerable sympathy for him, sometimes, as I have found, in quite unexpected places.

Although his followers have dwindled in actual numbers, he is the most widely discussed Negro in the world today. Two recent missionaries from Africa, one of them a man for whom I hold the highest respect, told me of the hold that Garveyism was taking in Africa that was a revelation to me.

Convict No. 19359

And as I listened to Convict No. 19359 speak in his resolute, well-informed way of the doings in the world of Negroes—of affairs in Abyssinia, South Africa, Liberia, the West Indies, Brazil, as well as of India, Egypt, and the League of Nations—I realized that Garveyism is still very much alive. Of his original program he had evidently yielded not one step.

"When I get out of here," he said, with all that old fire that had held his great audiences spellbound in Madison Square Garden, "I mean to do a thousand times more." This was in direct answer to a question about his steamship program.

These activities, however, will take place on British territory, unless Uncle Sam relents, as, according to Garvey himself, his deportation is settled.

In Pink of Health

The self-appointed ruler of Africa is considerably thinner. Gone are most of his paunch and his beefy shoulders, but he looks several years younger and in the pink of health. Time, he says, does not hang heavily, as he has abundant time for reading after duties, which, he said, he was not permitted to name.[2]

"Before I came in here," he said quite cheerfully, "I had no time whatever for reading, but now I can keep well posted on everything," and he evidently does. This, of course, is as near as I can recall his words, as I was stopped by the guard when I took out paper and began to write.

Number 19359—the Harlem fans might try that[3]—feels that he has not been fairly treated by that part of the Negro people who opposed his movement. Such, he declared, had never looked into his program, but had based their objections on rumor, or on what his enemies had said. As to the latter, he charged that they had first called him a "nobody," then later a "West Indian," and when he still continued to gain a following, "a crook."

As to the two volumes of his "Philosophy and Opinions,"[4] he said that the Negro press had been silent about it, while his wife had a scrapbook filled with clippings from the white press here and in Europe.

The N. A. A .C .P.

When I asked him what he thought of the N. A. A. C. P. he said that he thought it was an excellent and highly necessary movement, but that the leadership was wrong, declaring that the present leaders were only interested in succeeding themselves in office and pushing only those cases that would bring them plenty of notoriety.

"The N. A. A. C. P." he said, "encourages Negroes to move into white neighborhoods, and to do such things as got the Sweets[5] into trouble, then turns around and cashes in on them." For this remark I felt that the advocates of residential segregation in Washington D.C., and elsewhere would give him plenty of publicity.

As to the $5,000 given to Dr. W.E.B. Du Bois for the study of Negro education—is it in the South or South Carolina?—and which appeared in the September Crisis, he wanted to know why that sum should have been necessary, since Du Bois had lived in the South and was familiar with conditions there. He was plainly elated at the article appearing in the PITTSBURGH COURIER. Vann (Robert)," he said, "has dragged to light facts which I had long felt to be true."[6]

Liberia

Of Liberia, he said President King[7] had deceived him; gladly accepting him at first, but ousting him for bigger game. As to the Firestone Company,[8] he said that it would have been better had Liberia only leased the land, but as things now were it should try to get the tire company under governmental control.

Regarding the rumor of his not being permitted to return to Jamaica, British West Indies, he said that there had been similar talk in 1921, but he had visited all the places it was said he could not go and had returned to America without any trouble. It was at this point he complained of the "baseless rumors perpetually floated about him," one of which was that President Coolidge had offered him a pardon if he would leave the country.[9]

His Domestic Affairs

As to his first wife, he said she was motivated by "pure notoriety," and that he had been legally divorced from her prior to his second marriage.[10]

When I suggested that he would have fared better had he got a lawyer, he insisted that here for once the maxim that the man who is his own lawyer has a fool for his client was wrong. If he had had a lawyer, it is his belief that he would have got "sixty years," as there was much on the inside that an onlooker would never have understood.[11]

At the end of an hour the guard warned us that our time was up, and No. 19359 returned to what will be his home for another two years at least, while the three of us passed again through the iron gates to see again the magnificent lawn and the wooded expanse in all the glory and gold of an Indian summer. I, for one, absorbed in the thought that the once humble West Indian peasant that had just disappeared behind the clanging gates had started something that, liked or hated, is destined to affect the future of humanity in no mean way.

["Is There Such a Thing as Negro Art?,"] (Review of *Jazz* by Paul Whiteman), *Opportunity*, December 1926

In this book review, Rogers reiterates two of his main themes: the significance of jazz (a subject of which he wrote at length in "Jazz at Home") and the contributions of Blacks to world and particularly American culture. His favorable review of Whiteman is not surprising since Rogers agrees with his aim to "elevate" jazz; however, Whiteman, like Rogers, feels somewhat ambivalent about the attempt to raise jazz from its "lowly" origins, which are often considered morally dangerous. This phenomenon of jazz' initially being considered "dangerous " because of an ability to lead people, particularly young ones, astray would be repeated with other forms of popular music, such as rock and roll and hip-hop, that had Black origins. Although Rogers tries to couch his disappointment that there is not more discussion of Black practitioners of jazz such as James Europe in the book, he does leave us with that final thought—how the contributions of African Americans are often ignored by even well-intentioned whites.

["IS THERE SUCH A THING AS NEGRO ART?"]

Is there such a thing as Negro art?

Is jazz art?

These two questions, seemingly unrelated, but nevertheless closely so, have created a storm of discussion, which if I mistake not, is going to be further stirred by this book, for while Mr. Whiteman does not say in so many words that there is a Negro art, he insists that jazz is art, which, in its essence, he says, was brought in the holds of slave-ships to America three hundred years ago.

Ergo, if jazz is art, then there is Negro art.

And whether there is Negro art or not, it is indisputable there is a certain spiritual meaning that has been deposited by the Negro in America, a certain buoyancy, spontaneity, and joy of living that has re-inspired the staid, mechanical, intellectual Caucasian, stirring him to a merrier mood, and causing the blood to course with joyous rhythm through his veins. This Negro spirit, if I may use the phrase, practically dominates the amusement world in America and Europe today. Mr. Whiteman has brought out this art excellently, and given full justice to the Negro.

Jazz, Mr. Whiteman says, expresses the spirit of America more than anything else—the spirit of youth which must be up and doing. In his own words: "Jazz is the spirit of a new country. It catches up the underlying life motif of a continent and period, molding it into a form which expresses the fundamental emotion of the people, the place and time so authentically that is immediately recognizable."

Of course this spirit had always been there slumbering in the depths, like some precious chemical awaiting the unlocking power of some agent, the agent in this instance being the Negro spirit.

Jazz, being a distinctive American product, fosters originality, says Mr. Whiteman. And being distinctively American, it was like the prophet having no honor in his own country, for he says that it was not until leading European composers, notably Darius Milhand and Igor Stravinsky[1] used it with stirring effect that the American high-brows with their inferiority complex began to see its value.

Very interesting is Mr. Whiteman's account of his invasion of the sacred perfumed perlieus[2] of Aeolian Hall[3] with his first jazz concert, his great nervousness, and the conquest of the audience which included artists like Damrosch,[4] Heifetz, Kreisler,[5] Rachmaninoff and Stokowski.

Mr. Whiteman says the grand aim of his life is to elevate jazz to one of the fine arts, he wants to see "jazz compositions written around the great natural and geographical features of American life—written in the jazz idiom."

But, he points out, jazz is already art, for it is dependent upon adaptations taken from the great masters, "Yes, We Have No Bananas," for instance, he says, owed its popularity to passages from Mendelssohn's "Wedding March" and "I Dreamt that I Dwelt in Marble Halls."[6] Jazz is a reality, a quickening and more vivacious interpretation of music. Who, but a devotee, listening to one of the dreary fugues of Bach, but wished that the organist jazzed it a bit, giving it some life?

Like everything new, jazz has had not only its detractors, but its alarmists, who attributed to its influences almost every crime under the sun. It has put, so they say, the sin in syncopation; it causes intoxication; wrecks the American home, leads young girls astray, causes divorce—one Chicago judge declared that three-fourths of the divorce cases in his court were due to jazz—and an organist in Spokane, Washington, brought suit against a choir-leader, charging that in syncopating the classics the choir-leader had hurt his artistic sensibilities. The fact is that jazz, this new conqueror in the amusement world, rising from the lowest stratum and invading almost over night the places of kings and the haute monde has never been forgiven for its lowly origin. Mr. Whiteman says he has a large collection of clippings of the bad things said against jazz and that whenever he wants to have a hearty laugh he takes it out and re-reads them. Nevertheless, the laugh will also be on Mr. Whiteman, for though he gives the impression that he thoroughly believes in, and is passionately devoted to jazz, yet he reveals that subconsciously he has a doubt as to the propriety. For instance, he says rather naively, that it is not quite fitting to jazz everything, among them being airs like "Onward Christian Soldier," and the Tannhauser march.[7] Nevertheless, he says there "would be no sacrilege or lowering of dignity in jazzing the 'Song of India'[8] or 'Dixie' though the latter tune is deep in the hearts of the Southern People."

Of course Mr. Whiteman's opponents will ask for nothing better than an admission of that sort.

Jazz all in all is one of the most fascinating books I have ever dipped into, carrying the reader along by the same power that has made this new music, of which Mr. Whiteman is the leading exponent all over the world.

The book is as much an autobiography of Mr. Whiteman as it is of the rise and development of jazz. Most interesting are the recitals of his difficulties in getting his famous band together, and of the manner in which he was first struck by jazz in a dive dance in San Francisco. The Negro reader will wish that the author had said something about the Negro popularizers of jazz as the late James Europe, but of course there is no end to what one might include in almost any book.

"J. A. Rogers Discusses West Indian Women," Pittsburgh *Courier*, February 26, 1927

Rogers, in this essay, provides a window into the lives of West Indian women both at home and abroad. He points out that due to the general pattern of migration, men tend to leave home in much larger numbers than women initially. This is also true of West Indian women, who did not come in significant numbers to the United States until the beginning of World War I. Rogers argues that these female immigrants often lagged in terms of financial success behind their male counterparts as well as native-born American women, blaming this discrepancy on the fact these early women immigrants tend to be less skilled than many of the women who stayed behind. To compound matters West Indian women often resisted domestic work, the most frequent source of income for unskilled immigrant women, because such labor was looked down upon in their homelands. Furthermore, he states the early immigrants were often darker complexioned, generally making them less desirable for hire by white Americans. As employment opportunities decreased in the West Indies once World War I began, better skilled (and lighter-complexioned) female immigrants tended to migrate and were often more successful in finding work. These immigrants excelled, in particular, in the needle trade, and Rogers points out a number of West Indian women who have succeeded in a variety of fields in the United States. Unfortunately, the tighter immigration law did not allow this trend to continue.

Since there is generally more information on the early male immigrants, this essay focusing on the women is of added significance. For more on these pioneering women immigrants, whose contributions are generally underestimated by Rogers, see Irma Watkins-Owens, "Early Twentieth-Century Caribbean Women: Migration and Social Networks in New York City." *Islands in the City: West Indian Migration to New York*. Ed. Nancy Foner (2001); Paule Marshall's "Black Immigrant Women in *Brown Girl Brownstones*," *Caribbean Life in New York City: Sociocultural Dimensions*. Ed. Constance R. Sutton and Elsa M. Chaney (1994): 81–85; Rhonda Reddock, "Diversity, Difference and Caribbean Feminism: The Challenge of Anti-Racism," *Caribbean Review of Gender Studies* (April 2001); Henrice Altink "The Misfortune of Being Black and Female: Black Feminist Thought in Interwar Jamaica" *Thirdspace* (January 2006). Several of the women, such as Eulalie Domingo, are mentioned in the articles.

"J. A. ROGERS DISCUSSES WEST INDIAN WOMEN"

Native of Jamaica Says Lack of Educational Advantages Drop Them Behind American Women in Achievement; Too Keen On Color Customs and Prejudices of Old Country Live Longer With Them Than With Men; Marry Their Own Countrymen.

Much of what one could say in a general way about the West Indian woman in America has been included in Dr. Harrison's article on the West Indian male, which recently appeared in the Courier.[1]

Nevertheless, there are a few specific facts which might be added.

The immigrants from any country, European or otherwise, are usually the men, hence the number of West Indian males in America are far in excess of the women. Prior to 1909, the number of West Indians of both sexes was very small, and it was not until America's entry into the war that they began to arrive in any appreciable numbers. They now number 125,000 or less than one-eightieth of the total Negro population. The majority is to be found principally in New York City and Florida. Of course, in speaking of West Indian, one generally thinks of British West Indian.

The earliest West Indian women immigrants were of the servant type—it is a sociologic fact that the upper classes, male and female, usually stay at home, visiting other countries as tourists. Because of color humiliations, West Indians who can afford it, rarely come to America. Their children, they send to be educated in Europe.

But due to unemployment caused by the war, and the high cost of living without a corresponding rise in wages, the middle class West Indian woman began to arrive about 1916, and were coming in increasing numbers until stopped by quota restrictions. It is significant that almost the only people in the New World, who are affected by the quota, are the British West Indians, who number less than two and a half millions.

If the colored American woman is miles behind the colored American male—of some eighty Negroes in WHO'S WHO IN AMERICA, only one is a woman—then the West Indian woman is leagues behind the West Indian man, both here and at home. In comparative accomplishments, she lags behind the colored American woman, too.

This might be explained almost wholly on the ground of early training. In almost every British country the woman is regarded as inferior to the man, openly. She is taught "to stay in her place"—something as it was in America in the 90's. West Indian women do not vote. Further, it is considered a disgrace for any woman with social pretensions to do work of any kind. Were not servants, which are cheap and plentiful, made for that? Women, generally, in English countries, are taught to heed the Kaiser's three K's—Kirche, Kinder, Kuche (church, children, cooking).

With true British training, the West Indian woman has a dislike for domestic work, greater even than that of the American colored woman. Many have come from families that had two or three servants, hence, when they come to America and find nothing else but domestic service, they either enter it as a makeshift, and if they find nothing else, return home as soon as possible.

In New York City, a very large number work in the needle trades which they might be credited with having opened up for the colored American women. For while the West Indian woman is conservative along sex lines, she is far less so along color lines than the colored American women, having fortunately escaped the damning influence of the Jim-Crow car with its back-seat psychology toward life in general. The West Indian woman feels that as a woman certain positions ought to be open to her; she makes a try for them while the tendency of the colored American woman is rather not to try.

The first West Indian women were very little noticed, not because they were of the servant class, but because of their dark skins; the servant class of the West Indies usually comes from persons of this complexion. In America, where black is unpopular among both white and black, they found no more democracy than in their own class-ridden country. But since the war, the lighter complexioned ones are coming, and have been receiving much better attention.

These light women, however, unlike the colored American woman, are far from being inclined toward a union with the dark American male, with his penchant for "high yellows."[2] Many of these women have had it ingrained in them that black is inferior, in short, their attitude toward dark men is about the same as that of the white Americans would be toward the light-colored West Indians, themselves. One of the very last things a light West Indian girl will think of doing is to marry a black man. Professional men might stand a chance—might, because there is the typical case of a certain West Indian girl—a girl, who had never done work of any kind, who would not marry a certain professional in Harlem, although she confessed to liking him, her objection being that he was too dark. Class in the West Indies is strongly wrapped up with color, but with certain subtle distinctions that do not obtain[3] in America.

West Indian women, generally speaking, are better educated than the colored American women, for while they have had little of the splendid opportunities the latter have had, say in the North, they have made better opportunities with that little. Since economic opportunities in the islands are poor, the tendency is to keep children in school. Moreover, in British countries, generally, a higher value is placed upon education, and on those having education, regardless of color. Culture and education go far toward atoning for blackness of skin, so West Indians strive for education.[4]

Hence, as was said, much of the backwardness of the West Indian woman must be attributed to sex training.

This writer cannot think of a single West Indian woman who has achieved anything approaching significance in America, while the males who have done so are comparatively numerous. She has produced no Matzeliger, revolutionizing the shoe industry, or no Bert Williams,[5] who with his American colleague, Walker, did so much toward paving the way for the present Negro position on the stage, such as it is. Perhaps the most significant thing that can be credited the West Indian woman is being the mother of the two Johnsons, James Weldon and J. Rosamond.[7]

Among the leading West Indian women in America may be cited Mrs. Eulalie Domingo, an accomplished pianist, who holds a degree from the Royal Academy of Music, London, Eng.; Mrs. Brawley, wife of Prof. Benjamin Brawley; the two Mrs. Garveys; Ethyl Oughton Clarke, singer; Mrs. Packer Ramsay; Mrs. Arthur Quallo, daughter of Dr. Grenfell, famous African missionary; Dorothy Hendricks, M.A.; the Edwards sisters, well known in Harlem real estate circles; Iris Hall, formerly of the stage; Inez Thorpe, lawyer, said to be the first colored person to win a New York State scholarship; Mrs. Mabel Keaton, head of the Tuberculosis Department of the Urban League; Mrs. Isa Gittens, Latin teacher; Misses Enid Thorpe, Mazie Christian and Elsa Burnett, teachers, and others either not now recalled or unknown to the writer.

There are also a goodly number of near-white West Indian girls who "pass," getting good positions as stenographers, secretaries and business managers in New York firms. Because of the bad economic conditions in the West Indies, many a mistress has come to America to find her former servant much better off than she is. The humor of a situation of this sort can only be fully appreciated by one who has lived in the West Indies.

The tendency of the West Indian woman is to marry West Indians, and mostly from their own islands. Apart from a certain difference over nationality, involving the attentions of the West Indian male, both groups of women get along pretty well together. An increasing number of West Indian women are joining American lodges and going to American halls and parties.

With less than 200 West Indians coming in annually, it is evident that the West Indian-American question, a very trifling thing compared with the issue facing both groups, will disappear within a generation.

"Who Is the New Negro, and Why?," *The Messenger*, March 1927

For many readers, the term New Negro originated with Alain Locke's famed anthology *The New Negro: An Interpretation* (1925), a collection in which Rogers was included. However, the term has much longer roots, and can be traced back to sometime in the latter half of the 19th century.[1] The term New Negro itself suggested many different meanings, but generally, it referred to a more assertive, independent, proud, confident, and optimistic image of African Americans than during the time of slavery and the few decades after. Rogers's description of the New Negro is one that is strong and willing to fight and die if necessary for freedom and equality. This New Negro is one that will forge organizations independent of control by whites and will advance the Black cause. He is not interested in the color bar, but seeks unity within the race. Rogers advises Blacks to stand up to political groups and organizations, including religious ones, that he feels hold them back, urging them to disregard any labels that may be thrown at them except for one: "sheep." Instead, they must demand "social equality" and "social justice."

"WHO IS THE NEW NEGRO, AND WHY?"

One hears much these days about the New Negro. Who is he, and who knows him? In slavery times there was a type of Negro, who worshipped his master and his family. He was a tattle-tale also, and whenever he saw one of his fellow-slaves do anything, he ran to the master, for which he would be rewarded with a ham knuckle, or a suit of old clothes. The betrayers of Nat Turner and John Brown were Negroes. The first person killed by John Brown was Hayward Shepard,[2] a Negro.

This type was also made a slave-driver, then he became a tyrant of tyrants. When he became a slave-holder, as many did, he was even more exacting than the whites. When the Civil War broke out, this dog-like creature stayed at home protecting his master's family and property while the master was fighting to keep him enslaved, or he joined the ranks of the Confederacy. Benjamin Tillman later introduced a bill, to make these black Confederates "white," a quite unnecessary step, internally.

On the other hand there was a type of slave—stubborn, rebellious, liberty-loving—who, like Nat Turner and Denmark Vesey,[3] kept his master awake at nights, worrying lest they should rise up, massacre him and his family, plunder the plantation and take to the woods, as was so often the case, particularly in Hayti, Jamaica and Guiana.

The Old Negro is the present-day type of the first; the New of the second. Faces, like styles, may change but the human nature underneath remains practically unchanged.

One may recognize the difference between Old and New in their bearing. The former, respecting color more than qualification, is apologetic when dealing with white people. He acts as if he were always in the way, as if he had no right to be on earth. One can hear the clank of the slave's chain in all that he says and does.

The New is erect, manly, bold; if necessary, defiant. He apologizes to no one for his existence, feeling deep in his inner being that he has just as much right to be on earth and in all public places as anyone else. He looks the whole world searchingly in the eye, fearing or worshipping nothing nor no one. Self-possessed, he makes himself at home wherever circumstances place him. In a word, he respects himself, first of all.

The Old Negro, on the other hand, worships the white man, because of his absence of pigment. He is like the old colored mammy, who seeing the Minister from Hayti at a social function in Washington was horrified that a black man should be associating on terms of equality with white people, many of whom were his inferiors.

The Old Negro has a contempt for his own people, and in speaking of them he uses the same terms of contempt that his spiritual predecessors did. Shut your eyes when he speaks, and you'll hear a cracker talking.

The New Negro wastes no time worrying about his color. He realizes that a human being if he is to be visible at all must have a coloring of some sort, hence to him, one shade of coloring is the equal of every other. If light-complexioned he does not deem himself better than his darker brother.

The Old Negro when insulted, grins and apologizes; the New either ignores it or acts in a way to make his manliness felt. The Old submitted supinely to massacre as in the New York and Philadelphia riots, and the Palestine,[4] Springfield[5] and East St. Louis ones. The New arms himself and prepares to exact as many lives as possible, as in Washington, Chicago, Longview,[6] Houston, Brownsville. All of which makes it clear that the possession of a college degree or of polish and refinement does not necessarily make a New Negro. Also he may be old or young. Manliness is a quality that inheres in the very fibre of one's being—a quality that like wine, improves with age.

The New Negro would rather lose his tongue than betray his people in their struggle for freedom and equality. Should any amelioration come to him because of superior talent, it turns to gall in his mouth when he remembers the sufferings of the rest of his people.

The Old, hat in hand, is always begging white people, a sort of glorified cripple with a can. Because of this he always has two different messages, one which he gives to white people, the other to colored ones. He is a living lie.

The New Negro supports movements conducted by his own people, because he realize[s] that these are the only ones that are ever going to speak out frankly and forcefully on his grievances. White persons, in such matters as economics, religion, politics, range all the way from the rabid radical to the rank conservative. So far as race is concerned, however, the vast majority is but of one complexion—the conservative, hence organizations supported by them for Negroes, have at bottom, the same Nordic goal, that is keeping the Negro "in his place," or at best a little lower than the angels. The New Negro realizes that the finest work, the real work for the advancement of the group will have to be done by its own members. It's an old saying: The man that pays the piper calls the tune.

The Old Negro is too thankful for small mercies; he believes that the employer does him a favor in hiring him. He is always praising enemies of the race like Cole Blease,[7] or Tillman or Vardaman,[8] because of some trifling sop given by these individuals to some isolated group or person, while doing all they can to keep back the group, as a whole. The New Negro, on the other hand, is satisfied with no concessions or patronage of any sort. He wants neither more nor less than his rights as a man and a citizen. And this difference between the Old and the New enters into their respective attitudes toward the times in which they are living. While the New Negro prepares to live, to live vigorously, and dangerously, if necessary, to make the whole weight of his presence felt while he moves on this earth; the Old prepares to die, and go to heaven where he will at least be a white man in complexion. "Wash me," he sings, "and I shall be whiter than snow."[9] He tries to get a corner on religion, and sinks his money in churches, which brings no returns and are shut four-fifths of the week. He is as priest-ridden as the Italians of the Middle Ages, and enjoys it. The New on the other hand, invests his money in homes and factories. He tries to get a corner on business and education that will fit him to compete successfully with the whites, while the Old is singing psalms and repeating like parrots the religious nonsense that the enslavers of his forefathers used also to enslave their primitive minds.

The Old Negro is chiefly interested in what Abraham, Moses, David, Jehoshaphat and other fictitious and semi-fictitious creatures of a barbarous tribe did in Palestine thousands of years ago. So far as his thinking is concerned he is a walking mummy. The New Negro relegates all these things to their proper, infinitesimal place in the scheme of things, and is interested most of all in life as it stirs around him. He jettisons Matthew for Marx; David for Darwin, and prefers Douglass to Lincoln. He studies economics instead of wasting his time with epistles.

The New Negro joins unions either of his own, or forces the whites to take him in, and once in never rests until he gets fairplay. He realizes that if white men have to create unions in order to get justice from white men like themselves, then this step is even more necessary for Negroes. The Old Negro, on the other hand, is an individualist. He pulls off to himself and begs the employer for work, thus paving the way for his being used, not as a union, but as an individual, to break strikes.

The Old Negro, once having reached what he believes to be the top of the ladder, spends a great deal of his time kicking off other climbers. He wants to rule the roost alone, to be greatest in the kingdom of heaven, while the New Negro, remembering his own hard struggle, is eager to give other aspirants a helping hand, even though the newcomer gives promise of eclipsing him. In other words, he is a good sport. He is, further, not afraid of contradiction, and does not believe he is an oracle on what will solve this so-called race problem. He is ever eager for new information.

The Old Negro falls glibly for all the agencies used by white friends to sidetrack the mind of the Negro group from its real problems such as over-stressing of Negro art, spirituals, piffling poetry, jazz, cabaret life, and the puffing into prominence of mediocre Negroes. The New Negro again relegates these to their proper place. He realizes that the race question is almost solely an economic one, and is satisfied with nothing less than equal opportunity for employment with equal wages. He sees that in all those things that make for the benefit of the nation, as a whole, there is no color discrimination. That is, as in paying taxes, no one asks his color; it is only in getting a return that there is discrimination. In short that in all those things that make for the white man's benefit, he is a white man, but in those that make for his, he is only a Negro.

The Old Negro is also more interested in "high-yallers," football, boxing, handball, in mastering the intricacies of the black bottom and the Charleston, in making signs in "frats" and lodges and splitting hairs about points of order in such places, in parading in gaudy uniforms, and in slicking his hair than in doing something vital towards getting himself and his group out of the rut of semi-slavery. Improving his mind by reading good books and acquiring a knowledge of the history of his racial group, is to the Old Negro, a real pain.

The Old Negro protests that he does not want social equality; the New, seeing that this is but another phrase for social justice, demands it. No social inequality for him. He feels that the first and foremost of all duties is to seek freedom, hence he has a perfect right to take any step, however violent, to rid himself of tyranny. With Thomas Jefferson he repeats, "Resistance to tyranny is obedience to God."[10] Like the five colored immortals, Anderson, Copeland, Green, Leary, and Newby,[11] who joined John Brown in his raid on Harper's Ferry, he stands ever ready to head or to join any movement that will strike for freedom.

The New Negro is not afraid of such bogey labels as rebel, atheist, pagan, infidel, Socialist, Red, heathen, radical, realizing that what they really connote is "thinker." He will be anything else but a sheep.

And where is the New Negro of whom we have been hearing so much? Is he an ideal or a reality? This much is evident, that many who have been making a noise like New Negroes have proved to be but asses in lion's skins.[12] When a lion appeared they took to the woods.

"Is the Star of the Folies-Bergere Really Married?," Pittsburgh *Courier*, July 16, 1927

In 1927, Rogers embarked on his second tour of the Continent, staying until 1930. He had been sent to Europe and North Africa by Robert L. Vann, editor of the well-established Negro newspaper the Pittsburgh *Courier*, to be an international correspondent. He was one of the earliest such African American journalists. His travel writing, as Thabiti Asukile notes, "was part of a [Black] tradition that began in the early 19th century" with writers such as Frederick Douglass and William Wells Brown ("Black International Journalism" 327). Part of Rogers's job was to write about the Black community living in Europe and to speak about topics to Black readers back in the United States. Josephine Baker (1906–75) may have been the most internationally known Black person alive in the 1920s. Born in poverty in St. Louis, Freda Josephine McDonald started her career in local shows before moving to New York and getting rave reviews for chorus roles in Black musicals on Broadway. The singer and dancer moved to Paris in 1925, performing in *La Revue* Nègre. She became an overnight sensation with her risqué routine, including the finale, the Danse Sauvage, which she performed wearing only a banana skirt, in a number of clubs and music halls, most notably the Folies-Bergère and the Moulin Rouge. Given her great fame, it is not surprising that Rogers, while living in Paris, would see one of her shows and seek her out for an interview.

Rogers's gossipy discussion with the star largely revolves around the controversy over whether or not she was actually married to Giuseppe (Pepito) Abatino. Many people considered this "marriage" just a publicity stunt to try to revive a flagging career. The evasive star never gives Rogers a clear answer forcing him to go beyond the interview to draw his own conclusion. Abatino proved to be not a count, but a stonecutter from Sicily, and it is unlikely the two ever wed since Baker was still married to her second husband, Willie Baker, at the time. Abatino would go on to be her manager and sometimes lover from 1926–35 and helped to provide a measure of personal and professional stability in Baker's life. No matter the relationship between Baker and Abatino, there is something sad about the desperate need for stars to stay in the public spotlight, a message which resonates even further in our age of mass media and ephemeral careers.

Baker returned to the United States in 1936 to perform with the Ziegfeld Follies, but was disenchanted by the racial situation in America as well as the negative reception to her show. She returned to Paris the next year and lived the remainder of her life in Europe except for tours. Baker adopted twelve children from various ethnicities and became a national hero in France for her resistance work during World War II. For more on her, see Bennetta Jules Rosette *Josephine Baker in Art and Life* (2007), Peggy Caravantes *The Many Faces of Josephine Baker* (2018), and Jean-Claude Baker and Chris Chase, *Josephine Baker: The Hungry Heart* (2001).

"IS THE STAR OF THE FOLIES-BERGERE REALLY MARRIED?"

Rogers Discloses Amazing "Truths" of Josephine Baker's Reported Marriage to Count Repeated Denials and Affirmations Put Dancer In Embarrassing Position—Search of Records Does Not Reveal License—Popularity Said to Be Waning.

Is Josephine Baker, star of the Folies-Bergere, really married, or is the story of her reported marriage only an advertising stunt? Is the Count de Salvatini, or Abatino, only a cabaret dancer and a no-Count, that was to play the part of a Count in a movie picture, or is he, as Miss Baker claims, the descendent of a noble Sicilian family?

A few days ago three English speaking papers, the Paris edition of the Chicago Tribune, the New York Herald, and the Continental edition of the London Daily Mail, carried stories to the effect that

Miss Baker was married to the "Count." Later, that day, accompanied by Charles H. Johnson of Atlanta, Ga., here on a visit I called on Miss Baker at the Folies-Bergere, when in answer to a letter I had written her that morning, she said: "Yes, we're married." Previously both Dr. Johnson and myself had been talking to the "Count," who was waiting for Miss Baker in a taxi, and he said that he had been married to Miss Baker. Among the things he wanted to know was whether the papers I represented were in Paris. This question he asked me several times, each time I told him that they were in America. Our introduction to the "Count" was made by Spencer Williams.[1] Miss Baker also told me that the stories in the white papers were true, her only objection being the manner in which they showed her as speaking.

Later Spencer Williams, well known song writer, told us that he was a witness at the wedding and on Dr. Johnson's inquiry told us several other things highly complimentary about Miss Baker. Two of these were that Miss Baker had saved more than seven million francs—the Count and herself being very careful managers—and that Miss Baker had bought a villa in Monte Carlo. The only people who would be found speaking against Miss Baker, said Williams, are the colored people in Paris. We left with the firm conviction that Miss Baker was married to the "Count."

One fact struck me at the time, none of the French papers carried anything about the marriage, except in the advertisement carried in them by the Folies-Bergere. This read in English:

"The truth! The black star, Josephine Baker, has made only a white marriage[2]—and she will continue to appear in "A Burst of Folly" at the Folies-Bergere."

Three days later, however, one of the leading French papers carried on its front page (issue of June 24), the following story of which this is a correct translation:

—It was a trick! Josephine Baker is a Countess only in name—

Is Josephine Baker really become [*sic*] Countess d'Albertini, as the newspapers say?

That is what we have asked the dancer, who received us with a great burst of laughter, followed it is true with a little confusion.

"Yes, I am a countess," she told me at first. Then with a little pirouette she added:

"At least in the movies—a movie play that Maurice Dekobra[3] has written and still without a title, and in which my very nice manager, Pepito Abatini, and I are going to play.

"Listen, do you know a gentleman with brown mustache, who resembles Adolphe Menjou.[4] It's he, my husband in the films, isn't it?

"Then how amusing it was to be married. I have even let the city believe that story a little. Ah, how false news spreads! What I told several friends as a joke all the world has taken as serious."

She pouted as a frolicsome child who fears to be chided. "Will the public be angry, you think? It has been so nice."

Her voice became almost suppliant. "How funny it is to be called 'Mrs.' to receive telegrams from all parts of the world. Don't all young girls have a desire to be called 'Mrs.' some time?"

"They are already talking of getting me a divorce." A burst of laughter. "Don't you think it would be difficult to get a divorce with the film still unfinished, since I am 'Mrs.' only in the film." And she concluded laughing:

"What is perhaps true, that is the best way of getting married after all."

On reading this article I at once called at the American Embassy, where the "Count and Countess" were said to have been married by Ambassador Herrick.[5] "Ridiculous!" I was informed there, "even the son of the ambassador couldn't be married here."

Next I went to the American Consulate, where I met George W. Mitchell, native of North Carolina, who has been a receiver in the consular service for twenty-one years. "They were not married here," he said, "and what's more four French detectives have come here to find out if the story is true. Miss Baker gets a big salary, I understand, and a change of name would make a difference in her income tax. The detectives tell me that they have searched every mayor's office in the city, and there is no record of any marriage. Besides if Miss Baker was married don't you think it would be at the Italian consulate?"

My next visit was in the office of the Daily Mail to hear how they had got the story as well as the picture of the dancer and the alleged count. "I am glad I didn't touch that story," said the editor, "it was just an advertising trick. I am glad that we said under the picture that we got the story from the Tribune."

At the Tribune I saw the editor, Mr. Ranger. "We have lost all confidence in Miss Baker," he said, "we heard of the story and sent a reporter down there. He asked Miss Baker if she were really married, and she said, 'Yes, don't you think it is a wonderful thing.' And so we carried the story believing it to be true."

At the office of the Herald I heard a similar story. "There was a big bunch of reporters down at Miss Baker's cabaret," said the editor. It will be noted, however, that not a single French paper carried the story of the alleged marriage.

Shortly before I had called on Miss Baker and she had told me that she was engaged to an Italian count, who is an artist. She also said that she had been offered $1,500 a night in some place, Vienna, I think, though people would hardly believe that to be true. The fact is that she has told every reporter, including myself that she had married a count—a story that now seems to be highly improbable, and only an advertising stunt that the management of the Folies quickly capitalized.

The truth is that Miss Baker has been steadily losing vogue in Paris. When I visited the Folies I was much disappointed to find that it was not her, but an English dancer, Jack Sanford, who was the hit of the show. Her dancing was not as good as that of many girls I have seen at the Lincoln[6] or the Lafayette[7] in New York, though I heard that her dancing last year was very good.

When I arrived in Paris a lady who knows Miss Baker well says that the account carried about her last year in the New York World and reproduced in all the colored papers was grossly exaggerated. The general impression is that the present incident is going to do her a great deal of harm. The English speaking editors, are of course, all angry over the incident, and to indulge in a little free language, you can't kill them for that.

Finally, just before mailing this I called at the Folies-Bergere and saw Spencer Williams who admitted that the Paris-Soir was right. "The story of the marriage was just an advertising ruse," he said, "though when Miss Baker announced it that night I really thought it was true."

In the meantime "the Count," who is only a minor employe in a department of the Italian government is much worried over the affair for reasons which shall be nameless. As was said, he asked me several times which paper I represented.

From "The Negro's Experience of Christianity and Islam," *Review of Nations*, January–March 1928

Rogers was a free thinker or atheist albeit having an interest in the Bahá'í faith[1] (Perry *Hubert Harrison, Voice of the Harlem Renaissance* 115; Moore Turner 67). He had expressed an antagonism against Christianity as early as *From Superman to Man*, where he had observed that "The slogan of the Negro devotee is: Take the world but give me Jesus, and the white man strikes an eager bargain with him." He begins this essay in his typical fashion, providing a historical background. He speaks of the origins of Christianity, including a Black Jesus and Virgin Mary. This "early Christianity knew no colour line." However, over time, and particularly in the New World, racial inequality and slavery were introduced. Christianity, especially Protestantism, became a malignant force for people of color. Next, Rogers discusses Islam, which "has never known a colour line for reasons that go deep." He points out several areas of commonality between traditional African values and customs with those of Islam, stating "Islam is nearer to the Negro not only ethically but psychically." Despite what Rogers believes are the obvious advantages of Islam as opposed to Christianity for Black people, he maintains Islam also has its flaws such as the continued practice of "polygamy and chattel slavery." In addition, Christianity does provide some material advantages for its adherents over Islam. Rogers ultimately comes to the conclusion that a decision between two such bad choices "cannot be so easily reached." Instead, he offers his own solution for man's salvation: not to place one's hopes on any of the major religions "but in the scientific exploitation of matter, working hand in hand with the spirit of universal brotherhood and equality."

"THE NEGRO'S EXPERIENCE OF CHRISTIANITY AND ISLAM"

In its earliest stage Negro slavery made no pretense: its motive was economic, and it frankly showed this. The planters of the Indies and the American colonies needed labour, while the traders of England, France, Holland and the other nations saw profit.

But eventually it was forced to mask: the evils of the traffic were growing and the more humane people of Europe and the colonies began to protest in the name of Christ. In an age when life revolved around Biblical precepts this was [a] formidable argument and the slaveholders and dealers to save themselves replied in kind. They pointed out that in taking away the Negroes from Africa they were really saving them from being eaten by one another; that in Africa they were being decimated by diseases which civilisation with its science would prevent; and that as they were already being held slaves in their own degraded land, servitude in a civilised one was really a step in advance, ample proof of which had been furnished by early peoples as the Greeks, Anglo-Saxons, and the Jews, who had all reached the heights of human dignity after passing through an apprenticeship of slavery.

But the slaveholders carried the war even further into the camp of the objectors. They asserted that Christ had commanded that the gospel should be preached to every creature and that by taking these Negroes to a Christian land where this knowledge could best be imparted they were obeying the Divine command in all its fulness. Their arguments were irresistible and the subsequent outlook on slavery for which they were responsible may best be summed up in the words of one of the New England poets which ran something like this:

The slave ship goes from coast.
Fanned by the wings of the Holy Ghost.[2]

In thus taking away the Negro with the alleged aim of christinising him an important fact may be noted: he was being removed from the influence of another religious system which, too, holds the doctrine of

One God. The slave traffic to America continued well beyond the middle of the 19th Century and it is not too much to assume that a good many of the slaves brought from the West Coast must have been Mohammedans. Further, the descendants of these Negro slaves, now Christians, would in all probability be Mohammedans had they remained in Africa. In view, therefore, of the arguments of the slave-holders referred to above, and the general belief today that the taking away of the Negro has proved beneficial, a brief comparison of his experiences under Islam and under Christianity together with a consideration of his present status under both, might prove interesting.

In weighing Christianity and the Negro care must be taken to distinguish between the general attitude of the Christian Church prior to the discovery of the New World, and after. Many of the earliest Fathers of the Church were, in all probability, of Negro ancestry. St. Augustine, Tertullian,[3] Origen,[4] and St Cyprian,[5] the great standard bearers of Christianity, were all Africans. St. Augustine was a Numidian,[6] and it is frequently said in responsible circles that he was of Negro descent. Just as the Mohammedans venerate Bilal,[7] so the early Christians venerated Simon, the Cyrenean,[8] who in their day, was depicted as a dark Negro. By many of the early Christians both Christ and the Virgin Mary were depicted with Negro features.

St. Maurice,[9] commander of "the Theban Legion," and revered as one of the staunchest of the Christian martyrs, was known as a Negro. An abbey was founded in his honour at Aganaum, now St. Maurice-en-Valais, near Geneva, on the spot where he is believed to have been killed. He is the celestial saint of parts of Switzerland, Italy, France, and Germany. In a picture painted by Grunewald[10] which was part of the altar decoration of the Cathedral of Halle, Germany, and which now hangs in the Old Pinakothek, Munich, St. Maurice is pictured a sooty black, with Negro features and wooly hair.

In short, early Christianity knew no colour line. The Christian, whether Teuton, Roman, Moor, or Abyssinian, was welcomed as a brother in Christ. It is true that Christians at this time practised slavery but they made no difference as to colour or race in the matter.

This absence of a colour line continued through the centuries and when Negroes were again introduced as slaves in Europe in the middle of the 15th Century the policy toward them remained the same. Although Negro slavery lasted in Southern Europe for three hundred and thirty-one years (1442–1773), eighty-five years longer than in the United States, there is apparently no record of any disturbances due to colour.

The most cordial feelings seemed to have prevailed. Azurara,[11] an eyewitness of the arrival of the first slaves from Guinea, paints a touching picture of their intense grief, but goes on to relate how soon after they accepted Christianity, were taught trades, adopted by families, and even "married to the women of the country."*

Throughout Christian Europe, both at this time and later, the aspiring Negro received marked consideration. Leo Africanus,[12] whose book on Africa, was the standard work for nearly three centuries, was the protege and godson of Pope Leo X. Under Peter the Great, Hannibal,[13] ancestor of Poushkin, became a general. The European Negro produced painters, poets, soldiers, theologians and writers of note receiving warm praise from the Abbé Gregoire[14] and Blumenbach. In his Anthropological Treatise[s] the latter said that he had a library of his own filled with the works of Negro authors.

Turning now to the New World one sees a quite different picture.

Two dates must be mentioned here: 1503 and 1619. The first marks the introduction into Latin America; the second into Anglo-Saxon America. In the former region the greed of the white colonist was tempered by his religion, Catholicism, which still retains in America much of the spirit of the early Church above mentioned.

The Anglo-Saxon, on the other hand with none of these traditions, tended to regard the black slave as a creature a little less than human. There was another reason, too. Christianity, in theory, is Oriental, stressing what Schopenhauer calls the denial of the will;[15] it adjures its followers not to lay up for themselves treasures on earth, but to practise charity. The temperament of the peoples of North-western Europe, however, is "assertion of the will," the religion of Odin and Thor is in their veins, and to practise giving rather than getting, is difficult. Hence, Christianity, with them, has largely been a system of aggrandisement, not only as concerns the darker races, but the weaker groups and individuals of the white race as well. The Anglo-Saxon, so-called, controls much more of the globe than any other group. "How the European has been able to acquire colonies," says Nietzsche, "is explained by his nature which is that of a beast of prey."[16]

It must be noted, nevertheless, that the Anglo-Saxons, unlike the Latins, emphatically did not wish Negro slaves at first, but once having had them became more avid than the rest. It was against the express orders of the governor of Virginia and the wishes of the people that a Dutch ship landed the first slaves in Jamestown. White labour was then plentiful in the British Isles.

This labour, brought to the colonies, was reduced to slavery in all but name, and when Negro labour came on the scene the latter fell into the lowest rank, elevating the status of the white slave, as in primitive times the captives taken in war brought an improvement in the status of the women of the conquering tribe.

At first, also, strenuous efforts were made to prevent racial intermixture. White men who cohabitated with Negro women were soundly whipped, while the white woman was heavily fined and banished from the colony. In the case of marriage with a Negro she became with her husband a slave for life.

Like the white indentured servant, the Negro was at first not held as a slave for life. Later, however, laws were passed for making him one in spite of the fact that he had embraced Christianity. The slaveholders again using the Bible as an authority pointed out that St. Paul had advised the slaves of his time not to change their condition if they could, and that he had caused Onesimus,[17] a runaway slave to be returned to his master. "Servants, be obedient to them that are your masters,"[18] was the injunction. Many of the churches, themselves, held slaves, and while ample provision was made for teaching them Christianity, laws were passed making it a crime to teach them to read even the Bible, itself.

With the exception of a few favoured house-servants no Negro, free or enslaved, was permitted in the white church. E.S. Abdy,[19] an English visitor to the United States in 1833 tells the story of a Negro in Boston, who in some way had acquired a pew in a white church to the disgust of the other members. All attempts to oust him legally having failed the officers of the church painted the inside of his pew with wet tar on Sunday morning; the Negro thereupon stood in his pew, but when he returned the next Sunday he found that the flooring had been sawn away. Boston, then, as now, was the most liberal city in America in its attitude toward colour.

The free Negroes were forced to build their churches in which to worship the same God. Once a number of them while at worship in a white church were forced to leave even though they were at prayer. One of the number was Richard Allen,[20] who was thereby inspired to found the African Methodist Episcopal Church (1794), one of the most influential religious bodies in America, today.

I have in my possession a copy of a letter written by a white Baptist minister to a Negro one that is typical, not only of the South where the incident occurred but of the nation. The latter, visiting a soul-saving meeting in the church of the former, took a seat on the main floor, whereupon he was requested to go to the gallery where seats had been reserved for Negroes, he was told. In the Southern States, Negroes are not permitted to sit on the first floor of public buildings.

Instead of complying the Negro preacher left the church and wrote a strong letter of protest. The white minister, in answer, said that he saw no cause for complaint as many of his white members chose the gallery by preference, and that in Scotland gallery seats are considered the best. He said further that if what the Negro was seeking was social equality, that would not and should not be granted as it would lead to intermarriage, which was detrimental to both races. He insisted, however, that both were brothers in Christ, which did not include social equality.

An odd fact about the incident is that the Negro minister is so white himself that both men might have been brothers.

Were Christ to return in the guise of the dark-skinned individual many believe He was, He would find himself barred from most churches in America pretty much as He would be unwelcome because He was a Jew. With the exception of the Christian Science, and the Catholic Churches in the North, as well as the Community Church of New York,[21] the sight of a Negro in a white church is rare, indeed. And even in the churches mentioned the Negro attendance is few, as the feeling is that there must be present those whites who are prejudiced. Today the Negroes, according to the Negro Year Book have 45,000 churches, a membership of 4,800,000, and church property valued at $87,208,377. Colour has prevailed over Christ in making a division so complete that the two "races" might well belong to opposing religions.

The most insistently Christian part of America today are the Southern States. It is from this region come the blue laws, the Ku Klux Klan, the anti-evolution laws, and the "monkey" trials.[22] It is also the section from which came the strongest protest against America's ratification of the Treaty of Lausanne with Turkey on the ground that Turkey is anti-Christian and persecutes the Armenians.[23]

It is also in this region which Mencken calls "the Bible Belt,"[24] that most of the lynchings and burnings-alive, occur. Here also peonage thrives, and entire families are sold into slavery, instances of which occurred in 1927.

America's entry into the world war was marked by the massacre of more than five hundred Negroes in East St. Louis,[25] according to a Congressional report and her exit in 1919 by more than fifteen race-riots, one of which occurred in the national capital while President Wilson was formulating his plans for world peace. In another at Chicago more than fifteen hundred persons of both racial groups were killed and injured.

Several attempts have been made, and large sums have been spent by the Negroes and their friends, to have a law making such riots and lynchings illegal.[26] President Coolidge has repeatedly declared himself in favour of this enactment but Congress, which opens each day's session with prayer in the name of Christ, has persistently evaded doing this. Without lynching and mob force the exploiters of Negro labour would be powerless as the Constitution of the United States gives the Negro equal privileges with the white man.

Today in spite of splendid material and intellectual progress the Negro still finds himself a pariah, particularly in the South. "Who's Who in America" lists eighty-eight Negroes. There are poets, singers, authors, financiers, physicians and divines of distinction but attainment counts for almost nothing in face of the tremendous fact of colour. They are forced into the cramping confines of jim-crow institutions which deny them human dignity and equality in all save prices, in which case they must pay at the same rate as the whites, and sometimes much more as in the cost of housing. The census of 1910 gave 69,929 Negroes engaged in professional service. The number in 1927 is probably four or five times as many.

As an instance of the rigid manner in which colour is made to take precedence over intellectual and other qualities I may give the following personal experience: In 1926 while making a tour of the Southern States I was taken by a friend of mine, a book-dealer, to see one of the officials of the State Library in Richmond, Virginia. My friend was anxious to have introduced in the library one of the books I had written. The official received us courteously, and said that although it was contrary to custom he would purchase a book then and now for the library, adding that the library already had the first edition, and would be glad to add a copy of the fourth.[27] A little later, wishing to see just how much the book had been used I went into the reading-room, and quite forgetful of the fact that I was in the South took a seat as I was accustomed to do in other libraries whereupon an assistant beckoned to me and told me that I would have to leave as my being there was against the law.

Islam

Islam has never known a colour line for reasons that go deep. Ranking, perhaps, next to Mohammed in the affections of the Moslem world is Bilal Ibn Rahab, a Negro, and Mohammed's alter ego, treasurer, adviser, muezzin,[28] and almost earliest convert. Mohammed thought so much of Bilal that he granted him "precedence in Heaven." Later, when Omar was Caliph and Khobab, another staunch adherent of the Prophet visited him, Omar, rising from the throne deferentially seated Khobab thereon, saying that there was only one other in Islam more worthy of the favour, and that was Bilal. The words of the Adzan, or Call to Prayer are uttered throughout the East today precisely as they fell from the lips of Bilal nearly thirteen centuries ago.

Another and perhaps more important factor contributing to the absence of colour prejudice is that Islam rose to power in a region where from time immemorial many of the rulers were what are known as Negroes today, as many of the wearers of the double crown of Egypt, and the kings of Numidia and Lybia. Black and white had been meeting and mating as equals along the southern shores of the Mediterranean thousands of years before the coming of Mohammed.

From the moment a Negro becomes a convert to Islam there is nothing to prevent his attaining the highest privileges, social and political, to which a white Moslem may attain. Not only were Negroes made governors of provinces under the Mohammedan Empire, but kings. "I admonish you," said Mohammed on the approach of death, "to fear God and yield obedience to my successor though he may be a Negro slave."

While the Bible sanctions the enslavement of Christians, the Koran expressly forbids the holding of the faithful in bondage. As to churches, there is not a single exclusively coloured mosque in all Islam, the Negro entering freely into all with the white man. When the late Mahdi[29] saw a poor Negro kneel beside him in the mosque he said to him: "In this place we are all one." Contrast this with the attitude of the white Baptist minister mentioned above.

Islam is nearer to the Negro not only ethically but psychically. It is necessary to distinguish here between the Negro of the Old World and that of the New. Islam's command is simple: There is but One God and Mohammed is His prophet[30]—no intricate belief in the Immaculate Conception and a Holy Trinity. Islam also tolerates polygamy and slavery, that is, the Negro's property rights for these primitive forms of property persist in Africa.

The Mohammedan paradise with its feasting and its houris[31] also make a stronger appeal than the Christian heaven with its milk and honey, and absence of sex pleasures, to a people who live much more strongly in the physical senses than in the intellect, pretty much as the music of Irving Berlin makes a stronger appeal to the Caucasian masses than that of Beethoven.

Other points of affinity are that the Arab lives in his tent; the Negro in his hut; both believe in the circumcision of male and female, and both are at times wildly excitable in their religious manifestations.

These are some of the reasons why Islam has succeeded in ousting Christianity in the region where it was perhaps strongest. Less than a century after the flight from Mecca Christianity had almost disappeared in North Africa. Indeed its influence had begun to decline fully two centuries before the coming of Mohammed.

Today of some sixty million or so African Negroes believing in the doctrine of One God less than two millions are Christians. After nineteen centuries of missionary effort the majority of Christians in Africa are the small number of Europeans there.[32] Islam, it is true, propagated itself by fire and sword in Africa, just as Christianity did in America. In these later years, however, it is relying like Christianity on persuasion.

The case for Islam is simple. As was said, it imposes no peculiar hardships on account of colour, no handicaps in the pursuit of happiness. One finds less colour prejudice in England than in America; less in France than in England; less in Germany than in France, and in Turkey, the stronghold of Islam almost none. In the opinion of many American Negro musicians who have been around the world the Negro in Turkey enjoys a closer equality with the whites than in any part of the Christian world.

Christ said: "Inasmuch as ye have done it to the least of these my brethren ye have done it unto me."[33] If this ought to be the criterion of Christian conduct then it must be said that it is a non-Christian religion who is living most fully up to it where the Negro is concerned.

The case against Christianity could have been made much stronger. One could have said that while Islam discourages the use of intoxicants the Christian nations have derived great profit from its sale in Africa and elsewhere to the detriment of the blacks; one could have said that while Islam inspires manliness, Christianity tends to make servile imitators as in the United States where a large percentage of Negroes straighten their hair, bleach their faces, ape the whites, and generally despise themselves and the members of their group**—the general opinion of African travellers is that the Christianized native is an inferior product, spiritually, to the Islamic Negro, or the raw one—one could have said that in addition to whiskey, that syphilis, prostitution, consumption, and other Western ills usually follow in the train of the Christian missionary, yet, in the face of all this the singular conclusion must be arrived at: the Negro is better off in the West than in the East, actually and eventually.

Among the reasons are that modern civilisation is firmly opposed to polygamy and chattel slavery.

Christianity has not been entirely brutal. It was the Christian nations, chiefly England, who in combat against themselves, Mohammedans Arabs and Negroes, who have done most to suppress slavery that open sore of the world,[34] as Livingstone called it; it is Christian influence that has done most to reduce inter-tribal wars, a not unmixed blessing as the Christian nations have not only pitted the Negroes against themselves but brought them to Europe in the last war to take part in their own quarrels.

Slavery and polygamy are forms of property rights too crude for our age. Even wage slavery is meeting with less and less tolerance. The West has more to offer the Negro than the East not because it is Christian but because it is in Western lands that Science has reached its highest development. It is in Western lands that *the masses* of the Negro group are better off hygienically, educationally, and economically.

The United States, to use a conspicuous example, has been a hard school for the Negro. It is a prison—but a prison where he eats and sleep[s] sumptuously in comparison with the Mohammedan Negro. And it is because his body is being better cared for that the American Negro is making better progress. Mankind has progressed, not by following the path of least resistance but by doing what was difficult, morally, physically and intellectually.

The Islamic Negro has social equality; the Christian Negro, little or none. The respective positions of the two groups may be likened to two brothers, both poor, one of whom is his own master; the other, a servant in a rich man's home. Given both the will to advance, the latter is certainly better off.

But, on the other hand, might not much of what has just been said be purely Western bias? Polygamy was cited but has not the Christian colonist always been a polygamist so far as the Negro woman is concerned? Nearly every slaveholder in America had two families, one white, the other black, a custom that took such firm root that it exists to this day. The American white man, broadly speaking, craves sex association with the Negro woman, but he will have her, and does have her only as a concubine, a condition that is polygamy in all but name.

Slavery was also mentioned. In addition to the fact that slavery still exists in Christian Sierra Leone, and will not pass out of existence until the last day of 1927,[35] are not some free Negroes in Christian lands really worse off than enslaved Negroes in Mohammedan ones? In the United States the Negro is discriminated against in the matter of employment. Are not certain human beings who walk the streets drearily day after day in search of work really worse off than the Mohammedan Negro who has a kind master?

The Negro was also said to be better off hygienically in Western lands, but what of the fact, that his deathrate in the majority of them is almost double that of the whites in spite of his stronger physique?***

The Christian Negro was also said to be better off, economically and educationally, than the Islamic one. He is, for instance, in the United States, but happiness or what passes for happiness on this planet is the goal of our existence, and is one always happy in proportion to one's wealth and education? Is the American Negro with his two billion dollars of accumulated wealth, his fine colleges, and the indignation against ostracism and injustice forever gnawing at his heart, happier than the Islamic one?

No, the decision cannot be so easily reached. Nor does it seem important that one should be reached. In the new day to which we all look forward, black or white, it will not be a matter of Islam or Christianity or any other form of dogmatism. Religious dogmatism is founded on mystery—the mystery of the world and of life. But Man is now taking these for granted; he is devoting more time to work and less to wonder; he is realizing that it is not in word-spinning about any Deity, that lies the path to happiness, but in the scientific exploitation of matter, working hand in hand with the spirit of universal brotherhood and equality, whose observance is the command not only of Islam and Christianity but of all the other great religions.

ROGERS'S NOTES

* Azurara's Chronicles: Chaps. 25, and 26 (Hakluyt Ed.).

** The first individual fortunes made in America by Negroes were in hair-straightening products.

*** The United States Census reports give the following figures:

	1910	1911	1912	1916	1920
White	14.5	13.7	13.5	13.5	12.8
Colored	24.2	23.6	22.9	20.5	18.4

"Communism and the Negro," New York *Amsterdam News*, January 30, 1929

It is difficult to pin down Rogers to any particular political philosophy. As Joyce Moore Turner states, "he eschewed joining any political party" (68). It is clear from many of his remarks that he believes the capitalist system has done much harm for Blacks through slavery and color prejudice. He stresses that racism originated in the New World as the slave trade developed. In *Sex and Race* he comments, "there is color prejudice only where economic interests are involved." While there are aspects of Black Nationalism that he finds appealing, including Black pride and Black ownership of industry, the concept of racial separatism is anathema to him. Socialism also has some appeal, but when, in Rogers's perception, he sees unions and the party favoring whites, he dismisses it. Like religious organizations, Rogers looks at political systems including Communism with deep suspicion.[1] He laments that radicals tend to look at books praising the Negro as "black chauvinism" ("The Suppression of Negro History"; "How and Why This Book was Written" *World's Great Men of Color* Vol. 1). He sees Communism as more of a religion with fanatical followers than a political or economic system and maintains that the best way for Blacks to approach it is with caution and to try to use it to his best advantage. However, they should always be wary that these groups are not using them for their own purposes, and not put "their neck in the Communist yoke." Though Rogers kept his distance from Marxist organizations, the FBI maintained a brief file on him in the 1940s because of his interest in "social equality."[2]

"COMMUNISM AND THE NEGRO"

Last October I mentioned in the Amsterdam News the fact that the Communists are attempting to organize the Negro workers of the world in one vast union, and I gave the gist of their program. I also mentioned one of their journals, The Negro Worker,[3] published in French.

Since then I have received a letter from the Palace of Labor in Moscow from the editor of The Negro Worker telling me that when I stated that The Negro Worker is published by the International Secours Rouge (Communist) I was wrong.

The Negro Worker, says the letter, "is the official bulletin of the International Trade Union Committee of Negro Workers of the Red International of Labor Unions.

"You also stated that the publishers of The Negro Worker are a 'white' organization. This also is incorrect. The Red International of Labor Unions is an international revolutionary working class organization of all nationalities.

"The report of the work of the Fourth Congress of the Red International of Labor Unions convened in March, 1923, states that 'represented in the Congress was the trade union movement of the countries of Europe, Asia, North and South America, Australia and Africa. Well represented were the Pacific, colonial and semi-colonial countries.'

"It is needless for us to say that our program calls for a determined fight against all racial discriminations and inequality practices in the labor movement, such as are prevalent in the American Federation of Labor against Negro workers."

The latter also goes on to tell of a resolution adopted by the Executive Bureau of the Red International for getting the Negro into the Communist fold.

Since Negro workers, it says in part, comprise a very powerful force in the fight against capitalism, "thanks to their economic, political and racial oppression," and since the Negro workers of the United States, Africa and the West Indies will achieve equality with the white workers only by means of an organized and relentless struggle against the whole system of capitalist oppression, therefore, it is resolved to set up a committee of Negro workers composed of two representatives from the Negro workers of the United States, and one each from South Africa, Guadeloupe, Martinique and Cuba.

Haiti, East Africa, Portuguese Africa, the Belgian Congo, Liberia, French Equatorial Africa, and those countries of Latin America where there are considerable numbers of Negro workers (Brazil, Colombia, Venezuela, etc.) are also to be drawn in.

Joint unions of white and Negro workers are to be formed, and in places like South Africa, where the law prevents black and white from being in the same union, independent black unions are to be formed.

The Negro Worker, published in various languages at Moscow, is being broadcast to Negroes all over the world.

The question is: What effect will Communist agitation have on the world-wide color problem and what benefit, if any, is the Negro going to derive from it?

This, indeed, is difficult to forecast. But one fact is certain: Those nations having colonies with a large colored population are not going to relish Communist doctrine, to say the least.

Indeed, if my own personal opinion is asked, I would say that England, who has most to lose, is already so panicky that she's afraid of her own shadow.

And England has cause to be panicky. Of some 475,000,000 persons in the British Empire there are about 425,000,000 colored. Of that number perhaps one in a thousand really loves a white man, for while it is rare to find a white man who loves a dark-skinned person, it is far rarer to find a colored man who loves a white one. The Hindus number some 300,000,000 souls, yet I have reason to believe that the white race would have considerable trouble drumming up a few thousand Hindus who had any genuine love for it.

Communism is the new religion. Economics is its god and Karl Marx is its prophet. Speaking purely as an observer, as one who would not lift a finger either to help or hinder it, I believe that with increasing industrialism Communism is going to spread over the world. It talks to the pocketbook, a language that people of all climes and all religions can understand.

It is beginning just as Christianity did among the lowliest of the earth. Today in London, Paris, Berlin, Brussels and other large cities the Communist sections are the poverty-stricken ones. A great majority of those living in the wretched East End of London are Communists. They, by the way, sent to Parliament the only dark-skinned man who has ever been seated there.

Communism, too, has had its martyrs. In the recent Chinese revolution Communist women died with all the fanaticism of the early Christians and Mohammedans.

The Communists mean to make of Moscow what Rome is to the Catholic or Mecca is to the Mohammedan. Napoleon tried to make Paris the capital of Europe, and the Communists are out to make Moscow the capital of the world.

And very shrewdly they preached anti-militarism in England, France and other lands, while keeping in Russia one of the strongest armies in the world. Is it any wonder that the big powers are showing so much fear? They are showing the same fear that the Roman emperors did at the rise of Christianity.

The Communists, of course, mean to use the darker races to further their schemes, but the darker races must be prepared to use them instead. They must learn how to use them to further their own cause of freedom. Race prejudice is a weapon that can be made to cut both ways. Just as the white man has been using the darker man to oust his own people, as in West Africa, so the darker man must learn to use the white man against other white men to win his freedom.

The Communist, while in Europe, is free of color prejudice like other Europeans, but when he comes to live among dark men he is pretty much like the rest. I have met some very prejudiced Communists in America, though Communism, like Christianity, condemns color prejudice.

Communism has much dogma and indigestible bunkum, like other religions, but it has sounder and more practical meat than any of the others. It has economic doctrine that Negroes, above all others, ought to get acquainted with.

But as to putting their neck in the Communist yoke, that is something else.

"Ahead of Its Time," New York *Amsterdam News*, April 10, 1929

Rogers starts out his interview/review with Claude McKay by complimenting his fellow Jamaican for writing the novel *Home to Harlem* (1928). However, since McKay asked Rogers for his "frank opinion," it was inevitable that he would tell McKay his complaints about the book. *Home to Harlem* was the first Black best-seller, but it was very controversial because of what was perceived by many to be its overemphasis on an unsavory side of African American life, including violence, drugs, and wanton sexuality. Rogers felt that some of these depictions were "too much." He advocated the more traditional literature of "uplift" that provided "real aspiration." In that sense, he was in the conservative camp including Marcus Garvey and W. E. B. Du Bois who preached racial propaganda rather than artistic freedom allowing writers to present any facet of Black life in as honest a fashion as they chose. The latter aesthetic philosophy was favored by many of the younger Harlem Renaissance writers. Rogers's views are similarly expressed in his negative evaluations of such works as Eric Walrond's *Tropic Death* (Pittsburgh *Courier* March 25, 1927), and Langston Hughes' *Fine Clothes to the Jew* (Pittsburgh *Courier* February 12, 1927). Rogers, Garvey and Du Bois were all frustrated by McKay, who they felt was catering to white audiences instead of using his talent to advance the Black race as they believed he had done in his militant poem "If We Must Die," written in the bloody Red Summer of 1919. Rogers gave a more favorable view of McKay in an earlier discussion of his book of poetry *Harlem Shadows*, which contained "If We Must Die" (Pittsburgh *Courier* June 18, 1927). Since the two men both lived in France for years, they would encounter each other occasionally, but they never developed a friendship. Not only did they differ in their political and artistic views, but Michel Fabre notes that "McKay was annoyed by Rogers's perpetual wonderment in finding the French so nice, while he (McKay), who had been in contact with them for several years, knew better" (139–40).

"AHEAD OF ITS TIME"

"It will take the Negro in America another thirty or forty years to see 'Home to Harlem' in its true light—to appreciate it in the spirit in which I wrote it," said Claude McKay, speaking of the volume of adverse criticism he had received from Negroes on this book.

McKay, recent winner of the Harmon Prize[1] in literature, has returned from a trip through North Africa, Spain and Italy, and is spending a few days in Paris before returning to his home in southern France.

He said that he had been surprised at the attacks that had been made on him, since he had written only what he had seen. Some of his critics, he said, had accused him of "selling out to the white man," while others had charged him with being prejudiced against colored Americans. "Those who make the latter charge," he said, "however, will be forced to admit that I did not make saints or paragons of the West Indians in 'Home to Harlem.' I described them in the same impartial manner that I did the Americans, colored or white."

He went on to say that he was interested chiefly in what is known as the lower class of Negro: that his sympathies were very strongly with that class; but, as a realist in literature, he had to record what he saw.

"Take the leading character, Jake," he said; "underneath all his shortcomings you'll find a solid layer of sound principle. There are certain things done by some of the upper class that he refused to do. And, above all, he loved his race, and passionately watched its advancement."

As we sat together in the Soufflot Cafe, on the Boulevard St. Michel, he asked me my opinion of the book—"my frank opinion."

I replied that I had found the book interesting, full of joie de vivre, with the words vivid and well chosen. I also said that I found it true to life, except in one or two places, one of which was the instance in which two West Indian women stripped themselves of all their clothing and fought in a Harlem backyard. "That was too much," I said.

"Well," he replied, "I saw with my own eyes such a sight in Jamaica, West Indies, and I merely used the writer's privilege and transferred the scene to Harlem."

I answered that I knew Jamaica well, and that I had found there no less a desire on the part of the women to hide certain parts of their bodies. I cited instances, one of which was how we lads in the West Indies would go on market days, when the rivers were down, to see the market-women cross with lifted skirts, and how skilfully these women would hold their dresses to outmanoeuvre our curiosity.

"Nevertheless," he replied, "I saw it, and would be very glad to give you the addresses of others who saw that fight." As a writer, however, experience has taught me the truth of the old saying: Truth is stranger than fiction. Simply because a thing has not come within the range of my experience, does not make it improbable or untrue.

Continuing my criticism, I said that, while I thought the book on the whole was based on fact and that while I believed that the writer should be free to write about everything in life—censors, prudes and exploiters of humanity—that "Home to Harlem," coming when it did, was distasteful superfluity. That is the angle of Negro life, I said, that the white writers have nearly all treated—the angle that it is to be expected that they will continue to treat, simply because that is what a white reading public, with preconceived notions, wants.

Moreover, I said, when a Negro writer dips into the garbage-pan (such as is to be found on the doorsteps of all peoples) to the exclusion of the finer sides of life, that is just what the white exploiters of Negro labor wants. White writers hold up such books as Exhibit A, as Schufeldt [*sic*] held up Hannibal Thomas's book,[2] and use them to create still stronger sentiment against Negroes, thereby making it more difficult for them in their battle against prejudice. "The final result of such books," I said, "is to hit the Negro in the pocketbook. They are all for the benefit of the white man."

"But what is the Negro writer who is interested in portraying this phase of Negro life to do?" McKay demanded. "That is why I say that 'Home to Harlem' is ahead of its time. But, as for me, I see but one hope for the Negro, and that is for him to tell the truth about himself. The French do that and, as the result, they are the most intellectual people in Europe."

I replied that I thought that Negro writers who dealt with the more objectionable features of Negro life needed more balance. "For instance, the only Negro with any real aspiration in 'Home to Harlem' is a Haitian, and he ended as a flat failure. On the other hand, what is the real truth? There are thousands and thousands of Negroes in America who, most of them coming from just such surroundings as the characters in 'Home to Harlem,' have worked their way through bitter struggle and discouragement to positions of equality with both Negroes and Caucasians with far superior advantages."

I went on to say that, personally, I got little or no inspiration from 'Home to Harlem.' The hero, Jake finished with the aimless existence of a Bohemian, which is precisely the old, old idea that most white people have about Negroes.

There is no doubt, however, that McKay takes a deep and passionate interest in his people; that, as a "full-blood Negro," he feels keenly the injustices that darker Negroes in particular suffer, even though he happens to be in a land where a black man meets a minimum of color prejudice. Of this I am convinced after several talks with him.[3]

"Home to Harlem' was written chiefly for white consumption. It had to be to get recognition among Negroes. Those, however, who declare that its author "sold his race" would do well to reread the book (provided they had already read it) in a calmer state of mind, or read his poem, "If We Must Die"—a poem as spirited as any to be found in any language, and which has been translated in many languages.

McKay's new book, "Banjo,"[4] deals with the Negroes of a similar type in Marseilles, France, and will appear soon from the press of Harper Brothers. From what he tells me of it, it is likely to prove another best seller. Some 50,000 copies of "Home to Harlem" were sold, He is also to write a series of articles on North Africa for Harper's Magazine, and is planning to visit the United States soon.

"The Paris Pepper-Pot," Pittsburgh *Courier*, June 15, 1929

Rogers was a world traveler, but clearly his favorite city was Paris. He spoke French with a degree of fluency and enjoyed a sense of freedom there that as a Black man he did not feel in the United States or England. He established himself as a member of the small community of Blacks who were visiting or living in Paris in the 1920s and '30s, writing a short-lived column, the first article of which is included here, called "The Paris Pepper-Pot," in the Pittsburgh *Courier*, where he indulged in the gossip and goings on in this Black community. He solicited articles from his readers that he hoped to include in the column. In "The Paris Pepper-Pot" Rogers demonstrates a lightness and humor that is not always evident in his other, more serious, writings. Here he can indulge in the life, especially the nightlife, of the city he loves. In addition, he is able to provide a Black insight into what life was like in Paris for these intrepid American vagabonds. Unfortunately, Rogers was generally not successful in obtaining reader contributions to the column, and it ran for only about three months.

"THE PARIS PEPPER-POT"

As we are just moving into this column today the folks will have to take pot luck.

This is all the more so as we intend to be a real pepper-pot. But wait, we'd better explain what is a pepper-pot.

Pepper-pot is a favorite dish south of the Rio Grande. That is, if one can call it a dish, for it is composed of a variety of tasty what-nots.

During the week mother throws all the odds and ends of meat—beef, pork, chicken, mutton, rabbit, game into a three-legged pot that sits in the ashes near the wood fire. Then on Saturday she puts in the vegetables, bits of yam, breadfruit, cocoe,[1] ochroe,[2] and a variety of greens, not forgetting a liberal supply of fresh, wild bird-pepper[3]—and sets the pot on the fire.

In an hour or so there arises a delicious odor that can be smelt a mile off—an odor in which that of pepper predominates. The family then gathers around the pot. Each dips in his spoon just as his African ancestor did centuries ago, and whatever he brings up, down it goes. If there is any left, back it goes with the pot into the ashes to serve as a basis for next Saturday's dinner. And so you may be eating some of last year's pepper-pot, who knows? A pepper-pot may have ancestry, and then again it may not.

Besides, the Paris Pepper-Pot is going to run true to form. The first duty of a good columnist is to have others do his work for him while he draws pay for it. So we extend a hearty invitation to all who have no other outlet for their bright and clever thoughts to send them to us—bits of witty verse, anecdotes, and anything of striking human interest.

And we do not intend to let them work for nothing. Oh, no. We promise them the finest of all remunerations—a thrill. For what can rival the pleasure of seeing one's name in print? Lest it be thought I'm joking we'll add that even we old-timers do not exactly hate to see our names in print, though we've seen it a thousand times before.

Indeed in asking your contribution we may even be on the way to become a benefactor to humanity. Think! By contributing to the Paris Pepper-Pot you may be actually starting on a career as a great humorist, a great writer, or even a poet.

Blessed is the man who makes a laugh grow where none grew before. As a racial group, we have the reputation of being humorous but you'd never guess it by our writings. So send in your short articles and witty sayings to the Paris Pepper-Pot in care of the editor of this newspaper.

Enfin,[4] just a word of warning. Contributors must not get nervous if their articles do not appear the day after they are sent in. Some bits that go into the Pepper-Pot may not be eaten for weeks and weeks. Besides you know the saying: A watched pot never boils.

While waiting for the avalanche of wit and humor to pour in, we'd better get busy. The editor suggested that we begin with a series of articles on Paris. So since there is no help for it, here goes:

Paris has the distinction of being the only city in which we have not been bored. In Chicago, where we once lived, time hung heavy on our hands. The same is true of London. It was a little less true of New York. In Berlin, Rome, Vienna, Milan, Brussels, things were a little better. But being in Paris is like being on a perpetual holiday.

There are amusements to suit every taste in Paris. They range from the sublime to the silly, from the sacred to the sexy.

Are you interested in art and literature? Well, there are museums and libraries galore. Are you religious? You can ask nothing better; the churches are always open. Are you thirsty? You can buy a drink any time of night or day ranging in price from $16 to two cents.

Do you like walking? The parks and promenades are the finest and most beautiful in the world, chief of which is the Champs-Elysees. Do you like theatres? You can see Shakespeare, Hugo, Racine, Moliere, any night. But perhaps your tastes run, well—to things a bit more frivolous? Then you can go to places where the ladies frolic in fig leaves, and if you are exacting, you may see them dance in less.

And prices are arranged to suit every pocket. Some of the places are so cheap you go in for the price of a pack of chewing gum; others are so dear that the French, thrifty by nature, will not pass them lest even the odor of the bill strike them on the sidewalk.

There is Montmartre. This is the jazziest and sexiest spot on earth and the first place visited by every good American. Cut out Montmartre and you'd make an awful dent in the tourist trade, which is about 90 percent American.

Paris has an awful reputation although the average Parisian is not a bit worse than the average citizen of Hicksville, Oshkosh, or any place you may name. He goes to bed early because he has to punch the clock early, just like you.

But Paris' reputation is the making of Paris. Give it a better name and the hotel-keepers, the tourist agencies, the rich jewelers, the modistes[5] and dress-makers would certainly set up a howl. For with the present war against cabarets and sexy places in America, Montmartre is doing a finer business than ever.

Montmartre's night life reminds us of Harlem and Chicago's South Side. When the respectable Nordic wants to cut loose he goes to Harlem.

When the Englishman wants to have a good time he comes to Paris though a Montmartre would be unthinkable in straight-laced England. France is the land of personal liberty. Every one minds his own business.

The principal music halls of Montmartre are the Folies-Bergere, the Casino de Paris, Moulin Rouge and Moulin Bleu. All frankly cater to the nude and the jokes are—well—a trifle high. If you don't understand French, however, you'll keep as straight a face as if you were listening to a sermon while all around you, are laughing.

Scores of ladies throng the stage. Some have figures eclipsing the Venus de Milo, and almost eclipsing her in the matter of clothing, or rather lack of it. Some of the chorus girls, who, by the way, are mostly English, do wear a garment about one-fiftieth the size and thickness of the ham in a railroad ham sandwich.[6] Josephine Baker, who starred at the Moulin Rouge, finally took the record for the amount of clothing she wore. Miss Baker wore two bananas, one in front, the other in the rear, attached to a string.

Colored musicians and others from America play an important part in furnishing the pep for Montmartre's night life. In our next I'll tell something about them.

"The American Negro in Europe," *American Mercury*, May 1930

Rogers wrote of his experiences in Europe, particularly in England and France, the two nations where he spent the most time, in a number of essays. He tends in these writings to contrast life for Blacks in the United States with their treatment in Europe; inevitably, he maintains the British are closest to the Americans in their racial prejudices. In this article, Rogers is particularly harsh on the English, feeling they are even more prejudiced than Americans. He generally overlooks offenses by the French, who are his paradigm of racial relations. Clearly, in this lead article, he was given the space to go beyond the facile conclusions given in some shorter pieces and draw out his arguments more thoughtfully and at greater length. No doubt his observations were also aided by the fact he had now spent several years living in Europe, and he had learned more about the countries and had time to reflect on his experiences there. Still, he does slip into some questionable judgements such as evaluating racial prejudice based on instances of interracial relationships and dancing with a partner of a different race. H.L. Mencken,[1] the well-known, white editor of the *American Mercury*, had long been an admirer of Rogers and solicited him to write this piece for the periodical, paying him the then princely sum of $500 (Pittsburgh *Courier* Oct, 24, 1964). Rogers's publication in such a mainstream venue would also greatly add to his visibility beyond his usual African American base.

"THE AMERICAN NEGRO IN EUROPE"

The Aframerican who goes to Europe for the first time finds himself in a state of bewilderment as great as that of a lifer out on parole, or a canary tossed out of its cage. No more bars to beat against; they have disappeared as if by magic. In their place is a sense of freedom that is almost alarming.

Trained to resist race prejudice or to submit to it, he now finds himself without an enemy to attack or a fetish to bow to. Timidly he watches, fearing, and almost hoping, for some sign of discrimination—something that will make him feel at home—but as the days go by he meets, so far as his color is concerned, such respect, such courtesy, such appreciation as he would not receive even from his fellow-Negroes in America. He begins to realize that he may go anywhere he wishes. Months pass and the days are like Paradise. At night he awakes with a start, dreaming he is back in America. When, at last, he takes [a] ship to return he feels like an escaped convict going back to his jailers.

In 1928 two colored American women and I made an automobile tour of Western and Southern Europe. In parts of Germany, Holland, Austria and Northern Italy we were so surrounded by crowds of curious natives that the police had to save us from suffocation. And this curiosity was not of the American kind that reaches for the coil of rope and the tar pot: whenever we took pictures the crowd was eager to get into them. At the Hofbräuhaus[2] in Munich, German men crowded around my two companions and began kissing their hands. They followed us out on the street and were so persistent in wishing to go with us to our hotel that our German chauffeur was forced to make it plain that we wanted to go home alone.

All over Northern Europe a Negro of no particular worth may find himself taken up just because he is a Negro. The late Maximilian Harden,[3] writing on the so-called atrocity of stationing French black troops on the Rhine, ridiculed the color objection. He said that the black man was not unwelcome to German women, and told how primitive Negroes would be missing from Hagenback's Circus,[4] only to be found in the homes of society women.

In Stockholm not long ago the Americanized proprietor of a restaurant refused to serve a ten-year-old Negro dancer called Little Esther,[5] who had been having a great success elsewhere in Europe. A Swedish nobleman who was present, by way of protest, invited the child, her mother and her manager, both colored, to his home. The newspapers of the city without a single exception condemned the proprietor, and several of them cartooned him. One of them declared the incident to be "the greatest scandal Stockholm has ever had," while the leading paper, the *Dagblad*, made a canvass of the chief hotels and restaurants, all of which said that they would not object to serving a decent Negro,[6] and least of all the popular little dancer. Several correspondents wrote to the papers asking the Negroes not to think that the attitude of the proprietor, one Branda Tomton, represented that of the Swedish people. Among those who came to see Little Esther play were the King and Queen, and when she was leaving thousands of school children came to see her off, bringing flowers. The crush was so great that the police had to be called to permit the train to start.

At a recent social function in Vienna at which the ex-Crown Prince of Germany was present, he danced with a colored American girl, who is studying music there, while her male Negro escort danced with the white women present. The Prince of Wales and his father, the King of England, have danced many times with colored women during their tours of the Empire. The same is true of the Crown Prince of Italy, the King of Spain, and others. On his visit to Europe Booker T. Washington was invited to dinner by both the King of Denmark and the King of Sweden. But when he dined with President Theodore Roosevelt at the White House there was a storm in the American press and the white South foresaw the downfall of white civilization.[7]

It is, indeed, safe to say that the white European has less aversion to, or fear of, the black than *vice versa*. Livingston, Stanley, Cameron,[8] Du Chaillu,[9] and many other African travellers have told how whole Negro villages, including even the dogs and hens, took to flight at the sight of a white man. Throughout Africa the Negro woman who has a child by a white man usually becomes an outcast, and so does the child. In Continental Europe not only is the white mother of a mulatto child well treated, but the child itself is valued because of its brownness. Much of this, to be sure, is not true in England. But even there the white woman who marries a Negro is much better received by her white neighbors than she would be by Negroes in America. Here American Negroes imitate the American whites, as they do in so many other things.

This is not to say that many Europeans do not shy at their first contact with a Negro. I recall once walking out in Paris with a French woman. We came to a café through whose open door we could see several black laborers. Forgetting my own ancestry, she cried:

"Look at those blacks! They look like the Devil!"

"So you don't like black people?" I inquired.

"I'm afraid of them," she replied, and then added quickly: "but after all they're human beings like ourselves, and should be treated as such."

In any case, the aversion of such Europeans to the genuine black is not nearly as sharp as that of the West Indian or the Latin-American mulatto to the same black. Even in the United States there are mulattoes who are more prejudiced against the blacks than many white persons. Generally speaking, the European prefers the brown Negro to the black one. But many prefer the black, and in Russia the blacker the better. A Negro in Europe will meet ennuis aplenty, especially if he has no money, but these troubles certainly will not arise from his color.

Negro jazz players are better paid that white ones. Had Josephine Baker, one-time queen of Paris night life, been a few shades lighter it would have made a vast difference in her fortunes. The colored woman, regardless of worth, who can pass for white in America, is regarded as a prize by Negro males, but in Europe the high yaller, unless she is unusually gifted or beautiful, finds herself but one of millions of other pale-faced women on a continent where mere whiteness of skin is valued pretty much as water in Holland or sand in the Sahara. Black women in Europe receive attention that would not be accorded worthier white women.

From Sweden to Italy a Negro meets with prejudice only in Americans and in an occasional white South African or Cuban, who is often touched with the tar brush himself. Not long ago one of the latter attacked a Negro diner in a Paris night club, and next morning found himself facing a colored judge, a native of the West Indies. A party of Aframericans, visiting Rheims, was taken by the guide for dinner into a dining-room in which there were thirty Yankees. Instantly there was an alarm and a palaver was started to bring about the retreat of the Negroes. The latter insisted on staying, however, and the thirty white men walked out in a body, to the astonishment of the natives.

A well-known American Negro who had been stopping on the Boulevard Raspail in Paris, came down one morning after he had been there for two weeks and found a note asking him to leave. The proprietor protested that he was losing his American trade. The Negro refused to leave, and the proprietor later apologized to the black man's lawyer.

When white Americans objected to the presence of this same Negro in a Bremen hotel and again at one in Berlin, the proprietors told the Americans to leave if they did not like it. At the Hague, when they protested against a Negro doctor who had been living in a hotel there for more than twenty years, they were again asked to leave. In the best known of the Brussels night clubs, when one of the hostesses refused to dance with an educated native of the Congo, she was reprimanded by the proprietor and came near losing her place.

When the Haitian consul-general at Antwerp was recently refused entry into a Paris dance-hall patronized by Americans and the matter came up in the French Parliament, the proprietor had an uneasy time and hastened to deny that he had drawn the color line. Instead of using the fact as an advertisement, as he would have done in America, he untruthfully explained that the Haitian had been mistaken for another Negro who, he said, had created a disturbance the night before.

White Americans despise or affect to despise the frizzly hair of Negroes, and the Negroes, as good Americans, follow suit. But most

Europeans, so far as I can judge, hold an opposite view. Once a German woman placed her hand on the wooly head of a friend of mine and told him that he ought to be ashamed to have hair like that, adding that it was she who, as a woman, ought to have it. In Europe, I saw many white women with their hair so frizzled that one would have thought they were of Negro ancestry. On Oxford Street in London there is, or was, a sign reading: "Straight Hair is a Nuisance."

An Aframéricaine in Paris went to a *coiffeuse* to have her hair done. After the shampoo the *coiffeuse*, instead of straightening it, proceeded to kink it more, to the great consternation of the dame, who could not speak French. Several times I have taken colored American girls to French *coiffeurs* to have their hair done. The *coiffeurs* knew nothing about hair-straightening, and invariably wanted to know why Negro women should demand the reverse of what white women wanted.

Once, in conversation with a number of French Negroes, I remarked:

"Well, as for me, I don't care what color I am."

Instantly one of them, a high government official, who is always elegantly dressed, replied:

"Well, I *do* care. As a dark-skinned man I attract attention. Were I white I would pass unnoticed like the white man."

The British Negro, on the other hand, is usually ashamed of his color, and it is most amusing to meet in London coal-black Africans, Oxford accent and all, who pretend that they are Englishmen.

If one excepts Southern Spain and Portugal, which are Negroid (for more than three centuries—1442–1773—a stream of Guinea blacks poured into these lands, not counting the Moors), the European countries with the largest percentage of Negroes are France and England. The former has, conservatively, 75,000 including 15,000 Senegalese troops, while England has as many or more.

In the matter of treatment no two countries could be more unlike. The French people have a highly developed sense of equality. It may be true, as some say, that France, with her falling birth-rate, has need of the black man for the national defense, but the attitude of the Republic toward the Negro has always been just. When the mulattoes of Haiti came to France during the days of the National Convention, pleading for equality with the white planters and ignoring the blacks, the Convention not only granted their demand but declared all the blacks free also.

II

Under the monarchy the Negro was also well received in France. One of the best known courtiers at Versailles under Louis XVI was the Chevalier Georges de St. Georges,[10] son of the Marquis de Langey and a Negro slave. St. Georges was the champion swordsman of his day, an accomplished rider, skater, violinist, and composer. He once set the fashions both in England and France and was a personal friend of the Prince of Wales, afterward George IV.

At least three Negro generals, two dark and one light-colored, played important rôles in the Napoleonic Wars. They were Thomas A. Dumas, father of the novelist; Magloire Pelage, who commanded a division in the Peninsular War[11]; and Dugommier, commander of the Army of the Pyrenees.[12] France's best known general before the last war was Alfred Amédée Dodds,[13] a Senegalese mulatto. Dodds won, or safeguarded, for France the greater part of her West African empire, and was Inspector-General of Marines. During the Boxer Rebellion[14] in 1901 he commanded the Allied forces, including the Americans, for a short time. During the last war he was a member of the War Council.

A black West Indian, Colonel De. M. Mortenol, commanded the air defenses of Paris during the war, with white American aviators under him. The chief of staff of General Nivelle, who commanded for a time at Verdun,[15] was another dark Negro, Lieutenant-Colonel D'Alenson. I have been told that there is a Negro admiral named Amiot, now in retirement, as well as a naval captain, Pellieres Lacournee.

The Negro from the French West Indies is admitted, or rather conscripted, into the same companies with white Frenchmen, and has, on the whole, the same opportunity for promotion. In French politics Negroes also hold high places. There are three of them in the Chamber of Deputies and one in the Senate. One of them, Alcide Delmont, was in the first Tardieu Cabinet.[16] Others have served as under-secretaries of state, or as secretaries to the Premier.

The present first assistant to the Minister of the Interior is a mulatto, M. Isaac, son of ex-Senator Isaac of Guadeloupe. The chief of the penal department for the colonies is a dark Negro, M. Etienne Attuly, with offices in Paris. His brother, Robert, is chief justice of the Cameroons. M. Hector Simoneau is paymaster-general of the Department of the Aube.[17] He was formerly prefect of a department, which is something like the Governor of a State in America. M. J. Germany, formerly inspector of customs in France, is now inspector-general of customs for French West Africa. M. Louis Beaudza is *redacteur-principal* for the Grand Chancellory of the Legion of Honor. There are several Negro professors in government colleges and universities—for example, Isaac Beton, Cenac-Thaly, Deslandes, and Roche—and several colored magistrates.

On the French stage the Negro plays and dances with white people as an equal. There was Chocolate,[18] the noted clown, now dead, and Joe Alex,[19] a dancer in the *bals de l'opéra*, both blacks. The best known living actor is the magnificent Senegalese, Habib Benglia. Benglia plays leading rôles with white actors and actresses. In 1925, when agitation was strong in America against Paul Robeson's kissing the hand of a white actress,[20] Benglia, clad only in a loin-cloth, was playing at the Folies-Bergère, wearing still less. At times his fair white colleagues, some of whom were English, sat on his knees or extended their bodies over his, and it was not necessary to call the undertaker.

In all dance-halls of Paris Negroes may be seen dancing with white partners. In one hall, the Bal Blomet,[21] there is as conglomerate a mass of humanity as may, perhaps, be found anywhere. Because of the invasion of this place by whites the Negroes recently opened another hall on the Boulevard Blanqui to which the whites can come only on the invitation of a Negro friend.

Mixed couples attract no attention on the Continent. In the dining-room of a hotel in Amsterdam I once saw a tall, handsome white man come to breakfast with his wife, a rather insignificant-looking black woman, and the rest of the Dutch people at the table bade them good-morning and kept chattering on as if the entrance of the pair was the most normal thing in the world. There are a considerable number of mixed couples in Paris, and although I spent more than three years in the French capital I never heard of or read any adverse comments.

There is little doubt that if the number of Negroes were to be greatly increased, and there were to arise a competition for jobs, trouble would ensue, but this would be equally true if any other nationality were to come in large numbers. The feeling against the Italians in the south of France is not too cordial because of the large numbers of them there competing with the natives. Some of the Negroes in Marseilles complain of race discrimination, but when this is investigated it is found to be due largely to the conduct of these men themselves. The better class of Negroes there fare like Negroes in other parts of France. Recently, according to the Paris *Midi*, a white man of the town who shot down a black *maquereau*[22] under peculiarly cold-blooded conditions was nearly lynched by a mob of whites. The French are a very tolerant people. If they were not, some of the Aframericans in Montmartre would have been deported long ago. They would certainly have been if they lived in England.

The nearest approach to color prejudice that I met among French-speaking persons in France was the feeling of the West Indian mulattoes against both their black fellow-islanders and the Africans. There is not much cordiality between the West Indians and Africans in France.

Germany got her African colonies late and lost them too early for the Negro to play any part in the affairs of the Fatherland. The ex-Kaiser, however, had several Negro favorites, one of whom was Sabacel-Cher, who was bandmaster of his crack regiment. Among his bodyguard at Potsdam was Mambo, and an American Negro named Wilson. Ira Aldridge, Shakespearean actor, born in Maryland, was warmly received by King William of Prussia, who ordered a gold medal struck in his honor. Aldridge was one of four to receive that distinction, the others being Humboldt,[23] Liszt, and Spontini.[24] This happened while slavery still existed in America. Aldridge was similarly received by the Kings of

Denmark and Sweden, the Czar of Russia and the Emperor of Austria. He married a Swedish countess.

George Bridgetower, a noted violinist, was a personal friend of Beethoven, who, it is said, intended dedicating the Kreutzer sonata[25] to him. But a young woman of whom Beethoven was fond showed too much attention to the Negro violinist and caused, it is said, the great musician to change his mind. Bridgetower was a great success on the Continent and in England, where he was for a time private musician to the Prince of Wales, afterward King George IV.

During the reign of Maria Theresa of Austria, a Negro ex-slave, Angelo Solliman, played an important private part in politics and was the companion of her son, the King of Rome, later Joseph II. In Southern Germany, St. Maurice, a black Negro, is one of the leading Catholic saints. A drawing representing St. Maurice, by Grunewald, hangs in the Old Pinokothek, Munich, while at the St. Maurice-en-Valais, near Geneva, is an abbey founded in his honor.

In Russia, a Negro slave, Hannibaloff, ancestor of Pushkin, became general of artillery in the army of the Empress Elisabeth; his son was also a general and designed the fortifications of Cherkov. Another Negro, Yermaloff,[26] was one of the lovers of Catherine the Great.

III

When one turns to England the picture changes. Of all the colonial powers she gives perhaps the least opportunity for advancement to her Negro subjects, although she is the oldest of these powers.

For instance, the little islands of Guadeloupe and Martinique, with a combined population of half that of Jamaica, have five members in the French Chamber of Deputies and two in the Senate, but the 420,000,000 colored people in the British Empire have no representation in the British Parliament or any home rule. With the exception of Africa House in London, where one or two natives are employed in minor positions, no Negro holds in England any government office. Once, however, I heard of a Negro who was a physician for the Board of Health in one of the poorer districts.

In the British army the highest grade possible to Negroes is that of sergeant-major, though it is said that since the late war natives in certain African regiments are being promoted to the grade of second-lieutenant. During the war one of two West Indian Negroes served as officers, due largely to pressure from their colonies. In most cases attempts were made to reduce these men to non-commissioned rank, and some were actually reduced.

General Dodds, already mentioned, was the grandson of an Englishman and an African woman. His father migrated to Senegal, where he was born. Had he remained in his native Gambia, and had the general been born there, the highest grade possible for him under British Army regulations would have been that of sergeant-major.

In the British colonies black men are sometimes given positions of importance, but rarely, if ever, over white men, as is the case with the French. As I have said, a Negro is chief justice of the Cameroons, with white judges under him; while another is inspector-general of customs for all French West Africa, with white subordinates. This is unheard of in the British Empire. Britain's policy is that of our own South, or one had better say the South's policy is that of England, for it was from England that America inherited her color prejudice. America, so far as the advancement of the Negro is concerned, is more liberal than England, even though race prejudice is more evident in America, England, too, has had her race riots and lynchings.

The everyday lot of the Negro in England is far worse than in America. Employment is almost unobtainable; when there is a job the Negro is the last ever to get it. And if he gets it he is likely to be forced out very soon by the whites, who want to know why a Negro should be given work when Englishmen need it. Most Negroes in their own colonies are staunch British subjects, but when they arrive in England the majority of them become bitterly anti-British and anti-white. Negroes were brought to England in large numbers during the war, but no sooner had hostilities ceased than the English began to attack them. Race riots swept East London, Cardiff, Liverpool, South Shields, Hull and elsewhere, precisely as they swept the United States about the same time.[27]

Recently in London at the home of a friend I consulted a scrap-book with clippings from the English press on the Negro: they read like extracts from Ku Klux publications, or the pronouncements of Southern Congressmen. The marriage of black men and English girls was bitterly denounced. One writer in *Tit-Bits*,[28] under the caption "Should White Women Marry Black Men?" called the union of such a pair "a revelation of horror and disgust," "a scandal and a disgrace to English womanhood," and then asked, if such things were allowed to go on, how it would be "possible to maintain as one stern creed in the policy of the Empire the eternal supremacy of the white over the black?"

There are three or four classes of Negroes in England, including students, mostly medical, who complain of color discrimination, chiefly in their hospital work, just as in America. There are about fifty doctors, some of whom have good practices, thanks in this case to their color, for the English masses are superstitious and believe that black brings good luck. Hence these doctors, though graduates of universities, are looked upon rather as voodoo men. At the races some of the bettors will touch a black man for luck as others touch hunchbacks.

Another class of English blacks, and a large one, is composed of fakers. They sell charms, good-luck powders, black beans, fake medicine, tooth-powders, corn-cures, and may be met with in all parts of the British Isles, particularly at the Sunday morning markets. Others sell tips on the horses, or dope, or live off women. Talk with an English Negro long enough and he will almost always say that if it were not for some Englishwoman he would not be able to stay in England.

Here are the exact words of one of them to me, which I give because it is typical of the feelings of many:

"If it were not for the white women we'd die. That is an absolute fact. The men would massacre us, though the Negro is a terrible fighter. I have three colored daughters and I teach them to hate and disdain all white people except their mother."

This man's children and others complain that they are teased and tormented at school because of their color. Coleridge-Taylor,[29] the great Negro composer, met with the same persecution, and once some English boys set his frizzly hair on fire, "just to see if it would burn."

Still another class are the seamen. Some of the toughest, most disreputable Negroes on earth are to be found in the ports of the British Isles. They fight, brawl, carouse, beat the loose women who support them, and generally give the police a great deal of trouble. It is hardly to be wondered at that in some of these cities the English people bar them from their houses. But as the men themselves sometimes explain, it is conditions that have made them what they are.

By far the most interesting of the Negro fakers in England calls himself Rass Prince Monolulu.[30] He speaks fluently French, German, Spanish, Italian, Yiddish and other languages. He is a privileged character. Dressed in a most fantastic suit of the loudest colors possible, with a horse and horseshoes embroidered on his back, he sells tips at the races. Often he buttonholes the King, the Prince of Wales, Lord Lascelles,[31] Lord Lonsdale,[32] the Aga Khan and other leading sportsmen. His portrait, snapped with such personages, has appeared in the English illustrated periodicals. A double-page colored supplement to the London *Tatler* of June 5, 1929, showed him surrounded by England's foremost sportsmen.

Monolulu is witty and injects a great deal of humor into the life of an otherwise staid nation. I have seen him in Hyde Park surrounded by a laughing crowd. He has made a great sum of money which he wagers freely. His motto is: White for pluck; black for luck. When he visits Ireland he wears a costume which is half green and half orange split vertically, to show his goodwill to both the orange and the shamrock.[33] Monolulu has been in most countries of the world. When he was in Germany, where he helped to introduce the peanut, which he vended from city to city, the war broke out and as a British subject he was interned. He married a rich German girl who later lost her money. He got into the second German revolution, for which he was tried and sentenced to death, but he managed to escape.

Negro tourists who visit London are likely to be refused admittance to hotels. Recently a well-known Negro editor from America, R.S.

Abbott,[34] was turned out of three London hotels and refused admission to more than twenty others. Returning to America on an English ship first-class, he and his wife were refused service with the regular passengers in the dining-room and had to eat in the grill-room. Negro girl students who visited London last Summer were barred from many hotels, and Marcus Garvey reported similar treatment the previous year. He had no trouble in Paris. An accompanist of Roland Hayes[35] was asked to leave a London restaurant, while Paul Robeson says that he was refused service at the Savoy and other places. The Labor Government took official notice of this discrimination and tried to prevent it.

The better class of English people deplore any ill-treatment of the black man, but that is about as far as sympathy goes. The truth is that our white Southerner, with all his prejudices, is accustomed to seeing the Negro around and will not let him starve, while to the Englishman he seems remote and not worthy of consideration. In this respect the Englishman is pretty much like our Northerner. Away from the large cities, however, the treatment accorded the Negro in England is not much inferior to that he gets on the Continent. In the remoter places much depends on the individual.

As in the colonies, the English people make a difference between the mulatto and the black, and the former may go almost anywhere without hindrance, although I met one mulatto who said he was refused admittance to a Salvation Army lodging-house because of his color. Hindus, also, meet with considerable race prejudice and in Paris I once heard a Hindu leader of the Indian Home Rule Movement[36] speak of color prejudice in Edinburgh and ask Hindu students why they went to the British Isles to study when they encountered no such prejudice in France.

American Negroes are generally viewed with a special distrust, particularly if they are ex-Britishers, but England is more generous toward the American Negro artist than America. Roland Hayes was little appreciated before he got English recognition, and Paul Robeson's vogue in London has greatly increased the American appreciation of him. Two of the headliners in the English theatres, Layton and Johnstone,[37] would certainly not have been so well received in America. In the law courts also, there is no discrimination. In cases involving white women, Negroes are frequently acquitted where they would be punished in America, right or wrong.

IV

The largest Negro settlement in the United Kingdom, perhaps in Europe, is at Cardiff. It is an evil-looking dump, with ugly two-story cottages and alleys full of refuse, which bears the appropriate name of Tiger Bay. This name, it is said, came from the terrible fights that used to take place there between seamen. The regular Negro population is about 4,000, with a floating one of several thousand more. This figure includes another settlement nearby, named Barry.

Cardiff is said to be the best town for Negroes in the United Kingdom. Colliers, belonging to many small companies, leave here for all parts of the world, and many Negroes are employed. All of them are in the Seamen's Union, but only the roughest work is given them, at a monthly wage of nine pounds, ten shillings. A few are employed as stewards, while still fewer have captains' licenses. But this doesn't matter, for it is a cardinal British principle never to give a "native" a job that a white man can fill.

Negroes were living in Cardiff before the coming of the steamship, and some now there have been there for more than fifty years. Most of the men have white wives; the rest, colored ones who were born there of white mothers. There are apparently no foreign colored women. Throughout Europe race mixing is just the reverse of what it is in Africa. In the latter one sees the white father, black mother combination. In Europe it is the white mother, black father. On the Continent, as I have said, there is no objection; the English, however, make vigorous protest, and this is one of the great objections to the Negro in England.

But the girls usually have their way, leaving their parents to become reconciled to their unions, which they usually do. England has had more than one Rhinelander case.[38]

The white women themselves are vigorous in defense of their black husbands and go waspishly after those who attack them. One Cardiff editor, who wrote an article against Negro men, was faced by an angry delegation of these women, who made him to understand that the Negroes were taking better care of them and their children than white men would have done. They take great interest in their men's activities, and at the Marcus Garvey hall in the East End of London, they shouted the "Back to Africa" battlecry as enthusiastically as the men. Indeed, the London leader of the Garvey movement was himself married to a white woman.

As for white men, they rarely, if ever, marry mulatto girls. The black man, in England, generally goes out with the children and leaves his wife at home. To avoid insults both are rarely seen together in public. But at Tiger Bay there is no segregation. White and colored families live in the same cottages. Children are plentiful, all the colored ones being mulattoes. Here and there a black child may be seen, but its mother is sometimes white. The father, coming from the Sudan or West Africa, is himself so black that the mother's white blood does not show.

There are about 600 such colored children. In one street of three blocks—Nelson street—there are seventy-two, one man alone having twelve. Colored and white go to the same school, but there are no colored teachers. Here, as in other parts of the United Kingdom, Negroes have no position of even minor importance. The children look strong and healthy, and on Sunday they are well dressed. Indeed, the only persons at Tiger Bay who have the appearance of wrecks are the white men.

There is little opportunity for these children, even when they win scholarships and are taught trades. The boys usually end by going to sea, while the girls go into domestic service, marry, or go on the stage. There are three groups among the Negroes and hostilities between them are perhaps sharper than the feelings of prejudiced whites towards them. These classes are, those from the West Indies, who are usually the more educated; the Christian Africans, who come from West Africa, and make up with shrewdness for what they lack in education; and the Mohammedans, who came mostly from East Africa and that part of Asia which lies around the Red Sea.

The West Indians look down on the West Africans; at home they have been taught to think of them as cannibals and heathen; while the Africans, in turn, regard them contemptuously, calling them the descendants of slaves and hirelings of England who assisted her in taking away their land. Both West Indian and West African, however, unite against the Mohammedan African, who is accused of undermining both in order to get work. It is charged that the Mohammedan will pay to get the job, will work harder, and will be satisfied with wretched living conditions on board ship. The hostility between the groups is strong. As one Cardiff paper pointed out, not without justice, one objection to having the Negroes there is the constant fear of a clash between them. Nevertheless, during the Cardiff riots, all of these blacks stood solidly together and defied the white men to come in, with the result that they suffered less than elsewhere. Most of the Negroes killed or wounded were outside the Black Belt at the time.

One of the richest men in Tiger Bay is a West African, originally a seaman, who can neither read nor write. He owns several houses, has one of the finest race horses in Wales, and a prize Alsatian dog, and lives in a beautifully furnished home. He has five mulatto daughters to whom he has given good educations and occasional trips to the Continent.

One of the great problems of the Cardiff authorities is how to keep white women out of the cafés, There is an early closing law for the pubs but the café owners get around it by boot-legging liquor in their soft drink places. On three blocks of the main street there are forty-two of these cafés. To quote the *Western Mail and South Wales News*:

> It was the lack of power to require refreshment houses to close at a specified time that enabled Maltese, Indians, and Chinese to keep open their establishments to such a late hour, and thus attract immoral women, licentious white men, and colored men with uncurbed sexual passion

> dominating their actions. The Chief Constable says there should be a law to prevent the employment of white women in colored men's lodging houses and cafés. Practically every one of the cafés in the areas had been convicted for selling intoxicating liquors. . . . Again, under the present law a white woman could cohabit with a colored man if they rented a room, which became their own home. . . .

None of these problems could have arisen anywhere on the Continent.

"Ruminations: Takes a Poke at 'The Emperor Jones,'" New York *Amsterdam News*, September 27, 1933

Rogers wrote on numerous cultural as well as social and political issues. His comments on theater, music, art, and literature demonstrate his views on matters of aesthetics. He believed that the image of the Negro was important in these works, and he maintained, like other race leaders such as Charles S. Johnson (editor of the National Urban League's periodical *Opportunity*) and Howard University Professor Alain Locke that the demonstration of Black cultural genius could significantly raise the status of the race. Not surprisingly, Eugene O'Neill's highly popular play *The Emperor Jones* (1920) would draw his interest. After Shakespeare's *Othello*, *The Emperor Jones* was probably the most talked about play written by a white author that depicted Blacks. The role of Brutus Jones, a West Indian despot modeled on the short reign of the tyrannical Haitian president Vilbrun Guillaume Sam (March 4 to July 27, 1915), was performed in the stage production by Charles S. Gilpin, a widely respected African American actor. The play was a box-office smash. By the time it was adapted as a film in 1933, which is the work Rogers is speaking of here, the role was performed by Paul Robeson, the most famous Black actor of the era. Gilpin and Robeson both had objections to the language and portrayal of Black characters in the play, but O'Neill insisted on keeping his work intact. Rogers's comment that if O'Neill had truly understood Black life he could have created a better, but not as popular, play is intriguing. Rogers is indicating that works of art created by whites but largely utilizing Black characters intentionally perpetuate racist stereotypes in order to be successful with white audiences.

This article was from a series of Rogers's called Ruminations (or Rambling Ruminations). For more of them, see *J. A. Rogers's Rambling Ruminations: Rare Writings from the Collection of Joel Augustus Rogers*, edited by Jeff Menzise (Mind on the Matter Publishing 2013).

"RUMINATIONS: TAKES A POKE AT 'THE EMPEROR JONES'"

Writing about "The Emperor Jones" in 1921 I said that while I enjoyed immensely the fine artistry of Charles Gilpin[1] in so far as it was regarded as portraying, not a Negro, but a member of the human family, trying to escape his hunters, real and ghostly, that I did not like the play for fundamental reasons. Now twelve years later, after having seen the movie version, it is my unpleasant task to say that I find still stronger cause for disliking this alleged masterpiece of Eugene O'Neill.

My objections are clear and definite, and I am going to state them even at the risk of being considered a Philistine by the arty, emancipated chappies. First, "The Emperor Jones" represents defeat and pessimism, which is not true of the Negro, for in spite of persecutions that would crush many other people he presses buoyantly on, hoping and working for a better day, even though there is no sign of it on the horizon. Apropos, it will certainly be objected that the play is not intended to be typical of the Negro's life. Maybe not, but let us look at the next reason first:

This is that nearly all the old stock-in-trade as crap shooting, gin-guzzling, immorality, cutting, killing, fear of ghosts and other supposed Negro characteristics are dragged in in heavier quantities than usual, not to mention the refrain of "Nigger, nigger, nigger," which runs through the whole piece from beginning to end. The single departure from the old, old darky stereotype is when Jones overhears his white boss on the private car planning with an associate to put over a crooked deal on the stock market, and promptly talks up for a share of the loot. Otherwise this play is on the whole but a repetition of the things said by Thomas Dixon, Vardaman, Tillman and others of a generation ago who harped so much on this single string. These writers and politicians used to boast of their friendliness for Negroes, and unless I am mistaken so, too, does Mr. O'Neill.

Commercialism of Worst Sort.

Again, this picture, though it pretends to be art, is commercialism of the worst sort. The audiences who will see it are mostly white, and care has been taken to see that they will get the fare they want, that is, what they have been trained to think that Negroes are. If ever I live to see but one American film showing not only the depths, but, also, the heights: not only the disgraces and the shortcomings, but the aspirations and the achievements of Negro life, become popular with the average white audiences then I will gladly take all this back.

Eugene O'Neill, I am firmly convinced, does not know the Negro. He shows that clearly in both this play and "All God's Chillun Got Wings." Had he, say, the knowledge of John L. Spivak,[2] author of "Georgia Nigger," or of E.B. Reuter,[3] and even T. S. Stribling[4] on this subject, he would, with all his dramatic skill, have produced a far less successful play. In that case he would have had real facts to work with and would, in all probability, have produced characters that would have sat heavy on the stomachs of a prejudiced and generally uninformed white public. In short, Mr. O'Neill would not have been a box-office attraction so far as writing on the Negro was concerned.

Let us get this following fact straight: The Negro was brought to America for his labor. One of the weapons used in keeping him at a stage where his labor and the sex-life of his womanhood could be exploited most effectively was propaganda. Today, three centuries later, this propaganda is being carried on for the same purpose. Hence, the stage Negro—the crap-shooter, the gin-bibber, the good, happy-go-lucky darkey—still lives on. This much is certain: take any book, play, or picture about Negroes, regardless of the color of the author, and it will be found that if it is popular with the whites, it is not so with the self-respecting Negroes, and vice versa. It is an unwritten rule of the theatre that a Negro must not appear in a master-class role where whites are involved.

But one asks, how long will box-office receipts continue to be the criterion of not only good art, but of truth in America? Again, is it not about time that the white producers and the dramatists, out of artistic self-respect, if not from a sense of realism and honesty, stop dragging about the battered mummy of this stage Negro?

Negroes Have Good Movie Material.

As to the work of the actors, all of whom are Negroes, save one, it is good, and in parts even excellent. But it is no phenomenon. After such pictures as "Hallelujah,"[5] and the work of Clarence Muse,[6] as well as that of foreign Negroes—Africans, Cubans, French, West Indians, and others—we know that the Negro group has as good a movie actor material as any other group. What would be amazing, however, would be to have seen these Negroes showing enough self-sacrifice by refusing to use their talents in a play that was helping to perpetuate such conditions as Scottsboro.[7] No matter what is said, it cannot be denied that the term "nigger" is one of contempt in America. There is not a single one of those actors who were hurling "nigger" over the screen at the audience who would not be offended if so called by a white person. Uncle Tom's body lies a-mouldering in the grave, but his soul goes marching on.[8]

Here's a test. Paul Robeson deserves every whit of the praise showered on him by the white critics for his acting in this film. Let Paul come to New York, however, open a theatre, and give the play which I know deep in his soul he wishes to put on showing the aspiring and constructive side of the Negro life, and great as his genius and popularity are, he would be playing almost to empty houses.

Found Situation Different in France.

Theoretically, the actor, like the lawyer, should play what he is called on to, whether it is for or against his group. But when the game is unfair, he's a fool if he does play. For instance, if in France I saw a Negro actor playing a despicable role, I think nothing of it, because Negroes also play the superior parts. Benglia, the great Senegalese actor, always appears in a role in which he is the equal, and often the superior of the whites in the cast, and he would accept no other. That is, he appears as one of the master-class, while in America, no matter how capable the Negro actor is, he must be of the servant class, unless his role is burlesque, or he is defeated finally, as in the play in question.

This situation will never be corrected until the Negroes develop their own theatre for the presentation of their own life, as they know it.[9]

As to the play itself there is nothing extraordinary about it. Not only is it far-fetched, but it ended in a welter of nonsense at which I found myself yawning and the audience snickering.

From 100 *Amazing Facts About the Negro With Complete Proof: A Short Cut to the World History of the Negro* (1934)

Many Black readers first became acquainted with Rogers through this small pamphlet. Distinguished Harvard Professor Henry Louis Gates Jr.[1] recalled his first experience with Rogers: "For black families in the middle of the twentieth century 'Mr. Rogers' was a columnist for the legendary Pittsburgh *Courier*, his pithy and always interesting tidbits of African-American history armed them with facts about the black experience that seemed more like fantasies" (3). Doubtless many readers had the same reaction as Gates to Rogers's astounding nuggets of Black history in 100 *Amazing Facts*, often described as the Black version of Ripley's *Believe it or Not*. As Gates said, "'Did [Rogers] sometimes embellish what he found? Yes; Rogers wasn't above shock journalism. Did he miss key details? Absolutely. . . . But he was as serious a researcher as they come, as serious as W. E. B. Du Bois and Carter G. Woodson" (3–4). This is abundantly clear from the plethora of sources Rogers marshals as "proof" for his facts. The sections below on the Arts and Medicine show the vital contributions of Blacks in those fields while the section on Ancient Civilizations attests to the importance of Black people to world civilization, and makes the controversial claim that the ancient Egyptians were Negroes. Rogers had visited Egypt to do research in 1930. If one believes, as Rogers did, that Egypt is indeed the cradle of civilization and that the Egyptians were Negroes, then the Black man can be seen as "the founder of civilization"; as a result, "Rogers concludes that the white man's civilization is only a continuation of that which was passed on to him by the Negro" (Peters 21–23). The section on Religion speaks of a Black Jesus and the influence of

Blacks on Western Civilization. The fact that the pamphlet, like most of Rogers's writings, has gone through numerous editions and is still in print is testimony to the continued popularity of his work. This text is taken from the 1962 revised edition. Reprinted by Wesleyan University Press (1995).

100 AMAZING FACTS ABOUT THE NEGRO WITH COMPLETE PROOF

The Arts

6. The Negro was the first artist. The oldest drawings and carvings yet discovered were executed by the Negro peoples over 15,000 years ago in Southern France, Northern Spain, Palestine, South Africa, and India. The drawings are on rocks, the carvings on bone; basalt and ivory.
7. The oldest known representation of the human body is that of a Negro woman. It was carved by a Negro sculptor of Grimaldi[2] race from 10,000 to 15,000 years ago. It is called "The Venus of Willendorf" after the place in Austria where it was found, and is in the Vienna Museum.

Proof

In a reconstruction of Grimaldis by Alfred Rutot, a Grimaldi Negro artist is shown holding The Venus of Willendorf. (For reproductions of them see, Crisis Magazine, Feb. 1920: Dr. Frances Hoggan: Prehistoric Negroids and Their Contribution to Civilization, pub. in New York.)

E. Faure says: "The Venus of Willendorf, the most ancient human form in sculpture that we know." History of Art, Vol. 1, page 13, (N.Y. 1931.)

Dr. Verneau says, "The Grimaldi race is clearly a Negro one. The skeletons of the two Negroes of the Grotte des Enfants are complete and in a state of preservation which permits the describing of their characteristics with certitude." (L'Homme, Race, et Coutumes, pp. 24–37, Paris, 1931.)

Prof. E. Pittard of the University of Geneva, Switzerland, gives abundant support to Verneau in "Les Races et L'Histoire," pp. 81–86, Paris, 1924.

Histoire Universelle speaks of "Austria being inhabited by Negroes in the Paleolitihic Age." (Vol. 1, p . 55.)

G. F. Elliott says: "Whoever they (the Grimaldi) were their grave goods were the wealthiest and richest of their day and generation." (Prehistoric Man And His Story, p. 162.) Drawings strikingly like those in the caverns of Southern France, Spain, and Palestine have been found in South and East Africa. See also C. Van Riet Lowe; Illustrated London News, p. 606, April 29, 1933. F. Hertz: Race and Civilization, p. 101.

The late Prof. R. B. Dixon of Harvard University says that the presence of the Negro in Paleolithic times "has been universally admitted on the northern Mediterranean coast. . . . It continued to be a clearly discernible factor in the population of Western Russia until the Middle Ages—Racial History of Mankind, p. 478. N. Y. 1923.

Griffith Taylor says, "Next in order in Europe would seem to be the Negrito race, of which more evidence is accumulating every year. . . . We may label the fourth stratum, Negroid. These people must have been quite abundant in Europe towards the close of the Paleolithic . . . skulls of East Brazil show where similar folk penetrated to the New World."—Environment and Race, pp. 222–3. Lond. 1927.

The explorers, Neuville and Stekelis, discovered in a cave at Umm Qualifa at Wady Khareitum in Palestine, similar prehistoric drawings of elephants, rhinoceri, and other African animals. (London Times, October 6, 1932.)

8. Beethoven, the world's greatest musician, was without a doubt a dark mulatto. He was called "The Black Spaniard." His teacher, the immortal Joseph Haydn, who wrote the music for the former Austrian National Anthem, was colored, too.

Proof

Frederick Hertz, German anthropologist, in "Race and Civilization," refers twice to Beethoven's "Negroid traits" and his "dark" skin, and "flat, thick nose." (pp. 123 and 178.)

Frau Fischer, an intimate acquaintance of Beethoven, describes him thus, "Short, stocky, broad shoulders, short neck, round nose, blackish-brown complexion." (From R. H. Schauffler, The Man Who Freed Music, Vol. 1, p. 18, 1929.)

In speaking of the immortal Haydn who was Beethoven's teacher, Andre de Hevesy, says: "Everybody knows the incident at Kismarton or Eisenstadt, the residence of Prince Esterhazy. In the middle of the first allegro of Haydn's symphony, His Highness asked the name of the author. He was brought forward.

"'What!' exclaimed the prince, 'the music is by this blackamoor? Well, my fine blackamoor, henceforward, thou art in my service.'"

Carpani, who originally related this says that "Haydn's complexion gave room for the sarcasm." And that Haydn had the title of "second Professor of music but his new comrades called him The Moor." (G. Carpani: Le Haydine, etc. Letter 5. Milan, 1812.)

Referring to the above incident, Alexander W. Thayer, perhaps the foremost authority on Beethoven, says, "Beethoven had even more of the Moor in his features than his master, 'Haydn.'" (Beethoven, Vol. I, p. 146.) By "Moor" was meant "Negro." Until recent times the German for "Negro" was "Mohr."

Paul Bekker, another very noted authority on Beethoven, says that "the most faithful picture of Beethoven's head" shows him with "wide, thick-lipped mouth, short, thick nose, and proudly arched forehead." (Beethoven, p. 41, 1925, trans. Bozman.) Thayer adds that Beethoven was an ugly, little man, and no one would be more astonished than the great composer should he return and see how he has been idealized by sculptors and painters.

Beethoven's family originated in Belgium, which had been ruled by the Spaniards, who had large numbers of Negro soldiers in their army there. Theophile Gautier speaks of a Belgian type characterized by brown skin and dark hair "a second race which the soldiers of the Spanish Duke of Alva have sown between Brussels and Cambrai."

In short, the general description of Beethoven, even to his frizzly hair, fits that of many an Aframerican or West Indian mulatto. In the Southern States, Beethoven would have been forced to ride in the jim-crow car.

See also: Rogers, J. A. "Sex and Race," Vol. 1, pp. 288, 289, 302 (1941) for other data on Beethoven's Negro strain, one of which is from the New York Times. Also p. 8 for portrait of Beethoven drawn from life by Hofel, which clearly shows the Negro strain. For more extended proof as well as a picture of Beethoven's life-mask see Sex and Race, Vol. 3, pp. 306–309.

Ancient Civilizations

12. Cheops, a Negro, built the Great Pyramid, one of the Seven Wonders of the Ancient World. It is 451 feet high, has 2,500,000 blocks of granite, each two and a half tons, covers 13 acres, took 100,000 men thirty years to build and was completed in 3730 B. C.

Proof

The portrait of Cheops shows his Negro strain. See reproduction in Flinders Petrie: Abydos, Pl. XIV, Pt. II. London, 1903.

In the Ethiopian hall of the old Boston museum, I saw in 1924 a bust with the inscription, "Negro princess of the Cheops family." The new museum there has two limestone busts, one of a Negro prince, and the other a Negro princess of this family. See also G. H. Beardsley, The Negro in Greek and Roman Civilization, p. 12, Baltimore, 1929.

The testimony of eye-witnesses as well as that of modern science is that the Egyptians were Negroid, that is to say, largely mulatto, and the Ethiopians, unmixed Negroes.

Herodotus (484–425 B. C.) very distinctly says that the Egyptians had black skins and wooly hair. (See No. 47.)

Aristotle, who was born 324 B. C. and still ranks as a great scientist clearly says too that the Egyptians were "very black" and the Ethiopians, "wooly-haired" (Physiognomy, Chap. VI.)

16. Negroes lived in America thousands of years before Columbus. Central American monuments show numerous carving[s] of them as gods. When Columbus came to the New World, Negroes had been crossing from Africa to South America a distance of 1600 miles. The first white men to reach the American mainland, tell of seeing Negroes. Columbus who visited South America said that he had heard of them there.[3]

Proof

On the presence of the Negro in America before Columbus, C. C. Marquez, says, "The Negro type is seen in the most ancient Mexican sculpture. . . . The Negroes figure frequently in the most remote traditions of some American pueblos. . . . It is to this race doubtlessly belongs the most ancient skeletons of very different structure of two of the Red American races which have been found in various places from Bolivia to Mexico." (Estudios Arqueoligicos y Etnograficos, pp. 270–73, Madrid, 1920.) See also Prof. R. B. Dixon: Racial History of Mankind, pp. 400, 401, 409, 441, 449. Dixon emphasizes the fact that there was an early Negro strain in the Rhode Island, Massachusetts, and Central American Indians.

Columbus says, "He wanted to find out what the Indians had told him that there had come to it from the south and southeast Negro peoples." (Journal of the Third Voyage, p. 6.)

Peter Martyr, the amanuensis of Columbus, tells of Negroes living in Central America before the introduction of slavery and says, "There were the first Negroes seen in the Indies," (Descubriemiento de la Mar del Sur, in Lord Kingsborough's Antiquities of Mexico, Vol. VI, p. 291.)

Prof. Leo Weiner of Harvard University says, "The presence of Negroes with their trading masters before Columbus is proved by the representation of Negroes in American sculpture and design; by the occurrence of a black nation at Darien early in the 16th Century, but more specifically by Columbus' emphatic reference to Negro traders from Guinea. . . . The chief cultural influence was exerted by a Negro colony in Mexico." (Africa and the Discovery of America, Vol. III, pp. 365–369, Philadelphia, 1920–2.)

Colonel A. Braghine says that he saw in Ecuador a statuette of a Negro that is at least "20,000 years old." He adds, "Hitherto the ethnologists imagined that Negroes appeared in the New World only during our own epoch when they were imported as slaves . . . . Some statues of the Indian gods in Central America possess typical Negro features and certain prehistoric monuments there undoubtedly represent Negroes. . . ." (The Shadow of Atlantis, pp. 40–42, N. Y. 1940.)

V. Riva Palacio says, "It is indisputable that in very ancient times . . . the Negro race occupied our territory (Mexico) when the two continents were joined. This race brought its own religious cults and ideals. (Mexico a traves de los siglos, vol. 1, pp. 63–67. Mexico, 1887.) "The Mexicans recall a Negro god, Ixtlilton, which means black-faced." p. 163.

Medicine

33. Imhotep of Ancient Egypt, was the real Father of Medicine. He lived about 2300 B. C. Greece and Rome had their knowledge of medicine from him. In Rome he was worshipped as the Prince of Peace in the form of a black man. His Ethiopian portraits show him a Negro. Imhotep was also Prime Minister to King Zoser as well as the foremost architect of his time. The saying, "Eat, drink, and be merry for tomorrow we die," has been traced to him. Hippocrates, the so-called "Father of Medicine" lived 2,000 years after Imhotep.

Proof

Gerald Massey says of Imhotep, "The child-Christ remained a starrily-bejeweled blackamoor as the typical healer in Rome. Jesus the divine healer, does not retain the black complexion of Iu-em-hotep (Imhotep) in the canonical Gospels, but he does in the Church of Rome when represented as a little black bambino. A jewelled image of the child Christ as a blackamoor is sacredly preserved at the headquarters of the Franciscan order and true to its typical character as a symbolical likeness of Iusa, the healer, the little black figure is taken out in state with its regalia on to visit the sick and demonstrate the supposed healing power of this Egyptian, Esculapius, thus Christianized. The virgin mother who was also black survived in Italy as in Egypt. At Oropa near Bietta, the Madonna and her child-Christ are not white, but black as they so often were in Italy of old and as the child is yet conditioned in the little black Jesus of the Eternal City. Surely the profoundest sigh of an ever-warring world went up to heaven in the cult of Iu-em-hotep (Imhotep) who was worshipped as the giver of rest, the Kamite prince of peace." (Ancient Egypt: The Light of the World, Vol. II, p. 754, London, 1907.)

The statuettes of Imhotep in the Cairo Museum show his Negroid features. They are reproduced in G. Daressy's, Catalogue General des Antiquities Egyptiennes des Antiquities Egyptiennes du Musee du Caire, Plate IV, 38,045 to 38,050 and Plate V.

[Rogers includes Imhotep in *World's Great Men of Color*, vol. 1).

36. Dr. Daniel Williams, Chicago surgeon who died in 1931, was the first to perform a successful operation on the human heart.

Proof

Medical Record, March 27, 1897. The patient was James Cornish. Dr. Williams lived in Chicago. I knew him personally for many years.

Religion

47. The oldest and most noted statue in the world bears the face of a Negro. It is the Sphinx of Gizeh, which was worshipped as Horus, or Harmachis, the Sun-God of Light and Life. It was erected about 5,000 B. C.

The Devil which is now depicted as black, was once portrayed as White. When the black man dominated the planet he painted the forces of evil, white. When the whites came into power they shifted the colors. But as late as 1500 the Ethiopians still depicted their gods and heroes black, and their devils and villains, white. Father Fernandez, a Catholic missionary, who worked amongst them at this time, says, "They paint

Christ, the Blessed Virgin, and other saints in black form; and devils and wicked men, white. Thus Christ and his apostles are black and Judas, white. Annas, Caiphas, Pilate, Herod and the Jews are white, while Michael is black, and the Devil, white.

Proof

Count C. F. Volney[4] speaking of the mulatto appearance of the Egyptian people said, "but when I visited the Sphinx I could not help thinking the figures of that monster furnished the solution of the enigma, when saw its features precisely those of a Negro. I recalled the remarkable passage of Herodotus in which he says, 'For my part, I believe the Colchi to be a colony of Egyptians, because like them they have black skins and woolly hair,'—that is to say, the ancient Egyptians were real Negroes of the same species with all the natives of Africa." (Voyages en Syrie, etc., pp. 74–75, Paris, 1787.)

J. P. Widney says, "They (the Negroid races) once occupied a much wider territory and wielded a vastly greater influence upon earth than they do now. They are found chiefly in Africa, yet traces of them are to be found through the islands of Malaysia, remnants, no doubt of that more numerous black population which seems to have occupied tropical Asia before the days of the Semites, the Mongol, and the Brahminic Aryan." (Race Life of the Aryans, Vol. III, p. 238, New York, 1907.)

Schure, noted French writer on religion and mysticism, says "The Blacks invaded Southern Europe in prehistoric times and were finally driven back by the Whites. Remembrances of them have disappeared from popular tradition. The Blacks, however, have left two ineffaceable imprints in Europe: the horror of the dragon which was the emblem of their kings, and our idea that evil, or the devil is black. The Negroes returned the insult to the White race by making the devil, white. During the time of their sovereignty the Blacks had religious centres in Upper Egypt and in India. Their cyclopean cities embattled the mountains of Africa, the Caucasus, and Central Asia." (Edouard Schure: Les Grand Inities, p. 6, 113th edition. Paris, 1931).

The statement of Father Fernandez is quoted from M. Russell: Nubia and Abyssinia, p. 275, New York, 1833.

50. Psalms that read like those of the Bible were written by a Pharoah Amenophis IV, better known as "Akhenaton, the Heretic King," 1300 B. C. or more than 400 years before David was born. Akhenaton, who was the father of Tut-Ankh-Amen, was extremely Negro in type. He is called "the most remarkable of the Pharaohs."

Proof

For a comparison of one of the Psalms of Akhenaton with the 104th Psalm in the Bible see Arthur Weigall: Life and Times of Akhenaton, pp. 134–136. New York, 1923. Also J. H. Breasted, History of Egypt, p. 373. New York, 1926.

[Rogers includes Akhenaton in *World's Great Men of Color*, vol. 1.]

"Italy Over Abyssinia," *Crisis*, February 1935

Over time, the rise of fascism in Italy by Benito Mussolini in 1922 and Nazism in Germany by Adolf Hitler in 1933 caused Rogers to change some of his views about Europe. Even his initial reactions to these leaders were somewhat moderate. Rogers had, for example, written an article about the Italian leader ("Mussolini: Italy's 'Benevolent Despot'" New York *Amsterdam News* May 25, 1927). However, Mussolini's invasion of Italy in 1935–37 was a turning point for many Black leaders such as Marcus Garvey who were initially drawn to Il Duce's (the Leader's) Nationalistic Agenda.[1] With Ethiopia now at center stage and seen as a potential bulwark against fascism, some whites began to embrace Ethiopians as "white." Such views were challenged by Blacks including Rogers (*The Real Facts about Ethiopia* 3–8; Putnam 425–29).

After the Berlin Conference of 1884–85, Africa had been carved up by the European powers. The only non-colonized nations remaining in Africa were Liberia and Ethiopia (Abyssinia). The long-standing independence of these two nations was a source of great pride to Blacks worldwide. However, when Italy sought its own colonies, there was little left, only what would eventually become Libya, Somalia, and Eritrea. The Italians eyed Ethiopia and invaded it in 1895–96, but they were roundly defeated. By the 1930s, the Italians, a growing Western power with a modern army, never forgot the humiliation of having been defeated by African natives armed mostly with spears. Mussolini, with his nationalistic agenda and with a greatly expanded army and air force, would invade Ethiopia again in 1935. As Italy was in the process of preparing their invasion, Rogers reminded his readers of the disastrous results of the first invasion by the Italians who were outmaneuvered by the Ethiopian Emperor Menelik II and his crafty general Ras Makonnen. Though Italy in 1935 was much more powerful than it was in 1895, Rogers argues that the French and British governments will resist a takeover of Ethiopia by the Italian forces. However, this French/British resistance to Italian aggression was something that would never come to pass, and Ethiopia was eventually occupied by the Italians. Rogers later published a pamphlet *The Real Facts About Ethiopia* (1936). See also Rogers's "The Americans in Ethiopia" (under the pseudonym Jerrold Robbins), *American Mercury* May 1933, and Aric Putnam "Ethiopia is Now: J. A. Rogers and the Rhetoric of Black Anticolonialism During the Great Depression" *Rhetoric and Public Affairs* 10.3 (Fall 2007): 419–44.

"ITALY OVER ABYSSINIA"

The present dispute between Italy and Abyssinia[2] has already caused two fatal clashes: one at the Italian consulate at Gondar[3] where one Italian was killed and two wounded, and the other at Walwal,[4] in which 200 Ethiopians and 30 Italians were reported slain. Abyssinia has made apology and reparation for the first. The second is clearly an Italian aggression as Walwal is sixty miles within the Ethiopian border. Italy has been occupying this area against Ethiopian protest. The recent discovery of oil there has spurred the Abyssinians to oust the Italians.

Both clashes, it will be noted, have occurred on Abyssinian soil, the first to the north, the second to the southeast. The inner details, however, will probably not be known until they are aired at Geneva. But even a superficial knowledge of this East African quarrel predicts that the League of Nations will be faced with the toughest nut in its history, that is, if the disputants mean to act as defiantly as they talk. For if Geneva succeeds in cracking the outer shell it will find within a kernel of dynamite, namely Japan.

Let us trace very briefly the first contacts of Italy and Abyssinia. Italy, coming late into the race for Africa, picked up land that neither France nor England cared for, namely Tripolitania, Eritrea, and Southern Somaliland,[5] all three of which are rocky, broiling desert, and are great liabilities. Italy, like Japan, yearns for territory in which to colonize her teeming and rapidly increasing millions. But none of the three colonies named is really suitable for Europeans.

Last of Ungobbled Africa

As it happened, however, two of these, Eritrea and Southern Somaliland, lay, the first to the north, the second to the southeast, of Abyssinia, which, in all respects, was just the kind of territory which Italy craved. Its soil, climate, and mineral resources were famed of old. Its uplands with their light frost in winter and sunny, salubrious climate the year round, were particularly desirable. Moreover it was three times larger than Italy itself. Being near home and with millions of blacks to exploit, it permitted Italian expansion of the most favorable kind.

For reasons that will be given later on, neither France nor England had seized Abyssinia though England probably could have done so in 1868 when she penetrated to Magdala.[6] It was, in short, the last bit of Africa left ungobbled by Europe.

Italy, settling in the regions named, spun her web. She began by lending the Emperor Menelik[7] $1,000,000 for which she received the Asmara[8] region and a promise that Menelik would make no treaties with the other powers without her consent. Abyssinia soon discovered that the treaty was against her and diplomatic bickering followed. Then came an open break about 1894 when Menelik, instituting a postal service, had a stamp struck with his own effigy. Italy, who had not been consulted, resented this show of independence on the part of the black monarch. High words followed. Count Crispi,[9] then Italian Premier, seized the occasion to reach out for his heart's desire. He invaded Abyssinia, and seized as hostages three Ethiopian princes who were studying in Switzerland.

The Italians won at first. Flushed with this victory, which was magnified into a triumph, the Italian Parliament decided on the annexation of the ancient kingdom. It voted $4,000,000 to carry on the war and sent out 25,000 men, under General Barateri.[10]

But Menelik, meanwhile, had been rousing and uniting the warring elements within his newly won empire. They responded 120,000 strong, armed mostly with spears, under the command of Ras Makonnen,[11] a born commander and strategist, who from then on simply outwitted Barateri. Crispi, wishing to strengthen his ministry by a coup, accused Barateri of "military rheumatism" and demanded of him "a decisive victory."

Victory at Adowa

Faced by Ras Makonnen, Barateri was then in a most precarious position. Nevertheless on February 29, 1896, Barateri, seeing what seemed an unguarded hill dominating the Ethiopian position, advanced with his 20,000[12] men to seize it. But this was a trap prepared by the astute Makonnen. No sooner had the Italians shifted to the valley than the 120,000 Ethiopians engulfed them. Packed tightly in the narrow pass, and almost unable to use their arms, the Italians were speared like sheep. Less than 3,000 of them straggled back to Italian territory. This was the battle of Adowa.

The prisoners, following an Ethiopian custom of fifty centuries, were castrated. Italy, beaten by what she regarded as a horde of black savages, was keenly humiliated. Crispi was mobbed and driven from office, and the Italian soldiers mutinied rather than go to Africa. When General Balciderra, Barateri's successor, declared that it would take 250,000 men, five years, and $1,100,000,000 to be revenged, Italy was glad to make a treaty that galled her proud Latin spirit.

Is it any wonder, then, that Italian desire for Abyssinia has increased with the years? Certainly Mussolini's envoys at the great military review held in honor of the coronation of the Emperor Haile Selassie at Addis Ababa in 1930 must have told Il Duce how the fiery Ethiopian warriors in the homage to the throne had vaunted how they had slain and gelded the Italians. Every Abyssinian knows that Italy means to seize their country if she can and is aroused against her.

What now of England and France? It was commonly reported that both had agreed to give Mussolini a free hand against Abyssinia. But even the merest knowledge of the situation will show that neither is likely to risk this. In fact, Premier Laval,[13] in his recent conference with Mussolini denied this, and declared that Italy, herself, was pledged like Britain and France, to guarantee Ethiopian independence.

English and French Interests

England's interest in Abyssinia is a very vital one. Fantastic as it sounds, Britain's fate is intricately bound up with that of this black empire. In the Abyssinian highlands amid surroundings of rare tropical beauty is a lake from which the Abai, or Blue Nile, rises. This is Lake Tsana. British territory to the north and all of Egypt is absolutely dependent upon this river. Egypt, it cannot be too emphatically stressed, is the Nile. Hence the diverting of this outlet of Lake Tsana—which is possible—would cause the greatest imaginable disaster to the Anglo-Egyptian Soudan and Egypt. In 1902 England made a treaty with Ethiopia over this lake. Thus in 1927 when an American firm was merely awarded a contract to build a dam there in order to regulate its flow it caused great alarm in London.

Egypt and the Suez Canal are of the utmost strategic importance to the welfare of the British Empire. England has 15,000 of her own soldiers stationed there. Why? Because that is the route to India, and India constitutes two-thirds of her empire. Were Italy to grow strong in the Red Sea, as she would be if she owned Abyssinia, how easily she would be able to cut off England from her prize possession! England certainly wants no strong rival in the Red Sea, and for this reason may be counted on not to support serious Italian aspiration in the North-eastern Africa.

The same for a different cause is true of France. She and Italy are commercial rivals in this region. Italy has actually given Abyssinia a free port and zone at Assab to the north in competition with the French port of Djibuti to the south, at which latter place the Ethiopians must pay duty on all their exports and imports. Djibuti, which is one terminus of the Franco-Ethiopian railway, is now absolutely dependent upon Abyssinian trade for its existence. It is moreover an important link with France's Far Eastern colonies. Would France be willing to risk the decline of this port, as she would, by aiding the rise of Italy? Moreover there is the 500 miles of railroad to Addis Ababa, half of which is owned by France and the rest by Abyssinia. Italy is eager to connect her northern and her southern colonies by a railway running through Abyssinia, but she is blocked by an agreement that France made with Menelik against railroad concessions to other nations. As late as 1925, England and Italy secretly divided Abyssinia into spheres of commercial influence to the detriment of France. The latter made strenuous protest to Geneva, and both MacDonald[14] and Mussolini stuttered explanations and backed down. French influence prevails at Addis Ababa. Would France be likely to relinquish that in favor of Italy?

Outpost of Christianity

Again France and Italy are thinly-veiled enemies. Both were very near war in 1931–32. France's Italian border is as heavily fortified as her German one is. Mussolini has his eye on the Nice-Mentone area in the French Riviera. This was ceded to Napoleon III by Italy, and Italy has never become reconciled to the loss. Now the possession of Abyssinia would increase enormously the power of Italy in Europe. Are not the French statesmen likely to foresee this ? Those who think highly of the Laval-Mussolini warblings might well recall the fate of the Hitler-Mussolini ones of last October.

But independent of all the above-mentioned facts England and France have always been eager to preserve the sovereignty of the King of Kings of Ethiopia. In addition to the European problem in East Africa, there is a pressing native one: Mohammedanism against Christianity. Now Abyssinia has been a Christian Verdun against Mohammedanism for the past eleven hundred years. Once past Abyssinia and the Mohammedans would have swept the whites out of East Africa, especially so in 1885–89 under their great Mahdi.[15] As late as 1916, while Europe was at war, an attempt was made to turn Ethiopia to Mohammedanism. The Mad Mullah,[16] a Mohammedan Negro of Somaliland, after several victories over the British, threatened to push the whites out of East Africa. Lidj Yassu,[17] then emperor of Abyssinia, and a firm believer in the policy of "Africa for the Africans" made an alliance with the Mullah. As a result he was deposed. Civil war followed and in a bloody battle fought at Sagalle on October 27, 1916, in which 20,000 were killed. Lidj Yassu was beaten and the Christian forces secured in their power. As the king of England is pledged to support the Protestant religion so the emperor of Ethiopia swears to maintain Christianity. Let Abyssinia once throw in her lot with the Mohammedans and the white man's day in East Africa, and perhaps all of Africa, would soon be at an end. Hence, the reason for the Europeans asserting that the Abyssinians are a white people, though in features, hair, and color, they generally show more of what is known as the Negro than the Aframerican of the northern states.

The high preservative value placed on this black kingdom by the European is further reflected in the following: the total exports and imports of Abyssinia do not exceed at the most optimistic figure $10,000,000 a year. This is less than that spent by the 330,000 Negroes of Greater New York in a month. A white country with a similar low commerce would have but a vice-consul. Yet England, France, Italy, Germany, and the United States all have legations there. During the 1930 coronation at Addis Ababa the gold braid displayed by the Europeans rivalled that of a reception at Buckingham Palace or the Elysee.

Japan Cornering Markets

This matter of trade brings us to the subject of Japan. Japan is now the chief business competitor of the white nations in the Indian Ocean. Already she dominates the East African trade. Her cotton goods have crowded out European and American ones in the Abyssinian market. The white man's commercial day in the Indian Ocean is ended, unless he is willing to increase the purchasing power of the natives by giving them higher wages and a better price for their products, which he is not likely to do. Today, the natives, who are very poor, even according to European standards, must buy, if at all, low-priced products such as those furnished by Japan, China, and India.

Already Japan has a concession of land in Abyssinia the size of New Jersey. Nippon aims at nothing less than control of the Indian Ocean. Further the Ethiopians are more friendly to the Japanese than to the white man. Most Africans, black, yellow, or brown, and even white, detest European whites and with cause. Is there an understanding between Japan and Ethiopia in case of an attack by Italy? We do not know. The European powers, however, recently used their influence to prevent the marriage of an Abyssinian prince and a Japanese noblewoman.[18]

Finally, were Italy even given a free hand would she attempt the conquest of Abyssinia. Answer: the time is past when European nations can send large armies into Asia and Africa. They need them against their enemies in Europe and also against their discontented citizens. How Yugoslavia and the rest of the Little Entente[19] would rejoice to see Italy engaged in a great war in far-off Africa! The huge amount of men, money, and time necessary would drain an Italy which is already greatly strained. The Ethiopians, though no match for Italy, have the terrain and the climate in their favor, and are much better prepared than in 1896. The Italians, it is true, are very strong in the air, but airships are not a decisive factor in war.

The war against Abdel-Krim[20] ruined Spain, and Spain had no European enemies then. Most political prognostications are vain, but we predict that were Mussolini to engage in such a war and he did not win, and that quickly, he'd fare worse than Crispi. In short, our belief is that due to increasing restlessness at home, Mussolini is up to the old game of drawing a red herring across the trail. Moreover, was it a mere coincidence that all of this happened before the Laval-Mussolini conference at which France has made a few slight concessions to Italy?

"J. A. Rogers Gets Exclusive Interview with Emperor," Pittsburgh *Courier*, March 7, 1936

Rogers was the first African American correspondent ever assigned to cover a foreign conflict, being hired by the *Courier* to write about the Italo-Ethiopian War (1935–37) for the paper's 76,000 readers. His specific task was to get an exclusive interview with Haile Selassie (1892–1975), installed as Emperor in 1930. Rogers had gone to Ethiopia for Selassie's coronation in 1930 and later received a Coronation Medal from him in New York in 1954. It took many months for Rogers to arrange this interview, which required a great deal of security, but he was finally able to manage it. Clearly, Rogers saw this as a highlight of his journalistic career. It is an important interview, especially having been conducted by a Black foreign correspondent and taking place on the battlefield. Americans and Europeans, both Black and white, had a great stake in this war, and Ethiopia had overwhelming international support. Selassie had a messianic status for many of his followers as he traced his ancestry back to the biblical days of King Solomon. Rogers treats the Emperor with all the proper protocol, showing due deference. Rogers asks questions not only about the war but also about American Blacks. The Emperor shows an understanding of African American culture and demonstrates an appreciation for the support he has received around the world. He is open to accepting aid from other countries, and gives an invitation for African Americans to migrate to the country when stability is restored after the war. Unfortunately, Selassie's European allies chose to appease Italy to avoid conflict. Without this aid, Ethiopia was conquered by the Italians, and Selassie was forced into exile in 1936 until he and his European allies (now at war with Italy) retook the country in 1941. Selassie ruled Ethiopia until 1974 when he was ousted after a coup. He died in prison in 1975.

"J.A. ROGERS GETS EXCLUSIVE INTERVIEW WITH EMPEROR"

Rogers Used Disguise to Interview Haile Selassie

I have just completed the greatest experience of my life . . . an interview with Haile Selassie, benign Emperor of Ethiopia!

I arrived at Addis Ababa the day before Thanksgiving, hoping to be granted the interview for which I had traveled thousands of miles.

To my regret, the duties of war had called His Majesty to his troops in the north. I was commanded to wait. I waited.

I had to wait, because the entire Italian army was in search of this ONE superb "man of destiny." They were searching for him to put him to death.

Finally, I received word to proceed to the spot selected by him for my interview. Disguised and under strict cover, I proceeded to the spot, where I had the honor of being the first newspaperman to be granted a PERSONAL INTERVIEW.

"Get Interview" . . . My Instructions

In leaving America, I was specially charged by *The Pittsburgh Courier* to seek an interview with His Majesty, the Emperor, and to request his answer to certain questions in the interest of the millions of His Majesty's sincere admirers in America.

When, therefore, after months of waiting, I finally received word that I had been ordered by His Majesty to proceed to the place of the interview I was elated.

Arriving at the place designated, His Majesty welcomed me cordially and offered me his hand. After a few pleasantries, I remarked:

"Your Majesty, among the many millions of your warm friends in America are twelve million peoples of African descent. I wish I had the power to express to you, Sire, how deeply devoted they are to you. Your wise and able statesmanship, your courage, your firmness, your efforts to prevent the war, and your noble Christian conduct have endeared Your Majesty to them.

"At this time, when Ethiopia is struggling so gallantly to maintain her seven thousand years of unbroken independence, these children of the African motherland are eager to know in what way they can serve, because they feel that Ethiopia's fight is their fight also."

Knows of Sympathetic Attitude

"I know well of America's sympathetic attitude towards Ethiopia and I am very grateful for it," replied the Emperor in a voice and with a smile that expressed his pleasure far more than the mere words.

"The devotion of the Aframericans to our cause has touched me and my people profoundly.

"At present, our most IMPERATIVE NEED is the care of our unoffending people . . . the women, the children, the aged . . . who have been driven from their homes and lands by the Italians, and also those who are lying wounded in hospitals from Italian bombs. The war has fallen hardest on these innocent people; and at a time when our financial resources are taxed to the limit in our efforts to repel the invader."

Instantly, I recalled how America had aided similar stricken ones in Belgium and France during the great war . . . nations that were in a far superior financial position to Ethiopia. I queried:

"Your Majesty, during the Great War, America was very generous to the French and the Belgians that had been driven from their homes and cities by the invader. French and Belgian orphans were even adopted by proxy by Americans and money sent for their support. I am very sure, therefore, that in this strikingly parallel case America will do the same. Would Your Majesty kindly express his wishes in this respect?"

Grateful for Financial Aid

"Very well. We have an Ethiopian Red Cross. We have also an Ethiopian Women Workers' Association, composed of brave, self-sacrificing women. My daughter, the Princess Tsahai,[1] has the honor of being at the head of this society. I shall be grateful for any financial aid sent to these organizations."

"Would Your Majesty prefer that the money be sent directly to Ethiopia?"

"Yes, to these associations. At Addis Ababa one can buy almost everything necessary for the care of the wounded, as well as clothing and shelter for the refugees."

Would Accept Service of U.S, Doctors

When I left America last October, the doctors of Harlem were preparing to send certain of their numbers to Ethiopia. Thinking of them now, I inquired:

"What of the Aframerican doctors? Would Your Majesty accept their services? There are many who would willingly come."

"Certainly," he replied readily. "We would appreciate deeply their services. At the same time I would like to suggest that their ambulances be well furnished with medical supplies for a period of six months."

His Majesty reflected a moment before continuing.

"I would also advise that these doctors obtain from the American Government the authorization that will enable them to serve in accord with Article XI of the Geneva Convention. If this is not done, their ambulances must then work under the Ethiopian Red Cross."

"Is there some other way in which Aframericans can serve, Your Majesty?"

"By helping to enforce the sanctions," was the immediate reply.

". . . When the Last Italian Leaves"

I changed the subject to that of the war itself.

"When do you think the war will end, Sire?" was my next question.

Without a moment's hesitation came his firm response.

"WHEN THE LAST ITALIAN IS OFF ETHIOPIAN SOIL, then and not until then, can we talk of peace.

"I would be a traitor to my country; to my brave men who have given, and are daily giving their lives; to all my ancestors since Solomon and the Queen of Sheba; and to every principle that lovers of their country in all ages and all lands have ever fought for, if I did otherwise."

Resolute words these. But it was impossible to detect a suspicion of defiance in the Emperor's voice. He uttered the words as calmly as one who says, "No, thanks" to a particular question.

The muscles of his face retained their expression of tranquility. No motion of his slim hands or his graceful body indicated inward emotion. One of the most pronounced characteristics of Haile Selassie is his thorough mastery of himself.

"Will Not Accept Any Limitation"

My mind flashed back to Mussolini as I had seen him years ago, addressing his crowd before the Palazzio Venetia[2] and as I had seen him in recent months in the news reels. I thought of the bravado, the flourish, the theatrical manner in which Il Duce would have flung his defiance.

Yet in the very calmness, the very lack of pose of Haile Selassie, could be felt the determination of one who would never yield, because he fully realized the sacredness of the principle involved.

My next question seemed almost useless after this, but I asked it nevertheless.

"Would Ethiopia ever consent to become a protectorate or to be placed under a mandate?"

In the same even tones came the reply, **"Ethiopia will never accept any limitation of her sovereignty."**

Talks of Tuskegee, Howard, Joe Louis

The Emperor changed the subject to speak of America and the Americans of African descent.

In the course of the conversation, it was very clear that His Majesty was well-informed about Aframericans and that for many years he had taken a keen interest in their activities and their progress.

He spoke about Tuskegee Institute and its splendid industrial education; of Howard University and its fine medical school; of Mrs. Mary McLeod Bethune and her school in Daytona, Fla. (The school is Bethune-Cookman College).

He expressed his deep thanks to the pastors of the colored churches for their prayers in behalf of Ethiopia and the Y.M.C.A.'s and Y.W.C.A.'s.

He thanked the Aframerican newspapers for their editorials in favor of Ethiopia, and spoke of the colored writers and singers, such as Paul Robeson, Roland Hayes, Caterina Jarboro[3] and others.

Nor did he forget the subject of sports . . . of JOE LOUIS . . . and other current topics.

HE ASKED THAT HIS WARMEST THANKS BE EXPRESSED TO ALL HIS FRIENDS IN AMERICA THROUGH THE COLUMNS OF THE PITTSBURGH COURIER!

Welcomes Trained Americans

I then seized the occasion to ask a question nearest to my heart and that of most Aframericans.

"Your Majesty," I said, "in the United States there are thousands of graduates who come annually from our universities and industrial colleges.

"Some of these young people . . . and there are older ones as well . . . are well qualified in engineering, architecture, agriculture, chemistry, medicine, aviation and other fields. There is a great lack of opportunity for them in America.

"On the other hand, Your Majesty, here you have a large country which is very little developed.

"You have here the country of the future . . . a country which seems to be lacking in nothing save the intellectual and industrial development of its inhabitants. Therefore, Sire, may these Aframericans just mentioned look forward to the day when their energies will find an outlet in Ethiopia?"

"Assuredly. When we are left free to continue the improvement of our country, which has been so rudely interrupted by war, the Aframericans will be considered along with the other friends of Ethiopia.

"I am opposed to all distinctions based on race, religion, color or previous condition of servitude. It is one of my chief desires to maintain in our part of Africa a system based upon the merit of the individual; to establish a country where all God's children shall live in the harmony and the brotherhood that God intended them.

Ethiopia A Black Man's Land

"In the various offices of my government you will find the different races and colors working in harmony. Ethiopia, through her firm faith in God, will arise from this severe test stronger than ever.

"And in the 'New Ethiopia' colored Americans who are qualified will find their place."

I could not help but be struck by the truth of this statement. In the restaurants, cinemas, bars and other public places in Addis Ababa, Dire-Dowah[4] and other towns, whites and blacks, Ethiopians and Europeans, fraternize and sup in peace. Haile Selassie has always preached racial and national brotherhood to his people, who, by the way, have had much cause in the past 50 years not to be particularly fond of white people.

Every European here realizes that it is largely due to the broad Christian hospitality of Haile Selassie that he is able to dwell here in safety at this time.

For myself, I felt proud that in this "Black Man's Land" such a fine example was being set at a time when racial discord seems to be on the increase.

Severe Laws Against Slavery

Still another matter in which I felt all Americans are keenly interested occurred to me, viz: the bugaboo of slavery.

I knew for a long time of the strenuous efforts of His Majesty for its abolition. I knew of his proclamations and of his drastic laws against slave-trading and slave-raiding. I knew of the punishment meted out to offenders. I also knew well that slave-holding is punished more severely in Ethiopia than in any other part of Africa under European domination.

I knew that slavery exists throughout nearly all of Africa, and particularly in the Italian territories of Eritrea and Libya.

But wishing an expression on this from His Majesty, I asked the question.

"We have very severe laws against slavery," responded the Emperor, "and they are rigidly enforced."

Part of Italian Propaganda

"This accusation of slavery is a calumny disseminated by Italy for political ends. At the same time, it may be well to observe that Ethiopian slavery . . . indeed the more correct word would be service (His Majesty used the French 'servage') . . . differed greatly from western or plantation slavery. Often a 'slave' was a member of the family and was treated as such. Some of Ethiopia's greatest chiefs and cabinet members began as 'slaves.'

"In certain distant parts of my empire, where the central power is not yet fully established, there are doubtless a few rare slaves to be found.

"But generally speaking, the only slaves . . . if we may indeed use that word in this respect . . . are those who have remained of their own will, with their former masters. Such may go whenever they please and no one may detain them. No one in Ethiopia can now say legally: 'This is my slave.' As for the slave trade, that no longer exists."

Ethiopia Wants Port Out of War

"What of the League of Nations?" was my next question. "Has Your Majesty still confidence in it?"

The answer: "The proof is that I still continue to address myself to it."

"Does Ethiopia hope to get a port as a result of the war? Does she look forward to having Massowah?"[5] I asked.

"A port is essential for the future progress of Ethiopia. The peace terms will include provision for one."

The end of the interview approached. Already I had taken too much of the time of this man . . . the busiest in the world.

But I could not leave without expressing my appreciation of some of the remarkable things I had seen in Ethiopia. I mentioned the invigorating air of the mountains; the beauty of the deep-blue skies; the magnificent clouds and the fragrance of the roses and other flowers, adding: "Ethiopia has the most astonishing runners I have ever seen."

Work of Peace and Progress

Continuing, I said: "I hope some day to see her in the marathon of the Olympic Games.[6] I also hope to see the day when Ethiopia will be sending her young men and women to Europe to be trained in singing. From the timbre of certain Ethiopian voices . . . particularly the feminine ones . . . I am sure that Ethiopia has something new to offer the world in grand opera."

His Majesty smiled his thanks.

"In the midst of this cruel war, we are still looking forward to the time when we can resume our work of peace and progress, and the education and elevation of our people."

"One last question, Your Majesty," I said, preparing reluctantly to leave. "Do you contemplate visiting America some day? I assure Your Majesty that Americans, regardless of race, would give you one of the most cordial welcomes possible."[7]

Wants to Visit America Some Day

"To visit America," said His Majesty graciously, "has always been one of my great dreams. If ever the occasion comes, be assured I shall not miss it."

I left the presence of this great ruler feeling more elevated in spirit than I had ever been. I had met in the flesh and had the rare honor of shaking the hand of the man who had the most difficult job on this planet, and who withal had so acquitted himself as to win the general respect, aye the affection . . . of all mankind.

And what I, in particular, was proud of was the fact that he was a true "Son of Ethiopia" . . . reared and educated in Africa and born of a direct lineage that thousands of years ago gave to the world the first true conception of kindliness and brotherhood.

"Rogers Describes His 'Adventures in Jim-Crow Land,'" Pittsburgh *Courier*, August 8, 1936

Rogers was well acquainted with the Jim-Crow system on the trains through his years of working as a Pullman porter and from his own frequent journeys as a passenger. He had suffered racial prejudice as an employee of the rail system, but now he shows how this segregated system affects Black passengers as well. Jim-Crow (the policy of separate but equal) was established in 1896 in the landmark *Plessy v. Ferguson* case. It is appropriate that the issue in the case revolved around public transportation, of travel on the rails. Public transportation, this time on buses, was also, of course, at the core of the Rosa Parks case (1955–56) as well. Perhaps public transportation is the nexus where the races and differing social strata come together most, displaying society's most democratic as well as its most segregationist policies.

By its nature, the transportation system brings those from a variety of social, ethnic, and racial groups into a relatively confined area. Rail was the most common means to move around the country until after World War II, and it exposed the ludicrous nature of segregation, especially when traveling between the North and the South, where Black people would have to move to different locations on the train depending upon which state they were in. To compound matters, many decisions had to be made by self-identification as in this article. Would a conductor, for example, question whether a light-complexioned person such as Rogers was really Black if the person claimed to be white? A mistake by the railroad employee on such a matter would have serious repercussions. The hesitation of the employees in the essay to question the narrator reflects this concern. The narrator's honest depiction of his own internal struggles over whether to "out" himself or not or whether to accept special treatment over others of his race is very powerful and sheds light on what it was like to travel in the South by public transportation while Black in the Jim-Crow era, when even the most educated, well-off African American was assigned poorer accommodations than the lowest white person.

"ROGERS DESCRIBES HIS 'ADVENTURES IN JIM-CROW LAND'"

Writer Laughs at Bewilderment of Train Conductors

In the last century, Charles Dickens found much to laugh about in the crudities of American culture as he traveled over this country.[1]

In this year of our Lord, 1936, and of civilization 251,000, there is still much comedy here if one has the stomach for it.

Leaving Chicago recently for New Orleans I bought a first-class ticket and a Pullman straight through on the Illinois Central. Save for four drunken white Southerners who got on at Chicago flourishing a whisky bottle and using filthy language in the presence of women, whom they feign so much to respect, all went well, so far as I was concerned, until about 6 p.m. I was in my seat when both the train and the Pullman conductors came to me.

"What nationality are you?" asked the train conductor.

"American," I replied absentmindedly looking up from "The Life of Voltaire,"[2] which I was reading. For the moment I had imagined myself back in Europe where it is quite common to be asked one's nationality on the train. Definitely then I recalled that I was on an American train, where it was most unusual to ask such a question. I looked up at the two men. They seemed ill at ease.

Doubtful of Race

"You're not what they call a Negro?" stammered the train conductor, playing on the safe side. Then and only then the situation dawned on me. I had crossed the Mason-Dixon line. I was no longer in the United States. I was in the brave, the courteous, the chivalrous South.

I realized then that all I had to do to be permitted to continue my journey as a normal human being would be to say that I was a South American, a Central American, or anything else save "an American citizen."

Anyone But An American Negro

Unknown to me, the porter had already tried to square matters by telling the two conductors that I was "a French West Indian." These train officials had come to me merely for confirmation. But I decided that to deny my real citizenship would be too much of an easy way out. Moreover, I do not want any privileges that are denied other human beings, regardless of color, and most of all those of my own so-called race.

Years ago this would have made me boiling mad. But since then I had seen life in a bigger and larger way than most Southerners and even most Northerners are ever likely to see it, and this petty conduct tickled me hugely. I laughed aloud and said: "Sure, I am a man of African descent. What you call a Negro in America."

Certain of his ground now the train conductor replied: "You can't ride in here." There was that in his voice which made me feel that he expected me to get up instantly and turn tail like a beaten cur.

"I can't, eh?" I asked laughing. "Did you ever hear the story of the man that was in jail. A friend of his seeing him behind the bars said "They can't put you in here!' 'But I am in here all the same!' replied the prisoner. "Well, conductor, like that man. I am here—and with my ticket. And here I stay."

"You can't. It's against the law," said the conductor, uttering the word "law" as if it were some sacred idol. He added, "Some white persons might consider themselves humiliated because you are riding in here and bring suit against the railroad company."

Crazy Legislation

I thought of some of the world's finest places, trains and ships in which I had been: of some of the distinguished individuals in whose homes I had been received as an equal, and then here in this backwash of civilization with these coarse drunken white men near me to be told that I was breaking the law because I was riding a train as any ordinary human being in any ordinary civilized country could do—all this I thought was high comedy—the comedy of conceit—conceit of those who consider themselves the salt of the earth, but who when measured by the most ordinary standards of human conduct are only of the stature of pea-nuts, and I laughed merrily.

"Law?" I said scornfully, "Gentlemen this is not law, but plain lunacy."

I turned my back on them and picked up my book. "I am going to stay right here." I added, "There's only one thing to do, messieurs, and that's to get your mob. You'll find me right here."

The two began to confer. It was clear that they were embarrassed. "Well, give him the drawing room," said the train conductor. When this accommodation was offered me, my first impulse was to refuse since the purpose was really to jim-crow me, but I remembered the drunks in the adjoining berths. I was going to make an address in New Orleans the next day and had already seen myself passing a sleepless night because of them. Further, might not some one shoot me or harm me during the night while I slept. I was in the South.

And so I accepted the drawing room which incidentally cost four times as much as the berth, and required an extra first class ticket. But I took care not to confine myself there, for at times, I went back to the club car.

In justice to both the train conductor and the Pullman conductor I will say that I later discovered that both had performed a distasteful duty. The porter told me that the Pullman conductor had done his best not to have me disturbed, saying that I had a perfect right to be in the car. In any case we all three parted as gentlemen should.

Suit Against Company

But the Illinois Central and the Pullman company got even with me on my return. O. C. W. Taylor, New Orleans high school principal, under whose auspices I had come to speak in New Orleans, tried for two days to get me Pullman accommodation in vain. My own efforts were no more successful and thus I was forced to ride second-class in the day coach (jim-crow).

But the last laugh is up to me. The lawyers tell me that I have an excellent case against the company for while it sold me a first-class return ticket it forced me to ride second-class. The new railroad rates have created a first-class on the trains and Louisiana so-called law calls for separate but equal accommodation.

Railroad accommodations for colored people have improved little, if any, in the South since I saw them 25 years ago. In my next article I will tell you of my further adventures in jim-crow land.

"J. A. Rogers Rips 'Veil of Hypocrisy' From 'Best-Seller,'" *Pittsburgh Courier*, February 27, 1937

Margaret Mitchell (1900–1949) published only one novel, the blockbuster *Gone With the Wind* (1935). The book, set in the South during the Civil War and Reconstruction period, won the Pulitzer Prize for Fiction in 1937. The even more popular film based on the book was released in 1939. Mitchell's book is a prime example of the belief in the "Lost Cause," a highly Romanticized, nostalgic look at antebellum Southern life. The Civil War was seen as being fought for a just, noble cause. Slaves were happy, the men gallant, and the ladies charming. The image depicted in Mitchell's book is deeply disturbing to Rogers who was disappointed that the novel missed an opportunity to correct distorted historical views of the South. Instead of dismantling the nostalgia of the Lost Cause, the work helped perpetuate a mistaken notion of Southern gentility and kindness toward Blacks in the post–Civil War days. The spectacular success of *Gone With the Wind* (book and later film) helped make it seminal to adherents of the Lost Cause who continued to cling to this myth, supported by among others, works of fiction by Thomas Dixon, the film *The Birth of a Nation* (1915), and the writings of the pro-Southern historian Ulrich B. Phillips. The Lost Cause continues to resonate across the nation, particularly in the South, as is evidenced by the current debate over Confederate flags and monuments. Rogers revisits this thorny issue in his essay "Civil War Centennial, Myth and Reality" (1963) in this anthology. For a parody of Mitchell's novel from a Black perspective, see Alice Randall's *The Wind Done Gone* (2001).

"J.A. ROGERS RIPS 'VEIL OF HYPOCRISY' FROM 'BEST-SELLER'"

Says 'Gone with the Wind' Doesn't Tell Truth About Dixie

Quotes from Ku Klux Reports in Congress to Prove That Woman Author Toyed With the Truth—Book Highly Prejudiced

The winner of a war, a prize-fight, a race, or any other contest is inclined to forget and forgive, but a loser never does. He feels that he must justify himself by countless explanations, which call for still more explanation.

In no instance is this more true than in the case of the South in the Civil War. The North, victorious, soon forgot; the South, seventy-two years later, still fights on in a wordy warfare, whose bitterness is excelled only by its childishness.

Dog-like Negroes Idealized

The current best seller, "Gone with the Wind," is the latest sample of this long line of attempted justification. But as a bit of propaganda, Miss Mitchell's book not only does not offer anything new, but it lacks the fire of the earlier defenders as Hinton Rowan Helper[1] and Thomas Dixon.

In "Gone With the Wind," as with its predecessors, the Negro fares badly, particularly in the Reconstruction period. The '"good" Negroes of Miss Mitchell's book are the door-mats, the lick-spittles, the faithful dogs, the Uncle Toms and all those who were too dumb and too spiritless to know that as human beings they had a right to be free: whilst the "bad" Negroes are those who refused to let the whites treat them as if they were still slaves. Miss Mitchell's better class of Negroes "scorned freedom." She says on page 654:

"The former slaves were now the lords of creation and, with the aid of the Yankees, the lowest and most ignorant ones were on top. The better class of them, scorning freedom, were suffering as severely as their white masters. Thousands of house servants, the highest caste in the slave population, remained with the white folks, doing manual labor which had been beneath them in the old days. Many loyal field hands also refused to avail themselves of the new freedom but the hordes of 'trashy free issue niggers' who were causing most of the trouble, were drawn largely from the field-hand class."

Alleged Rapes

Again on page 656: "But these ignominies and dangers were as nothing compared with the perils of white women, many bereft by the war of male protection, who lived alone in the outlying districts and on lonely roads. It was the large number of outrages on women and the ever present fear for the safety of their wives and daughters that drove Southern men to cold and trembling fury and caused the Ku Klux Klan to spring up overnight."

Ku Klux Leader Denies

Good. On this subject let us pass over the testimony of such dependable Northern writers as Tourgee,[2] Schruz,[3] Blaine[4] and Major John R. Lynch[5]: hear from one of who was no less than the one-time head of the Klan. Gen. J. B. Gordon, Confederate leader. At the Congressional investigation of the Klan in 1871, Gordon testified "One of the things which I mentioned and which Gen. Clanton[6] also mentioned was the behavior of the Negroes during the war: the fact that which, when almost the entire white population old enough to bear arms, was in the army and large plantations were left to be managed by the women and children, not a single insurrection had occurred, not a life had been taken, and that, too, when the Federal armies were marching through the country with freedom, so to speak, on their banners."

Question—"Scarcely an outrage occurred on the part of the Negroes at that time?"

Gen. Gordon: " . . . Scarcely an outrage. When I made that speech at Montgomery, I may say, without intending to compliment myself that when I referred to the handsome behavior of the Negro during our absence in the army and his protection of our families at that time, my remarks were heartily responded to, and with great feeling by every man in the convention."

Question—"Do you mean the colored men responded to them?"

Gen. Gordon: " . . . No sir, I mean the white men in that convention."

(Ku Klux reports, Vol. VI, page 320.)

Now since the Negroes did not attack the white women, when the white men were absent, is it likely that they would have attacked them when the white men had returned? Of this, Gen. Gordon, himself, also testified "They behaved so well that the remark is not uncommon that no race on earth relieved from servitude under such circumstances, would have behaved so well."

In short, Miss Mitchell is more Ku Klux than the greatest of the leaders. Gordon, too, was speaking of what he saw. Miss Mitchell is writing 70 years later from what she heard or read.

Miss Mitchell's history is so crassly prejudiced that one hesitates to attack it unless one also makes himself as ridiculous.

Other Defects

I have other causes for disappointment with this book. I bought it, took it home, and settled back to read what I had been led to believe was a modern treatment of the Civil War . . . a novel that I hoped was going to help get us out of this morass of futile discussion on to solid ground . . . one that would point the great moral and economic lesson to be learned by all Americans, regardless of sectional or color differences from this tragic struggle. But I found only the same recriminations, the same old wringing of the nose.

Both Sides Guilty

We all know that both sides were to blame. The North had forced slavery on the South until it had become the chief Southern institution . . . then . . . when it had become disadvantageous to the North, it wanted to get rid of it. Slavery had to go, however, and the South chose the roughest way . . . not alone because it wanted to maintain slavery but because it wanted independence. As Gordon, himself, says in his autobiography,[7] "the South could have "saved slavery" at any time during the war "by simply laying down its arms and returning to the Union."

And as for the atrocities of the Northern Army which Miss Mitchell paints so vividly, were there not as great ones on the Confederate side? Did not Sherman say that war is hell? The Yankees had their march to the sea and the Rebels their Fort Pillow Massacre.

During the Reconstruction period, there were all kinds of rascals, white and black, Southern and Northern, and some good heroic folk, too. What I had looked for was a work in which all these types were depicted.

Real Reason for Klan

As for the Klan, we know now that it was formed by Southern and Northern capitalists to bring back a condition akin to chattel slavery for both the Negro and white masses.

Author Tells Too Much

My chief disappointment with "Gone With the Wind," however, is on artistic grounds. For instance, I found it much inferior to a similar work, Thomas Dixon's "The Clansman." Dixon's book was concise. It went to the mark like a flaming arrow. But "Gone With the Wind," sprawls on and on, like a mid-western city . . . Cleveland, Chicago, St. Louis or, like Philadelphia, and with as little beauty. I very strongly disagreed with Thomas Dixon, still I found his book gripping. I had positively to drag myself through "Gone With the Wind." It is true that there are passages of great skill and even genius in it but one had to patter through [a] wilderness of triviality to reach them. At least 500 pages could be lopped off with great advantage.

Lacking in Humor

"Anthony Adverse"[8] was, of course, interminably long. But its length was relieved by the many countries into which it took the reader. "Gone

With the Wind," however, in its 1037 pages, keeps one in the dull, dispiriting atmosphere of the post-war South. Anthony Adverse, also, took one at times to stirring heights of spiritual regeneration . . . a quality I did not find in Miss Mitchell's book.

And as for humor even Miss Mitchell's Negroes have as much of it as a glass eye.

"The Suppression of Negro History," Crisis, May 1940

In the opening statement of this article, one of Rogers's seminal pieces, he sets forth a belief that would undergird all his work: "History, or what is said of us nationally, racially, socially, or individually, is often the most important factor in our lives." He maintained that whites had seriously injured Black people by denying them their proper history, either by omitting or distorting it. Without it their sense of self and of self-worth were damaged. At the time Rogers was writing this essay, the concept of a "Negro History" was even open to question. Many whites, and not a small number of Blacks, were not sure how much Blacks had actually done. Some certainly would be hard-pressed to provide evidence of notable Black people. Publishers and newspaper editors also added to the problem by printing only sensational headlines about people of African descent. Rogers tried to restore this missing history by chronicling the achievements of scores of Black people that have been removed from history. He is probably best known for his popular history aimed at the common man. Here, Rogers is writing a more academic, research essay, complete with notes, more the way of the traditional historian. While it may not be as engaging as, for example, his sketches on famous Black personages in *World's Great Men of Color*, he still amazes the reader with the information he provides. His depth of knowledge and the enormous amount of research he has done is staggering. And even if a few of the cases he cites may seem dubious, everything he says is far more credible than the comment of esteemed British historian Arnold Toynbee about the lack of any contributions by Blacks to world civilization.

"THE SUPPRESSION OF NEGRO HISTORY"

History, or what is said of us nationally, racially, socially, or individually, is often the most important factor in our lives. The most effective way of keeping down a people, regardless of race, and forcing it to sell its labor in the lowest market is continually to publish bad things about it. He who robs me of my good name, said Shakespeare, leaves me poor indeed.[1]

Of this art of debasing a whole people, the American slaveholders were the past masters. Using the Bible as their authority, they painted such an awful picture of Negro ancestry that even some of the Virginia aristocrats had a lively time side-stepping charges of being touched with the tar brush. George Washington, in his diary, January 12, 1760, tells how one haughty Virginia colonel, Catesby Cocke, walked out of Washington's home "disgusted" because he saw there "an old Negro" who resembled him strongly. Colonel George William Fairfax, Washington's bosom friend, was another. Fairfax, who was nephew of Lord Fairfax, Virginia's richest landowner, was born in the West Indies, it was said, of a black Negro mother. Most of the native-born West Indian whites, then as well as now, had a touch of the tar-brush, more or less evident. "In view of his distinguished ancestry, this scandal was particularly annoying" to the colonel, who moreover hoped to inherit his uncle's title and estates. He went to England, it is said, to prove to his uncle that he wasn't a Negro; nevertheless, the property went to another. (Rupert Hughes, Life of Washington, Vol. I, p. 183; Vol. II, p.21).

Still another who was "accused" of being a Negro was Thomas Jefferson. In his case, however, it was clearly pure politics. Jefferson had a fondness for fair black femininity, quite unconcealed, particularly for Sally Hemings, the celebrated Black Sal,[2] and Jefferson's enemies argued that one so fond of Negroes must be of Negro strain himself.

With this as typical of the spirit of the time anything about the achievements of the Negro was simply out of the question. Indeed, any history that did not paint Africans as cannibals and savages who had been dragged out of Africa to save their souls would be almost downright atheism. Solemn-faced divines from Massachusetts to Georgia pounded the Bible at the command of the tobacco-growers to prove that the Negro "was descendant of Ham and thus doomed to be a hewer of wood and a drawer of water for the white race, forever." To talk of Hannibal, Esop, Delphos,[3] Buddha, Akhenaton, or Christ, as being Negroes, was equivalent to flying in the face of the Almighty. Negro history had no more chance than the proverbial cockroach at the roosters' ball.[4] In short, the black man was entirely cut off from his past and liberally dosed with white religion to make him a cross of something between a faithful dog and a grinning mule.

The American slave-holder did not stop there. Like the average white southerner of today he was an ardent propagandist abroad of his doctrines of white superiority. He took his racial creed to England, along with his slaves, and succeeded in reviving Negro slavery, which had been abolished there by Chief Justice Holt in 1707.[5] In short, the American slave holding interests made such a thorough black-out of everything favorable to the Negro in literature that now, centuries later, it functions as almost brand new.

Negro History a Reality

Nevertheless, "Negro history," was a reality even as the so-called New World was there despite its absence from maps of the world prior to Columbus. Mankind has been living on this planet not less than half a million years and there is ever increasing proof that the first human beings were Negroes, and that all the other human varieties, including the proud Aryan, are their offspring. Professor W. K. Gregory in "Our Face from Fish to Man"[6] traces on a chart the evolution of man from the Tasmanian Negro. And there are many other scientists from Schopenhauer onwards who have done similarly. Of course, for many Nordics, it is easier to believe that their ancestor was an ape rather than a Negro.

In the dawn of history we find the whites idealizing the blacks. It is possible to produce much painstaking authority to prove that all or nearly all the earliest gods and messiahs from Japan to Mexico, including Jehovah, Christ and the Virgin Mary were what are now called Negroes.[7] The earliest gods of even Ancient Greece were black. Homer tells how the Greek gods used to go to Ethiopia, their ancestral home to feast and enjoy themselves at intervals. Even the curling of the hair, so common among the later Greeks might have been done in imitation of the Negroes. Apollo's face is distinctly Caucasian but his hair is artificially curled until it is a tight pepper-corn. Now the founder of the famous Delphic oracle, the rites of Apollo, was Delphos, a full-blooded, wooly-haired Negro whose effigy appears on a Greek coin of 500 B. C. (C. T. Seltman: Athens, Its History and Coinage, pp. 97, 200. 1924). The Christ on a gold coin of Justinian II, Byzantine emperor, has the same pepper-corn hair, a distinctive characteristic of the Negro of the purest type as the Bushman and the Andaman Islander. The Venus of Willendorf, the oldest known statuary of the human form, of about 10,000 to 15.000 B.C. has the same kind of hair.

George Washington in his Barbados Journal told how the white ladies "affect the Negro Style." In Europe I saw white women got up to look like black ones, particularly during the Paris Colonial Exposition of 1931. Some white women had their hair so tightly curled and skin so darkened by sunlight or lotions that it was a distinct surprise to see them later in low neck dresses with the white streak left by the shoulder-straps of the bathing suit.

There is so much of Negro history to be garnered that I am convinced after thirty years of research that it would take several industrious historians a life-time to gather it. Gerald Massey rightly says, "To the despised black race we have at length to turn for the birth of language, the beginnings of all human creation, and as the Arabic saying puts it let us 'honor the first although the followers do better.'"

Historians Have Blind Spot

So heavy was the black-out laid down by the slave interests, however, that almost none of this Negro history glimmers into the histories written for popular white consumption, including Wells' Outline of

History.[8] The popular white writer has actually developed a blind spot where the Negro is concerned.

The following incident will illustrate my point. I must insist in advance that though it sounds most ridiculous I am telling it just as it happened. Some years ago I attended a lecture on Brazil given by a professor from one of New York's most enlightened colleges and with a reputation for being radical. During the question period I brought up the subject of the Negro strain in John VI, who once ruled Portugal from Brazil. The professor said, "Impossible! He was not a Negro. He was a Bourbon!" In reply I quoted from the Duchess d'Abrantès, one of France's greatest women writers, and wife of the French ambassador to John's court at Lisbon. She said of John VI, "his enormous head with its Negro hair, which, moreover, was quite in harmony with his thick nose, and the color of his skin." (Son enorme tête, surmontée d'une chevelure de nègre, qui, au reste, était, bien en harmonie avec ses lèvres épaisses, son nez africain, et la couleur de sa peau," Memoires, p. 200, Paris, 1837). I added that a large proportion of the Portuguese population was then Negro, that John's portrait bears out the Duchess' description, and that the Duchess knew the Negro type as she had lived in Haiti. Still the professor held to his point. "No," he said, "he was not a Negro. *He had adenoids!*"

Equally amazing is the case of Professor Arnold J. Toynbee[9] of London university. If Toynbee's work is an index of his mind he must be utterly free from color prejudice; nevertheless, like H.G. Wells, he is also a victim of the slaveholders' blackout. In his study of history (Vol. 1, pp. 232–238), Toynbee flatly asserts that the Negro has made no contribution to past civilization. He says, "When we classify mankind by colour the only one of the primarily races given by this classification which has not made a contribution to any of our twenty-one civilizations is the Black Race . . . ."

"Within the first six thousand years the Black Race has not helped to create any civilization while the Polynesian has helped to create one civilization; the Brown Race, two; the Yellow Race, three; the Red Race and the Nordic White Race, four apiece; the Alpine White Race, nine; and the Mediterranean White Race, ten."

Four Deleted Words

Match this with what Sir Arthur Evans,[10] one of the greatest archeologists has said. In his presidential address to the British Association of Science, 1916 (p. 15), he says, as regards even Western Europe, "We must never lose sight of the fact that from the earliest Aurignacian Period[11] onwards a Negroid culture in the broadest sense of the word shared in this artistic culture as seen on both sides of the Pyrenees." What also of the researches[12] of Dieulafoy[13] in Persia, not to mention others!

Yet another illustration. F. A. Wright, in his introduction to the works of Liudprand,[14] Bishop of Cremona, (p. 11) omits mention of the color of Phocas, Byzantine emperor. He quotes Liudprand's whole description of Nicephorus except the four small words "in color a Negro." In place of these he has three dots. Nicephorus Phocas[15] was an Arab. Liudprnad visited him in his capital at Constantinople. There was much Negro strain in the Byzantines. The southern part of their empire, Greece, was dominated for years by Negro sea-rovers, who landed in Thessaly in fifty-four ships in 904 A.D. (Schulumberger: Un empereur byzantin, p. 34–35). The Byzantine emperors took their title of Basileus from the Ethiopians.

Still another case of the hundreds I could cite is that of Robert Browning.[16] Browning was of West Indian ancestry. Frederick J. Furnivall, a contemporary of Browning and head of the Browning Society, after a lengthy discussion of Browning's ancestry, said Browning's Negro strain was a "certainty" to him. (Browning Society Papers, Feb. 28, 1890, Vol. III, pp. 31, 36. London). Thomas Carlyle almost [*sic*] spoke of Browning's dark skin. Nevertheless, many of Browning's admirers and biographers, most of whom have never seen Browning, have almost frothed at the mouth at Furnival's statement.

For unblushing, barefaced suppression of Negro history the palm, as in so many other cases where truth is involved, goes to Hollywood.

Cleopatra, who is known throughout history, was at least a mulatto woman, becomes a pale Nordic. So are all of the Three Wise Men, one of whom is depicted in all or nearly all, the great paintings as a Negro. Frank Morgan[17] plays Allessandro dei Medici, Duke of Florence, and mulatto son of Pope Clement VII, in the most approved Hitler complexion. Quite different are the films of Italian make. In D'Annunzio's[18] film Cabiria, Massinissa, celebrated King of Numidia, was played by a Negro. Massinissa provided the balance of power whereby Rome defeated Carthage.

Radicals No Better

So much for the conservative white people. What of the radical economic whites? Are they any better? Personally I have found them to be even narrower. While the conservative whites consider Negro history to be "social equality," the radicals denounce it as "black chauvinism" even while some of them talk about self-determination in the black belt.[19] A book on great Negroes is dubbed "inferiority complex" by the radical whites and some of their Negro converts. Was it a sense of inferiority that inspired Plutarch to write his Lives?[20] Radicals keep their nose so close to the economic grindstone; they talk so much about the belly that one would imagine it is the only organ in the body, except when it comes to laudation of their own leaders. They would put these economic blinders on the Negro, too. Most of the literature they get out about him is defeatist. Reason: the Negroes will be discouraged in their own leadership and become easier tools. The stressing of crime, degeneracy, and injustice at the expense of the more favorable aspects of the Negro's life serves to make many Negroes feel that the economic nostrums of these radicals are their only salvation.

White publishers, too, complain that Negroes will not buy books about themselves. Most of these books tend to hold the Negro just where he has always been. After three centuries of the preaching of defeatism one needs inspiration. People who have been thrust into dark holes crave sunlight.

The Negro Lends Aid

And speaking of crime and defeatism that brings us to the subject of what the Negroes, themselves, do to suppress the favorable in their own history. My experiences on this alone would fill a book. The chief offender in this respect is the Negro press, whose policy, broadly speaking, is almost identical with that of the white press, namely, to give crime and scandal precedence over achievement.

Some years ago at a press conference in Chicago, a Negro reporter took the white editors to task for mentioning color in the case of Negro offenders.

The late Victor Lawson, publisher of the *Daily News* quietly asked, "If we did not carry the color of the offender where would the Negro press get its news? Besides while we give the matter only a paragraph or two, you make a headline of it." After that, the Negroes were as mum as mice. I was working on a Negro paper at the time and this was its precise policy. Our editor, and he was no different from the rest, felt that week lost when some Negro did not kill another or some Negro minister or other big shot was not mixed up in a scandal. Negro journalism has come a long way—a very long way—since John Brown Russwurm and Frederick Douglass. Today it is only a job.

Negro journalism is also far more personal than white. Some of the editors are more touchy than a dictator of a small Latin-American state or a petty African chief and will order to be suppressed news of those individuals who differ with them however slightly. The younger crop of Negro newspapermen too, know as a rule, little or nothing of Negro history and hate to be corrected. In 1937, a leading Negro newspaper copying from a white one, said that Sargeant Wanton[21] of Washington, D.C., was the first and only Negro to win the Congressional Medal of Honor. I sent four typewritten lines to the paper saying that instead of one there were forty-one Negroes to win this highest honor. The article was never published. I called at the office and left a stamp for its return. The stamp disappeared, too.

Then there is the rivalry in the camp of the Negro historians. There are the Brahmins and the Sudras,[22] or the fellows from the big white colleges with big degrees and those who have none. The Brahmins, in turn, are divided. In short, the researches of none of the groups mix, or are endorsed by the others, even when drawn from the same sources.

Again, any number of Negroes also resent hearing that this and that great man were Negroes. They had been taught that they were white and hate to have their ideas changed. They much prefer to sit back in the easy chair of their own inferiority. I have several times been attacked in print or conversation because I said from the extensive documentation I have on the subject, that Christ was originally worshipped as black, or that Beethoven, according to the description of him by his contemporaries, must have been a dark mulatto. In 1919 when I was writing sketches of Negroes [such] as General Dumas, Antar,[23] Bilal, Kafur,[24] one Aframerican wrote from Germany to a Negro newspaper, saying I was talking all fable. Of course, his white professor had never told him so, ergo, it couldn't be so.

Latin America "Touchy"

In the suppression of Negro history, Latin America comes a close second to England and America. Most of the peoples of these lands are of mixed Indian, Negro and white ancestry, and sometimes very much offended at candid photos that show up their Negro strains, a fact also true of the British West Indian. Dr. Francia[25] of Paraguay, most terrible of the Latin-American dictators, had a blue-blooded Spaniard, who had once snubbed him, shot because he took him for a mulatto, which Francia probably was. Francia further decreed that white Spaniards in Paraguay should marry only Negroes and Indians. Hence most of the great Latin-Americans, including even San Martin[26] and Sucre[27] are doctored up to look like white movie stars of the technicolor.

Some Mexicans in California once protested because I said that Vicente Guerrero, liberator of Mexico and its third president, was a mulatto, my authority being Biographie Universelle, Larousse, and

Guerrero's less idealized portrait. Similar it was with what I said of Bolivar, the George Washington of South America. Now comes a distinguished authority on Latin-Americas, S.G. Inman, who says in his book, "Latin America" published in 1937, page 46, "The two most gifted men of Latin America, ranking high among the geniuses of the nineteenth century, were born in the Caribbean—Simon Bolivar of Venezuela and Ruben Dario[28] of Nicaragua. Both probably had Negro blood although it is often considered unpatriotic to say so—this, no doubt because of the desire to appear well in the eyes of the European and the North American."

If you don't want a fight on your hands don't mention "Negro" blood to the average Cuban or Porto Rican in the United States even if he is three-fourths black. He wants to be white.

In the matter of hushing up Negro ancestry, the South African is even worse. Some of the oldest and most aristocratic families of the Cape are the descendants of white men and native women, who were made "white by law" in order to clamp down more effectively the exploitation of the native blacks.

Negro ancestry will come into its own, and Negro history is the means that will bring it about. All peoples were once despised, even the English, chief despisers of the Negro. Macaulay[29] says, "In the time of Richard I, the ordinary imprecation of a Norman gentleman was, 'May I become an Englishman.' His ordinary form of indignant denial was, 'Do you take me for an Englishman?'"

From *Your History: From the Beginning of Time to the Present* (1940)

In 1934 Rogers began a weekly illustrated column, "Your History" in the Pittsburgh *Courier*. Rogers wrote the text and illustrator George L. Lee[1] (1934–40) and Samuel Malai[2] (1940 onwards) supplied the artwork. The series is perhaps the best example of his attempt to popularize African Diasporic history. Rogers had a long background in art, and he realized the importance of using illustrations in his work, particularly in such writings as *Sex and Race, World's Great Men of Color,* and *Nature Knows No Color-Line.* These images often added evidence for the points Rogers was attempting to make about the contributions of Black people (Asukile "Black International Journalism" 328). Illustrations could not only clarify his points and engage his readers, but they could help him reach an audience that sometimes lacked strong literacy skills. By utilizing a comic strip format, Rogers was able to disseminate important information about Black history to a wide audience, particularly Negro youths. The cartoons not only were a very palatable way to educate readers about Black history, but they also countered the popular racist comic strips such as Winsor McKay's *Little Nemo in Slumberland* (1905–27), featuring a Black character Jungle Imp, who was "portrayed as a cannibal who uttered nonsensical phrases" (Asukile "Black International Journalism" 333). The impact of "Your History" is demonstrated by the positive reaction to it from readers, students, teachers, and Black historians. As Frederick James Carroll writes, the column "inculcated generations of readers with an appreciation of Pan-Africanism"(66). In 1940,

Rogers collected the columns in the volume *Your History*. The name of the column was changed in 1962 to "Facts About the Negro," and it continued even after Rogers's death. A second collection of Rogers's cartoons, also called *Facts About the Negro*, was published in 1960.

From *Sex and Race: Negro-Caucasian Mixing in All Ages and All Lands* (Vol. 1, 1941; Vol. 2, 1942; Vol. 3, 1944)

The three-volume publication *Sex and Race* was Rogers's most ambitious work, examining the origins of "race" and of racial mixing. Its stories, some scandalous in detail for the time, also made it his most controversial writing. Even more controversial than the text itself was the use of sometimes "salacious" drawings and photographs of women from around the globe. However, the real objection to Rogers's work was to its findings. As he says in his "Remarks on the First Two Volumes," many readers could just not accept "that this or that noted person was, or might have been, of Negro ancestry." This was a problem Rogers faced with many of his writings, but none more so than in this work. Despite the criticisms of the book in some quarters, it had a great impact on many readers. As just one example, Malcolm X stated that it was "one of the works that opened his eyes to black people's history" (cited in Sandoval). Historian St. Clare Drake said the book showed "[s]olid scholarship combined with considerable speculation based upon photographic evidence" (98).

Rogers had conducted much of the extensive research for what would become *Sex and Race* during his years in Europe and North Africa. The book explored his long-held belief that there is no scientific basis for the concept of "race," that there has been so much sexual intermingling that it is impossible to have a "pure" race. Subsequent scientific studies have demonstrated unequivocally that there is no evidence for distinctions based on race; however, with the rise of fascism and Nazism in the 1920s and '30s, the utilization of science to justify racial discrimination was again on the rise. Rogers's knew that he had to counter these arguments. *Sex and Race* again lays out the case, with mountains of evidence and copious images, that there is no pure race, as Hitler and many pseudo-scientists argued. Rogers also maintains that none of the racial mixtures is superior to another. To Rogers, "color prejudice is not natural and is a modern phenomenon" (Peters 17).

Of all the sensational stories told in *Sex and Race*, two of the most scandalous are those of the Black Nun and Hannah Elias, dubbed the Black Cleopatra. Rogers himself sets them off as separate chapters, unlike most of the other narratives in the three volumes, and develops them at greater length. The Black Nun is the love child of Queen Maria Theresa of France and her Black servant Nabo. That he is a dwarf only adds to the intrigue. Unfortunately for the Black Nun, she is never able to gain any advantage from her royal lineage, and ends up living the rest of her life in the convent. While there are a number of accounts of the Black Nun, including ones by Voltaire and the Madame de Maintenon, her parentage cannot be definitively ascertained. Rogers also wrote of the story in chapter eight of *Nature Knows No Color-Line*.

The murder of a famous, wealthy white man (later found to be the wrong man) by a jealous Black suitor of Hannah Elias was made for tabloid fodder. It is anticipatory of the famous murder of architect Stanford White in 1906, which is alluded to in Rogers's narrative. The story of Hannah Elias, (told through the words of her former house-keeper), illustrates the inexplicable, powerful allure of interracial desire. The secrecy needed in such affairs contributes to the tragedy. Elias' obsessive desire to be white also demonstrates the madness of self-hatred over color. Elias, however, may have gotten the last laugh as it is rumored that she took her fortune to Europe accompanied by her Japanese butler, Kato (Shomari Wills *Black Fortunes*, 2019). The story has also been fictionalized in novels by Jonathan Lee, *The Great Mistake* (2021) and Barbara Chase-Riboud *The Great Mrs. Elias* (2022).

Rogers's "Remarks on the First Two Volumes of Sex and Race" is important in setting forth his research process and in voicing his frustration with "[c]ertain orthodox scholars, white and colored" who had objected to the first two volumes of the book. Their objections, he notes, are not based on the quality of his research but on the sources he has chosen. He speaks frankly about the problems he has faced as a scholar who lacks formal training and is thus denied funding and access available to mainstream scholars. He also discusses how his findings are often upsetting to many readers' set expectations of history, not wishing to discover many of their white heroes were touched with, as he would say, "the tar-brush."

In his essay at the close of Volume III, "Race, A Spiritual, Not a Scientific Problem," Rogers turns from his usual scientific argument about race. Since even a number of formally educated people practice race prejudice, he proposes that we look at the issue from a moral perspective. People should be treated equally based on our common humanity, rather than by "race." He will support anyone, regardless of their "scientific beliefs," who follows their sense of morality and treats all people equally. Moreover, he reminds members of the stronger race now that they were not always in this power position and may not be in the future. He does all this while using some of his most stirring language.

The text used for volumes I and III are from the first editions. Volume two is from the fourth edition. The three volumes have been reprinted by Wesleyan University Press (2011), not from the first editions.

VOL. 1: "THE BLACK NUN—DAUGHTER OF MARIE THERESA, QUEEN OF FRANCE"

In Titus Andronicus, Shakespeare depicts a Roman empress who had an illegitimate mulatto child.[1] Here is a true story of a Queen of France, who had one.

The affair was hushed up at the time, of course, but enough of it leaked out to make a first-class scandal. In later years it was expanded into several romantic versions. Here, however, is the story stripped of romance as told by G. Le Notre[2] of the French Academy.

Several years after the death of Marie-Theresa,[3] says Le Notre, when Louis XIV had married secretly his favorite, Madame de Maintenon,[4] a peasant, who said he was a blacksmith, appeared at the gates of Versailles and asked to see the King. The guards bade him begone but he insisted so hard that they took him to Marshal Duras, chief of the palace.

Duras, seeing the shifty looks and loutish manner of the peasant felt sure that he was an imposter, but bade him tell his story.

The man refused at first but finally stammered out a tale of a spirit he had seen, and of a message it had given him to give the King. Duras drove him away with a warning to keep his mouth shut.

A few days later, however, the King sent for Duras, and to the latter's astonishment ordered that the peasant be found and brought before him forthwith.

This was done, and the peasant told his story to the King, who at the first words turned pale and shook all over. The story was that on a certain date he was going home through the woods when he saw a very bright light. As he came nearer, he discovered that it was a woman who had on bright garments and whose face shone like the sun. This spirit, he said, revealed itself as the dead Queen, and bade him give the King a message.

Louis XIV, who was very superstitious, continued to tremble. The man concluded, "And, sire, the Queen's spirit has appeared to me again. Both times it has given me the same message. It says you must make your second marriage public."

At that a lightning change came over the King. From being frightened, he grew very angry, and lifting his stick, struck at the man. It was a trick, court intrigue, he felt. The supposed vision of this peasant was a dream he, himself, had had. Someone hearing him tell it, had told it to this peasant and sent him here with it, hoping to trick him into announcing his secret marriage.

The peasant dropped to his knees and insisted he was telling the truth. "Sire," he said, "the Queen told me that if you didn't believe me to tell you she had sent me *in the name of the Negro woman of Moret.*"

Again, the King turned pale. He bade the peasant never to mention the story to anyone and to make sure that he never would [,]sent him off to solitary confinement in the Bastille.

The preface to this strange incident, says Le Notre, went back twenty years before when the Grand Admiral of France arrived from Dahomey bringing with him a dwarf which the King of that country had sent as a present for the Queen.

The Queen, pleased with the little black, dressed him in silken robes, ornamented with precious stones, costly bracelets and arm-bands, and a magnificent turban for which Madame de Maintenon gave him an aigrette[5] of rubies, pearls, and diamonds.

Soon other ladies of the kingdom, following the Queen's example got little Negroes, too, to carry their trains and to show off the whiteness of their skins. This explains, says Le Notre, why Mignard[6] and the painters of the time included Negroes in their canvases. "It was the mode, and became a veritable frenzy among the fashionable which lasted until a misadventure befell the Queen."

When the Queen was about to become a mother again, she became strangely restless, and kept repeating:

"I no longer recognize myself. I experience strange disgusts and caprices such as never happened before. If I were to do as I wanted to, I would be cutting somersaults on the carpet, like my little Negro, and eating green fruits and living birds like him."

"Ah, Madame," replied the King, "you make me shiver. Forget your foolish fancies or you will have a child, bizarre and unnatural."

The King was only too right. When the child was born, it had a dark brown, African tint. The King recoiled in horror at the sight of it, and stamped about in rage. The Queen swore she was innocent. The doctors to pacify the King told him it was atavism, a throw-back. The King seemed about to believe this when someone unfortunately mentioned the Queen's dwarf, Nabo. "Why," said one doctor, "the color of the child might have been caused by the black man's looking at the Queen."

"A look!" exploded the King. "It must have been a very penetrating look." The King demanded the dwarf brought before him. "He is dead,

Your Majesty," said someone. The dwarf had been spirited away some time before.

The King was for having the child strangled as the fruit of adultery, and threatened the impeachment of the Queen, and the punishment of all her Spanish attendants. When he had stormed about until he was exhausted, the Queen's confessor took him aside, and assured him of the Queen's innocence. The mother, he said, had been bewitched. Evil spirits had caused the baby's color. One of the doctors assured him that it could be made white by an application of antimony.[7] The King, somewhat calmed, decided to spare its life, but said that it could not be kept in the palace. Accordingly it was sent to a convent and a notice was inserted in the Gazette de France that it had been born dead.

A first-hand account of the birth is given by the King's own cousin, Mademoiselle de Montpensier. She says:

"The Dauphin told me of the trouble they had with the illness of the Queen and the crowds that were there when the King arrived: how the Bishop of Gardes, his first almoner,[8] now Bishop of Langres, almost fainted with sorrow because the Prince and everybody laughed: that the Queen had been angry, and that the royal infant that had just been born, resembled a little Negro dwarf that M. de Beaufort had brought her from foreign lands—a little Negro that the Queen always had with her, and who was well-built for his kind of dwarf and Negro; that the child would not live and that I should not mention it to the Queen. When the Queen was a little better I went every day to the Louvre to see her. She told me that everyone had laughed at seeing the child, and the great pain their laughter had caused her."

The child lived. The King went once to the Convent of Moret to make sure that she was really alive. But she was kept a prisoner and pined for freedom and restoration to what she believed was her rank. One day, when the Dauphin (heir to the throne) was hunting in a nearby forest, and she heard who it was, she burst into tears and said from behind the bars of her cell: "It is my brother."

The Duke of St. Simon, statesman, and one of the leading figures of the King's Court, said:

"Speaking of the secrets of the King, it is necessary to make amends for something else I had forgotten. Everyone was astonished at Fontainebleau this year, to see that hardly had the princess arrived than Mme. De Maintenon took her to the little convent of Moret, where there were likely to be no amusements or persons of her acquaintance. She returned there several times, which awoke curiosity and rumors—Mme. Maintenon went often to Fontainebleau and finally one got accustomed to seeing her go there.

"In the convent was a professed nun, a Negro woman,[9] unknown to everyone and who never showed herself to anyone. Bontemps, first valet to the King and governor of Versailles, to whom I have spoken and to whom the domestic secrets are known, had placed her there quite young after paying a large sum, and a regular pension. He took great care that everything that could add to her comfort was provided. The late Queen went often to Fontainebleau to see her, and after her, Mme. De Maintenon.

"The Dauphin went there several times, and the princess and the children, and all asked for this Negro woman and treated her with kindness. She was receiving more marks of distinction than the best known or the most distinguished person there.

"It is said that she was the daughter of the King and the Queen, that her color had caused her to be hidden there, and after her disappearance, to be published that the Queen had had a miscarriage. Many of the people of the court believe this. But whatever it be, it remains a mystery."

Voltaire believed that the Black Nun was the daughter of the King by a Negro woman. Speaking of the King's children, he said, "It is believed, and with good reason, that the Nun in the convent of Moret is his daughter. She was very dark, almost black, and resembled the King. The King gave her a dot[10] of 20,000 crowns and placed her in the convent. The belief that she was of royal birth gave her a pride of which the Mother Superior complained."

Voltaire adds that he visited the convent himself and saw her. He was accompanied by M. Caumartin, treasurer of France, who, he explains, "had a right to visit the convent."

But, says Le Notre, if the Black Nun had been the illegitimate daughter of the King by a black woman, would the Queen and her children have shown so much affectionate interest in her? "Would the Queen, Marie-Theresa, the Dauphin, the Duke and the Duchess of Bourgoyne, have shown the same attachment to her? Besides, the King had other adulterine children. Furthermore, she bore the name of both the King and Queen: Louise-Marie," he says.

Touchard LaFosse, who wrote an intimate account of the reign of Louis XIV, says, "Let us record here what is generally believed about the birth of this child. Duquesne had given to the Queen a young Negro, named Nabo who was very pleasing in his manners, and amused Her Majesty in the solitude in which most of her time was passed. When this African learned to speak French, his chatter was funny, naive, and full of vivacity; he finished, it is said, by pleasing the Queen so much that all her virtue could not protect her from yielding to a weakness that the finest gentleman of Christendom would have solicited in vain.

"Nabo died suddenly, and soon afterwards, Her Majesty gave birth to a girl so black that Dr. Felix thought it his duty to say that it had been born dead. The black child was sent to the nuns of Moret, who reared it in ignorance of its origin. . . .

"How much of this story is true, I cannot say exactly, but it is positive that a young Negro lived near to the Queen, that a black girl-child was sent to Moret at the same time the Queen had a child; and that every year, Bontems, (the King's confidante), took her a large sum in gold and a necklace of coral."

The queen was much more to be pitied than blamed. Being quite plain, she was neglected by the King. The Duchess of Orleans, the King's sister-in-law, said of her:

"Her teeth were very ugly, being black and broken. It was said that this was caused by her constant eating of chocolate. She also frequently ate garlic, and was short and fat, and her skin was very white."

"No woman in the kingdom," says Des Grieux, "had more to complain about than Marie-Theresa. She was married to a despot whose egotism went as far as cruelty. . . . No man was admitted to her company and she was forced to enclose within herself the ardors of her imagination and control the fire of her Spanish temperament, whilst around her lords and ladies of the court whirled in an atmosphere of voluptuousness . . . A single servant had the privileges of coming into the Queen's room before she was out of bed; a young Negro, very short in height, but otherwise well-built. The consequence of this familiarity was that Marie-Theresa had a mulatto child."

Grave says: "The little Negro of Marie-Theresa is well known. . . . Receiving little attention from the Grand Monarch, she consoled herself with Nabo."

Victor Hugo asked: "What [is] the use of being a Queen if one cannot permit one's self to be treated familiarly by a Negro?"

According to Beaujoint, the Black Nun was honored "as one of those Black Madonnas[11] attributed to St. Luke, which performs miracles and attracts pilgrims. There is no Black Madonna that is not miraculous. The color compels it."

She figured in one of the most romantic love stories of later days. It is said that the King's nephew, the Duke of Chartres, fell violently in love with her on a visit to the convent, and spirited her away. When, however, the King refused to give his consent to the marriage, the Duke was forced to return her to the convent, where she remained until her death.

Her picture hangs in the art gallery of the Library of St. Genevieve in the Latin Quarter of Paris. It represents a black woman with bright eyes, a prominent nose, thick lips and a long chin. The lower part of the face is unmistakably Negroid. Specimens of her handwriting are preserved.

The original documents about her disappeared as mysteriously as her supposed father, Nabo. All that remains at the Library is the original cover, which bears the title: "Documents concerning The Princess Louise-Marie, daughter of Louis XIV and Marie-Theresa."

ROGERS'S NOTES

Le Notre, G., "La religieuse Noire"; Le Monde Illustré, 12 Fevier, 1898.
Beaujoint, J., "Alcoves de Reine", p. 431, Paris, 1879.

La Chatre, M., "Historie de Papes", etc.Vol. 9–10, Paris, 1842–43.
Des Grieux, "L'Amour dans tous les temps", Vol .I, p. 1432, Paris, 1888.
Lacroix, P., "Oeuvres Illustrés de Bibliophile Jacob-La Folle d'Orlèans, Vol. III, Paris, 1851–52,
Montpensier, Mlle. De, "Memoires", 1664 (Tome V, p. 118–119, Paris, 1728).
"Intermediare des Chercheurs et des Curieux," Vol. 60, pp. 684, 917, Paris, 1909.
Blumenbach, "Anthropological Treatises," p. 111. London, 1865.
St . Simon, "Memoires", Vol. I, p. 258, years 1697–81.
Touchard La Fosse, "Oeil de Boeuf," Tome II, pp. 192–193. Paris.
Boinet, Amedée, "Catalogue des Oeuvres d'Art Bibliothèque St. Genevieve", Paris.
Voltaire. Siècle de Louis XIV. Vol II. p. 186. Paris, 1784.

Note: That laughter in the Queen's chamber was possible during the birth of the Black Nun may be explained by the fact that a late as 1856, Queens of France gave birth publicly so that their subjects could see that another child wasn't being foisted on them. Should the child be born suddenly, the navel-string would have to remain uncut until the crowd was summoned. When Marie Antoinette had her first child the crowd of peasants in the room was so great that she fainted from suffocation. Madame de Campan reports, "Two savoyards got up on the furniture in order to see over everybody's head." (Memoires sur la Vie de Marie Antoinette, pp. 158–58, Paris, 1876. Intermediare des Chercheurs et des Curieux, Vol. 41, p. 761, 899.

VOL. 2: "HANNAH ELIAS, THE BLACK ENCHANTRESS, AT WHOSE FEET MILLIONS OF DOLLARS WERE POURED"

Several stories can be told of the fortunes bestowed on Negro women by their white lovers. There was the colored woman who received the deed to a fine hotel; another who was given a splendid home in the suburbs of a Northern city and now lives there with her mulatto children surrounded by every luxury; still another is one whose Negro husband was bought off by a white man whose fortune is said to run into the hundreds of millions; but the most amazing by far was Hannah Elias. She received millions and one of America's most prominent citizens was killed over her. In fact, the story would be noteworthy even without an interracial angle.

On November 13, 1903, Andrew Hassell Green,[12] multi-millionaire, white, was shot and killed in front of his Park Avenue home by Cornelius Williams, Negro, and a furnace-tender.

Green was New York's leading citizen. He had been city comptroller; had belonged to the city's leading eleven societies; had secured the $2,000,000 Tilden trust for the New York Public Library; and was the Father of the Greater New York idea. At his funeral were the governor of the state; the mayor of the city, and hundreds of the most prominent men of the nation; while the flags of the city flew half-mast. Later a monument was erected to him in Central Park.

Williams, the odd-job man, claimed that Green, the civic leader, had stolen the affections of his Negro sweetheart, Hannah Elias.

Who was Hannah Elias? New York and the nation burned to know.

District Attorney Jerome, later to become famous in the Thaw case,[13] set his forces in motion. Hannah Elias was finally discovered in a splendid mansion at 236 Central Park West, one of the choicest residential areas of the city. Neighbors questioned by the detectives said that she was one of a large staff of servants in the building, two of whom were Japanese, and the remainder white.

Entering the mansion, the detectives found it lavishly and expensively furnished. But there was something about it different from any they had ever been in before. One whole quarter of it was decorated in the style of ancient Egypt in the days of Antony and Cleopatra. Some of the servants were dressed in costumes of that period and carried the large, long-handled feather fans one sees in ancient Egyptian paintings. One bedroom was done entirely in what was believed to be like Cleopatra's with a fountain spouting scented water. The parts of the mansion done in modern style as well as the glass, and the silverware, reflected equally great wealth. Later one New York firm, Sheppard, Knapp & Company, said that it alone had sold $30,000 of the furnishings for the place. As for furs and diamonds they were there galore. Who was the owner and the employer of this large staff of white and Japanese domestics? The detectives expected to hear some great name. They had the shock of their lives to learn that it was Hannah Elias.

They were even more astonished at further developments. Not only did she own the mansion but she had two fine apartment buildings at 73 West 68th Street and 138 West 53rd Street all paid for. Still further search revealed that she had accounts in one hundred and twenty-nine banks. The total sum she had in them was not made known but it must have been millions in the money of our time. The New York Sun said that the list of banks "reads like a bank list taken from a directory."

Enterprising reporters set about discovering every possible detail about Hannah Elias, and her story as it was told in the press reads like that of the king and the beggar-maid. This woman who lived so sumptuously had come up from the depths.

The New York American reported in part, "Hannah Elias was born in Philadelphia in 1865, her mother being a Negress and her father an Indian. She was born amid scenes of squalor in the heart of the Negro quarter of the Quaker City. She was fairly well-educated at the House of Industry and at nineteen was sent out to earn her living.

"She was arrested for stealing her mistress's gown to wear to her sister's wedding and was sent to prison . . . She became an inmate of the Philadelphia Poor House . . . " She had once married a railroad porter named David by whom she had had a child.

The newspapers of the city, even the conservative New York Times, made her their feature for days. The New York American called the affair "stranger than any story told by the most lurid fiction writer." It finally discovered a white woman, who had been Hannah Elias' housekeeper, for three years, Mrs. Belle Marshall, who said she knew the inside story and was willing to tell it. She did, and gave the most intimate account published.

Hannah Elias, she said, had been given vast sums of money by white men and had the notion that she was "a sort of Cleopatra. Where she ever got the Cleopatra idea is hard to understand but the fact that her hold over white men caused them to give her unlimited supplies of money probably furnished the basis for the notion," she said.

Mrs. Marshall added that Hannah Elias had almost no education.[14] "She could read after a fashion, but she couldn't read with anything of facility literature that was above the dime novel standard, and consequently she was always having some one read to her things about the enslaver of Mark Anthony [*sic*]. She carried her notion into an imitation that was as near the original as she could figure it out.

"She had a scented fountain in her room, and used to make her servants dress in Egyptian costumes and stand about her fanning her with a huge feather duster that she had bought in a Japanese place downtown.

"This bit of by-play used to amuse her wonderfully. She really hadn't many ways of entertaining herself, notwithstanding her vast fortune, for she couldn't go out into the street without having her feelings hurt."

Hannah Elias, she continues, tried to delude herself into the belief that she wasn't colored. She called herself Spanish and had no Negroes around her, not even her daughter, Clara—but only white people and Japanese. The Japanese were in imitation of the craze of white American society to have Oriental servants.

Mrs. Marshall added, "The one thing that caused her to grow hysterical with rage was to have someone take her for a Negress. In order to prevent things of this sort she rarely went into the street and when she did she travelled in a closed carriage. She never went into the big stores and even had a complete dental outfit in her house, chair and all, in order to avoid going to the dentist's. She never went into a theatre, although she was strangely fond of the drama of a certain sort, but she denied herself this simple pleasure through fear of having someone recognize her as a mulatto.

"She paid $200 for the pompadour wig she wears. Under that wig was a mass of hair as kinky as any ever seen upon the head of a Negress. She would have paid any amount of money to have straightened out the kinks in her wool, and did pay an enormous amount to a man who said that he could change her color to white. Once when a boy went past the house singing:

"Coon, coon, coon. Ah wish mah color could fade,"[15] she almost had a spasm of rage. That song hurt her more than anything else.

"The man that offered to bleach her was a wonder. She paid him $100 a day for two months and had to wear a mask all that time. At the end of that time the mask came off and she was just the same mulatto. She was wild with rage that time: the doctor had the money and there was no way of getting it back."

Later Hannah Elias, did say that one white doctor had bled her of $103,000.

Mrs. Marshall adds, "Hannah Elias hated white women in a way that gave her great satisfaction in employing them in the house in order to humiliate them. I have seen her hire white girls, and after a few days call them to her and dress them up in fine clothes and hang jewelry all over them. She would then tell them that the clothes and the gems were theirs and tell them to go home to their folks and show them what she had done for them. But at the door Kate would catch them and strip off the clothes and the jewelry, while she listened, convulsed with laugher, at their cries of rage.

"She was always buying books of etiquette, but never had any chance to use them. It was better than any monkey dinner that was ever pulled off to see her eat at home and attempt to follow out all the instructions in the books. Frequently she would have all her servants dine with her, making them dress for the occasion. Then she would have a dinner that was as formal as a Newport affair[16] for an hour or so. Then the liquor having circulated freely, the function would degenerate into an orgy not pleasant to describe."

Hannah Elias, amid all her luxury had a yearning for the days when she lived on humble fare. As a contrast to the sumptuous meals, says Mrs. Marshall, "were the tin-pail meals she used to eat. Every little while she would send one of her servants down to the section in which she used to live with a tin pail to buy her a mess of 'possum stew or fried fish such as she was accustomed to in the days when she kept a boarding house. This she used to eat out of the pail in a total forgetfulness of the book of etiquette.

"She had a library full of books, but never read them. She used to read dime novels and detective tales and was always fancying herself the heroine of some of the yarns she read. Once when an Italian professor tried to get her to marry him, she fancied that he was trying to lure her to Italy and kill her in a dungeon there. When he was last seen he was making long jumps and running fast."

Hannah Elias she adds, was a good dancer especially after she had imbibed her favorite drink—just plain what was known as 'nigger-gin.' Then she would "entertain all the servants doing buck-and-wing dances[17] and jigs. She was one of the best Negro dancers I ever saw. There are few on the stage who can equal her."

Her favorite servant was her Japanese butler, Kato. "He was employed about the time Hannah Elias moved in. She had a Japanese craze at that time, and had thirty-five of them in the place. Finally she picked out Kato and let the others go."

She gave Kato plenty of money, said Mrs. Marshall. "She bought him all sorts of clothes and on one occasion gave him $10,000 worth of diamonds. She also gave him money enough to go to the Paris Exposition[18] and furnished him with a valet."

In addition, she had a cottage at Rockaway where in the summer she posed as a Spanish woman of great wealth.

From time to time Hannah Elias would steal away from her rich surroundings and mix with her old underworld friends. Though no Negro, not even her own dark-skinned daughter, was permitted in her home, she seemed to have helped other Negroes and poor whites as well. The New York Sun said, "The Elias woman had a large number of hangers-on who lived in more or less comfort on the bounty squeezed out of wealthy victims. The company included Japanese, Negresses, Negro men and prize-fighters, black and white."

But as to who were the white men who gave her money no one could say. Mrs. Marshall did give one name but nobody had ever heard of him.

Was Andrew H. Green, the highly respected socialite and church member among them? At the hearing Cornelius Williams, the slayer, swore that Green was the man who had stolen the affections of his old sweetheart and placed her in surroundings where he could no longer reach her. He said that he had seen Green at the boarding-house Mrs. Elias once kept, that she had told him Green had given her $250, and had once invited him to take a peek at "the Old Fogey," as she used to call Green. Soon afterwards, he said, Green had taken her away. Then for years he had searched for her. Finally he found her and that she told him that "Green would pay her lawyers, and take care of her suit if I began one, and it made me mad to think that a man like Andrew H. Green was shielding her. I resolved that he should tell me where she was." The New York Sun said, "Before the Elias woman accumulated her crew of rich white men, Williams believed he was her lover."

The mystery continued for the next several months. Then it broke. On June 1, 1904, the New York dailies carried headlines that ex-Senator John R. Platt,[19] millionaire glass manufacturer, retired, member of an old New York family, had brought suit in the Supreme Court against Hannah Elias to recover the sum of $685,385, his money, which Hannah Elias had squandered between the years 1896 and 1904. In the suit Platt submitted a bill of details with the various sums and the dates handed over.

Platt, he was then eighty-four, said he had first met Hannah Elias in 1888, or sixteen years before. And the way in which he had met her was as sordid as it was singular.

He said that as president of the New York Volunteer firemen—a high honor in those days—he had received a delegation of visiting firemen from California. He had taken them one night to see the sights of the town and in the early morning they had wound up in an establishment of Negro women—a "coon joint" as it was called—kept by a Negro woman.

Among the girls in the place was Hannah Elias. He went with her and several times afterwards. Then he lost track of her.

Nine years passed. Then one day he read an advertisement in a newspaper "telling of a certain person on Third Avenue who could cure rheumatism by massage." He answered the ad in person, and lo, the advertiser was no other than the long-lost Hannah Elias.

She gave him a "massage" then. It did him so much good that he returned again and again, and finally loosened up to the tune of $685,000 or several million dollars in the money of the present time.

Later he was forced to admit on the stand that the massage was of a quite special nature and that the relations were "somewhat tenderer than those between a massage artist and a patient."

Platt's first outburst of gratitude to his masseuse had taken the shape of a boarding-house, then diamonds and furs, and two other buildings, one of them the Central Park mansion. Platt said that when he had met her again in January 1896, "she had pretended to be enamored of him and had assured him that he had completely won her affections and was her only true friend on earth." Believing it at the time, he said he had "assumed intimate relations with her." Since then, he charged, she had blackmailed him. "She was a colored woman," he said, "and I was afraid that unless I gave her said sums of money she would expose my relations with her and I feared the disgrace of such exposure."

Hannah Elias denied all. She declared that Platt used to throw money at her feet and beg her to take it. Platt had been friendly with her up to the time of the Green shooting which had brought the police in. Her lawyer said, "Old Man Platt came to the house regularly and fairly showered her with money. All the talk about her scaring money out of him is false. She didn't have to. He was a fool about her and he is yet. I doubt if he can face her now and say she blackmailed him for I believe he is still under her control if he is in her presence."

To the charge of squandering, Platt now added the more serious one of blackmail. However, it seems that he was egged on by his relatives and District Attorney Jerome, who it is said was trying to make political capital out of the case. In fact, Platt was a most unwilling accuser. Twice he refused to sign the indictment.

When the police came for Mrs. Elias she locked herself in, and the police battered in the doors and took her away, while vast crowds gathered before the mansion and sold pictures of her, Platt and Green.

The case came up for a hearing before Magistrate Ommen.[20] The aged Platt, a pitiful figure, took the stand. When asked whether he had signed a complaint against Hannah Elias, he said, "No," then added, "Ask my lawyer." Asked also whether he had signed the indictment, he said, "I don't remember." He stammered and contradicted himself until the trial developed into a comedy, and the prosecutor was forced to ask for a dismissal. Mrs. Elias was never even called to the stand. She left the court with all her money and property intact, while Platt was hooted by the crowd.

[Rogers's Note:] Close-up descriptions of Hannah Elias appeared in most of the papers. The N. Y. American (June 8, 1904) said, "That she ever passed for a Cuban or a Spaniard was inconceivable. The woman who stood outside the railing in Magistrate Ommen's court yesterday gave no evidence of possessing beauty or attractiveness. She looked every day of the thirty-nine years she confessed to.

"Short and stout and even dumpy, she possessed nothing more of a figure than a badly-made sofa cushion . . . That she was not an octoroon or even a quadroon was plainly evident yesterday when she stood in the light from the large windows of the courtroom. She is darker than a mulatto and her features are a strange blend of Negro and Indian."

Nevertheless, judging by her early pictures, she must have been attractive.

Were there other rich men who had given Hannah Elias money? All we have on this subject are unsupported statements. A veil of secrecy fell over the affair it seems by the consent of both sides soon after the hearing. One prominent Broadway lawyer was named in the press however, and J. Frank Wheaton, who took up the case on behalf of the Negroes of New York claimed that he had the names of three others, "one of the most prominent citizens of the city, now dead; a politician, whose standing is of a sort to make the exposure a national scandal; and a merchant who holds a leading position in this city, all millionaires." Their names are not given in the article.

Hannah Elias had one child living with her in the Central Park West mansion, Gwendolyn Toyo Elias, born October 15, 1902. It had been registered as white and the father as Platt. But gossip said that the real father was the Japanese butler.

As for the shooting, it was said to be [a] case of mistaken identity. Platt was said to resemble Green and to have had a relative by that name who lived next door to the slain man. Jerome was censured in the press and elsewhere for what was regarded by many as persecution of Mrs. Elias. Among the Negroes the case was discussed for a long time. One of the latter remarked, "How many are the Hannah Eliases and the Senator Platts who have never come into the courts?"

In November, 1906, the New York Supreme Court confirmed Hannah Elias' title to all the property. (N. Y. Evening Journal, November 21, 1906).

VOL. 3: FROM "REMARKS ON THE FIRST TWO VOLUMES OF SEX AND RACE"

"*Our race is essentially slavish; it is the nature of all of us to believe blindly in what we love, rather than that which is most wise. We are inclined to look upon an honest, unshrinking pursuit of truth as something irreverent. We are indignant when others pry into our idols and criticize them with impunity, just as a savage flies to arms when a missionary picks his fetish to pieces . . .* " Galton.[21]

Certain orthodox scholars, white and colored, have not liked the history as given in the two preceding volumes of "Sex and Race," as well as in my earlier books. One English editor after reading the "100 Amazing Facts About the Negro," wrote me that it made him feel as if the white race had never accomplished anything. Others said that I claim everybody who has ever done anything as Negro, nevertheless, I had never said, or dreamed of saying, that Homer, or Pericles, or Aeschylus, or Julius Caesar, or Alfred the Great, Shakespeare, Milton, Michael Angelo, Bach, Handel, Wagner, Washington, Lincoln,[22] Edison, Franklin D. Roosevelt, Einstein, or thousands of other noted white men were of Negro ancestry; nor did I attribute to Negroes any role of any importance in Europe, itself, from say the sixteenth century onwards. Yet because I maintain a few individuals, whom they had all along believed to be of unmixed white strain, I have been called "fantastic" and "credulous!"

And I have been ridiculed not on the result of research, not on examination of the sources which I have given abundantly, but on sheer belief. These scholars did not happen to run across such facts in their reading, in a word, the research I had done was off the beaten track of the college curriculum, therefore, it did not exist.

Perhaps I exaggerate, perhaps I am really being fantastic when I say this of the orthodox scholars, well, I shall give a not uncommon illustration and let the reader judge for himself.

In 1943, Gunnar Myrdal, noted economist of the University of Stockholm, Sweden, aided by 75 experts, working for five years, completed for the Carnegie Corporation at a cost of $209,000, a work on the race problem entitled "An American Dilemma"[23] and published by Harper and Brothers. On page 1393 of this book (1st ed.) I am listed as an example of those who write "pseudo-history, fantastically glorifying the achievements of Negroes."

On what grounds was this judgment arrived at? On anything I had written? No, I was judged on a non-existent book—a book that no mortal could ever have seen.

Here are the facts: In 1927, I finished a manuscript entitled "This Mongrel World, A Study of Negro-Caucasian Mixing In All Ages and All Countries." At about that time I was asked to fill out a blank for "Who's Who in Colored America," and intending to publish the manuscript soon I listed it as being published. However, circumstances prevented my doing so. Thirteen years later, due to the much greater research I had done on the subject, I changed the title to "Sex and Race." Parts of the manuscript I used in Volumes One and Two of that work and discarded most of the rest. In short, when "An American Dilemma" was published not even the manuscript of "This Mongrel World" existed. Nevertheless this *non-existent manuscript* is listed as a *published book* in Myrdal's bibliography. What had happened? In reading through my biographical sketch in "Who's Who in Colored America," Myrdal, or some of his assistants, saw the title and on that alone condemned me. Not a word was said of any of my published books. They probably didn't take the trouble to look into any of them.

Now what is the difference between an attitude of this sort and that of any uneducated man, or any bigot, who would similarly condemn Myrdal's work, or that of any other scientist in such off-hand manner? So far as I am concerned, none whatever.

Furthermore, though I have no philanthropist or foundation, or staff of experts behind me, I go to as great pains as any of the most conscientious of these experts to get my facts straight, checking and re-checking, and travelling hither and yon to see with my own eyes whenever possible what I am writing about; and quoting only from the original sources and from those I have reason to believe are the most reliable. One can do no more. Of course, there will always be errors, but when seventy-six experts, working with unlimited funds as in "An American Dilemma," make errors surely a lone worker, like myself, might be forgiven a few.

Another reason why some object to the facts as given in my books is that they feel that their own learning is being impeached. If such facts were true, why, they certainly would have known them. One able Negro musician, who had a fine education in England, admitted to me later that when he heard me say for the first time that Beethoven was colored, he was "offended." Had he not long been acquainted with Beethoven?[24]

In 1930 while I was carrying in the Negro press a series of articles on great Negroes, an Aframerican, studying in Germany, and now a college professor, wrote the Pittsburgh Courier, leading Negro weekly, that my stories were dubious even though I had included Bilal, Dumas, Pushkin, General Dodds, Chevalier de St. George, Henri Diaz,[25] and others who are very plainly mentioned in biographies as being of Negro ancestry. The simple truth is that he didn't know the first thing of the true ancestry of these individuals but never having heard it, why, that alone made what I said false. As for my statement that the Virgin Mary and Christ were once worshipped as black and that at the present time pilgrimages are made to the shrines of the Black Virgins in France, Spain and even in Germany, that seemed a veritable Munchausen tale.[26] One Negro columnist, a Catholic, actually resented the idea that the Madonna could have been black. Had he not all his life seen her depicted as white?

Still another reason for their rejecting my researches is that they didn't want the present knowledge in their brains disturbed. They had been taught that the Negro's position in history had been that of a slave and it was much more pleasant to go on believing that than to investigate.

Race prejudice is responsible too, in part. There are those who at the merest mention that this or that noted person was, or might have been, of Negro ancestry, at once set their backs up like an angry cat. So racial are such people that when one attributes Negro ancestry even to an ancient Greek or Egyptian it is "social equality"—a lowering of their own personal dignity. One white woman angrily resented the idea that Alexander Dumas, the great novelist, could possibly have been of Negro ancestry.

The classic example of this sort, however, is Mary Preston,[27] a Southern white woman, whose readings on Shakespeare were popular in her day. Miss Preston twisted "Othello" to suit herself. While admitting that Shakespeare did make Othello "black," that was positively not what Shakespeare meant so far as she was concerned. She said (italics hers): "In studying the play "Othello" I have always *imagined* its hero a *white man*. It is true the dramatist paints him black, but this shade does not suit the man. It is a stage decoration which my *taste* discards; a fault of color from an artistic point of view. I have, therefore, as I believe stated in my *readings* of this play, dispensed with it. Shakespeare was too correct a delineator of human nature to have colored Othello *black* if he had personally acquainted himself with the idiosyncrasies of the African race. We may regard, then, the daub of black upon Othello's portrait as an *ebullition* of fancy, a *freak* of imagination—the visionary concept of an ideal figure . . . Othello *was a white man*."*

Wherein we ask does such an attitude differ from that of any blind believer in revealed religion?

Of course this attitude is hugely amusing. It is one of a piece, too, with the feeling of certain Gentiles when they take up a book on Jewish biography and see for the first time that this or that great pioneer, scientist, or soldier whom they had all along fancied to be non-Jewish was a Jew.

The result of this attitude toward "Negro" history is that the better-known historians, sociologists, and anthropologists, with few exceptions, have been great claimers of Negroid peoples as white. The idea has been to maintain white supremacy. Pick up any national or world history and you'll find even the Ethiopians, who such early writers as Xenophanes,[28] Aristotle, Herodotus and Strabo,[29] tell us were black and wooly-haired, that is, the type now called Negro are white. They still say the Ethiopians are white though they are uniformly blacker and more wooly-haired than the American Negroes.

Whenever, too, Negroes are mentioned as having appeared anywhere, whether in prehistoric America, the Caucasus, or Albania, they are invariably spoken of as "slaves." For instance, Ignatius Donnelly[30] in trying to prove that the so-called New World was known to the people of the Old reproduces from the ancient Mexican monuments certain portraits of Negroes which he calls "idols."** But in the same breath he says they were "slaves" who "were brought to America at a very remote epoch." (Please note the contradiction "slaves" who were "idols!") His reason for saying they were slaves is that "Negroes have never been a sea-going race," for which statement he hasn't a shred of evidence. Of course, the "slave" had to be brought in to square with white imperialism and the exploitation of the darker peoples even though what he mentions occurred in prehistoric times. The Negro must always be marked down so that his labor can be had in the cheapest market.

The motive for this twisting of history is that white imperialism must be shown as being of old, aristocratic ancestry. This imperialism was built upon the backs of the darker races. A noted example was the British empire, of whose 500,000,000 people, eighty percent are colored. Now some of these colored people as the Ethiopians, Egyptians, East Indians, and Moors were the originators of Western civilization; they were highly civilized when the Europeans were savages***—a fact that cannot be denied as long as the works of Julius Caesar and Tacitus[31] exist. But it would never do to show that the lord and master once had very humble beginnings as it must be shown that the originators of civilization were white—that the white has always been on top. Therefore, for the purpose of adding lustre to white imperialism, the Ethiopians, Egyptians and the others are called "white" but for the purposes of profit they are treated as colored. Thus the white imperialist eats his cake and has it too.

It is a blow to the pride of certain white Americans, Englishmen, and Germans to hear it said that persons and individuals they had all along fondly believed to be "pure" white were not so. Because I said on the testimony of white people who knew Beethoven, as well as on the reports of his ancestry by German scholars, that he showed evidence of Negro strain, I have received letters as cross as if I had attacked the writers themselves.

Any talk of Negro progress angers many. If the blacks advance who will they have to be better than? There will go their splendid isolation of fancied superiority. Even worse, they already see themselves losing out, a state of mind expressed by Bacon when he said, "Men of noble birth are noted to be envious towards new men when they arise for the distance between them is altered and it is like a deceit of the eye that when others come on they think themselves go back."[32]

So thorough has been the penetration of white imperialist propaganda that only a small percentage of the white or the colored in any part of Western civilization today have any idea that any other than white people had a hand in the originating of civilization. Although I had been an omnivorous reader from my earliest years I was well past twenty before it began to dawn upon me that the darker peoples could have had a part in it. Even now I can recall my astonishment when this occurred to me.

Even as the white manufacturers have bleached out our salt, sugar, flour, so the white historian has bleached out world history. The dark or mineral portion has been rejected. Of course this process has produced a product beautifully pleasing to the eyes of those who have been psychologized to admire it, but which, nevertheless, is constipative and harmful to both the physical and the mental digestion.

But as there are those who, realizing the value of the minerals that have been rejected from our foods, have placed them in again, thereby increasing the health value, as say how bran has been restored to the bleached, starved-out white bread, so in like manner I have attempted to gather up the Negro, or dark, rejected portion of history in the hope that some day they will be restored to world history, thereby permitting a less clogging effect on the mind.

Such being my purpose I do not ever claim that I am writing world or national history. Call it the bran of history if you will. As for those who will regard this "bran" as proving that the white race has never accomplished anything and that the Negro did everything, I can do nothing about it.

I can say, in addition, that I dislike too much the whitening of history, I have too great a loathing for racial propaganda, ever knowingly to indulge in it. Moreover, the facts I have given have been culled nearly always from white writers, some of them very ancient, who related facts as they saw them, and who did not worship at the shrine of white imperialism, or did not think of the effect of what they said would have in later years.

To get those little known facts I have travelled tens of thousands of miles in many lands; consulted books and printed matter so vast in number that were I to try to say how many I would sound like a Munchausen; visited the leading museums of many of the civilized lands, and engaged in research in their libraries and ever going to great pains to get my facts as humanly correct as possible. In short, I felt I have looked into books and dug up buried knowledge that many college professors or doctors of philosophy do not know exist because just as there is a life in the deeper depths of the ocean of which the average fisherman knows nothing so there are depths in the ocean of research of which some of the most learned have never dreamed. For instance, it is estimated that in the National Library of France alone there are 8,000,000 books and pieces of printed matter. How much does the most educated man now alive know of the totality of knowledge in these books? Very, very little. One is ever learning. Truly, as Sir Isaac Newton once said as he looked out on the ocean that there he was picking up pebbles on the beach as it were while the vast ocean of unexplored knowledge lay before him.[33]

Those who will forget their orthodoxy for a while and read my books might not find them so fantastic after all. And even should they reject them they might still profit to the extent of knowing the arguments on the other side and thus be able to refute them, not by denunciation, but in a manner more compatible with common sense

ROGERS'S NOTES

* Studies in Shakespeare, p. 71, 1869. Apropos of this a noted psychoanalyst once objected to my saying during a discussion period that when Shakespeare said, "Black men are pearls in beauteous ladies [*sic*] eyes," he actually meant black men. No, he said, there were no Negroes in England in Shakespeare's time, and he was positive about it. I informed him that there was not only Negro slavery in England at the time but that G. B. Harrison, an Elizabethan authority, thinks that Shakespeare himself, had a Negro sweetheart. (For sources see Sex and Race, Vol., 1, p. 201, 1941, and Vol. II, p. 400). [The quotation is from *Two Gentlemen of Verona*, Act V, Scene II].

** Donnelly, I. Atlantis, pp. 174–5. 1882.

*** Julian Huxley and A. C. Haddon say, "It is asserted vociferously in certain quarters that the Nordic 'race' is gifted above all others with initiative and originality and that the great advances in civilization have been due to Nordic genius.

"What are the facts? The fundamental discoveries on which civilization is built are the art of writing, agriculture, the wheel and building in stone. All these appear to have originated in the Near East, among peoples who by no stretch of the imagination could be called Nordic or presumed to have but the faintest admixture of Nordic or proto-Nordic genes" (We, Europeans, p. 94, 1935).

VOL. 3: "RACE, A SPIRITUAL, NOT A SCIENTIFIC PROBLEM"

> *"As a people striving to shape our actions in accordance with the great law of righteousness we cannot afford to take part in or be indifferent to the oppression or maltreatment of any man who, against crushing disadvantages, has by his own industry, energy, self-respect and perseverance struggled upward to a position which would entitle him to the respect of his fellows, if only his skin were of a different hue."*
>
> —THEODORE ROOSEVELT.[34]

The so-called science of race is founded on "racial" differences but since difference is the most obvious thing in Nature and since every individual on the planet differs from every other not only in looks but in psychology racial science can be but *academic*; at best a matter to enliven one's interest regarding his fellow-man. The simple truth is that most of this "science" of race is mere exercise for the pen and the jaw, not to mention boondoggling by scholars who are thereby enabled to get handouts from philanthropists, who had squeezed the money from laboring people. If these superficial differences, called race, did not exist, says Bonger,[35] "The countless laymen and amateurs who now get so excited over race problems would hardly give them any attention."

Is this an argument against the study of so-called racial differences? Not at all. Everything on the planet should be studied and explored. But the trouble began when the anthropologists began to talk of inferior and superior races, when numbers of them sold out to the exploiters of humanity. In fact, the trouble went even deeper because as soon as one begins to talk about superior and inferior qualities whether inside or outside a "race," there are always those inferior creatures—creatures who can only feel themselves big by looking down on others, who will pick up these so-called superior attributes and apply them to themselves. Even some of the great scientists have this inferiority complex as the late Henry Fairfield Osborn, director of the American Museum of Natural History, or Ales Hrdlicka,[36] of the Smithsonian Institution, or Professor Charles Richet, Nobel Prize Winner.[37] In botany and mineralogy, these men would have been real and impartial scientists but the moment "race" entered they were led by their feelings and began to think in terms of inferior and superior with the result that in this respect they sank to the level of the ignorant, race-prejudiced man on the street.

I have therefore, decided, after more than forty years of study and reading on the subject that "race" is ethical and spiritual, not scientific. Arguments in favor of racial inequality are capitalistic and as I am absolutely opposed to the exploitation of human beings, no matter how unlike to myself in appearance or point of view, I, therefore favor those who stand for racial equality even when they are academically incorrect, and oppose those who favor racist inequality even when they are academically correct.

"Inferiority" or "superiority" has nothing whatever to do with the question. My dog is hopelessly, immutably inferior to me in nearly every respect, should I on that account give it less than one hundred percent kind treatment?

Though I value as much as any other the good things of civilization I cannot lose sight of the fact that in its present workings, it is more destructive than constructive. The more advanced nations are like a horde of wolves in the chase, the members of which will immediately stop to rend and eat any of the pack that shows signs of weakening—cold, heartless, cruel, grasping.

What deluges of woe has [*sic*] not the leading nations visited upon the darker peoples of the world? What mountains of crime and cruelty mark their footsteps over the earth! The Indian exterminated or herded into cramped corners: the Maori relentlessly butchered; the Australian and Tasmanian blacks killed wholesale like flies with strychnine; India scourged and plundered in the name of a Christian God; China cheated and forced to poison herself with opium; the Eskimo pilfered from; Africa, hospitable Africa, robbed, raped, maimed, her children killed for sport or strewn alive on the bosom of the Atlantic—food for sharks. Brutality, Brutality, unrealizable Brutality! For every ounce of good that the white man's religion or culture has done for the darker races it has exacted a ton of agony. If blood be the price of Culture, Lord God, they have paid in full.

"How the European has been able to establish Colonies," says Nietzsche "is explained by his nature which is that of a beast of prey."

To summarize my conclusions regarding race mixture: Race mixture makes for change and change is inevitable, unpreventable. Whether change in any form—race-mixing, politics, religion, diet—is good or bad depends on those who experience it. Some will welcome it; others will hate it. Some who welcomed it will in time hate it; and some who hated it will in time like it. But as to whether it is good or bad in a universal sense no one knows. Perhaps it is, as Nietzsche says, beyond good and evil.[38]

Man, we are told, evolved from seaweed, a most likely theory. The power of change was great enough to bring him from that state to this.

What proof have we that change has lost its potency? Beside such a feat as evolution, race-mixture as a form of change is hardly worthy of mention.

Thus I am not interested in whether race mixture is good or bad, whether mixed peoples are superior or inferior to unmixed ones. What I am interested in is that minds will become so enlightened that race-mixture as a form of change may be able to operate on the highest ethical and spiritual lines even when it appears disadvantageous to racial and national prestige.

The developed, if it is to survive, must be reinforced perpetually by the undeveloped, therefore, inasmuch as cultures have their period of birth, development, decline and death like the individuals of which they are composed, it would be no more desirable to have the whole world highly civilized at the same time than it would be to have all the land under cultivation, all the villages swarming with skyscrapers, all the ore in use, or every individual with a brain developed to its limit. In short, the underdeveloped peoples, like any other natural resource, are but Nature's reserve—her balance in the bank.

Hence they should not be despised.

There is no individual or aggregation of individuals but were once in a state as infantile and primitive as the lowest now, just as the world's champion pugilist was at one period of his existence so feeble that an aged grandmother could have whipped him.

Patience and kindness should mark all dealing with these primitive peoples. It should be remembered that if there is a law of progress in the universe there is also a law of retardation. It should never be forgotten that Nature seems purposely to create conditions to keep some peoples back until their time shall have come. To some peoples, as to some individuals, she has given too much, and they have accomplished little, as the Tahitians; to others like the Eskimo, she has given too little, and they also, have accomplished little.

Of those who oppose race-mixture, I ask: What about the principle of exogamy, or marriage and sexual union outside the tribe or race that has always gone on, as well as what about the almost universal objection to the intermarriage or to sexual unions between near relations. Similarly, to those who say that race-mixing is better than no mixture I will ask what about the people of endogamy or marriage within the tribe or race, which has always gone on and is the stronger of the two, locally.

Scientific argument in favor of race-mixing or against it is but a development of these two natural laws, which have existed ever since we were in a savage state. Scientific argument in favor of race prejudice, as that made by Elliott Smith,[39] is but a development of the endogamic principle, plus a desire on the part of such scientists to look out for their own interests by standing in with the ruling class. As to our Gobineaus,[40] Stoddards, Hoffmans,[41] and Madison Grants, if we were to trace their type back spiritually a few thousand years we would find that the sole difference between it then and now is the additional information it has gathered on the subject. In essence, however, it has remained unchanged by time or the advance of knowledge, and probably cannot change. In other words you'll find these scientists in embryo among the most primitive peoples. It is the human will, not knowledge, with which we are dealing.

Stronger peoples have always forced weaker ones to yield them their labor and their sex at the lowest possible price. Meanwhile they boast of their alleged superior stock. Since the economic is thus used to dominate the biologic, how is it possible ever to get an unbiased evaluation of race-mixture? Thus it should no longer be outlawed and forced down into the gutter, but be permitted to move on a higher plane. The individual must be free to marry where he will, inside or outside his "race" and entirely to the dictates of his or her heart.

Miscegenation is perhaps but a creator of variety, serving as a distributor throughout humanity of those traits acquired by the different races in their respective environments—traits which it disseminates with as great a disregard of our changing economic values as a linotype machine distributes type. There is so far no proof that race-blending produces either inferior or superior offspring. This would mean in both the cases that the parents [*sic*] stocks were inferior. Are the proponents of the theory that race-mixing produces superior children prepared to argue that from two inferior sources one can get a superior product. Of course, there were such mixed-bloods as General Dumas, Frederick Douglass, Booker T. Washington and scores of others who were much superior to both their white fathers and black mothers but probably a greater number could be cited who rose no higher than the lower of these two parents. Couples, regardless of color, often have children inferior to themselves. Great fathers rarely have great sons.

There are two facts about race-mixing that seem certain: It permits the survival of the white man (in a modified form) in lands with too much sunlight; and it serves for the multiplication of the species in that it is for some a natural aphrodisiac—a sexual excitant—for individuals sated with mates of their own race. It would be interesting to learn the percentage of adventurers who are lured to foreign lands by prospects of association with native women. Advertisers for sailors and soldiers to go abroad are not unaware of this.

Given two persons, one white, the other colored, both of equal capabilities, then, as conditions are in America, marriage would ordinarily be to the social and economic disadvantage of the white. If opposers of intermarriage held to this ground their arguments would be valid, but as this sounds commercial, a moral coating is applied and such ideologies as patriotism, white superiority, truth, good citizenship, purity of the home and womanhood are dragged in. The halls of Congress have resounded to[o] much of this.

One who has visualized the flow and reflow of the mixing of white and black through the ages, will find it a perfectly natural process, and one that will go on. Here are two examples that certainly cannot be set down to accident or co-incidence: the coming in of the fairer-skinned Romans and Greeks to mate with Negroes in Egypt at the time when Egypt had become much more black than white; and the importation of the Negro to the New World, there to predominate in the tropical regions and to mix in with the white.

As for those who advocate intermarriage as a solution of the race problem they are not so broadminded as they think. At least this is too much of a concession to color prejudice. Intermixture means a change of racial type and why in a democracy should it be necessary to change one's color in order to get one's rights?

In other ways, too, the race question is so ridiculous that it makes one look silly even to take notice of it. For instance, even as the elephant is afraid of the mouse we find in America that nine-tenths of the nation with the army, the navy, the political machinery, and nearly all the wealth gives the appearance of being afraid of the feeble one-tenth, the Negro.

We are told, too, that white blood is superior, but in the same breath informed that one "drop" of Negro" blood makes a white man a Negro, which is equivalent to saying that if a citizen has ninety-nine white ancestors and one black, that one drop cancels all that the whites have contributed. Compare that with the Arabs who say that one drop of Arab "blood" makes one an Arab.

While every group has a perfect right to keep to itself if it so decides and to say with whom it will or will not marry, yet the instant it enters the life of another group, so surely does it forfeit that right, and the other group has a right reciprocally to interfere. It is indisputable that in the beginning the black man wished no association whatever with the white, and that the white has forced his company upon him even to the extent of bringing him to America. If the white man will not leave the Negro alone, but wishes to mix with him, the Negro has a perfect right, that is, if there is to be any justice, to say also under what conditions such mixing shall take place.

As for anthropological research while I am strongly in favor of it, I do not think that scientific pronouncements are going to help the race question much except in so far as they can be used to influence religious and ethical bodies, labor unions and other organizations, because, it its final analysis, the race question is not scientific, but highly sentimental. And I do not believe it will ever be otherwise because our dealings with others, regardless of race, are too highly charged with likes and dislikes.

To illustrate: The parts of the world in which the race question is most aggravated at the present time are the southern United States and South Africa. Suppose, by way of the impossible, all the students of race were to agree that the Negroes of both regions were superior in every way to the whites, would that alter conditions? I firmly believe it would not make the slightest difference because it is not "race" so much that is involved as vested interests in the labor of the blacks. These vested interests use all their propaganda to keep "race" alive, tempering it, of course, so that the stronger group will not directly attack the exploited group and thus endanger profits.

Therefore Science, like true religion, must come squarely out in favor of the under-dog. It must hammer in, without ceasing, the thought that there is but one race—the human race. It must realize that all its measurements, averages and statistics on "race," even if they were not so self-contradictory, touch only the outskirts of the question because what *might* be true of any group—Slavs, Jews, Negroes, Indians, Caucasians, Mongolians, Eskimos—as regards mentality, intellect, character, height, weight, skull, etc. *is never, never true of the individual members of those groups*. Why not even two peas in the same pod are alike.

It is the individual and his treatment we must never lose sight of.

If the science of "race" is to serve for the betterment of mankind it must ever be inspired by the cool head and the warm heart. Especially the latter. A kind, unselfish deed by the member of one racial group to another will often have a greater effect for good than a whole library of scientific books. Kindness will succeed where formal learning, however great, will often fail. Schopenhauer did not pay it too high a tribute when he said, "As torches and fireworks become pale and insignificant in the presence of the sun so intellect, nay genius and also beauty are outshone and eclipsed by goodness of the heart. Even the most limited understanding and also grotesque ugliness, whenever extraordinary goodness of heart declares itself as accompanying them, become, as it were, transfigured, outshone by beauty of a higher kind, for now wisdom must be dumb. For goodness of heart is a transcendent quality; it belongs to an order of things that reaches beyond this world and is incommensurable with any other perfection."

On the other hand, the most dangerous, the most pernicious and heartless thing in the world is intellect unaccompanied by high morality. This is the lesson the Nazis have taught the world to its bitter cost.

Happily, recent years have seen a change for the better. Anthropology is returning to the noble foundation laid by Blumenbach and Lamarck.[42] We are having an increasing number of these students of man, who are also humanitarians, as Ashley Montagu,[43] Otto Klineberg,[44] Earnest Hooton,[45] H.J. Muller,[46] Ruth Benedict[47] and Margaret Mead.

The good name and the democratic pretensions of the United States are at stake in this matter of Negro treatment. As long as a cultured and refined man who is "colored" is denied the freedom of an ex-convict who is "white" then its democratic pretensions are bare-faced humbug. As long as color distinctions prevail the upholders of the dignified constitution of the United States are co-workers with the miserable jim-crow law makers of the Southern States. As long as human beings continue to be burnt alive on the altar of white "racial superiority" as at Sikeston, Missouri, in 1942,[48] so long will the Statue of Liberty, torch in hand, be also symbolic of the lyncher.

Some day we are going to do for our brains what we do for our houses—give it a thorough cleaning. We are then going to toss out all the beloved rubbish about "race" now cluttering our thinking and preventing the attainment of true brotherhood and peace. Mankind is one. "The earth is but one country and mankind its citizens," says Abdul Baha.[49]

Oswald Spengler[50] in his mighty book, "The Decline of the West," shows the falsehood about race springing out of what he calls the period of Romanticism, and adds, "How utterly unimportant these are for what we call 'race' in higher mankind can be shown by a drastic experiment. Take a set of men with every conceivable race-difference, and while mentally picturing 'race' observe them in an X-ray apparatus. The result is simply comic. As soon as light is let through it 'race' vanishes suddenly and completely."

Here is another test of the oneness of mankind. Go to any large clinic in New York, Paris, or London, and you'll see individuals of the various 'races' there awaiting treatment. Are these patients treated according to "race"? No, the Caucasian, Mongolian, Negro, or Indian, or individual from no matter what part of the world, if suffering from the same malady is given the same kind of medicine, which, if he is susceptible of being cured, will cure him regardless of race.

Since, therefore, mankind is so truly one in its organism, must not its thoughts, sentiments, and inherent possibilities be fundamentally the same?

Americans of the future, looking back on our times, are going to marvel, aye, to laugh at our stupidity; how we squabble and fight and kill one another like half-wits over the color of one another's skin, as in Detroit in 1943.[51]

The solution of the whole question of race is so very simple that I hesitate to give it after all the ponderous tomes on the subject. Nevertheless, I offer it:

Since no man is responsible for his race or his physical appearance, then he ought to be accepted for what Nature has made him. The racially intolerant should remember that what cannot be cured must be endured. Who among us, of normal intelligence, is quite sure that he, himself, is a paragon of beauty, wisdom, and desirability?

The goal of life is happiness and when that is attained one can enjoy the maximum of contentment under any color of skin or mixtures of color of skin. The like is true of misery. That the Danes, the Dutch, and the Norwegians had a white skin did not lighten for them one whit the miseries of Fascist domination also suffered by the Ethiopians, who are black.

> "Oh blood of the people, changeless tide, through century,
> creed and race.
> Still one, as the sweet salt sea is one, though tempered
> by sun and place.

The same in the ocean currents and the same in the sheltered sea,
Forever the fountain of common hopes and kindly sympathies.
Indian and Negro, Saxon and Celt, Teuton and Latin and Gaul,
Mere surface shadow and sunshine, while the sounding unifies all.
One love, one hope, one duty theirs! No matter the time or ken,
There never was separate heart-beat in all the races of men."

—JOHN BOYLE O'REILLY.[52]

"Rogers Says: Exception Is Taken to Criticism of 'Black Boy' Written by Theophilus Lewis," Pittsburgh *Courier*, July 14, 1945

Rogers was brought into writing this evaluation of Richard Wright's autobiography, *Black Boy*, by means of a challenge. A reader disliked the negative review given of the book by well-respected Black critic Theophilus Lewis in the Jesuit periodical, *America*. The reader hoped that Rogers would come to Wright's defense. Rogers does challenge some of Lewis' assertions, particularly his contention that the book is not competently written. However, the more interesting part of the article is not Rogers's opinion of Lewis' review but when he launches into his own brief defense of the book itself. In some ways, Rogers would not seem a good candidate to support the writings of a social realist like Wright. He did not care for *Native* Son, and was lukewarm about the play based on it ("Rogers Says: I Found Nothing in 'Native Son' That I Could Object To" Pittsburgh *Courier* May 3, 1941). Rogers would certainly not agree with Wright's radical political perspective; nevertheless, he is generally impressed by *Black Boy*, maintaining that many Negro youths (as well as he himself) could relate to it. The book demonstrates what Rogers believes is the most essential quality in an author, "namely, to convey clearly and vividly what he has seen and felt." Ultimately, Rogers maintains that the book could "do an immense amount of good," and he hopes its popularity will be long lived and that it "stirs to action every lover of right and justice in this land."

"ROGERS SAYS: EXCEPTION IS TAKEN TO CRITICISM OF 'BLACK BOY' WRITTEN BY THEOPHILUS LEWIS"

Raymond Van Cleef (white) of Woodside, Long Island, N.Y. writes me, "The review of Richard Wright's 'Black Boy' by Theophilus Lewis[1] in the April 14 issue of 'America' reeks with prejudice. It is so unfair that it deserves some retaliation. In fact, Mr. Lewis should be severely rebuked for his intolerance." [I] find myself somewhere in the middle regarding this after reading Mr. Lewis' review and "Black Boy." Lewis treats the book largely from one angle and while I disagree with him in certain places, I feel that he is right most of the time from his angle.

Mr. Lewis' angle (or angles) is, in my opinion, neither quite realistic nor broad. However, he thinks that autobiography is a field "reserved for the mature author" and asks "Why should the author of 'Black Boy' . . . assume his life is important enough to make present and future readers curious about his rather uneventful childhood and youth?" I feel, on the other hand, that we ought to have more youthful autobiographies, especially when written with such frankness as Wright's. One of the most celebrated of all autobiographies, which had a great influence on her times, was that of Marie Bashkirtsev,[2] who died at the age of 24. Had she waited until she reached maturity it would never have been written.

I look at "Black Boy" primarily as a statement of facts—facts which, though unpleasant, should be chased out into the open where they can be seen and corrected. One colored reviewer called the book a lie. I think the burden of proof is on that reviewer because I, personally, found nothing in it that did not ring true or even sounded sensational. Most of the incidents will be familiar and even commonplace to many Negroes. What I got out of them as related by Wright, is that ever-nasty meanness of these members of a so-called superior race, who have been taught that they have no hope for survival unless they "put on the dog"[3] where Negroes are concerned, that low-down meanness and descent to despicable lies as exhibited by Bilbo[4] and Eastland[5] in the

Senate recently. Millions of Negro youth are experiencing in some way or other what Wright so vividly describes.

Lewis says further, "As autobiography, 'Black Boy' is neither interesting reading nor a competent job." As regards interest, I agree with him to the extent of saying that the first eight chapters would be less trite if condensed into say, two or three. But from the ninth chapter onward I found it most interesting and a sociological document of high merit.

As regards competence, I think "Black Boy" is extraordinarily well presented, too. Some white critics have called Wright the foremost American writer of today. This, of course, is a matter of opinion. But this is sure: He has to a marked degree that first qualification of a writer, namely, to convey clearly and vividly what he has seen and felt. He is, without doubt, one of America's greatest living writers. What's more, he came up the very hard way. Of course, there are those whose judgment will be swayed by some of the "indecent" facts in the book, but I have read Freudian accounts of the lives of some white boys and girls that would make what Wright relates of his seem mild.

Space will not permit here a discussion of the book, itself. It has many incidents which touched me deeply. For instance, the deception he had to practice to borrow books from the white library, there being none for Negroes. These "superior" white folk are so afraid that Negroes will get knowledge, so afraid that they will have aspirations other than to be porters and domestics. One, also, is impelled to ask what would Wright be now had he not the ambition to pick himself up and get out of the South. Released from the crushing prejudice of Mississippi and Tennessee his genius rose and grew erect like a plant from which a huge stone has been lifted.

"Black Boy" will, I am sure, do an immense amount of good. It will make those who have conscience capable of being awakened, realize what it means to be an ambitious, aspiring Negro in those hell-holes of the South. For several months now it has been second from the top on the best sellers' list. May it remain on that list until the truth it conveys stirs to action every lover of right and justice in this land.

From *World's Great Men of Color* (Vol. 1, 1946; Vol. 2, 1947)

Rogers is probably best known for his short, probing sketches of "great" Black men and women. He began these brief biographies in *The Messenger* magazine in 1924 at the urging of his friend and colleague George Schuyler. The feature became an instant success, and Rogers put together a collection of the articles in 1931 and later in 1935 (Parfait). This was eventually expanded into the 1946–47 compilation, described by distinguished historian John Henrik Clarke as Rogers's "greatest achievement" (1: ix). Despite the title, the 200 sketches include numerous famous women. The collection is important because in it, Rogers was able to concisely show readers, both Black and white, of the achievements of people of color. The sketches, while historical in nature, also display Rogers's narrative skill, no doubt adding to their popularity.

The essay, "How and Why This Book Was Written," explains how a Black teacher's casual comment that Blacks had no great people inspired Rogers's lifelong quest to disprove this statement. Rogers decided to do this by writing short "success" stories meant to inspire young readers, particularly Blacks but also whites. The essay also sets forth Rogers's lifelong belief in the power of education to help undo or at least mitigate the harmful effects of racism. Learning one's true history, one often left out or distorted in the case of Blacks, was a powerful way to do this. And, for Rogers, biography was the perfect tool. As Thabiti Asukile notes, anyone reading the work "would be forced to re-think the roles played by people of African descent in world history" ("Black International Journalism" 338).

Three representative sketches are included here. Rather than choose pieces on well-known figures such as W. E. B. Du Bois or Marcus

Garvey, lesser-known figures were selected, ones his audience then and possibly now might not know well. Rogers knew that what made someone "great" was largely a matter of opinion, but for him it generally meant someone who had a significant impact on a large number of people. There were many "greats" that could have been selected, but Hatshepsut, Jan Ernest Matzeliger, and William Monroe Trotter show a diversity of Black achievement, and demonstrate characters who all had to overcome challenges to gain their eventual success. Hatshepsut was an Egyptian queen who ruled her kingdom with great skill despite the male prejudice against her. Rogers was one of the early proponents that the ancient Egyptians were Negroes and should be included when recording Black success. Jan Ernest Matzeliger was a poor, struggling inventor, born in Dutch Guiana in 1852, who migrated to the United States and revolutionized the shoe industry by changing it from hand-made to mechanized. African American newspaperman and militant activist William Monroe Trotter certainly was not unknown when he lived, but he never reached the heights of fame of some other race leaders. Though he was born with some measure of privilege, he spent his life sacrificing his wealth and position for racial equality. As a result, despite the tragedies in his life, he helped birth several important Negro organizations These three individuals are only a few of the many "greats" brought to readers' attention through Rogers's research.

The texts used here are from the first editions, privately published by Rogers in 1946 and 1947. They were republished with some changes by The Macmillan Company in 1972.

"HOW AND WHY THIS BOOK WAS WRITTEN"

> *"A people will never look forward to posterity who never look backward to their ancestors."*
>
> —EDMUND BURKE[1]

I have often been asked what led me to begin my researches on what for a better name I will call Negro history. As I look back on it now I think it really began in my early childhood when it was firmly impressed on me by the ruling classes that black people were inherently inferior and that their sole reason for being was to be servants to white people and the lighter-colored mulattoes. The blacks, I was told, had never accomplished anything in all of history, which of course, began "with Adam and Eve in the Garden of Eden," and that such signs of civilization they now showed were due to the benevolence of Christian whites who had dragged them from Africa and cannibalism thereby plucking them as "brands from the burning"[2] of hell and eternal torment.

The Christian blacks, themselves, said amen to this and joined in spreading the doctrine. My Sunday School teacher, an almost unmixed Negro, told us that black people were cursed by God and doomed to eternal servitude, to white people because Ham had laughed at his drunken father, Noah. To clinch his argument he read to us from the Bible, which we were taught was infallible. Doubt but a single word, try to change but a tittle, and you were doomed to burn in hell forever and ever. The slavemasters and kidnappers had indeed done their work well. They had so incorporated their iniquities with the Christian religion that when you doubted their racism you were contradicting the Bible and flying in the face of God Almighty.

As for the devout Christian Negro who taught us that[,] so great an impression did he make upon me that I still remember his features and his name though nearly half a century has passed. Of course, it was understood that if one had a mixture of "white blood," which was true in my case, one's future was not so entirely hopeless[;] still he could not ever reach the heights of intelligence and accomplishments of an unmixed white person for any visible degree of Negro strain immutably consigned one to be "lower than the angels," that is, the whites. This latter degree of eternal inferiority included me. However, even at the risk of the eternal torture awaiting me I could not swallow what this sincere, but gullible, tool of the master class told me. Even then there was a streak of logic in me that prevented it. I had been told that God was good, why, then, I asked myself, had he doomed millions and millions of people to such an ignominious fate simply because their "ancestor" thousands of years ago had laughed at his father because the father had been acting like a pig. Was God so much in favor of drunken fathers?*

I had furthermore noticed that some of the brightest of my schoolmates were unmixed blacks and some of them were more brilliant than some of the white ones. The principal of the school, too, was a mulatto. I also saw around me black physicians and lawyers, all graduates of the best English and Scotch universities. If [the] Negro strain were inherently inferior why had these black people been able to accomplish these things, and be more advanced than some of the barefooted white adults I knew? Still I did not contradict this Sunday School teacher. I was not supposed to. My business was to swallow what I heard. One word of doubt and I would have promptly been dubbed "infidel," which was at bottom being worse than a criminal because a criminal could be saved and go to heaven while special torment in hell, a la Dante, was reserved for deliberate unbelievers. If you did not swallow all the good things the existing order told you, including the yarn about the whale swallowing Jonah and Moses turning his stick into a snake, you were not only not a good Christian but not a good citizen. I distinctly recall two individuals I had been specially taught to look down on: One was a man who used to argue with my father on the miracles of the Bible which he called "rubbish"; the other was a relative, a light mulatto, who had married a black woman. Race prejudice, religion, and good citizenship went together.

Of course the above will seem an exaggeration to many. Well, we can still find plenty of it in any English-speaking land. Millions of whites in the South, what H. L. Mencken calls "the Bible belt," pin their faith in the Ham story. One thing I have learnt from my travels, especially in civilized lands, is that stupid beliefs and superstitions never die no matter how mechanical progress advances. Even some of the world's great intellectuals find strength and comfort in the superstitions about race.** They remind one of the patient who when asked by a psychiatrist whether any members of his family suffered from insanity, replied, "No, they don't suffer from it; they enjoy it."

Jim-crow and upright Christian living are held to be indivisible by millions of whites, especially in the United States and the British colonies and dominions. As for the Mormons, their missionaries still teach that Negroes can't go to heaven because of "race." I ran across these Mormon missionaries in Germany in 1927 and a Minnesota white woman recently wrote me about their teachings in her state. In 1903 when burial service were held in a Baptist church in Salt Lake City for Eugene Burns, a Negro, the grandson of Abel Burns, faithful servant of Joseph Smith, founder of Mormonism, Patriarch Miner, president of one of the quorums of the Seventies[3] of the Mormon Church, walked up to the pulpit and to the consternation of the mourners began a highly sensational discourse to prove that Burns, as a Negro, "could not reach the state of exultation necessary to entrance into heaven" and that "his soul was doomed before birth." The only Negro who had ever entered heaven, Miner declared, was Burns' grandfather, and that was because of the latter's fidelity to the "Prophet" (New York Sun, Nov. 15, 1902).***

As I grew older I revolted more and more at this asininity concocted by "the master race" but I had no books at hand to contradict it, or no knowledge of any kind. To make matters worse I finally had from a Negro friend of mine a book in which this alleged inherent inferiority was stressed, and which, ironically, had been given to him as first prize for the best essay in which white children had also competed. Years later to make it still worse I read Thomas Dixon's "The Clansman," a highly emotional novel, in which all but the Uncle Toms were painted in a most horrible light and which said that if one had but a "drop" of "Negro blood" he was damned intellectually forever. There were also the books on Africa, "darkest Africa," by Stanley, and works by missionaries in which Africans were painted either as faithful dogs or horrible savages. Occasionally, I heard a newly returned missionary from Africa, who, at a Sunday morning service, would paint a most pitiable picture of what he called "the heathen," and how we should all contribute, and put into the collection plate "the feathers that would make the gospel fly." Incidentally when I did go to Africa I saw natives who lived better than a large number of whites in Europe, especially England and Italy, and who, unlike the whites could not even read the

Bible. As for the poorer blacks, I venture to say that their huts of grass, sticks, and clay, were no worse than the slums I saw in the East End of London.

Up to the time of these "racial" experiences I had been identifying myself with the characters in the books I read. For instance, in my great favorite, Shakespeare's Julius Caesar, I saw Brutus, Caesar, Cassius, and the rest not as "white" men but as individuals either to be emulated or shunned. In "Paul and Virginia"[4] my deepest sympathies went out to Virginia because I never thought of her as a "white" woman but as one whose high ideals had brought her suffering and death. From then on I began to see world figures not as men and women and began to search for some that were of Negro ancestry. However, there was not a single one to be found, so carefully had they been expurgated by the masters. Alexander Dumas the Younger was one of my favorites but not a single word was there of his Negro strain. Literature, religion, education had all been carefully bleached. At last, however, I did hear of one great mulatto whose "race" could not be hid because I knew people who had seen him, and who was then in the world news: —General Antonio Maceo,[5] Cuba's greatest military leader. However, it was not until years later I found in Chicago a friend who introduced me to books in which I found the names of several great men of Negro ancestry, past and present. In my spare time, and with no thought of writing a book, I began to collect some of these names. That was about 1911.

About a year later, however, I had a set-back from an entirely different quarter. I belonged then to a radical economic group composed of whites and Negroes. When during a discussion at one meeting I mentioned great Negroes and how I had been collecting their names, there was a great howl of disapproval from the whites and most of the Negroes. They called me a "chauvinist" and said that I was suffering from an inferiority complex.

Who were these great Negroes I was digging up? Tools of the capitalist order or they wouldn't be in capitalist books. In short, I was one of the most despicable of all creatures: A Negro who was a capitalist hero-worshipper. Furthermore, they said, such work as I was engaged in would be useless when "the industrial revolution" came and color differences mattered no more. A true radical would be studying Marx, Engels, and Lafargue[6] and preparing for the workers' utopia, which was just around the corner. Incidentally, that was thirty years ago. Some of these folks still believe in their workers' heaven as religious folk in theirs.

With my enthusiasm dampened by this rebuff I allowed much time to pass without doing any research on great Negroes. However, I noticed that books alleging inherent Negro inferiority continued to appear. And Dixon's Clansman had now been made into a flaming attack on Negroes in a motion picture, "The Birth of A Nation." All of these I felt should be answered not with sentiment as I noticed certain white friends of the Negro and Negroes themselves were doing in the Chicago press, but with facts. It seemed to me, too, that if the new order was going to be all that my radical friends said it would be, then one of its aims would be not to exclude or ignore the cultures of minorities but to conserve them as a knowledge of other peoples, their art, literature, accomplishments and helped to produce that variety necessary for a high state of civilization. I decided also that if those who objected to my researches were really interested in righting the Negro's wrongs in a concrete way they ought to welcome any knowledge that would equip them with means of refutation. I finally left the economic radicals, deciding their views were far too narrow for me.

About this time I also made what was to me an important discovery, namely, that the recital of the deeds of the great or the worthy was instinctive in humanity. I found that all peoples—English, French, Germans, Spaniards, Italians, Americans, Chinese, Jews, Moslems—had lists of their great and noted men. And more than that, even states of the union, cities, and small towns had their list of "greats," as well as doctors, scientists, lawyers, preachers, engineers, and almost every professional group. Why, even the radicals who had called me a chauvinist had their own heroes whom they were forever extolling and whom they worshipped as blindly as the conservatives their own heroes. What the radicals really wanted was that I should worship at their own particular shrine, eschewing all others. Also, I felt that if I were the victim of an inferiority complex, I certainly had a host of illustrious company dating back to Plutarch with his "Lives of Illustrious Greeks and Romans."

Another thought that decided me to continue my researches was that man's chief knowledge of himself was what has been done by man; that the good and the evil that others have done were our sole guide through life's wilderness. And was not the recital of great and stirring deeds the most gripping of all dramas?

To bring out the best in ourselves (and at times the worst, too) a study of the lives of the great of all races, ages, and climes is a necessity. Biography will ever be the highest and most civilizing form of literature. That is why Plutarch is still a best seller after two thousand years.

As regards "race," which was thrust upon me (I had never felt otherwise than as a member of the human race) I realized that the further back the Negro's past could be pushed, the more ridiculous would appear the old slave-holding dogma of Negro "inferiority." I saw, also, that the white overlords to inflate the ego of their own group had reached back to claim the coal-black Ethiopian; the mulatto Egyptian; the black Hindu; the Negroid Polynesian, not to mention certain individuals such as Esop, Terence,[7] Cleopatra, and Mohamet, as white. Later, I saw Mussolini trying to prime his people by telling them of their great Roman past; and Hitler puffing up his by calling them Aryans and claiming that the ancient Egyptians were really Teutons. In short, Negro history was only a rebuttal of this braggadocio of the white masters. Let me say here that I feel emphatically that any boasting by Negroes about their history is just as nauseating. Furthermore, those individuals who work themselves up to a state where they talk as if the deeds of an ancestor were actually done by themselves will probably go no further than that in doing something worthy themselves. One of the world's greatest needs has ever been unboastful, unbiased history.

I noticed, too, that there was an urge not only to delve in national and "racial" history but in individual ancestry, also. I thought of the great genealogical societies; of the immense number of books tracing genealogies even here in America; and of the money paid out by the newly-rich and others for a family-tree and a coat-of-arms. I was especially struck by one magazine founded in 1899, "The Mayflower Descendants," tracing minutely living Americans to the Mayflower, even though such strain after more than three hundred years is extremely attenuated. Yes, it does appear that a past is as necessary to man as roots to a tree.

Of course, it is true that people who boast of their ancestry do so because they realize their own inferiority. Such have been rightly compared to a potato plant whose best part is underground. However, it is undeniable that a knowledge of one's ancestors does have a certain psychological value, especially if such ancestors were worthy. Especially for youths would this be an inspiration. In short, as with almost everything else, ancestry is what you make of it.

I reasoned now that since so many other groups and individuals were tracing their past, why should the objection be so strong when the Negro did so [?] Was not such objection but another manifestation of the white superiority complex, even in the case of the white economic radicals?

As regards the lives of great Negroes, I felt, too, that the greater handicaps they had had to overcome because of color ought to be proof of an inspiration to right-thinking white people with their lesser handicaps. Queen Victoria made her grandchildren read Booker T. Washington's "Up From Slavery." In view of the foregoing and in spite of the taunts of the economic radicals, white and Negro, I continued my researches on great Negroes, purely as a hobby.

In 1924, however, while I was writing a column of criticism for the Messenger Magazine, George S. Schuyler,[8] the managing editor, asked me to do instead short sketches of noted Negroes. I complied rather reluctantly, feeling that the public, not only white, but Negro, also, would not be interested. However, the stories seemed to take. A South African magazine carried one of them and Time Magazine made mention of another.

When the Messenger was discontinued about three years later Schuyler then editor of a supplement, "The Illustrated Weekly," that went to some forty Negro newspapers wrote me [in] Paris, France, where I was then living asking me to write biographies for it. Still not liking the idea, I did not reply immediately and he wrote again, urging me to accept. I did and so successful were the biographies that many requests came in asking for the sketches in book form. Finally in 1931, I published a small paper-bound edition at a dollar, which sold very well. Two other editions had even more success. The last copies of this book were sold in 1938 and are out of print.

Something now about the research, itself. That was not easy since the story of the contacts of whites and blacks is usually told from the white angle. To get the material I had to browse through an immense number of books and other printed matter in the libraries of America, Europe[,] and North Africa, as well as long and persistent search through museums, old bookshops, churches and private collections. I knew, for instance, that the Negro had been important in Portuguese history but I sought in vain, at least in books of English text, for the name of a single great Portuguese Negro. It was not until I went to Portugal that I did learn of some.

From two works by Negroes I received much perspective and valuable leads. These were George Wells Parker's "Children of the Sun"[9] and William H. Ferris' two-volume work, "The African Abroad."[10] Later, I found three invaluable books by white authors on the Negro's past: Godfrey Higgins' "Anacalypsis"[11] and Gerald Massey's "A Book of the Beginnings" and "Ancient Egypt, the Light of the World."[12] From others as the late Arthur Schomburg, I also received some rare leads.

With regard to Parker I must make a belated apology. I once disagreed with him in the Messenger for saying that Cleopatra and Mohamet were of Negro ancestry. The simple truth is I had never looked into the matter but having so often heard that Cleopatra was "pure Greek" and knowing that her ancestor, Ptolemy, was Greek, I accepted it as fact, not knowing that the Egyptian Ptolemies were very much mixed, and furthermore that the Greeks were a nationality and not a so-called race, and that even as one can be "pure" American and be of mixed race so was it with the Greeks. Later, I did find evidence to make me believe that Parker was right about Cleopatra and most certainly about Mohamet.****

As a result of the above on my part, I can readily understand how preconceived ideas on the Negro's real past must constitute a barrier to the acceptance of a book such as this of mine. One truth that research has taught me is that however incredible things may sound there are very, very few situations in the life of humanity that could not be true. This is particularly true of miscegenation and the mixed strain it has brought into the ancestry of peoples and individuals. It is possible for the fairest Nordic to have had a Negro ancestor. This latter, by migrating to Europe and he and his offspring mating only with blonds, would in time produce blonds, who unless records were kept would know nothing of that Negro ancestor. A white migrating to Central Africa and his offspring mating, in like manner, only with blacks will in time produce blacks indistinguishable from his fellows. This process has doubtless taken place innumerable times in human history. There is no doubt in my mind either that even without miscegenation climate alone would effect such a change after fixed habitation over a very long period. Europe was once inhabited by an indigenous Negro people and by tropical animals and plants and might be again. Wherever coal is found was once tropical, including what is now the Arctic Circle. However, many find it impossible to believe that the forces of nature which were able to change black anthracite to a diamond of the purest water could have changed a coal-black Negro into a white man. There are scientists, too, who find it easier to believe that they had an ape for an ancestor than a Negro.

In 1945, when the New York Public Library carried an exhibit intended to prove the equality of "races," a Southern[er], who is editor of an atheist magazine and is very well read on science but who, while he has been able to throw off religion has not been able to throw off his racial superstitions, denounced the exhibit, calling it "side-show science . . . a disgraceful exhibit, farcical in its presentation" and an attempt to "Barnumize" science.*#

This brings me to what is usually meant by "Negro" ancestry. What most scientists and sociologists call a "Negro" (when achievements are being spoken of) is a highly specialized and very primitive type that has been isolated in Central Africa or New Guinea for thousands of years, as isolated as were the savages Julius Caesar saw in Britain.[13] Of this type there are, at most, but a million and [a] half, too few in number to have built up a civilization at any time. When, however, it is a question of what is not very creditable the Negro variety is made to include hundreds of millions of individuals, some of whom are more Nordic in color and features than many whites.

The scientists are as divided on who is a Negro as the theologians are on who is God. The ethnologists certainly cannot say because ethnology is but a mass of conflicting opinion based on the opinions of observers who were subject to many influences and made pronouncements according to their personal likes and dislikes of this or that people. What ethnology has to say on the alleged inferiority of certain people reminds one of the Haitian proverb, "When the rooster and the cockroach come to court, you don't have to guess which will win." What ethnology needs most is emancipation from an exploiting capitalism—a complete divorce from the slavemaster's legend of Ham.

As certain individuals who I know positively are of Negro ancestry but are fair enough to pass for something else will say that they were of Indian, Spanish, or South American ancestry, so do certain anthropologists in the case of evidently Negroid peoples as the Egyptians, Moors, Ethiopians and some Asiatic and Polynesian peoples, the entire idea in both cases being to duck admission of Negro ancestry. Even in the case of those paleolithic men, whose Negro characters were evident, they use such phrases as proto-Negroid.

These anthropologists, while pretending to scorn the Biblical story of the origin of man and his distribution over the earth, continue to use such terms as "Hamitic" for the Ethiopians and "Semitic" for the Jews. These terms, if they have any meaning at all are only as language-groups, precisely as Latin, Anglo-Saxon, Arab. It is as nonsensical to talk of a Jewish race as it is to talk of a Christian one.

As to who is a Negro in the United States I have come to the conclusion after long and careful thought that to be an expert on that subject the first qualification is to be crazy. Only those who are able to throw all logic, all reasoning to the wind, can ever hope to be authorities on that matter. I have more than once witnessed the amazing spectacle of one American calling another American fairer and more Nordic in features than himself a "nigger" and relegating him to the jim-crow car. Again, one can be very visibly a Negro and because he speaks broken English with a foreign accent, or doesn't speak English at all become legally white. I recall the case of a friend of mine, an unmixed Negro, who once lived in Sweden and speaks Swedish fluently. While travelling in the South the conductor sent him off to the jim-crow car. Pretending not to understand English, he replied in Swedish. Finally an interpreter was found, and when the conductor learned that the Negro, who is a native of the British West Indies, could speak Swedish in support of his statement that he was a Swede, he was allowed to remain in the white coach.

I know several West Indians and South Americans, visibly Negroes who were drafted into the white army and navy while other Americans who were fairer than many whites were placed in the Negro regiments. I recall the case of a Harlem newspaper photographer, who is as white as any of the Nordics, but is of Negro ancestry. He was drafted into [a] Negro regiment, but when he was taken South and went into the Negro quarter, he was arrested by the white M.P.'s as whites were forbidden there. Thereafter, to save arrest, he carried a paper, stating that he was a Negro. Had he permitted himself to be drafted as "white," however, he would probably have been punished. Many times, too, I have, myself, taken "white" for "colored" and the reverse.

Congressman Adam Clayton Powell was fairer than some of the anti-Negro Southerners in Congress yet to them he is of another "race."[*##] Even some of the cleverest whites don't know their own. In 1939, a chain of moving-picture theatres—the RKO—offered a prize for the American who looked most like Abraham Lincoln and who should win it but a Negro! Of course the judges discovered that too late.[*###] Several of the Southern states and some of the Northern ones have their own particular definition of what is a Negro and as I have shown in

Sex and Race in certain Southern states even the state constitution and the state laws differ on the subject. As for the United States Bureau of the Census it again has its own ruling which is that if one has a "drop" of "Negro" blood, he is a Negro. Someone has defined a "Negro" as one who, regardless of complexion, is not entitled by his ancestry to ride in a white coach in the southern United States. **This definition would be true of every personage in this book.** Of course, such a definition though true, is idiotic. I use it only by way of argument.

The persons who hold to the above doctrine happen to be also the ones who will usually attribute ability in the mixed-bloods to their white strain. To avoid this I have included no one with less than an eighth of Negro strain with the exception of Dom Pedro II,[14] who was about one-sixteenth, or perhaps one-thirty-second, Negro. I have given him as an example chiefly to show what would have happened to him had he lived, say, in Virginia, where the law provides that the remotest trace of Negro ancestry makes one a Negro. Dom Pedro married a white woman and that would have brought him five years' imprisonment in Virginia. Dom Pedro was no fairer or more Nordic in features than thousands of Virginia Negroes. I recall, too, the case of Jean Toomer, the novelist, a grandson of Governor Pinchback of Louisiana, whose Negro ancestry is a matter of record. When Toomer, who was fairer than millions of American whites, married a white woman in 1931 it was reported in both the Negro and the white press as the marriage of a Negro to a white woman. Toomer has since ceased to be a "Negro," which, I think, is logical.[15] My contention is that those who look white are white, and those who look mixed, are mixed; no matter on what side of the fence a fantastic American dogma places them. If we see a Negro with evidences of white strain, we'll say unhesitatingly that he is mixed. I carry my logic all the way and when I see a white person with evidence of what my eyes tell me, after fifty years of experience, is a Negro strain, I attribute the same to that person no matter in what society or in what part of the world he is. One's ancestry does not come out of the air. Though invisible, it is as real as anything else on this planet. Every "atom" of our ancestry could be accounted for.

Many, many millions of individuals over vast centuries—individuals who lived and breathed even as ourselves—built it up as surely as the insects built up a coral reef. Had there been the tiniest break in our ancestral line we could not have been the individuals we now are. In fact, we might never have been born at all.

No matter how proud one may be of his ancestry; no matter how far back he may trace it to great kings and chiefs who lived, he reaches inevitably a point of obscurity as dark as the darkest depths of the ocean. To talk, therefore, of a "pure" race or a "pure" ancestral line is abysmal ignorance.

Certain difficulties in research might also be noted. In lands where there is no color discrimination, color is rarely mentioned, except in the case of "pure" blacks, who were generally aliens. This is particularly true of ancient and modern Egypt and Arabia.

Outside the United States a mulatto is not a "Negro," and still less so is a quadroon or octoroon. If Pushkin's great-grandfather and Alexander Dumas' father had not been so prominent we would have lost knowledge of their Negro strain as we have in the case of hundreds of thousands of other Europeans. For instance, the English people between 1440 and 1834 absorbed the Negro slaves that had been brought into England at the rate of thousands annually. What do we know of the descendants of these Negroes and where their strain is now to be found, high or low, in the English population? Practically nothing.*####

Antonio Vieira,[16] Portugal's grandest personage, is an instance of how Negro ancestry could be lost to history. We should probably never have known of Vieira's Negro strain if the Spanish Inquisition, failing to suppress him in other ways, did not finally pounce on his dark skin and frizzly hair, hoping to prove through them that he was of Jewish or Islamic strain, which being "heretic," would call for his expulsion from the priesthood.

Discovering great men of color in Central and South America is not easy either because the white strain in the mixed-bloods in emphasized and the Negro one suppressed. What Sir Richard Burton[17] said of Brazil is, on the whole, true of Latin America: "Here all free men who are not black, are white, and often a man is officially white but naturally almost a Negro. This is directly opposed to the system of the United States, where all men who are not unmixed white, are black." Indian strain, also, was considered higher caste than [the] Negro one, hence Negro strain is often called "Indian" and even "West Indian." Take the case of Thomas Mann, great German writer and Nobel Prize winner. Mann's mother was a Brazilian creole who was sent to study in Germany. Now I am not saying that she was of Negro strain since I have not investigated that but because she was colored, or at least not white, it was inevitable that she should be said to be part "Indian" or part "West Indian" by his biographers.*&

In Cuba quadroons and even mulattoes are considered white, hence the census reports list the bulk of the population as white. The same is true of Puerto Rico. The result is a looking-down on Negro strain by such individuals.

In the United States an individual who is more Caucasian than some of the whites is rarely offended if called a Negro. The reason is that the white colonists of America thanks chiefly to continued and fairly large immigration did not need the mulatto to help them keep the blacks in check and thus did not elevate him to a caste superior to the blacks but generally lumped blacks and mulattoes together. South of the Rio Grande, however, especially in Haiti and the British West Indies, the whites there erected the mulattoes into a caste above the blacks and taught them to regard the blacks as inferior. The result is that today the mixed-bloods of Central and South America and the West Indies are generally offended when classed with blacks. In the British West Indies the census reports still list them separately.

Some of these near-whites are probably more sensitive of their Negro ancestry than they would be of a police record. Mention of it is more distressing to some than would be a large boil on the face of a movie star.

A case in point is Jose Maria Heredia,[18] a Cuban, who was a member of the French Academy. Heredia was usually taken as "colored" by both white and Negroes [in] France.*&& Ordinarily no mention might have been made of his color but it happened at the time that France's most prominent writer was one whose Negro strain was widely known because of his illustrious parentage, namely, Alexander Dumas, fils, who was president of the French Academy, or Forty Immortals.[19] Heredia, to make matters worse for him, was darker than Dumas.

When Heredia was elected to the Academy some of the Negro intellectuals of Paris, accepting the popular belief that he was colored, called on him to congratulate him. Heredia snubbed them and told them that he was not of Negro but of "conquistador" ancestry. Dumas, the Younger, on the other hand, was not only not sensitive about his Negro ancestry, but mentioned it in his first address to the Academy. The difference is that Dumas had not been taught to despise the pigment in his skin, while Heredia had been.

Pushkin was so proud of his Negro strain that he credited himself with more of it than he had. Colette,[20] France's leading woman writer, and Officer of the Legion of Honor, mentions her Negro strain, too, though one would hardly guess it. "The idealistic temperament of the Latin American, his pretension to a high civilization and to the status of caballero, creates a natural yearning for a white skin," says Garcia Calderon.[21] Europe is the Latin America's model. The first colonists taught even the whites born in the colonies to look down on themselves and to worship things European. The tradition still remains.

Because of this "yearning" to be white, the United States as a part of its good neighbor policy[22] caters to Latin American color pride. The 1940 United States census lists Mexicans as white, which of course will make anyone who has been to Mexico and seen the bulk of its population laugh.

Touchiness about Negro ancestry is, of course, still more characteristic of whites in the Southern United States. Southerners with dark skin or Negroid faces will assert that they are of Indian ancestry, as if the Indian were not also very much mixed with the Negro.

A study of Latin American portraits will also help little in discovering Negro ancestry. It is almost the usual thing to find Negroes, even unmixed, whose portraits are doctored to make them look like whites.

For instance, General Laurencio Silva, who from an incident in his domestic life, we know positively was a Negro.[*&&&] In the case of General Vicente Guerrero, president of Mexico, who was very definitely a mulatto, I defy anyone to tell from the pictures most current of him that he was not a European. It was only after long research that I found two pictures of him which bore out what is said of his ancestry. General Antonio Sucre of Venezuela, President of Bolivia, is being doctored up to look like a white movie star though he was a dark mixed-blood. The same is true of San Martin, liberator of Argentina.

The second and the third dictators of Paraguay, the Lopezes, were of Negro ancestry but you would never know it from the portraits. And even General Antonio Maceo of Cuba is being doctored up to look less and less like the dark mulatto he was. Thus, while noted men of Negro strain are not infrequent in Latin America it is a great task to locate them. I happened to know of Dom Pedro's Negro strain only because I ran across a description of his grandfather, John VI of Portugal.

In the Dominion of South Africa a condition even worse than in Latin America exists. The number of eminent South Africans who have a Negro strain must be considerable because the older the South African family the more likely it is to have one. Very few white women existed in the colony as late as the end of the seventeenth century. In 1633 there were only thirteen.

The same is true of Australia, where the first mothers of the white colony were aborigines, who were coal-black with Negro features and with hair, not wooly, but frizzly. In Tasmania the aborigines were definitely Negro with pepper-corn hair. Their women became the mothers of the first native Tasmanian whites.

As regards Islamic lands, locating Negroes was the most difficult of all. Not only is there no color-line in Islam but portraiture of any kind was absent until recent years, having been forbidden by Mohamet. As a rule, the only great Negroes who are mentioned as such in Islamic literature are "pure" blacks, the Zends or Zenghs, who were brought chiefly from Central Africa as slaves, and were later converted to Islam, as Lokman[23] and Kafur. Negroes born of a free Islamic father and a slave mother from the land of the Zenghs, may sometimes be distinguished also since the birthplace of slave mothers were [*sic*] mentioned. For instance, we know that Ibrahim Al-Mahdi,[24] half-brother of the famous Haroun Al-Raschid,[25] was of Negro ancestry since his mother, though also of royal ancestry, was a slave. However, there was much Negro strain in some of the highest Islam-born families, as the Abbasides,[26] rulers of the Mohammedan empire at the height of its power. If the Caliph Al-Mahdi, father of Haroun Al-Raschid, was not almost black himself, is it likely that Ibrahim would have been so dark as to be called a Negro by his nephew, Caliph Mamoun?[27] Caliph Al-Muktafi[28] also had a Negro mother. Ibn Khalikan[29] mentions several distinguished Negroes in his Biographical Dictionary, but no mulattoes, the inference being that these were regarded as "white."

As regards great men in the Far East, I have done almost no research on them. I have come across certain names in China and Japan such as Sakonouye Tamuramaro, the first shogun of Japan, but I did not follow them up. In India also, I did little on the Negroes among the Mohammedans there, while on Turkey I did no intensive research, though the number of great Turkish Negroes, some of whom were virtual rulers of the empire, is considerable. I have given the names of some of them in Sex and Race.[*&&&&]

As regards the evaluation of the personages in this book there will be, naturally, differences of opinion. Some might even go so far as dismiss most of them. For instance, the late Professor Edward M. East of Harvard University said that among the "15,000 or 20,000 Great Ones of the Earth,"[*%] there was only one of Negro strain, Alexander Dumas, pere. Toussaint Louverture, he dismisses, as being of only "fair calibre."

Now if we take East seriously it is necessary to know what was his standard of greatness? And did he arrive at it by some method other than haphazard? Where did he find his 15,000 to 20,000 great? Evidently in the encyclopedias. It would have taken him a lifetime to read up on each one and compile his own list.

Did he check on his 15,000 to 20,000 great to see whether his opinion differed with that of the editors of the encyclopedias? And did he go to the trouble of picking out the Negro names in these encyclopedias; or did he classify Negroes only by whom he had heard were Negroes? All of the leading encyclopedias have the names of several Negroes. This is true of the Encyclopedia Britannica, Larousse, La Grande Encyclopedie, Biographie Universelle, The Dictionary of National Biography, *the* Dictionary of American Biography, Enciclopedia Universal Ilustrada, *the* Encyclopedia of Islam, Who's Who, Who's Who in America, *and* American Men of Science. In this last eight Negroes were mentioned along with East.

Furthermore, what constitutes greatness is largely a matter of opinion. East's 15,000 to 20,000 could be whittled down to three or four or expanded to a million, depending on the appraiser. Victor Hugo in his "Shakespeare" narrowed down the world's greatest writers, poets, and artists to six and placed Shakespeare first. But Voltaire, who was as great as Hugo, ridicules Shakespeare and calls him a "ninny" and "charlatan with occasional outbursts of ability." Shakespeare's tragedies he called "monstrous farces that ruined the English theatre."[*%%] Also, Tolstoy, another immortal, says that Shakespeare was "inartistic," "trivial and positively bad," and that any praise of him is "false adulation."[*%%%]

Again, do we consider a man great because of the degree to which his life and actions affected humanity? If this be so, then how many biographers really endeavor to trace and to check up such for themselves? If they did they would find that some men of "fair calibre" who received only a few lines in an encyclopedia, and some who were not even mentioned, have affected mankind more than some who were ranked "great."

How many persons, for instance have heard of Fernandès[30] and Ni-cot[31] who introduced tobacco into Europe, thereby causing a greater effect on Europe, America, and Africa than Shakespeare? Or of Hargreaves[32] who discovered gold in Australia. The men who discovered gold in California or diamonds in South Africa probably had a more profound influence on world conditions today than any of Carlyle's heroes.[33]

Suppose for the sake of argument that Toussaint was not "great," yet did he not set in motion events that have had the most far-reaching effects on humanity today? His success against the French was chiefly instrumental in causing Napoleon to sell the Louisiana territory for a ridiculously small sum, without which the great America of today would not have been possible.

Had East been informed on Toussaint he would have found noted scholars who ranked him among the great. I would mention only three: Lamartine, who placed him above Napoleon; Wendell Phillips, who called him greater than Washington; and Auguste Comte, French philosopher and sociologist, who ranked him with Charles V, Coligny, Gustavus Adolphus, Walpole, Franklin, Washington, and Jefferson in statesmanship.[*%%%%]

Finally, it will be interesting, I think, to see how East came to say that there was only one great man of Negro ancestry. In 1918 E. B. Reuter wrote "The Mulatto,"[*@] which was intended to show the superiority of mulattoes over blacks, and gave several thousand names of prominent Negroes compiled by Negro writers and organizations including 139 given by W. E. B. Du Bois in his "Who's Who in Colored America" (1916). Now the Negroes who compiled the lists said little or nothing about Negroes outside of the United States, and Reuter, whether he knew of them or not, gave only what the Negroes had given. In nearly all of these lists there appeared many who had made only trifling success, and nearly all of whom it is safe to say, were mediocre and would probably have risen but little higher had there been no color prejudice against them. Such is the source from which East speaks so authoritatively. It is clear he knew nothing of his subject himself, and could go only as far as Reuter took him.

It seems to me that in sheer self-respect those who declare that such and such individuals were greater than others ought to be informed on the lives of the persons compared.

Another important factor in the true evaluation of a person's capabilities is the degree of opportunity afforded by his environment. For instance, had Napoleon been forced to remain on the island of Corsica, we should have known no more about him than we do about one of the bandit chiefs of that island despite the fact that he had within him all the potentialities of the Emperor Napoleon. He would have been but one of the innumerable flowers "born to blush unseen and waste its sweetness on the desert air."[34] Similarly certain personages in this book such as Queen Nzingha,"[35] Rabah Zobeir,[36] and Nat Turner might be ranked as insignificant, but the test is how well did they play on the small stage destiny had placed them?

In estimating greatness one should consider the intensity, sincerity, and capability an individual plays his role, whether that role be great or small. To exclude a great "small" man because life gave him a small role and include one whom it appointed to play a larger role seems to me to be idealizing the stage and not the individual. Snobbery, pure and simple. Had Napoleon been born black and a slave on Haiti, he could not possibly have been other than a Toussaint. Every character in this book has caused repercussions of greater or less[er] world importance; every one is of sufficient merit to have brought their inclusion in one or more encyclopedias.

I have also been asked not to include such figures as Chaka,[37] Dessalines,[38] and Samory,[39] since "they reflected no great credit on the Negro race." But while I dislike conquerors, tyrants, and dictators, whatever their color, I am endeavoring to write not "Negro" history but history in which people of a certain color played a prominent part—in which case, genius and ability must be presented regardless of the manner in which these were employed. We must remember, as Lord Acton[40] said, that great men are sometimes bad men. Furthermore, there are great men of whom much good has been said and yet I do not consider them worthy of imitation, as St. Benedict the Moor,[41] here included, who reached greatness through a sub-human humility that was in reality, pride.

As regards living persons, I have been advised not to include any of them as certain of those left out, might be offended. Rivalry of any kind is not the spirit of this book. Certainly there are living people who ought to be included and are not, but had I named 10,000 instead of only 200, the favorites of some would still have to be omitted. One can only hope that those who have been left out will show that they are worthy of inclusion in a really great book, by having no such feelings. The selection was my own and I do not claim to be an authority on who are great and who are not. Moreover, certain of these sketches were written before I had thought of certain persons not included. Variety of occupation also had to be considered to avoid monotony.

As regards my sources, I have given those I thought the most important. And I have checked them as carefully as is humanly possible in a work of this magnitude. I had also to be on guard for overstatement not only by Negro writers but by noted white ones, too. For instance, H.G. Wells says "In the eighteenth century he (the Negro) was the backbone of the British navy"[*@@] Even Mr. Wells' broadmindedness on "race" does not make this true. As for names of individuals who were supposed to be of Negro strain, I have received many from readers. When, however, I investigated I found that either their statements were too nebulous; or too difficult to be proved; or the individuals had too little Negro strain, which fact, as I said, led me to omit all but one such. The list of persons who might have been of Negro ancestry but are known as white that I have is a rather large one. I have said more on this matter in the appendix.

In conclusion, let me say that my intention was not to write highly critical and psychoanalytical, or even literary, essays, but rather principally success stories, chiefly for Negro youth. I hope white youth will find some inspiration in them, too.

And not only young people but adults too need the encouragement to be had from the lives of the great. Doctor Albert E. Wiggam[42] very rightly says, "The extraordinary and never-ending success of success stories in books, magazines, movies, soap operas, etc. would indicate that even the most obscure persons gain courage from them. In all ages, stories of heroism—success against great odds—have furnished most of the themes for literature and drama. On the other hand, nothing is more discouraging than stories that end in defeat and tragedy."

Of course, it is true that all the personages in this book did not win. Some fell short either through force of circumstances or defects in their character. But all were giants. I have been careful not to claim more for them than did those from whose books I gathered the facts.

ROGERS'S NOTES

* This fable of Ham as it is made to apply to black people does not come from the Bible but from Jewish legends. For its sources see Sex and Race, Vol. 3, pp. 316–17. For how black Southern mammies taught this Ham story to white children see: Andrews, M.P. Woman of the South, p. 190, 1920. See also Century Mag., Vol. 28, May-Oct. 1884, p. 859.

Incidentally, there was ground for setting in operation a similar fable against the whites by the dark-skinned peoples. Today, as Lord Raglan says, civilization is often thought of as being inherent in "a white skin and it is forgotten that the founders of civilization were brown skinned." Aristotle, whose people had received their culture chiefly from dark-skinned Egyptians, found Nordics intellectually and mechanically inferior (Politics, VIII, 7) and that was more than two centuries before Julius Caesar carried the light of civilization to those who now make most use of the Ham legend. Lord Raglan rightly says, "The Whites were, it seems, incapable of civilizing themselves . . . The savages of today seem to be in the same case as the whites were three or four thousand years ago." (The Future of Civilization in "The Rationalist Annual," p. 40, 1946). For the manner in which the Romans regarded the Nordics, see Sex and Race, Vol. 3, pp. 3–5, 251.

** Berry, B. (You and Your Superstitions, 1940) names many of the stupid beliefs still held even by many educated people. Especially is this so in the matter of physiognomy. You will find, he says, some of those listed in Who's Who *and* American Men of Science "who will not balk for a moment at the theory that kinky hair and black skin reveal low intelligence and musical temperament and that blond hair and blue eyes reveal intellectual and spiritual excellence."

*** Prejudice for Negroes is a cardinal tenet of the Mormon religion. Black people are considered accursed and so are all their offspring with white people. The Mormon prophet Joseph Smith had the "Lamanites," a white people, changed to black by God for their sins. The Book of Mormons, II Nephi, Chap. 5, verses 21–23, reads, "And he caused the cursing to come upon them, yea, even a sore cursing because of their iniquity. For behold they had hardened their hearts against him that they had become like flint; wherefore as they were white and exceedingly fair and delightsome that they might not be enticing unto my people, the Lord God did cause a skin of blackness to come upon them . . . .

" . . . and cursed shall be the seed of him that mixeth with their seed; for they shall be cursed with the same cursing."

Utah law punishes mixed marriages severely.

Negroes are permitted to attend Mormon services but they are not welcome as devout Mormons do consider them an accursed "race." They are ineligible for Mormon priesthood and incapable of redemption. Not so the Japanese, however, thanks to their lighter color. "Several Japanese," says Carey McWilliams (Nation, N.Y. Jan. 26, 1946, p. 98) "are members in good standing of the Mormon Church and eligible for the priesthood and are not segregated." Negroes, he says, are treated quite differently in Utah and in the Mormon Church.

**** Al-Jahiz, Arab writer of the ninth century, says that Mohamet's parents were black. See AL JAHIZ in this volume.

*# The Truth Seeker, April, 1945, p. 60. I discussed a similar attitude on the part of certain world famed scientists in Sex and Race, Vol. 3, Chap. 25.

*## When Congressman Powell married Hazel Scott, whose Negro strain is evident, an irate Southerner who saw their pictures in Life, wrote him, "Dear Senator Scott [*sic*]: I simply want to tell you that you are an eternal disgrace to the white race." (Afro-American, Feb. 23, 1946).

*### See account and this man's portrait in Sex and Race, Vol. 2, pp. 377–8.

*#### See Sex and Race, Vol. 1, Chap. 18. (1941) and Vol. 3, p. 15.

Let's take a concrete case: that of Charles Morett, a Negro child belonging to Lady Hilsborow of North Aston, Oxfordshire, who was baptized there on July 20, 1722. In the same parish register is a record of the baptism of his daughter, Eleanor, May 13, 1744 (Notes & Queries, 5 ser. Dec. 7, 1878). Morett's wife was very likely white, as Negro women were, and are, still few in England. What became of Morett's descendants as well as those of hundreds of thousands of similar Negroes during the centuries—as say, also, those of Francis Barber, servant of Dr. Samuel Johnson? In present-day England I saw the process of the absorption of blacks and mulattoes by whites. Coleridge-Taylor's descendants will doubtlessly disappear into the white "race" as did those of Dumas. My researches lead me to believe that the marriage, or mating, of the Negroes in the sixteenth, seventeenth, and eighteenth centuries with white women was the usual thing and that their mulatto offspring usually married white, until the Negro strain disappeared.

As regards names and surnames, the Negro children were baptized with ones characteristic of their color, as Morett (little Moor). Moorish (later shortened to Morris), Moore, Moor, Blackman, Blackie, Blackamore, Blackmur, Blackmuir, Blackmore. (See British Museum catalogue for list of authors with similar names). The Duke of Queensbury's ten-year-old blackamoor was christened "Blackmore." (Notes & Queries, 3 ser. Vol. VII, p. 198. Mar. 11, 1865). Is [it] not likely that certain white people who bore the names above-mentioned were descendants of these Negroes, as say, Sir Richard Blackmore, knighted by William III? David McRitchie, noted archaeologist, holds to this theory and gives a long list of British names derived from the black people who lived in England and Scotland even before William the Conqueror. (See his "Ancient and Modern Britons." Sources from him are given in Sex and Race, vol. I, pp. 198–200. 1941).

*& J. Cough (Thomas Mann, p. 12, 1933), says she was of German, Portuguese and West Indian ancestry and that her mother, that is Mann's grandmother, was "a Brazilian creole." See also Prof. Phelps on this subject. (New York Herald-Tribune, June 23, 1938).

*&& V. Thompson, white, writing on American artists in Paris, shows clearly that De Heredia was regarded as colored. He says, "There is no artist more talked of than Mr. H. O. Tanner. Perhaps this is because he is a mulatto and in spite of the example of Dumas and De Heredia, we are still surprised when the artist reveals himself under a dark skin"). (Cosmopolitan Magazine, p. 19. May 1900.)

Heredia's snubbing of the Negroes seems to have caused more than a little stir in Paris at the time, and while there I discussed the affair with several persons well informed about it, as Professor Cenac-Thaly, physicist, of the Sorbonne, and Louis Beaudza, chief editor of the Secretariat of the Grand Chancellery of the Legion of Honor, and all confirmed the belief that Heredia was colored and gave me additional stories regarding him. As late as 1935 I saw Negroes paying homage to Heredia's bust in the Luxembourg Gardens. Heredia might, or might not, have been of Negro ancestry. I have never looked into it. What I did learn, however, is that talk of his alleged Negro ancestry galled him.

Heredia, by all accounts, was about the color of W. E. B. Du Bois and resembled him somewhat and had a mustache like his. Heredia's portraits do not show a Negro strain nor do several of Du Bois' that I have seen. Again, take Paul La Fafargue, socialist, writer, and a distinguished contemporary of Heredia's. Lafargue's portrait looks like that of a Nordic, yet he was certainly a colored man, a native of Cuba. La Fafargue married Laura, second daughter of Karl Marx and Marx in a letter dated Sept. 5, 1866, refers twice affectionately to Lafargue as the "Negrillo," that is, little Negro. (Private letters of Karl Marx. Socialist Review, Sept. 1929, p.45). Portraits, especially etchings and wood-cuts[,] I have discovered are often deceptive.

As regards Heredia's statement that he was of "conquistador ancestry" and therefore white this would be poor proof. Many of the first Spaniards who came to the New World had a Moorish or Negro strain. There were also mixed-blood conquistadors, as Francisco Fajaro, Juan de Urquijo and Alonzo Ruiz Vallejo. As for Nuffo de Olano, who went with Baboa to the Pacific he was an unmixed Negro. Moreover, not a few conquistador descendants undoubtedly ended their lives in jail or on the gallows.

***&&&** See his portrait in Sex and Race, Vol. II, p. 26, and read what was said of his Negro ancestry on p. 25.

***&&&&** See Vol. I, pp. 286–7, 1941. "The Negro in Turkey,"

***%** Heredity and Human Affairs, pp. 199–200, 1927.

***%%** Lettre de M. De Voltaire a l'Academie Francaise, Aug. 25, 1776.

***%%%** Shakespeare and the Drama. N.Y. 1928.

***%%%%** Calendrier Positiviste (Douzieme Mois) Paris. 1852.

***@** See pp. 217–314.

***@@** World of William Clissold, Vol. 2, p. 614. N.Y. 1926.

HATSHEPSUT

The Ablest Queen of Far Antiquity (1500 B.C.)

Hatshepsut of Ancient Egypt was the greatest female ruler of all time, according to some Egyptologists. Among those whom she dominated was her brother, Thotmes III, "The Napoleon of Far Antiquity."

She is also said to have been the first woman in history to challenge the supremacy of the male, though arrayed against her were more than three thousand years of masculine tradition. There was no word for "queen" or "empress" in the language of her day—but she fought her way to power and held the throne of the world's then leading empire for thirty-three years.

Hatshepsut lived 150 years before Tut-Ankh-Amen, or 3500 years ago. Her father, Thotmes I, was the conqueror of the known world, and when he was stricken with paralysis, Hatshepsut became his chief aide. So efficient did she prove that Thotmes, in time, entrusted her with the management of the kingdom and made her co-ruler.

When Thotmes called the nobles together, he said to them, "This daughter, Khummit Amen Hatshepsitou, the Loving One, I put in my place . . . henceforth she shall guide you. Listen to her words and submit unanimously to her commands. Whoever adores her, I will adore, but he who speaks evil against Her Majesty will die."

Together father and daughter travelled over the empire, receiving homage, offering sacrifice in the temples, erecting monuments and buildings, improving industry and agriculture.

But Hatshepsut had several rivals, principally the two sons of Thotmes, one of whom, later Thotmes II, was born of a wife not of royal birth, and was a minor. The other, later Thotmes III, was the son of a slave named Asnut.

Thotmes III, hoping to oust Hatshepsut, staged a trick in the Temple of Amen to demonstrate that it was he, not she, who was the elect of God. Whilst he was at prayer one day in a secluded part of the temple, he had a priestly procession which bore a glittering image of the supreme God, Amen-Ra, swerve suddenly from the main aisle, as if drawn by some unseen power, and come toward him, whereupon he fell prostrate to the ground as if in a trance. It was then, the priests declared, that the God himself stepped out of his shrine, raised Thotmes to his feet, conducted him to the innermost altar where only the Pharaoh could tread, and bade him rule over Egypt.

This plot was extremely effective and Hatshepsut was faced with the alternatives of war or compromise with Thotmes. She ended by marrying him. The two now put their father off the throne but the old lion reasserted himself, drove them both out, and made Thotmes II, the real heir, ruler. The latter, however, was by all accounts, a weakling, and died, it is believed, by assassination.

At this period much of the record is lost and there is a gap in the story of Hatshepsut. When we next hear of her, she is again on the throne with Thotmes III, who is now so strong that he is able to restrict her to the position of Chief Royal Wife. However, by skillful intrigues she not only restores herself as co-ruler but finally thrusts him into the background as a mere husband, who is inferior to her prime minister, Nehusi, which name in Egyptian means, "full-blooded Negro."

Hatshepsut had yet another handicap besides that of sex, namely, ancestry. On her father's side, she was not of pure Theban stock, though her mother was. Her enemies, the priests of Amen, now seized on this "taint" in her lineage and plotted to dethrone her. To offset this, she began to publicize herself in the most sensational manner of that time: the building of temples, pyramids, and obelisks, the size and grandeur of which was regarded by the popular mind as a gauge of the ruler's power. Accordingly Hatshepsut decided to build a temple the like of which the world had never seen, and sent for her chief architect, Senmut, who to all appearances was a full-blooded Negro. Together, they chose a site which was not only appropriate but strategic. This was on an elevation three miles away from the stronghold of her opponents, the Temple of Amen-Ra. From this site her temple looked down on theirs.

Under Senmut's genius, Hatshepsut's temple developed into what is still one of the world's most remarkable specimens of architecture. It had a frontage of eight hundred feet and was for the most part hollowed out of the great cliff that overlooked it. Double and triple rows of columns lined the entrance, and the approach was marked by innumerable statues, wonderful terraces, and paradisiacal gardens. Colorful inscriptions decorated the interior, which abounded in architectural novelties.

Not content with this Hatshepsut decided to carry her triumph into the very camp of her detractors. She ordered to be made two obelisks, taller than any others in Egypt. Each was hewn from mighty blocks of rose granite and when completed took two great rafts, each manned by 900 men, to transport down the Nile. Hatshepsut intended these as a gift to the Temple of Amen-Ra but very astutely she had ordered them made so tall that they were higher than the temple, whose ruins, now known as Karnak,[43] reveal it to be one of the most colossal structures made by man. Accordingly, to make the obelisks fit, the roof of the temple was opened, and from this Hatshepsut's obelisks reared their heads as chimneys over a roof.

But that was not all. To make the obelisks still more conspicuous she had their tops encased in electrum, a metal costlier than gold. (Electrum was a composition of silver and gold. Silver being rarer than gold in ancient Egypt, it was more precious.)

In the bright sunlight of that rainless land the obelisks shone like glittering peaks. Their brilliancy, in the queen's own words, lit up the two lands of Egypt.[44] Whenever a resident of Thebes or a visitor looked out on the city, the most dazzling sight he saw was no longer the temple of Amen-Ra but her obelisks.

When the people entered the temple, they read on them this engraving: "O ye people, who shall see my monument in the ages to come, beware of saying, 'I know not, I know not why this was made and a mountain fashioned entirely from gold.' These two obelisks My Majesty hath wrought that MY name may abide, enduring in this temple for ever and ever."

The queen's popularity increased and she became firmly established. Great prosperity came to the land and gold was so plentiful it was no longer weighed but was measured in bushel-baskets. She wrote in her own praise, "It came to pass that Her Majesty was increased above all things; was beautiful to look at above all things: her voice was that of a god; her frame was that of a god; her spirit was like a god. It came to pass that she was a beautiful maiden."

But in spite of all this, she was still a woman with masculine prejudice against her. To overcome this she boldly announced that she was really a man. Whether Egypt was startled we do not know but this step crushed all further opposition. She donned male garb, changed her name, from Hatshepsitu to Hatsehpsut, its male equivalent, and announced that she was of virgin birth. Her father, she declared, was not Thotmes I, but the great God, Amen, himself. The latter had appeared to her mother "in a flood of light and perfume."

The whole story in its most intimate bed-room details was painted on the walls of her temple and may still be seen. The child shown as being born of this union is a boy. Thereafter her sculptured portraits showed her with a man's chest and beard. She also took the title "King of the North and South: Ka-Ma-Ra; the Horus[45] of Gold; Bestower of Years; Conqueror of all Lands; Vivifier of Hearts; Chief Spouse of Amen; the Mighty One."

But the feminine in her cropped up when she wrote of herself: "His Majesty, herself, put with her own hands of oil of ani on all her limbs. Her fragrance was like a divine breath; her scent reached as far as the land of Punt; her skin is that of pure gold; it shines like the stars in the hall of festival in view of the whole land . . . she has no equal among the Gods who were before since the world was. She is living Ra, eternally. He hath selected her for protecting Egypt, for rousing bravery among men. . . .

"I rule over this land like the son of Isis; I am mighty like the son of Nu.[46] I shall be forever like the stars which changeth not. . . ."

Hatshepsut sent expeditions to distant lands, one of which, to Punt, merits special attention. Punt was the traditional home of the earliest Egyptians and was located somewhere in East Africa. The mission was entrusted to her three favorites: Nehusi, the unmixed Negro who is spoken of in her inscriptions as "Prince Chancellor, First Friend, Wearing the Collar"; Senmut, the architect, who is depicted as holding the Queen's infant daughter, Nefruara, on his knees; and Thutiy, her treasurer. They left with five vessels of about 300 tons each, and returned with gold, myrrh, incense, incense-bearing trees, strange animals, and other products of that region. The full story of this expedition may be read on the walls of her temple at Deir-el-Bahari.[47]

In the fifteenth year of her reign, and the thirtieth of her rule, she held a jubilee. Her husband, Thotmes III, was permitted to burn a little incense to Amen-Ra as he joined the procession. She wrote triumphantly, "I have no enemy in all the land; all countries are my subjects: He (Amen-Ra) hath made my boundaries to the extremities of heaven; the circuit of the sun hath labored for me."

At last she died, her end hastened, perhaps, by Thotmes III. Succeeding to the throne, he killed off her friends, defaced her inscriptions, chipped her features from her portraits, and walled in her obelisks, doing all with such thoroughness that she was forgotten for three thousand years.

In 1906, however, an American excavator, Theodore Davis,[48] discovered her tomb and amazed the world with the story of this remarkable woman, a worthy predecessor of Elizabeth, Joan of Arc, and Catherine the Great.

Hatshepsut's grandmother, Nefertari-Aahmes, was Ethiopian, and is shown in her portraits as being very black. In addition, Hatshepsut was of southern Egyptian ancestry, which was and still is very much mixed with the pure Negroes of the Sudan, whose territory adjoined Egypt.

Of Hatshepsut and her temple, Robert Hichens[49] says:

> "To me most feminine she seemed when I saw her temple at Deir-el-Bahari with its brightness and its suavity; pretty shallowness and sunshine; its white and blue and yellow and red and orange all very trim and fanciful, all very smart and delicate: full of finesse and laughter breathing out to me of the twentieth century the coquetry of a woman in 1500 B.C.
>
> "After the terrific masculinity of Medinet-Abou; after the great freedom of the Ramasseum and the grandeur of its colossus, the manhood of the ages concentrated in granite, the temple at Deir-el-Bahari came upon me like a delicate woman perfumed and arranged, clothed in a creation of white and blue and orange standing ever so knowingly against a background of orange and pink, of red and brown, a smiling coquette of the mountains, a gay and sweet enchantress who knew her pretty powers and meant to exercise them . . .
>
> "A radiant queen reigns here, a queen of fantasy and splendor and of that divine shallowness, refined frivolity, literally cut into a mountain. . . . Instead of being uplifted or overawed by form, we are rejoiced by color, by the high vivacity of arrested movement; by the story that color and movement tell, and over all there is a bright, blue painted sky, studded, almost distractedly studded, with a plethora of the yel-

low stars of the Egyptians made like starfish. . . . Through this most characteristic temple one roves in a gaily attentive mood feeling all the time Hatshepsut's fascination."

One thing seems certain: Hatshepsut held her own until the last. Her tomb was discovered in the Valley of the Kings, where only the lordly males were buried. The queens had a burial place of their own.

Hatshepsut's dearest wish was to live in the memory of mankind. To the Egyptian, that was true immortality. And she has achieved this, for graven in imperishable granite, her story is as fresh and fascinating now as when it was written thirty-five centuries ago.

REFERENCES

Sir John Garstang, noted archaeologist, thinks that Hatshepsut was the princess who reared Moses (N.Y. Times, Jan. 27, 1932).

Theodore Davis says as regards the leader of the expedition to Punt: "Having once made the decision the queen had to choose the chief to lead her ships to the land of Punt. We have preserved the name of the chief, whom we see appearing before the queen with other high officials at a ceremony in the year IX. His name is Nehusi, 'The Negro.' He is entrusted with the transport of soldiers to Punt. It is not impossible that he was a real Negro. The Egyptians felt no aversion towards Negroes. We know that a king of the XIVth Dynasty, of whom the base of a statue remains, was called 'The Negro' and we have every reason to believe that King Taharka of the XXIVth Dynasty was one also . . . nevertheless, at the time of the XVIIIth Dynasty when a native race occupied the throne, it would be surprising if so important a command had been entrusted to a Negro and also that he should have such high titles for it is said he was 'prince, chancellor, first friend, wearing the collar,' he, therefore, belonged to one of the highest ranks of the administrative hierarchy."

This latter statement sounds contradictory. It is true that there was a social difference between the unmixed Negro who was not a native

Egyptian and the unmixed Negro who was: — The former was an alien. But the bulk of the Egyptian army was composed of these foreign-born Negroes, who were known as Matoi. We have pictures of them as commanders-in-chief of the Egyptian army. All through the East, these Negroes from the Sudan held high posts. For seven hundred years, and as late as 1906, the most trusted man of the sultans of Turkey was the Daroussada-Aghassi, or head eunuch, who by tradition was an unmixed Negro from the Sudan. He bore the title of Prince, Marshal, and was ruler of the holy city of Mecca. (Bull. *et* Mem. Soc. d'Anthrop. de Paris, March 14, 1901, p 237. See also EUNUCHS in index of Sex and Race.)

As regards Punt, it was known, says Davis, as "the divine land." The name, he says, "seems to indicate that it had played an important part in ancient Egyptian tradition" (p. 26)... "It cannot be doubted that the fauna (of Punt) is an African country so the five ships of Hatshopsitu landed in Africa."

Davis, Theodore, "Tomb of Hatshopsitu," London, 1906.
Maspero, G., "Histoire Ancienne des Peuples de L'Orient," Vol. II, p. 245.
Breasted, "Ancient Records of Egypt," Vol. II, p. 119, 144—Chicago, 1906.
Rawlinson, G., Ancient Egypt. Vol. 2, p. 215–16. 1880.

JAN ERNEST MATZELIGER

Inventor Who Gave Supremacy in the Shoe Industry to the United States (1852–1889)

In spite of handicaps which exceed those of the oppressed in almost every other land, there are always individual Negroes in the United States who are not content to settle down to a color-line job but have striven to play a man's part in achievement, regardless of all discouragement. These individuals are to be found in almost every field, including the very difficult one of scientific invention.

In at least one branch of industry, America owes its supremacy directly to a Negro, Jan Ernest Matzeliger. A pioneer in the art of shoemaking, he enriched America and other nations by billions of dollars, made a dozen or more millionaires, created work for hundreds of thousands, and contributed enormously to what is regarded as one of the distinctive features of civilization, namely the wearing of shoes. Massachusetts, center of the world's shoe trade, has been a particular beneficiary of his ingenuity.

Matzeliger was born in Dutch Guiana, South America, of a Dutch father and a Negro mother. Mechanically inclined as a child, he entered the government machine-shops of the colony at the age of ten, as an apprentice.

Ambitious to learn more, he left for New York City when his apprenticeship expired. Handicapped by his color and his lack of funds, he nevertheless contrived to learn a good deal about machinery.

At the age of twenty-five he went to Lynn, Massachusetts, and thanks to that more liberal environment, he found employment in the factory of M. H. Harvey, where he operated a McKay machine for turning shoes.[50] There his attention was naturally directed to shoe machinery. Noting the time-wasting method of lasting[51] shoes by hand, he decided to invent a machine to do it.

Such a machine had been the fond dream of many an ingenious youth, eager to make a fortune. Inventors had burned barrels of midnight oil and promoters had spent hundreds of thousands of dollars in the endeavor to change the lasting of shoes from hand to machine methods, as Blake and McKay[52] had changed the sewing of the uppers.

When Matzeliger announced his intention, his white fellow workers laughed at him derisively. That a Negro should succeed where some of the best white inventors had failed, seemed ridiculous. They boasted, moreover, that whatever else was done by machinery, nothing could ever supersede hand-lasting. The lasters felt secure in their position. These skilled craftsmen were the gentlemen of the shoe trade, earning from $20 to $40 a week, a very good wage then.

Securing a room over the old West Lynn Mission at the corner of Ann and Charles Streets, where he would be safe from too curious eyes, he worked nights studying, experimenting, and drawing. He had started out in a field never before entered by anyone.

With no other capital but his meagre wages, he was forced to make use of such material as he could get hold of. Pieces of wood and old cigar and packing boxes were mainly used. For six months he toiled strenuously until he had constructed a model which, though crude, gave him confidence that he was on the road to success.

Although he tried to work in secret, the hand-lasters learned of his efforts and sometimes dropped in to laugh at the odd-looking combination of sticks in the form of a machine. One of them, in racial contempt, dubbed it "the niggerhead machine," the name by which it was popularly known later.

Even Matzeliger's friends advised him to give up what seemed to them a foolish undertaking, and insisted that, after a long day's work at the factory he should have rest and recreation. One man, however, thought he saw some good principles in the collection of sticks and offered Matzeliger $50.00 for it. But Matzeliger, reasoning that if it was worth a $50.00 first offer, it probably would have a much higher value elsewhere, refused to sell.

He now planned to make a model in metal. Gathering odd bits of iron, he worked patiently, filing and fitting the parts unaided. Four years later he perfected a machine that would work. He was offered $1,500 for his invention of pleating the leather around the toe, which sum he again refused. Greatly encouraged by the widespread interest his model created, he started to build a better one. Perfection was his aim. For another six years he worked on his invention until a more simplified machine had been constructed.

With his new model it was easy for him to convince practical men that his invention would work successfully. A company was formed, consisting of himself, those who had advanced him money from time to time, and some others with large capital. It was soon found necessary, however, to build another machine, different in construction, which, when completed, worked almost to perfection.

One of the especial merits of the invention was that the pincers for pulling the upper, were positively closed by a smooth movement and did not tear even the most delicate leather.

Today, according to experts, no better method of handling loose tacks for fastening the upper to the sole has ever been invented. The twist and pull of the pincers reproduced exactly the peculiar and almost inimitable skill with which expert hand-lasters treat difficult upper leather in their lasting of shoes. No other machine has been invented that is capable of manipulating and shaping a shoe on all styles of lasts, and it is practically impossible to make shoes to meet commercial requirements without using Matzeliger's machine. After twelve years of persistent pursuit of a single idea, he had won.

With this new invention, the United Shoe Manufacturing Company rapidly drove competitors out of the shoe business until, a few years later, it controlled 98 percent of the shoe machinery business.

A tremendous expansion in the shoe industry followed. Shoe stocks proved a gold mine to investors. Earnings increased more than 350 per cent while wages increased but 34 per cent and the price of footwear decreased.

The machine was set up in factories but there were stubborn and prolonged strikes against it by the hand-lasters. One veteran laster said: "The machine revenges Matzeliger by singing as it works. I've got your job! I've got your job!"

F. A. Gannon says: "Sales of shoes abroad increased approximately $16,000,000 annually. United Shoe Machinery Company machinery and shoe experts were sent around the world and American shoe manufacturing methods were adopted farthest north in Norway, in tropical Central America, in England and all the countries of Europe, in Africa, Australia and even in China, Japan and the Philippines."

The United Shoe Manufacturing Company constructed a model manufacturing plant in Beverly, Massachusetts. It was built of reinforced concrete and employed 5,000 persons at a high average wage. Nearby recreational buildings, including a country club, a gun club, and motorboat club, were constructed, and a band and an athletic team organized—all for the benefit of the employees. The health of shoe workers under the new working conditions improved immensely, and tuberculosis, their worst menace, was greatly decreased.

One of the stockholders, Colonel McKay, left $5,000,000 to the engineering department of Harvard University.

And what about Matzeliger? The amazing young genius was not to enjoy his triumph. Close confinement and overwork had undermined his health. He was stricken with tuberculosis and died two years later, in September, 1889, at the age of 37.

In his will, Matzeliger left a few shares of his stock to the North Congregational Church, a white congregation that had befriended him. Years later this church, finding itself in financial difficulties, remembered the bequest and sold the stock for $10,860. A tablet in this church commemorates the inventor.

The Consolidated Hand Lasting Machine Company, in its bulletin, said of him: "The conviction is forced upon us that this man of iron will, this man of nerve, who could not be turned from his course, knew whereof he spoke and builded better than he knew, very much better than his most sanguine friends hoped for. Such men do away with old methods and institute new and better ones. Such men make missionaries and martyrs. Without such men we should be without material progress."

What Edison is to artificial lighting, Matzeliger is to footwear. This great Negro genius needs no monument. Almost every shoe worn by civilized men is his memorial. With hundreds of millions of people in civilized lands to be shod, think what it would mean if there had been no such invention as Matzeliger's and the old method of hand-lasting was still in vogue!

ROGERS'S NOTES

Through Matzeliger was mocked about his color, and his machine called "nigger-head" in derision, he came to be considered white as the great value of his machine grew. However, his death certificate listed him as a "mulatto." Also Waldemar Kaempfert, noted scientific writer, says he was "a poor half-breed son of a Dutch engineer and a native black woman . . . This messenger from a foreign land solved in principle the final problem of making shoes by machinery." (Popular History of American Invention, Vol. 2, pp. 429–430, 1924).

Gannon, F. A. "A Short History of American Shoe-Making," 1912.
McDermott, C. H. "History of the Shoe and Leather Industries," pp. 61, 106–07.
Jour. of Negro History, Vol. 2, p. 29. 1917, for proof of "mulatto," on his death certificate.

WILLIAM MONROE TROTTER

Most Unselfish of the Negro Leaders (1872–1934)

William Monroe Trotter, the most persistent, uncompromising, and unselfish crusader against racial injustice since Frederick Douglass, was born of parents who had been slaves. His fighting spirit was encouraged by his father, a Civil War veteran, who taught him that he had a right to enter any public place and that he should always insist on that right. He was also told that he should try to excel whenever he came in contact with white people. If beaten in a fight with a white boy, he would get another whipping when he came home. For this ideal of fullest rights for his people, he later sacrificed wealth, political preferment, friends, the ordinary comforts of life and finally, life, itself.

No other Aframerican leader of his time was as courageous as Trotter. There were worlds of difference between him and his prominent contemporaries, some of whom were ready to compromise in order to be able to enjoy comforts that the people for whom they were supposed to be speaking were very far from attaining. Unlike most of the other Aframerican leaders, also, Trotter had started life with a certain degree of affluence, and had been able to get an education with little or no financial difficulty. His father, who was recorder of deeds under President Harrison,[53] was earning about $10,000 a year.

As a youth, Trotter was exceptionally bright. At fourteen, he led his class in grammar school at Boston, Massachusetts, and was its president and valedictorian. At Harvard University, he won four important scholarships and was graduated magna cum laude. So excellent was his record that Harvard conferred a Master of Arts on him without further studies.

At the university he had also distinguished himself as a member of the Debating Club and was elected to the Phi Beta Kappa, being the first Aframerican to win that distinction. He was also president of the Harvard Total Abstinence Society.

Finding it impossible to get suitable employment on graduation because of color, he entered the real-estate and mortgage business in 1897 and was so successful that he soon became the second wealthiest Negro in Boston. But ever concerned about human rights, he did not confine his activities to making money. True to his ideas of racial equality, he founded the Guardian, a militant newspaper, in 1901, as well as the New England Suffrage League in 1903.

At this time arose a new Negro leader with a program which Trotter felt was a challenge to all that he stood for. This was Booker T. Washington, who was preaching to Negroes the doctrine of duty and the concentration on trade, agriculture, and self-development, rather than the seeking of citizenship rights.

Washington's gospel, as enunciated by himself, was not wholly one of surrender, however. Viewed from a certain angle it was practical. But what mattered to Trotter was how what Washington said was being construed by all those who were eager to keep the Negro in his so-called place. It practically meant that since the white people were "the Negro's best friends," he should always yield to them and let them decide what was best for him. In short, subservience.

Trotter knew further that many of these white "friends" had the same superiority complex as the white enemies, and that such "friends" usually insisted that in any clash of wills it was the Negro who should yield in the cause of peace and goodwill. As for the Negroes[,] he saw that since most of them took their cue from the whites and usually accepted the leader chosen for them by the whites, as Booker T. Washington had been, that Washington, doctrines and all, had become their hero.

His fighting spirit aroused more than ever, he decided to show America that there was an element of Negroes who did not accept Washington as their spokesman. Washington was to speak in Boston and a large audience of both "races" came out to hear him. Trotter and his lieutenants stationed in different parts of the church heckled

Washington and finally set off stench bombs which sent the audience coughing and sputtering outside. As for Washington and his friends on the platform, cayenne pepper liberally thrown there sent them gasping. A free-for-all fight followed in the aisles, and one of Trotter's men, a policeman, and others were hurt.

Trotter was thrown into jail. His trial attracted nation-wide attention. Found guilty, he was sent to prison for thirty days but he gained his end in that his views on rights for Negroes had been given a publicity they could not possibly have had otherwise.

He came out of jail more determined than ever. The Guardian became more militant. Forgotten was money-making. Into the insatiable maw of his crusade for justice he poured first of all, his ready money, then that from the sale of his properties. When this was not enough he threw in the money from the sale of his wife's properties and then of his mother's. The simple truth is that since his editorial policies were not countenanced by the whites and he did not receive any approval from them, he did not receive much support from established Negro leaders or from the Negro masses.

But his efforts bore fruit in other directions. As a result of his arrest some of the bolder Negro spirits organized the Niagara Movement.[54] Later, and no doubt as a result of this movement, the National Association for the Advancement of Colored People came into being with a membership of whites and Negroes.

This organization attacked Booker T. Washington and spoke up for the rights of the Negro vigorously. But Trotter resigned from it. He distrusted the white people in it. He felt that since the financial support of the organization came from them that they would dictate its policies, which, in the final analysis, would be to the Negro's disadvantage. He founded the National Equal Rights' League,[55] an organization that lived up to its name.

To his "call for arms" the response was weak. But Trotter continued to act as if he had a mighty host behind him. When "The Birth of a Nation," a rabid anti-Negro moving picture, appeared in Boston, he fought it so vigorously that he went to jail again. Nevertheless he won his case and succeeded in establishing a censorship to curb this kind of propaganda in the state. He next followed the picture to Richmond, Virginia, capital of the Confederacy, and fought it there even against the clubs of the police.

During the war, Trotter resolutely opposed separate regiments for Negroes. White and black, he pointed out, had fought side by side at Concord, Lexington, and Bunker Hill, and were even then doing so in the French army. As for those Negro leaders who had accepted segregation on the condition that there would be Negro officers he denounced them with withering scorn.

Trotter took his case to the White House. He had been going there to petition every President since Theodore Roosevelt. But Woodrow Wilson refused to see him. Three years before he had bearded Wilson at the White House on the segregation of Negro federal employees, which had come in with the Wilson regime, and his outspokenness in contrast to the soft, well-chosen words of the rest of the Negroes in the delegation had so angered the haughty Southerner in Wilson that Wilson walked abruptly from the room.[56] When rioting Negro soldiers shot up the white population of Houston, Texas, Trotter went to the White House and was largely instrumental in getting a reprieve for them.[57]

In 1926, on the 150th anniversary of the Declaration of Independence, Trotter was again at the White House with a mammoth petition addressed to Calvin Coolidge, asking that the spirit of that famous document be applied to the treatment of colored citizens. He also petitioned Coolidge and the Judiciary Committee of the United States Senate, to support an anti-lynching bill. His efforts in this direction served in no small measure to bring about the passage of the bill in the Senate, but which was defeated in the House.

Trotter's most notable exploit was his invasion of the Versailles Conference after the United States government had tried to block him. As one of the most important issues before that conference was the right of minority groups as expounded by Woodrow Wilson,[58] Trotter felt that the Negro ought to be considered with other oppressed groups.

Accordingly he appeared before the Foreign Relations Committee of the United States Senate to demand an additional clause in the Covenant of the League, granting Negroes equal rights in America.

The Senators gave him no satisfaction. He announced that he would take the matter to Versailles, himself. The government refused him a passport but he engaged as a ship's cook and reached France.

His mission did not succeed but his story told to the peace conference received world-wide publicity and caused Woodrow Wilson, who was acting as the champion of oppressed minorities whilst under his own administration the oppression of American Negroes had noticeably increased, considerable embarrassment.

In all these activities Trotter found an able and untiring helper in his wife, Geraldine, who had come of a refined, well-to-do colored family and had caught like him the vision of equal opportunity and justice for all Americans. She gave her money freely to the cause and then her beautiful home to suffer privations with her husband. She was associate editor of The Guardian. After her death in 1918, Trotter published her picture each week on the editorial page in loving memory.

Trotter attacked segregation no matter where he saw it and no matter in what guise. There was no beating about the bush with him. Whenever he spoke he made every nerve of his auditors stiffen against the evil he was attacking. Nor did he spare the white philanthropists who gave money for the building of colored Y.M.C.A.s, racial scholarships, and racial medals. These, he denounced as so many bribes given by the ruling class to silence the more articulate members of the group, and as being fatal to the cause of the inarticulate Negro masses. Naturally, none of the medals, scholarships, and prizes that were given to Negroes for accomplishments, or more properly speaking for good behavior, ever fell to Trotter.

Who's Who in America carried the names of nearly 100 Negroes, the majority of whom were only of average worth, but Trotter was omitted.

In the matter of so-called voluntary segregation, Trotter was equally consistent. Declaring that this was born of forced segregation, he insisted that it strengthened the position of the white segregationists. In consequence of this, most of the other Negro leaders, with an eye to present advantage, thought him erratic, while the masses, in whom a segregated psychology had been instilled through centuries, regarded him on the whole as a fool.

For instance, after he had spoken at a convention on the National Equal Rights League in Chicago about 1919, some colored women, ignoring his inspiring address, began to discuss him personally. One of them said that she thought him worthless because his clothes were shabby and soiled, and were quite a contrast to those of her pastor. Another added deprecatingly that she had seen him that morning in an ill-smelling, fifteen-cents-a-meal Greek restaurant. Here, however, was a cultured and talented man who, had he closed his heart to the injustices suffered by his people might have been a millionaire.

As the years went on Trotter's financial worries increased. During the depression of the 1930's he had extreme difficulty keeping his paper going. The Negroes, it was true, were beginning to appreciate him but not enough to support the work.

His health failed and he was still inconsolable at the loss of his wife whom he seemed to miss more and more with the years. Then in 1934, came the knock-out blow to this stout-hearted fighter: he lost control of his newspaper. With wealth, health, wife, newspaper gone, there seemed nothing else to live for. He staggered up to the roof of the three-story building in which he was only a lodger; later his shattered lifeless body was discovered on the ground.[59]

He had given his last défi[60] to life itself—life which had remained deaf to his ideal.

Like every other born crusader, Trotter had something of the fanatic in him. The cayenne pepper and stench-bomb attack on Washington proved that; but be it noted that the opponents of the Negro with their lynching and jim-crow were infinitely more intolerant. Finally, were it not for a spirit such as Trotter's—the spirit of the eternal rebel against wrong and injustices—mankind would still be slaves and serfs.

If those leaders who compromise with racial injustice in the hope of present gain either to themselves or their group are following the better path than [*sic*] the sacrifices of William Monroe Trotter have been in vain, and he deserves the name so often given him of fool and obstinate dreamer. But if an American citizen whose skin is dark, is entitled to the same rights as one whose skin is fair—for this was simply Trotter's stand—then unborn generations will revere him.

They will revere him not because he alone had the vision of an America in which there would be no color injustice, not because he worked harder than others to achieve it but for the persistency and purity of his ideals. No Puritan of New England ever had a greater scorn of compromise with evil than he.

From *Nature Knows No Color-Line: Research into the Negro Ancestry in the White Race* (1952)

Nature Knows No Color-Line examines the social interactions, and frequently the prejudices, that have occurred when different groups encounter one another. Often, according to Rogers, these biases would gradually disappear as the groups inter-mixed. In the essay "Where Did the Color Problem Originate? And Why" Rogers explores the history of racial prejudice. Instead of using complex Marxist or psychoanalytic theory, Rogers explains racial prejudice in simpler terms. Rogers gives five early examples of it. The first instance he can locate occurred over five thousand years ago in India, where the lighter complexioned Aryans discriminated against the darker Dasyus. He also goes on at some length about the discrimination against Blacks based on the Biblical stories revolving around Cain as well as Noah's son Ham. Rogers demonstrates that all groups have their own biases based on arbitrary and insubstantial interpretations, sometimes grounded on differing views of the same material. As he says, "Theology, whether it be Jewish, Christian, Buddhist, Moslem, Shinto, or just plain heathen, is largely an excursion of the folk-mind into the realm of the unsubstantiated, and the incoherent. Ideas picked up here and there are patched into a system." Such is the arbitrary and often irrational nature of race prejudice. John P. Claburn gives an interesting ecocritical interpretation of the book (234–38). The text here is taken from the privately printed third edition (1952). Reprinted by Wesleyan University Press, 2011.

NATURE KNOWS NO COLOR-LINE

"Where Did the Color Problem Originate? And Why"

The two varieties of humanity which have intermixed the most and longest are so-called Negro and Caucasian. There is some evidence that they mated in prehistoric times; that a Negro, or Negroid, people inhabited Europe when it was joined to Africa and was still tropical. As for the historic period, or about eight thousand years there is abundant evidence they did, especially in the Americas since Columbus.

In so-called racial intermixture there are usually two forces: exogamy or out-breeding and endogamy, or inbreeding. In colonial lands, the first is called miscegenation; the second, race purity. However, in those lands as in all lands where one's partner in marriage is not selected by his parents, like and dislike generally determine one's choice of a mate. Which qualities attract or repel are quite beyond precise definition, so much depends upon the individual, regardless of race, caste or religion. As Shakespeare said:

> Strange is it that our bloods
> Of colour, weight and heat, poured all together
> Would quite confound distinction, yet stand off
> In differences so mighty.[1]

Some of these "mighty" differences are not all physical. They are economic, social, educational and religious, also. Any of the latter can operate as strongly as the racial, which is supposed in colonial, or former colonial lands, to be the strongest of all objections. The peculiar thing about miscegenation is that some of its most vociferous objectors practise it.

In certain colonial and former colonial lands as in the United States, South Africa, and the West Indies, color of skin, (which is accepted as normal in Europe, where the population is white, or Central Africa where it is black) is a "mighty" difference, influencing not only mating but life in some of its most unexpected phases. For instance, the matter of the blond and the brunette among white women. When one reads in American papers of a man having an affair with some gorgeous girl, she is always blonde. When brunettes are mentioned it is almost with some sort of apology. Is this depreciation of the white brunette an extension of the prejudice against the Negro's color? Whiteness of skin has become a symbol of purity, goodness, and fine Christian living. "Wash me and I shall be whiter than snow," runs the hymn. Thus the more bleached the skin, the more bleached the character—Negro albinos, not included, of course.

But whatever be the reason the blondes are raved over in America, and the brunettes aren't. However, in the Scandinavian lands, where as one visitor remarked, "Blondes are a dime a thousand," blond skin and hair count for no more than does black among the blacks of Central Africa or yellow among the Chinese. Unmixed blacks in Scandinavia, I have noticed, attract attention and are usually welcome. They offer some variety to the color scheme, in certain villages in the West Indies where the people are dark I have noticed similar welcome given to a white visitor for the same reason.

Is color in sexual selection a factor only in colonial and former colonial lands? Evidently not. It probably goes back to the time when variety of skin coloring began to appear in the human race, or many hundreds of thousands of years ago. Since the first human beings were all of the same color it is clear that difference of color of skin is an important factor in human evolution. All human beings, except albinos, have some degree of color in their skins.

Another question. When and where was color first used as a social, economic and political factor? Many who have given thought to that say it started with the invasion of the dark men's lands—Asia, Africa, America—by the whites in the fifteenth century. Lord Cromer,[2] distinguished statesman, thought however, that the question had never been competently examined. "I am not aware," he said, "that any competent scholar has ever examined into the question of the stage in history at which difference of color . . . acquired the importance it now possesses as a social and political factor."* I think he is right. If it has been done I have not seen it.

The first recorded instance of color prejudice I have been able to find is in India of some five thousand years ago when the Aryas, or Aryans, invaded the valley of the Indus and found there a black people—the Dasysus, or Dasyus. In any case we find very clear evidences of it in Aryan writings. In the Rig-Veda (Book IX, Hymn, 42:1) Indra, their national god, is depicted as "Blowing away with supernatural might from earth and from the heavens the black skin which Indra hates." Hymn 42:1, tells of "Driving the black skin far away." The blacks were called "Anasahs" (noseless people). Book v. Hymn 29:10, tells how Indra "slew the flat-nosed barbarians."

India's caste system was based on color.** The word varna (caste) literally means "color." Arya varna (white skin); Krishna varna (black skin).***

"The Aryans of India," says the Encyclopedia of Religion and Ethics, "prided themselves on their fairer skins and more aquiline features and held in derision the black color and flatter physiognomies of the aborigines, regarded them much as conquering whites regarded blacks in Africa."

Thanks, however, to time and the Moslem invasion of the eleventh century color prejudice weakened. Aryan and Dasyu amalgamated into the present Indian population. Later, the incoming of the Europeans, did much to revive it.

The next evidence of it I have been able to find is in Ancient Egypt. Gerald Massey, perhaps the greatest of all authorities on ancient Egyptian lore, said: "On the monuments the dark people are commonly called 'the evil race of Kush' but when the Ethiopian element dominates the dark people retort by calling the light complexions, the pale, degraded race of Arvad."**** But this prejudice of fair for dark and the converse was, it is safe to say, never nearly as strong as in India. The whites did not come in any considerable number to Egypt until the Ptolemaic invasion of the third century B.C., by which time intermixture had already taken too firm a root for any appreciable degree of color prejudice, as I shall show later.

The third instance of color prejudice is to be found in the rabbinical writings. The early rabbis did very definitively and abundantly say that a black skin was the result of a "curse" on Ham by Noah. The signs of this "curse" said certain rabbis were "a black skin, misshapen lips, and twisted hair." The Bible says the "curse" was placed on Canaan, Ham's son, but some rabbis said it was placed directly on Ham. Rabbi Huja said that he came forth from the Ark "black-skinned."*# This would mean that Ham who had gone into the Ark fair-skinned had undergone this change of color in the only one hundred and ninety days that [he] had been in the Ark. Ham it appears, had been guilty of some sexual infraction while in there from having intercourse with his wife to sodomy.

Topinard,[3] French anthropologist, thinks, too, that the rabbis of the first century were the first to stress differences of race and color. Race, as we now use it, he says, was unknown in far antiquity, at least in the West. He correctly notes that Aristotle, Father of Natural History, and Hippocrates, Father of Medicine, do not mention "race" though both studied anatomy and the then known varieties of the human race, including the Negro.

The Greek had two distinct divisions of humanity—Greek and Barbarian, or citizen and alien. An Athenian who married an alien, regardless of color, was sold into slavery. It was for a long time the same in Rome. "Race" as based on color and physique is, in fact comparatively recent. The King James Bible of the seventeenth century does not mention it. Shakespeare used it only for family lineage or contests. So also do the first English dictionary by Nathaniel Bailey in 1736; and the second by Dr. Samuel Johnson in 1750.

To quote Topinard, "In the first century when Christianity was beginning to seat itself in Rome the doctrine of a separate creation for whites and blacks was defended by the Babylonian rabbis and later by Emperor Julian. In 415 A. D. when one council was debating whether the Ethiopians were descended from Adam and the theory they weren't was making progress, St. Augustine in his 'City of God'[4] intervened and declared that no true Christian would doubt that all men, of no matter what form, color, or height were of the same protoplasmic origin."*##

Emperor Julian, The Apostate (c. 331–363 A. D.) said on race, "For different natures must have existed in all those things that among the nations were to be differentiated. Thus, at any rate is seen, if one observes how very different in their bodies are the Germans and Scythians from the Libyans and Ethiopians."[*###] The first were whites; the latter two, blacks.

Also in a letter to a priest he said that "facts bear witness that many men came into the world at once I shall maintain elsewhere, and precisely, but for the moment it will be enough to say this much that if we were descended from one man and one woman, it is not likely that our laws would show such divergence; nor in any case is it likely that the whole earth was filled with people by one man; nay, not even if the women used to bear many children at a time to their husbands like swine."[*####]

St. Augustine replied that all human beings even "monsters"—so-called freaks of nature—were of "the stock of Adam's or Noah's sons" and that, "whosoever is anywhere born of a man, that is, of a rational mortal animal, no matter what unusual appearance he presents in colour, movement, sound, nor how peculiar he is in some power, part, or quality of his nature no Christian can doubt he springs from a single protoplast." He added, "All the varieties of mankind . . . unquestionably trace their pedigree to that one first father of all."[*&]

As a result of this dispute, monogenism, or a single origin for the human race, became a fixed Christian doctrine; and says Topinard, more than one doubter paid the supreme penalty for disbelief.

The fourth stage in the development of color prejudice seemed therefore to have occurred in Rome of the first century A. D. as a phase of the fight between Christianity and Paganism. Prior to that, however, Pagan masters held the belief that humanity regardless of color, were either Roman or Barbarian. Christianity, the new religion, decided that "of one blood" God made all the peoples of the earth and that all men were brothers in Christ. Moreover, the earliest Christians pictured the Virgin Mary and Christ as black, both being an evolution of the worship of Isis and Horus which was once common in Rome.

Before proceeding to the fifth stage in the growth of color prejudice let us endeavor to see why the rabbis made the "curse" on Ham a black skin. This is certain: Next to the Aryans the Jews were more color conscious than any of the ancients. Why? They had been slaves to the Egyptians and Ethiopians who are described in their legends as Negroes. Again, after they had established themselves in Palestine they were twice invaded by Egyptians and Ethiopians. Shishak, Ethiopian ruler of Egypt, ravaged the land, plundered Solomon's Temple, and took a great number of Jews slaves to Egypt. (II Chronicles, 12). Another Ethiopian King, Zerah, who came with "a host of a thousand and three hundred chariots" was beaten off. (II Chronicles, 14).

It could be that the Jews before they left Egypt imbibed some of the color prejudice mentioned by Massey but it could not have been strong among them because they were dark, or even black. One rabbi does say they were black at that time, that the passage "black but comely" from the Song of Solomon means, "I was black in Egypt but comely in Egypt."[*&&] There is no doubt that after four centuries in Egypt the Jews had mixed much with Egyptians and Ethiopians, whom their legends describe as "black" and "wooly-haired." Thus the main difference between Hebrew and Egyptian was not racial but religious, the form which economic exploitation then took. Miriam's objection to the Ethiopian wife of Moses, Zipporah, was not on color but on religion and more likely on culture. Talk of Semitic and Hamite as "race" is sheerest nonsense and is used only by "parrot" anthropologists.

Furthermore we have no proof that the original seventy Jews who went to Egypt were white. According to their legends they originated in Chaldea and there is considerable evidence the inhabitants of that region in earliest times were Negroid. In fact, some writers said the Jews were an African people. Strabo said many of his time believed they were.

How then was it possible for them to place a "curse" on a black skin? The answer is that centuries after they had left Egypt and being somewhat whitened by mixing with fairer skinned people to the north and with Europeans, they could now look back on the unchanged color of the Ethiopians and Egyptians in comparison with themselves; and their rabbis, that is their "scientists," endeavoring to explain how black people came about tacked on that bit of folk-lore of the "curse" of Ham. It is very important to remember here that the Masoretic[5] text, regarded as the correct one of the ancient Hebrew writings, (called by Christians "The Old Testament"), says nothing whatever of Ham or Canaan's color. It merely says that a curse was placed on Canaan. So, too, does the Old Testament (Genesis, 10:25). That the "black" skin was a later addition is indisputable.

Strongest reason of all is that the curse on a black skin could now be used as proof of retribution on the blacks for having enslaved them. "The Egyptians," said one rabbi, "were descended from Ham, who was pronounced to be a slave of slaves." Other rabbis say likewise.

Still clearer proof that this legend was used later as retribution is that the "curse" on Ham and "blessing" on Shem by Noah worked in reverse. The Hebrews, sons of Shem, were enslaved for centuries by the Egyptians, while there is no proof that Hebrews enslaved the Egyptians, whom they call the sons of Ham. Moreover, according to the Masoretic version, the curse is on Canaan. But the Canaanites lived in Palestine which is in Asia, not Africa. Being Asiatics and nearer to the whites of the north, they were doubtless lighter in color than the Egyptians. Why then the curse of blackness on the offspring of Canaan? Well, they owned the land of Canaan, which the Hebrews claimed Jehovah had given them. In olden times one way of inciting one group against another was to place a curse on it. The modern parallel is "excommunication."

The Arabs, who are ethnically related to the Jews and are largely Negroid, had their version of the Ham legend, which they applied to the blacks of the Sudan. Mohamet, they said, once stopped at a woman's house and asked her how many sons she had. She had three but fearing that Mohamet would take one to carry his baggage, she hid one and brought out two. The Prophet of God, knowing she had lied, placed a curse on the hidden son. While the other two would have fair-skinned offspring, who would be wealthy and be lords of the earth, that of the hidden one would be as black as "darkness," be sold like cattle, and be perpetual slaves to the offspring of his brothers."[*&&&] Of course the

Arabs also captured white Circasians[6] in Asia and sold them like cattle but here again logic and facts give way to belief, inspired by gain, in this case, enslavement of the blacks.

And just here an observation as regards the lighter Negroid Arabs and what they said of the unmixed blacks since it will explain the case of the Negroid Jews towards the latter also. It is not necessary for a people to be unmixed white to have prejudice for a black sin. Sometimes those with only an eighth of white ancestry have this prejudice, too. I have known dark mulattoes, especially in the West Indies, who were much more prejudiced than many European-born whites there. Lighter mulattoes in France had much more prejudice for African blacks than any white Frenchman.

Incidentally, the blacks had their theory of the origin of the whites, also. Thin lips, straight hair and a white skin, they said, originated from an albino ape, who was the ancestor of the whites. Christianized Negroes, dipping into the Bible, had their origin of the whites, too. All men, they said were originally black but that when God shouted at Cain in the garden of Eden for having killed Abel, he turned white from fright.[*&&&&] The rabbis, on the other hand, said that Cain turned black as a curse. Xenophanes of 550 B.C. rightly observed that men made their gods in their own image and that the gods of the Ethiopians were black and flat-nosed like themselves. Marco Polo said that the "natives of Malabar make their devils white and their saints black" like themselves.

Mungo Park[7] said that the Africans accounted for his white skin by saying that as a baby he had been continually dipped in milk. The prominence of his nose, they said, was due to its being pinched daily "until it acquired its present unnatural and unsightly shape." [*%] Parkyn,[8] a white traveller, said that Ethiopians said he had "cat's" eyes and "monkey hair" and that he had "lost his skin."[*%%]

Another belief was (and still is) that a white skin was caused by leprosy. Voltaire thought that African albinos were descended from "a race that had been whitened by leprosy." Many East Indians still believe that white people are the descendants of lepers. T.S. Ramanujam says,

"An Indian villager after seeing an Englishman for the first time asked me whether the gentleman 'was tainted with leprosy.'"*%%% Harold Cox tells of a high-caste Indian woman who on seeing white persons for the first time, said, "Why they have no skins."

Certain American Negroes also believe that a white skin was caused by leprosy. The ancestor of the whites, they say, was Gehazi, servant of Elisha, who was "cursed" with leprosy for having solicited money from Naaman (II Kings, 5:21).

Some Negro preachers and expounders of the Bible have even "proved" that white people will not go to heaven because Jesus placed a curse on their hair. As authority they quote the parable of the sheep and the goats (Matthew 25:32), where Christ said that when he comes again in all his glory he shall separate the sheep from the goats, place the sheep on his right hand and say to them, "Come ye blessed of my Father, inherit the kingdom prepared for you from the foundation of the world." Now there is this distinction: The goats have straight hair like the whites; the sheep, wool, like Negroes.

Of course, all these versions of the origin of color whether originated by unlettered blacks or by learned theologians show a common kinship. Theology, whether it be Jewish, Christian, Buddhist, Moslem, Shinto, or just plain heathen, is largely an excursion of the folk-mind into the realm of the unsubstantiated, and the incoherent. Ideas picked up here and there are patched up into a system. The theologian of whatever faith is largely a romancer. For him miracles do happen as in pagan myths and in fairy-tales.

ROGERS'S NOTES

* Ancient and Modern Imperialism, p. 140. 1910.

** The aborigines were not the barbarians Aryan legends say they were. These blacks, now known as Dravidians, had a mighty civilization of their own. From them came the Buddhas. James Bird (Historical Researches on the Origin of the Buddhas, pp. 5, 8, 12. 1847) says, "Buddhas of a black complexion are common in the Fresco paintings of Ajunta and that of the Arishtanemi, or race of vishnu, who is the twenty-second Jain saint[,] is described as of a black complexion on the authority of the Hemachandras vocabulary."

Of one black Buddha in the case of Aurangabad, he says, "Its features are large, its hair curly, its whole resemblance is so much allied to that of the African as to have given origin to the opinion of some that Buddhism had an extra Indian origin." In this cave there is also, he says the drawing of "an Abyssinian prince seated on a bed along with a fair woman to whom he appears to be married."

Godfrey Higgins says, "The religion of Buddha of India is well-known to have been very ancient. In the most ancient temples scattered throughout Asia where his worship is yet continued he is found as yet with that flat face, thick lips and curly hair of the Negro. Several statues of his may be met in the Museum of the East India Company . . . The religion of the Negro God is found in the ruins of his temples and other circumstances to have been spread over an immense extent of country, even to the remotest parts of Britain and to have been professed by devotees, inconceivably numerous . . . That the Buddhists were Negroes the icons of their God clearly prove." Anacalypsis, Vol. 1, p. 52, 1866.

For additional facts on the Negro, Buddhas together with pictures of them and the evolution of Christianity from the black Buddhas see Sex and Race, Vol. I, pp. 265–8. 2nd ed. 1940.

*** Rabindranath Tagore, Indian poet and Nobel Prize winner, says of color prejudice, "Our own history began with it and though India desperately tried some kind of mechanical race adjustment she has failed in giving birth to a living political organism owing to this abnormal caste consciousness that obstructs the strain of human sympathy and spirit of mutual cooperation. This is the reason why, in spite of the fact that India had produced a series of great minds, she has not produced a great organic history; and it has yet to be seen if such history is in the making in which peoples of different colours can have a perfect bond of life from across the seas." Spectator, May 9, 1931, p. 739.

Rice says, "In India, itself today a fair skin is considered desirable." Hindu Customs and Their Origins, p. 39, 1937.

The Spectator says, "To this day a high caste Hindu may speak disparagingly of a low caste man 'as a very black fellow' and may avoid pollution by his touch." May 28, 1931, p. 501.

P. L. Prattis says of his visit to India in 1949: "I talked with the editor of the Hindustani Times about matrimonial advertisements in which girls mention their fair and white complexions as desirable attributes in seeking a husband. It was my impression that this disposition was a carryover from the long British occupation. The editor said this was not true, that it has long been the tradition of Indians to place a premium upon a fair skin that fairness has been a sort of ideal written into India's literature by the poets."

The Indian movies, said Prattis, had "a milk-white cast." How could Indians, I asked myself, make a picture with a cast so unrepresentative of Indians, themselves? All the members of the cast looked like Italians and Greeks. They were a white set . . . But India is just running over with brown, dark brown and black peoples. The yellows and the fair are a minority so small that you don't even meet them on the streets. Take any handful of Indians and they are dark. . . . But you couldn't tell that from seeing one of their motion pictures . . . " Seventeen Days in Independent India. Pittsburgh Courier, Aug. and Sept. 1949.

Moslem India—Pakistan—thanks to its faith, is less concerned about color than India. When Islam invaded India about the ninth century A. D., Negroes were in the Moslem armies and their numbers increased as the conquest of the peninsula proceeded. Some Negroes rose to be sultans, two of the principal ones being Malik Ambar (1548–1628) and Malik Andeel (1494). There were also great generals, admirals, prime ministers and builders. Many of these blacks, says C. Stewart, "who , if they had fallen into the hands of Europeans, would have been condemned to service drudgery became the associates of princes and governors of provinces." (History of Bengal, pp. 100–08, 1813). For Malik Ambar, Andeel and names of other eminent Negroes of the Moslem past see Rogers, J. A. Sex and Race, Vol. 1, 96–99, 1946.

**** A book of the Beginnings, Vol. 1, p. 454. 1881.

*# Ginsberg, L. Legends of the Jews. Consult the Index, Vol. 7 for HAM, HAMITE, ETHIOPIAN, EGYPTIAN, CAIN (1938). See also Sex and Race, vol. 3, pp. 316–17. Also Freeman and Simon's Midrash Rabba for Story of the Ethiopian maid who thought herself fairer than her white mistress (Song of Songs, p. 690); and the story of the Negro slave to whom his Jewish master left his entire wealth except one thing in order to trick him, in Rapoport, S. Tales and Maxims from the Midrash, pp. 223–4, also p. 167. 1907.

*## De la notion de race en anthropologie. Revue d'Anthrop 2nd ser. Vol. 2, p. 589. Paris 1879.

*### Works of Emperor Julian, Vol. 3 (Against the Galileans) p. 357. 1903. Trans. by Wright.

*#### Julian, Vol. 2 (Fragmentum Epistolae), p. 297.

*& Works of Aurelius Augustine. City of God. Vol. 2. Book 16 pp. 117–18. Edited by Marcus Dods. 1871.

*&& Freedman and Simon, Midrash Rabba, Song of Songs, p. 51. 1939.

See also their Genesis, Vol. 2, p. 293.

*&&&Speke, J. H. What led to the Discovery of the Blue Nile, p. 341. 1864. Sir Thomas Browne examined this belief about Ham nearly three centuries ago and showed its falsity (Works, Vol. 3, pp. 242–8. 1928).

*&&&& Reade, W. Savage Africa, p. 24. 1864.

*% Park. Travels in the Interior of Africa, p. 56, 1799. Marco Polo, India, Vol. 2, p. 291. (Yale ed. 1871). Fernandez reported the same of the Ethiopians. See Sex and Race, Vol. 3, p. 122. See also Spectator, May 28, 1931 Other Indians have said the same.

*%% Parkyn, M. Life in Abyssinia (Lond. Quar. Rev. Vol 1. pp. 178–9; Vol. 3, 1854–55, p. 49).

*%%% Spectator, March 14, 1931, p. 402.

From *Africa's Gift to America: The Afro-American in the Making and Saving of the United States*, 1959

In this book, Rogers provides a history of the United States from its beginnings to the 1960s though the emphasis is up until the end of the Civil War; however, the perspective is from the view of African Americans. By means of this reinterpretation of America's history, Rogers fills in the gaps omitted from many standard texts of the time. The relatively simple vocabulary and the numerous illustrations make the book seem aimed at young adults; indeed, William Loren Katz says the book provides "an interesting picture of the Negro in Africa and America . . . " and is "a useful classroom tool" (22). It also has the feel of an alternative textbook to American history somewhat anticipating Howard Zinn's *People's History of the United States* (1980). In the selection given here Rogers discusses the infamous Triangular Trade between Africa, the West Indies, and Europe. Slaves would be taken from Africa and brought to the West Indies to work on the sugar plantations. This sugar, turned into molasses, would be sent to Europe (or, as in Rogers's description, the New England colonies) to be manufactured into rum. Then, the rum would return to Africa in exchange for more slaves. Much of the wealth of Europe and the Northern colonies revolved around the money made from this trade. Africa's "gift" to America is through its people—their talents, their skills, their very bodies. It was not given freely as a true gift, but was stolen. America could not be what it is without the often unacknowledged contributions of Africa's people. The book's publication, as Thabiti Asukile notes, "during the civil rights era was timely mainly because of the backlash and resistance of many white southerners to African American demands for an end to legal Jim Crow, U.S. apartheid" ("Black International Journalism" 341). The text Is from the First Edition, privately published by Rogers in 1959. Reprinted by Wesleyan University Press, 2014.

AFRICA'S GIFT TO AMERICA

Africa as the Economic Foundation of the United States

"The discovery of African labor was an American enterprise. It was the introduction of a hitherto unknown muscular force, proving on trial to be the most perfect agent of production then known to commerce . . . African labor fixed with eagerness the marvellous power in the varied and exhaustless wealth of the South"

—J. W. DuBOSE[1]

The United States, both as a colony and a young nation, wasn't highly thought of in Europe. When Thomas Jefferson was president he offered to give a site in Washington to any European nation that would build a legation[2] on it; none accepted. Many leading writers even considered the new nation hopeless, among them Count Gobineau, Sydney Smith,[3] and James McSparran.[4] Gobineau was expressing a sentiment long popular in Europe when he said "Americans represent the most varied specimens of the races of Old Europe of whom the least possible can be expected. They are the refuse of all the ages—Irish; Germans, often mixed-blood; some French; and Italians, who outnumber all the others. The mixture of all these degenerate types, gives, and will continue to give birth to new ethnic confusions. These mixtures have in them nothing good. Italian, Frenchmen, Anglo-Saxon will amalgamate in the Southern States with the Indian, Negro, Spaniard and Portuguese already there. From such a mixture one can imagine nothing but horrible racial results—nothing but an incoherent juxtaposition of the most degraded beings."* Still another writer called America, "the graveyard of the white race," and American-born Bayard Taylor[5] said an American is "an Anglo-Saxon relapsed into barbarism."

In the Bible it was asked what good could come out of Nazareth. In a similar vein, Sydney Smith, celebrated writer and wit, asked in 1820, "In the four quarters of the globe who reads an American book? Or goes to an American play? Or looks at an American picture or statue? What does the world yet owe to American physicians or surgeons? What new substances have their chemists discovered or what old ones have they analyzed? What new constellations have been discovered by the telescopes of Americans? What have they done in mathematics? Who drinks out of American glasses? Or eats from American plates? Or sleep in American blankets?"**

But less than a century after that, America was not only doing all it was said she couldn't do, but had taken the lead of all the nations on earth. Indeed, the rise of America from a wilderness over which roamed Indians and buffaloes to world power; and from a people once so pressed by hunger that some were driven to cannibalism*** to a nation with enormous surpluses of food is nothing short of the miraculous. Britain took 1920 years to become the world's foremost power—1643 years from Julius Caesar's invasion, 55 B.C. to the defeat of the Spanish Armada in 1588; and another 277 years to Waterloo, 1815. The United States took only 353 years, that is, from the founding of St. Augustine, Florida, to the end of World War I.

Coming centuries later, America had, of course, the advantages of man's knowledge accumulated since but she had also some terrific disadvantages, not the least of which was the long struggle with the Indians, which sometimes ended in massacre of the colonists as in Virginia in 1622.[6] In spite of hardships greater than those met by colonists south of the Rio Grande, the British North American colonies, a little over a century after the founding of St. Augustine, took the lead in the New World. Cuba, Hispaniola, Mexico, Puerto Rico, were colonized before the United States. They, too, had the advantage of man's accumulated knowledge. Why did they drop behind?

Those who attribute human advantages in "race" will say, America was a "white man's land," that her racial origin was North European. It is true that the Spaniards and Portuguese, pioneers in the lands to the south, were mixed with Africans from very early times and very much so after the Moorish invasion of 711 A.D., but why were the South Europeans at the top in 1492 and the Nordics so far below them? Also, why did the United States outstrip Canada, which has been and still is, more racially Nordic?

The Reason for America's Advance

Why did America take the lead so early in the New World? The answer is Trade.

Trade in what? The reply to that sounds so utterly preposterous now that one must be bold to state it. However, there were those living then who did not hesitate to say it as well, as certain candid writers of our time. *It was trade in Molasses.* A pro-American bulletin of 1731 said, "The molasses trade is the most (if not the only valuable one) of New England.**** And John Adams, second president of the United States, said, "I know not why we should blush to confess that molasses was an essential ingredient in American Independence."*# He added that Washington also thought highly of molasses. Which Washington certainly did. In 1776, he sent one of his slaves, Tom, by a ship-captain to be exchanged for molasses. (Washington, Writings of, Vol. 2, p. 211. 1889.)

The Molasses Trade

Why molasses? Molasses meant rum. Why rum? Rum was for exchange of Africans on the African West Coast. In short, it was the sale of Africans in the New World—the Slave Trade—that laid the financial foundation of the United States. It was Africa's great gift to America.

More will be said of this in the proper place.

The events leading up to the trade in rum and molasses are these: England, with Sir John Hawkins (1531–1595),[7] had taken the lead in the slave trade. The Royal African Company had the monopoly but it was unable to supply the demand and Parliament ordered the trade opened to all British ships "for the well supplying of the plantations and colonies with sufficient numbers of Negroes at reasonable prices."

New England Yankees who had inherited the maritime spirit of their motherland now entered this trade with such zest that they soon became rivals of the English merchants. The Yankees had discovered that molasses, the best article for making rum, was either being fed to the hogs or thrown away in the French sugar islands of the Caribbean, and therefore could be had very cheaply. The molasses trade, in turn, gave impetus to other New England industries as distilling, fishing, shipbuilding, lumber and horse—and cattle-rearing. In 1708, Governor Cranston of Rhode Island reported that his colony had built 103 ships since 1698. In 1749, Boston had 469 ships tied to the slave trade. G. F. Dow has a special chapter on American ships engaged in the trade.*## The New England merchants, says Louis B. Wright, had discovered "two commodities which enriched them and their ports, rum and slaves."*###

Thanks to rum and the slave-trade, New England became commercially dominant in the New World. She not only dominated the Caribbean trade but that of Virginia, the Carolinas, and the rest of the South. She had very few slaves herself. Her climate and agriculture did not make them profitable. In 1776, the six New England colonies had only 16,034 slaves as compared with nearly 300,000 in Virginia alone. Her type of industry made white servants, who were semi-slaves, more profitable. In 1652, Rhode Island abolished Negro slavery, not from humane reasons but because what she gained from it locally was trifling in comparison with what she made from the trade. In abolishing her own slavery, she had specially provided that "nothing in the Act shall extend or be deemed to extend to any Negro or mulatto slave brought from the coast of Africa into the West on board any vessel belonging to this colony."*####

This was the procedure. New England ships with their cargo of rum would sail to West Africa, where they would exchange it for slaves and such articles they could pick up as gold dust and ivory, thence to the West Indies where they disposed of them at high profit, then return with molasses for more rum, then again to Africa. This was known as the Triangular (or Three-Cornered) Trade. Molasses, be it noted, was slave-produced, too.

Distilling became the chief home industry of New England, especially of Massachusetts and Rhode Island. There were hundreds of distillers. Boston with her then small population alone had sixty-three. But they could not keep pace with the demand.

"The trade in Negroes from West Africa," says Weeden, "absorbed immense quantities of spirit. The African demand was very importunate." Letters of ship-captains of the period prove it. In 1752, when Captain Isaac Freeman wrote for a cargo of rum, he was told that he wouldn't be able to get that quantity even in three months. "There are so many vessels loading for Guinea we can't get one hogshead of rum for the cash." Captains were advised to water their rum. One satire ran, "Water ye rum as much as possible and sell as much by the short measure as ye can. An overwhelming Providence has been pleased to bring to this land of freedom another cargo of benighted heathen to enjoy the blessings of a gospel dispensation."

Dow says, "Molasses was the all-important feature of the slaving trade, which required rum as a means of barter for slaves for without molasses there could be no New England rum." He reproduces letters from ship-captains of the time telling how great a necessity they found rum. There are also letters from distillers. "In whatever branch of trade we now find ourselves," said W. B. Weeden, "we are impressed by the immense prevalence and moving power of rum, lumber, Negroes . . . all feel the initiative and moving impulse of rum . . . Rum distilling and Negro importation gave more than direct profits to Newport (Rhode Island), great as they were. They gave a tremendous impulse to more than legitimate industry and commerce and compelled the exchange to follow in the wake of the 'rum' vessel and slaver." Molasses, says James Parton, in his "Life of Franklin," "was the basis on which a great part of the commerce of America rested . . . . The single article of molasses did actually par, and was therefore the equivalent of the bulk of the numberless articles which Yankee traders took to the French West

Indies." (Vol. 2, p. 298. 1865). Pitman says likewise, "In the great slave communities to the southward, Americans found the only great and permanent market for all their staples. It was the wealth accumulated from West India trade which more than anything else underlay the prosperity of New England and the Middle Colonies."*@

New England made better rum, sold it cheaper, and pushed it so energetically that it began to displace English rum and even French brandy.

ROGERS'S NOTES

* I'Inegalite des Races Humaines, Vol. 4, p. 313, 1853.

** Edinburgh Rev. Vol. 33, Jan. to May 1820, in his review of Seybert's book on America. McSparran wrote "America Dissected," in 1753. Gustavus Myers discussed these detractions in "America Strikes Back."

*** Captain John Smith (1580–1631) wrote, "So great was our famine that a savage we slew and buried, the poorer sort took him up again and ate him; and so did divers ones another boiled and stewed with herbs. And one amongst the rest did kill his wife, powdered her and had eaten parts of her." The General Historie of Virginia. The Fourth Booke, p. 294 (1606–1625). Neill E. D., quotes the Virginia Assembly of 1623 in its complaint against Governor Thomas Smythe, "One man killed his wife to eat for which he was burned. Many fed on corpses. "Terre Mariae (Maryland), p 30. 1867. Other instances of eating corpses and killing Indians and eating them occurred as late as 1846. The Donner party, lost in the Sierras in the dead of winter, was driven to this. State of California Bulletin. The Donner Party Tragedy, pp. 10, 11; Croy, Homer, Wheels West, Stewart G. R. Ordeal by Hunger; Story of the Donner Party, pp. 132–35, 1960. This is significant because one great charge against Negroes was that their ancestors were cannibals.

**** Case of the Northern Colonies, p. 3, 1731.

*# Works of John Adams, Vol. 10, p. 345 ed. by C. F. Adams.

*## Slave Ships and Slaving, pp. 255–265, 1927.

*### Colon, Civiliz. of N. America, p. 105, 1949.

*#### Rhode Is. Col. Records, VIII, 251–2.

*& Development of the British West Indies, p. vii, 1917.

From *She Walks in Beauty* (1963)

Rogers sometimes tried his hand at fiction; however, *She Walks in Beauty*, written near the end of his life, is his first attempt at a traditional full-blown novel. The title, taken from a poem by Lord Byron, again gives a nod to Rogers's appreciation of the Romantic writers. In the Introduction to the novel, Rogers states his desire to write a historical novel utilizing a Black heroine, something that he feels fiction writers have ignored despite their presence in history. The mixed-race young girl Eva becomes a model for England's best known painter. Her beauty, in this story with elements of a fairy-tale, eventually helps to gain her a social status that this daughter of a slave once could only have dreamed. It is, in some ways, a fictional retelling of the story of Hannah Elias, from *Sex and Race*. Rogers had started his career by wanting to be an artist. Nowhere in his work does he demonstrate this painterly quality more than in this novel, with its lush descriptions of characters and scenery. However, even in his fiction, Rogers cannot neglect the favorite social issues of his essays and books. Miss Eva, a blend of the best of Africa, America, and Europe, is the consummate example of racial mixing so often discussed in his other works. Rogers also points out numerous places where real life women of color have had important influence over high ranking white Europeans. Thus, his fiction is treading ground familiar to him from such non-fiction works as *Sex and Race* and *Nature Knows No Color-Line*. The text is from the First Edition (Western Publishers).

SHE WALKS IN BEAUTY

Chapter One

Mr. Pym stopped before Eva's dressing-room almost without knowing it. Other mornings he had passed with only a glance at it. For months he had been wanting to fondle her. He stood there a little while, as if making up his mind then suddenly parted the draperies and peeped in. She was standing before the mirror in a filmy gown that accentuated rather than hid the tempting contour of her buttocks. Winking slyly he reached in and gave them a little pinch.

She spun around gasping, "What do you take me for, Mr. Pym?" she exploded.

"For the most beautiful and seductive of all your sex, Miss Eva," he said, brassily.

"No compliments from the like of you, Mr. Pym," she said indignantly. "Be gone."

Pym laughed lightly, "One question first, Miss Eva. What would it take to win you? A coach and four? Or a mansion in Mayfair?"

"And a castle in Ireland, sir. Also a handsome face and figure. Now go. Or I'll scream." And the not so handsome Mr. Pym continued to the studio.

Still angry she resumed her toilette. Then as she brushed her hair, her good nature returned. Pym had gone too far, but wasn't he only trying to express what many others had done with finesse—their admiration of her?

Compliments showered on her had made her very proud of herself. She was a mixture of three continents—Europe, Africa, and America—and was often told that the finest of the three continents were blended in her. Her maternal grandmother was a mixture of American Indian and African; her grandfather on her mother's side was African and European. Her father's father was European. She, herself, was born in England of an English father.

Her complexion, a light russet brown, was the envy of many paler English girls. Her skin was a smooth camelia-like texture; her face oval; her five feet nine supple with breasts provokingly thrust out like young African girls at the fair. Her soft dark-brown hair glinted with gold in the light, and fell to her shoulder in natural waves. From early childhood she had been complimented on her rare type of beauty. In a few weeks more she would be seventeen. She would forgive Pym this time, but was glad she had put him in his place. Smiling again, she gave a last look at herself in the mirror and followed him to the studio.

Sir William Hyde of the Royal Academy, for whom she and Pym were posing, was there, mixing the colors on his palette. She bade him a cheery good morning, lithely mounted the dais, threw off her light gown and took her pose. Pym climbed up after her and took his place beside her. Sir William resumed work on his picture: Phryne Before Her Accusers.[1]

He worked for nearly an hour, touching places here and there lightly and then suddenly laid down his palette, flung down his brush and shouted jubilantly "C'est fini! C'est fini!"

"Finished, Sir William?" echoed Pym.

"Yes, yes, not another dab, thank heaven."

Pym gathered up his Grecian robe, stepped down and returned to the throne chair at the fireplace. Dropping into it, he picked up his stein of unfinished ale. Eva shifted her sandalled feet, put on a flowing silk gown and going to the edge of the dais, sat there, dangling her feet. She was glad the painting was finished. After months of it, she wanted a change. Sir William would be going to France for a rest. She smiled and wished him a happy holiday.

"Thank you, Eva," Sir William pulled off his smock and tossed it to a stool. "I'll be away a fortnight. If it weren't for the vernissage—the varnishing, that is, I'd stay two months."

"In the meantime, Sir William, I'll be looking forward eagerly to your next picture."

"My next picture! There'll be none, my girl. This is my last."

"Your last, sir?"

"Yes, my very last."

Her face clouded. He had told her several times of another picture for which she was to be the model: Venus Callipygus—Venus of the Beautiful Buttocks. "Haven't you said that before, Sir William?" she teased.

"Yes. But this time I mean it."

Something in his voice said he really meant it. Her eyes lost their sparkle. How she was going to miss this studio! The happiest days of her life had been spent here. Its beauty had lifted her out of a dull world. How she loved its sparkling chandeliers, the carved rafters, antique brass lanterns; cosy alcoves; tall shining windows, velvet-draped, looking out on a sunlit Thames; blue-satin window seats; costly Persian rugs, hand-carved Renaissance chairs and chests. Its priceless sculptures and soft, mellowed tapestries especially delighted her. What she liked even more were Sir William's studio parties. The courteous gentlemen who paid her compliments and the elegant ladies far above her class who were so kind. A great emptiness came over her. She hung her head.

Sir William saw her dejection, "I'm very sorry, my girl," he said, feelingly, "you've been such an inspiration. I couldn't possibly have had a better model. Why, you made me feel at times as if Phryne herself had come to life."

"Thank you, Sir William," she said, as bravely as she could.

"And I must tell you this, Eva. Before I found you at the Gaiety, I had searched every theater in London. None of the many girls there suited me. All had some defect—thick or skinny legs, flabby breasts, or hips like mares. I wanted the Greek ideal—the perfect balance of high round bosom, strong arms, neck, legs, with muscles, not fat . . . and personality. Then I found you."

He saw her disappointment and thought of what he could do to help. He would recommend her to his artist friends. At the same time, he ought to give her a little fatherly advice. She was so young and impressionable. She had changed much in the few months she had been with him. A simple dancer then, she now seethed with social ambition. For that he blamed himself. He said a little teasingly, "Eva, I sometimes think you'd like to emulate Phryne. I hope artist life hasn't changed you that much."

Her mouth twitched. She looked away from him. Yes, she did want to be another Phryne. She wanted to set the world afire in admiration of herself. She felt she could. Like Phryne, she had started from the very bottom. She had come to London as Phryne had to Athens, a nobody. Now in less than three years she was in these affluent surroundings. Even as Praxiteles, most famous sculptor of ancient Greece had chosen Phryne for his Goddess of Love, so had Sir William, England's most famous painter, chosen her as his. Like Phryne she had youth, beauty, shapeliness. Why shouldn't she also rise socially? This picture of her would be shown at the Academy in the autumn. All England would be talking of it and wanting to know who she was.

But, alas, that was two weeks away. What should she do meanwhile? Go back to the theater? She didn't want to. Smiling a little at the compliment, she said, "Nothing is further from my thoughts than being another Phryne, Sir William."

"I'm glad of that, Eva. I was beginning to feel a little guilty . . . that I had praised that classic courtesan too much to you. She wasn't a very good girl, you know. But truth to tell, I'm rather carried away by her myself." She looked at the painting. It showed Phryne at the moment her defender, Hypereides, famous orator, and one of her lovers, had ripped open her robe, exposing her bosom. She had been accused by jealous rivals of profaning the Eleusinian mysteries,[2] the penalty for which was death. At the sight of her lovely bosom, the judges had acquitted her at once. She added, "Besides, Sir William, times have changed. Athens raised a statue of pure gold to Pyryne. I'd be lucky to have one of pewter."

"Alas, no such homage is paid to beauty today, my girl."

"In France it is, Sir William." She remembered the visit of French aristocrats in exile to the studio parties and how gallant they had been to her. English gentlemen were so much colder. "Beautiful women even of humblest birth have risen to be queens there," she added.

"That's true, Eva. In the meantime, my best wishes go with you." He added, feelingly, "I know what it means to be a girl of your class in London."

That stung her again. What was her class? In her fondest dreams she saw herself a great lady . . . a princess in splendid robes, glittering with jewels, a diamond tiara on her head. Her head drooped; her feet no longer dangled.

Sir William saw he had hurt her. He picked up his palette and began to scrape the paint mechanically. Hoping to soften what he had so unwittingly said, he added, "I've been thinking that modelling has a better future for you than the theater. That is, if you pose for the right artists. I'll recommend you to friends of mine."

"Thanks, sir," she said with pretended gratitude. "But I think I'll return to the theater." Posing was dull at times. It gave her too much time to think. Dancing was far more suited to her restless spirit. Besides she might learn to love it again. Of course, it was hard on the toes and gave her a ravenous appetite. And with prices in the chop-houses so high. She said, sweetly, "Sir William, you're the only one I'd care to pose for." She wanted to tell him she [*sic*] was the first decent man she had ever met. He had always treated her as a lady.

A burst of cynical laughter made both turn their heads. It was Mr. Pym. "Why the laughter, Mr. Pym?" asked Sir William, jovially. "I take it you want no more modelling either. As a disciple of Epicurus[3] you consider eating, drinking and making merry enough to occupy a man."

"To be sure, Sir William—unless I could go on looking at Miss Eva's charms. Then I'd make it my life's work!"

Mr. Pym, unwillingly retired from his profession, the law, because of certain irregularities, had posed as Hypereides, Phrynes['] defender and lover. His shrewd, convincing profile had attracted Sir William. But in front, his too long face and shifty eyes showed clearly the man he was. He drained his stein, put it down and came over to them. "Hard work is not for a smart man, Sir William," he said blandly. "Leisure is the only true wealth. Unless, of course, there are hidden rewards like an artist must get while painting beautiful women . . . had I the talent," he shrugged, "this will be the picture of the year, sir, both model and master outstrip the Greek."

Sir William smiled. "A too generous compliment, Mr. Pym. That is, for the artist. For the model, yes. Eva is handsomer that [*sic*] the original. Her skin, hair, body are er . . . er . . . the finest I've ever seen. Try as I would, I could not capture all their beauty, all their charm."

Pym went to the picture and gazed at it, rapt. There he was a finer and handsomer Pym standing beside the beautiful Eva for all eternity.

"Please, Miss Eva," he begged, "get up and pose just once more. Let these soiled eyes of mine feast again on the most peerless form in all Christendom."

Eva laughed indulgently. Sir William nodded approval. She rose, dropped the gauzy robe from her shoulders and took her pose with an air of mockery that wasn't in the picture.

Sir William laughed aloud. "Even Hypereides couldn't have saved you with that expression, Eva."

"Now she is indeed guilty of mocking the gods!" chuckled Pym. He sank his gaze into the sparkle of her hair in the candlelight and brought his eyes down almost with physical contact to the half-turned column of her neck, the lush, pouting breasts, the golden brown of her firm, flat abdomen, the arch of her thighs and shapely knees and toes, where the skin seemed as if lightly tinged with bronze. He wanted her so much it ached. But she wasn't for the like of him. He was fifty-two, three times her age. And he had no money. Age and poverty against dazzling youth. But at least he could help her if she would only listen. She was wasting her time dancing and posing. London was full of wealthy bucks, who would be eager to keep her in style, he had told her. But she had only laughed at him.

"May I rest now, Mr. Pym?" she jested, pretending he was the artist. Pym sighed, gave one last imploring look, and left the room to change to his street clothes.

Eva and Sir William exchanged amused glances. "He's smitten on you," said Sir William. She shrugged. She hoped this would be the last she'd be seeing of him. "By the way, " said Sir William, "I'll be back for the varnishing and am looking forward to seeing you there. I'll have an invitation sent to you."

"Thanks, Sir William," she brightened. When she saw him again he might change his mind. She excused herself and went off to dress.

In the dressing room, she poured water in the basin, but instead of washing she dropped on the couch and began to think of what Sir William had said about her class. What was her class? There was no time in her life when she didn't feel she belonged to the best. She had always identified herself with the princes and princesses in her fairy-tales. In the penny novels she devoured the poor but lovely girl who married the rich, handsome prince was herself. Her mother, Betsy, had stressed pride to her.

Her home in Sussex had been somewhat better than that of the neighbors. Her mother, who had been brought to England from Virginia by her white master, had taught her to feel that she was superior to all the other girls in the little town, that her dark skin was more attractive than theirs. Some of the girls had seemed to envy it too.

"Evie," her mother would say, "yer difrunt, God broke the mould when ye was borned; ye didn't yell when ye came out; ye laughed. 'Tis a good sign. The midwife claimed it be."

At eleven, she was the beauty of the little town. She did little services for others and remembered their birthdays, which made her popular. Her mother had also told her that her real father was not her husband, but a lord on whose estate she had been a milkmaid. "Evie," she had said, "yer blood is better than my husband, John Langston, could give ye. He married me before I was bigged, but he know it later and never kicked. God bless 'im for that! That was wot made me put up with him. Now ye see it ain't jes' me fancy that ye be difrunt. I was poor but I gave ye the best I could—good blood from the gentry. See that ye always hold up yer head."

At twelve a crushing change had come. John Langston was sent to the Fleet Prison for a long term. The good things he brought home hadn't been earned honestly. Instead of being in the king's secret service, as he claimed, he was a smuggler of wines and silk from France. Thereafter it was the Sussex Poor-Farm for herself and her mother.

Life was excruciatingly dull. It was up to work, to sleep, and to work again. Gaiety of any kind was frowned upon. Laughter wasn't for charity folk. The food was awful. Chiefly bread, made of flour and ground bones;

moldy cheese and potatoes. Tea was hot water colored with burnt bread crusts. There was meat only at Christmas and the King's Birthday.

Even more than the work, she dreaded Sundays. Then she had to listen to long dreary sermons on the punishment of the wicked. If she dozed off, she was soundly cuffed. Sick of so much goodness, she thought how wonderful must be some of the bad things she was warned against.

Day dreams were her only solace. She had been in London once and ever since she imagined herself living in one of the mansions there. At the poor-farm she found a torn copy of Perrault's Fairy Tales.[4] It was the greatest event so far in her life. She read the story of The Sleeping Beauty in the Wood until she knew it by heart. As she hoed turnips she could see herself in a beautiful chamber on a bed of gold and silver with silken hangings. Then a very handsome prince came to the bed on which she had been sleeping for a hundred years and as she lay there magnificently dressed and resplendently beautiful, he kissed her and she awoke and said, "You have tarried long, oh my Prince." Then all the ladies and gentlemen came to life and crowded around to pay her homage. To herself she was the Princess Eva. Then at fourteen, another change had come. The overseer at the poor-farm had started fingering her. Her mother seeing what that would lead to, advised her to run away. "Better go to Lunnon, Evie, and take yer luck there. An' don't do no more wrong than ye can help. But it's better to pick up a gent there then to bed with that overseer—that tup'ny[5] ole rake." She had helped her slip away one night after warning her against the inconvenience of pregnancy. She pressed into her hands a jar of mutton fat and sheep's wool[6] and told her how to use it. "Sen' fer me some day, me chile, iffen ye can." She walked all that night. At dawn she saw a farm house, and went in, and begged for work. It was harvest time and she was engaged. The farmer's son wanted to marry her. She felt he was below her but what else could she do? London was a big town and she'd be lost there. Then one evening, he led her into the hayloft and tried to make love to her. She started to yield, but suddenly decided she couldn't give herself to a mere farmer's son. She broke away from him and left for London at daybreak the next morning. She reached it by begging rides.

With no change of clothing and only a few pennies in her purse, her first night was spent at Damnable Dick's, a windowless cellar on Stinking Lane,[7] swarming with lice. Men, women, and children slept together closely packed after stripping themselves to the skin to prevent the vermin from filling their clothes. She wept. Oh, that life could be so cruel to one so young and full of ambition.

At last she fell in with a pickpocket, who made her his mistress and gave her the best food and clothes she had since a child. But he was caught and hanged. Thanks to the clothes, she was able to appear as an orange girl[8] at the Royal Gaiety, where her fine figure, and wit brought her to the notice of the director, who gave her a small part in the chorus. From this she went to posing in tableaux from the paintings of Fragonard[9] and other masters of the nude. Her great ambition was to be a ballet dancer. In her spare time she took lessons but the manager thought he could use her to better advantage with nude poses in tableaux. One evening after she appeared in Rembrandt's "Toilet of Bathsheba,"[10] a stranger had stopped her at the stage-door and asked her to be his model. It was Sir William.

During the months with him, she had had secret offers from his male friends, but had adroitly put them off. She felt that one day some worthy man might make her an honorable offer. She'd wait and see. Life had something great in store for her, she felt.

She remembered she must dress. But she'd take her own time. The persistent and pestiferous Mr. Pym must be given time to make himself scarce. She helped herself lavishly to the French soap, powder and perfume, but resisted the temptation to take some with her.

Dressed now, she went back to the studio. Sir William had gone, leaving a note of warm goodbye for her and the recommendation. Her spirits fell again. It looked like an age before she'd see him again. And in the meantime all she saw before her was monotony. Bitterness against him for having dropped her filled her. Then she remembered how much she owed him. He had taught her to walk with verve, to talk, dress, behave at table and most of all how to display herself to the best advantage. He had made a lady of her.

She went to the painting again. In it, Sir William had given her an air of distinction that inspired her. Yes, her mother was right. She had noble blood and Sir William had perceived it. She would live up to it. Certainly the future must hold something good for one with such rosy dreams. She touched the picture lightly with her lips, held her head high and walked to the door. A new phase in her life had begun. *She'd face it with courage.*

She opened the door but closed it quickly. Mr. Pym was there. She had underestimated his persistence. Now he would be there for the rest of the day. There was only one thing to do: appear not to see him. She opened her penny romance, pretended to be absorbed in it, and turned in a direction away from him. Unabashed, he fell in step with her. When she could ignore him no longer, she said, "Ah, it's you, Mr. Pym."

"Yes, Miss Eva. Remember what I said I'd do for you," he cooed. She closed the book sharply, "Mr. Pym, you'll excuse me now. I must go. I'm late . . . "

She walked sharply on. He caught up with her. "But Miss Eva, you must listen to me. It's for your own good."

She only walked faster.

"You must listen, Miss Eva," he pleaded in a fatherly voice, "this is a hard world. You have to take what you can get and bargain for that too, me lamb. It's like this, Miss Eva. You're a beauty, and sweet as one's own daughter. And I'm old, old as your grandfather, old as God maybe. I see things you don't. Fact is, I'm in love with you—as one is with some rare and beautiful painting. But that's beside the point. I want to help you—yes to help myself too. Of course it's a gamble. But even a gamble works sometimes when a sure thing won't. Like Sir William and his promise to you."

Struck again with her disappointment over Sir William, she listened more attentively. He went on, "I'll tell you something that was dinned into me when I was reading law. It did me a lot of good. It was: Examine a case thoroughly. Especially don't neglect seeming trifles. And whenever in doubt, take a chance."

That reminded her how she had taken a chance and come to London and had succeeded. Hadn't she better find out what he had in mind? Just now the only prospect she had was going to her room which would look more dismal than ever. "What is it?" she asked.

He knew that if he told her she'd refuse. She was proud. But women of a higher class than hers went there and had succeeded. "Oh," he evaded, "where we'll be going is just a bit up Kingsway."

"What sort of place is it?" she insisted.

"There'll be hundreds of people there. Some very rich."

"But what do they do there?"

He laughed lightly, "Ah, Miss Eva, the question is: Dare you answer the call of destiny? Girls, less attractive, less personable than you have made their fortunes there. I repeat: Whenever in doubt, take a chance."

"All right. I'll take a chance. But why are you so mysterious?"

He'd better not answer that. Where they were going he would present her as his wife. He'd say he had married her at the Fleet some weeks ago. It was a very ancient form of ceremony that needed no license, no ban[n]s, no witness, consent of parents, or other formality. It was still popular, even among the rich, because in such a marriage, a man couldn't be sued for debts contracted by his wife. A Fleet marriage[11] gave respectability without responsibility. And either party could be free again simply by giving the other a paper to that effect. But if he told her she might become balky again and that would call for explanation after explanation. The only thing was to change the subject altogether. Newsboys shouting the latest news of the war gave him a cue. "Hear that, Miss Eva," he said "we have captured Prince Lucien, Napoleon's brother.[12] That means the war will be over soon now. Have you lost anyone in the war?"

Without giving her a chance to reply he went on to tell of a fictitious brother of his who had been killed at Trafalgar,[13] and how he had left four orphans for whom he had been caring. He followed that with lengthy fabrications of his own service in the navy and the lands he had visited.

“Civil War Centennial: Myth and Reality,” *Freedomways*, Winter 1963

In 1957, with the 100th anniversary of the Civil War approaching, Congress planned a nationwide celebration honoring the event which would take place from 1961–65. The Centennial was designed to focus on national unity, on the reconciliation of the two opposing sides when the war ended. Instead, it showed the continuing division between the groups, the roiling tensions that remained between them, particularly that the South had never fully accepted the results of the war. Southern states poured a great deal of money into the Centennial, seeing it as an opportunity to celebrate the Lost Cause. They particularly supported events commemorating Southern victories in the early years of the war. General Ulysses S. Grant III, grandson of the head of the Union army, was chosen as head of the Centennial commission, but, ironically, he was a supporter of the South. By 1963, interest in the Centennial was minimal in both the North and the South. For more on this, see Robert J. Cook, *Troubled Commemoration: The American Civil War Centennial, 1961–1965* (2007).

In this essay, Rogers provides a reexamination of the events of the Civil War. He emphasizes that Lee and his men were traitors against the Union, and fought the war to preserve the system of slavery. Lincoln was reluctant to engage in the conflict and only did so to preserve the Union, not to abolish slavery. The slaves, the ones over whom the conflict took place, in fact, were the ones who had to bring about the resolution of the war. Rather than being passive vessels waiting to be granted their freedom, slaves actively fought on behalf of the Union, largely being responsible for their victory. The Emancipation Proclamation, often thought of as guaranteeing Negro freedom, was issued reluctantly by Lincoln, and only to encourage African Americans to fight for the Union cause.

It was ironic that the Centennial was being honored in the years 1961–65, precisely the time when the Civil Rights struggle faced some of its greatest challenges. Rogers's article reminds Americans of the true history of the Civil War, and how African Americans had to fight for their own freedom and that many of the issues that the war was being fought over were not resolved a century later. The essay is also a timely reminder for present day readers, that the legacy of the Civil War is still not ended as battles over how to best remember the conflict in history, monuments, museums, continue today, issues that Rogers raises in the piece. To see how the myth of the Lost Cause still lingers, consult Clint Smith's article "Why Confederate Lies Live On" *Atlantic* June 2021. It is entirely appropriate that this lead article was published by Rogers in *Freedomways*, one of whose founders was W. E. B. Du Bois. Its roster of contributors included such leading Black writers and intellectuals as Alice Walker, James Baldwin, Lorraine Hansberry, and C. L. R. James.

"CIVIL WAR CENTENNIAL, MYTH AND REALITY"

On September 7, 1957, Congress established a Commission for a Civil War Centennial, 1961 to 1965. The obvious purpose was to celebrate the fact that the Union had been saved; that America had remained a single nation instead of being split into two; that thanks to that victory she is now the world power she is. In short, the order of the day was Harmony.

But what was then happening on the race question made it very clear that the opposite was to be the result. The 1954 ruling[1] of the United States Supreme Court had caused a wave of attacks on Negroes and the burning of their homes and churches. Chief of these disorders was at Little Rock, Ark.,[2] which forced the Federal government for the third time to send troops to the South to protect Negroes. This last had caused great bitterness in the South, and Chief Justice Warren[3] had been denounced by Southern senators as a "Communist."

So clear were these signs that June Purcell Guild,[4] white Southerner, and author of "Black Laws of Virginia," predicted that the Centennial would become "a colorful picture of Southern propaganda." She said, "Every gold ingot in Fort Knox may be safely wagered that the South will attempt to use the Centennial as a superior chance to spread misrepresentation of law, history and science as they are related to American Negroes. . . . Signs are multiplying that the always politically shrewd South is planning to fight another anti-America, another anti-Negro vilification campaign.

"Actually there is in the South at this time so much massive resistance to Federal law and the right of the Supreme Court to interpret the Constitution that we are experiencing 'Down Here' a period similar in many respects to the Civil War. Everywhere you can hear people saying 'Eisenhower, Warren . . . should be taken out and shot.'" Flying the Confederate flag "has reached epidemic proportions," she said.

FINDING A CONFEDERATE "VETERAN"

The approaching Centennial found that the last veteran of the war on both sides had passed on. But the South needed a veteran to show that the Confederacy had "outlived" the Union. Such a one was forthcoming.

Some years before one Walter G. Williams, in a sworn statement, claimed that he had served with Hood's Brigade,[5] and that he was born November 14, 1846. Confederate-minded congressmen, with no investigation whatever, accepted his word, and rushed through a bill certifying him and giving him a pension. But a housewife, Mrs. Opal Beckett, then living in Ohio, called a Cincinnati daily, saying that she knew Williams, and had grown up with him on a farm in Franklin, Texas, adjoining that of the Williams family, and that William[s] had never served in the Civil War.

On this, Lowell K. Bridewell of the Scripps-Howard press, started to investigate. On a search of the Texas records, he found Mrs. Beckett was right. Further search in the National Archives revealed that Williams had never served in Hood's Brigade. Still further search in the 1870 census disclosed that Williams was born in 1855—therefore that his claim that he had served in the last eleven months of the war would have him enlisting when he was not yet nine. Still more he had named a non-existent county in Mississippi as his birthplace.

In spite of all this further honors awaited Williams. Another bill signed by the President[6] made him a national hero. It provided that his death should be a day of national mourning with flags at half-mast, and that he be given a general's funeral. However, Mr. Williams ungratefully up and died soon after the Centennial began. Age 105 instead of 116.

As if to crown all of this, the one appointed as chairman of the Centennial Commission was a segregationist, an anti-Semite, and showed much eagerness to please the Confederates—General Ulysses S. Grant III,[7] grandson of General Grant. While head of the National Planning Commission he had posted jim-crow signs in Rock Creek Park, Washington, D. C. Also in June, 1959, he had warmly endorsed an editorial in the Bulletin of the Loyal Legion[8] to the effect that "Jewish financiers" had started the Civil War to split the nation the better to control it.

A leading historian denounced this as "a travesty on the name of history . . . a vicious piece of anti-Semitism." On complaint by the Jewish press and organizations Grant finally admitted that several of the allegations "are unsupported by sound historical authorities and so are probably false."

It was in this atmosphere of distortion, historical falsehood, and determination to continue the robbery of the citizenship rights of Negroes, the Centennial began.

Congress had voted $100,000 a year for the Centennial Celebration: Maryland, $351,000; Texas, $1,500,000; and Mississippi, $2,000,000 for two years. Why did the poorest, economically, state vote the largest sum? Because it is the worst anti-Negro state—the home of Senator Eastland, most notorious foe of the Negro. And why for only two years? In the third year of the war defeat of the South began.

THE GLORIFICATION OF LEE

The first observance of the war, or more correctly, celebration in the South was January 9, when the Queen of the West,[9] a Northern steamer, was fired on. Robert E. Lee was lauded to the skies and made into a saintly figure—Lee, who a century before had been the North's most execrated figure and into whom the Northern soldier would have loved to plunge a bayonet.

Lee, as an officer, had taken an oath of loyalty to the army. When offered the command of the Union army, he refused, saying that he was a Virginian first. He said, "The property belonging to my children, all they possess all lies in Virginia. I cannot raise my hand against my children . . . . Save in defense of my state, I never desire to draw my sword again."[10]

Compare this with the words of another Virginian, Patrick Henry, in a similar crisis: "I am not a Virginian but an American."[11]

Lee had headed a revolt that had taken 600,000 lives and wounded many more. A Southern woman, Mrs. Pryor,[12] who had been through the war, said at the time that it had given the South "Poverty for riches, mutilation and wounds for honor and distinction; exile and loneliness for inherited homes and friends; pain and death for happiness and life."

Lee had said, "I think slavery a greater evil to the white than to the black race."[13] Yet he fought to keep slavery. The Constitution of the government he had chosen to serve, said, "No bill denying the right to own property in Negro slaves shall be passed." Also, Alexander Stephens,[14] the vice-president, had declared, "Our new government is founded on slavery . . . its foundations are laid, its cornerstone rests, upon the great truth that the Negro is not the equal of the white man."

Lee, once considered a calamity, is now made into a hero. A postage stamp bears his effigy. Why this glorification? Because he can be used for what the Southern politician and the racists, North and South, desire most: Keeping the Negro down. When racism shall have been downed, Lee will be given his historical due.

The same is true of the Confederate soldiers. Eisenhower in his Centennial Proclamation said of the war, "It was a demonstration of heroism and sacrifice by men and women on both sides who valued principle and whose devotion to duty is a part of our nation's noblest tradition." What political gush!

They fought to maintain slavery which was considered a great evil by right-thinking Americans then. And is still more so by such now! Since time has not made slavery more palatable how can fighting for it be a part of any nation's "noblest tradition"?

Shakespeare said that a man could smile and smile and yet be a villain.[15] One can utter the most pious sentiments and yet be a monster within. History has innumerable examples, one of whom is Lee. He was as guilty as Eichmann.[16] He is a hero to American Negrophobes precisely as Eichmann remains one to the hater of Jews.

The Confederate spirit in the South is still the chief weapon for keeping Negroes as near to slavery as possible and for getting politicians into Congress where, thanks to the seniority they get through the suppression of the Negro vote, they head important committees which decide national policy. In this respect the South won the war.

Politics has made the Civil War look like a fight between two friends who later shake hands. But what of the victim over whom they fought and who a hundred years later is still a victim?

GENESIS OF THE CIVIL WAR

The war really began over the admission of new states into the Union. The South wanted them to be slave states in order to increase its power in Congress; the North the opposite. Behind that was the fact that the Northern capitalist was exploiting the Southern slaveholder. The North owned the banks, the railroads, the ships and sold the slaves brought from Africa at a fabulous profit. In short, the agricultural South was really sharecropping for the rich, industrial North. Southern leaders openly declared that if they could cut free from the North they would save hundreds of millions of dollars annually.

But business in the North didn't want war. It would cut into their profits. The North went so far as to pass a Thirteenth Amendment making slavery perpetual in those parts of the Union that had slavery. The South rejected that. It also called a Peace Convention[17] which the South rejected. Senator James Hammond[18] of the South said then,

"The slaveholding South is now the controlling power of the world. The North, without us, would be a motherless calf, bleating about and dying of mange and starvation." All appeasement failed. The cry for independence went up. Independence for what? To continue the robbery of 3,000,000 blacks and the exploitation of the poor white. The South struck the first blow.

It is with this spirit the Centennial is being observed there. On February 12, the inauguration of Jefferson Davis was reenacted in Montgomery, Alabama, with riotous joy and braggadocio. T. B. Hill, cousin of U. S. Sen. Lister Hill, was chosen to represent Davis. The oath of office was administered by Walter B. Jones, Circuit Court judge, son of a Confederate veteran. Jones is the one who had fined and imprisoned Negro ministers and confiscated their cars and other property to pay the heavy fines he imposed on them—penalties which the Supreme Court recently declared illegal.

Jackson, Mississippi, had Secession Day in which 3,000 Grays marched in review before Governor Ross Barnett, while hundreds of Confederate flags waved to a lone United States one. The crowd went wild about "Dixie" and "The Bonnie Blue Flag."[19]

NORTHERN CENTENNIAL CELEBRATIONS

The first big event in which the North was to participate was the attack on Fort Sumter, S. C., April 12. But the Confederate spirit, rampant as ever, left the North no alternative but to withdraw. The North had Negro delegates, among them Mrs. Madeline Williams, Register of Deeds of New Jersey and former state legislator; Illinois had Charles Armstrong, state representative. Charleston through its mayor, Gaillard,[20] announced that no Negro would be received in a hotel, could not mix with the other delegates, and would not be seated at the banquet. The presence of Negroes said Gaillard "would be very embarrassing to all concerned."

President Kennedy wrote Grant, the chairman, insisting that the Negroes be treated as "citizens of the United States." Grant made half-hearted protest in vain. New Jersey, Illinois and New York said they would have no part in the affair. Kennedy ordered a separate observance. This was held at the Charleston Naval Station, a Federal base.

The New York Daily News had a good laugh at the affair. It said, April 26, 1961: "CIVIL WAR II. GRANT SURRENDERS. YANKS SECEDE."

The shot fired against Sumter a hundred years before still reverberated. Gen. Grant made a final surrender soon afterwards. He resigned. His praise of Lee and the Confederates hadn't helped him.

An amendment to prevent use of the Federal allotment in programs or activities not racially integrated was defeated in the House 67–8.

The next big observance was the battle of Bull Run. The event was one of immense rejoicing for the Southerners. And with good reason. Union troops had suffered terrific defeat there and ran back to Washington like frightened rabbits.

Since Sumter the Centennial is a "flop" in the North. To Mississippi's $2,000,000, New York had voted only ten thousand. The first observance in January 1961 (which this writer reported for the press), had apart from the troops, less than two hundred spectators. Two others, in New York City and in Albany, were equally tame and colorless. The Northern press since has said little if anything about the Centennial.

So far the Centennial is a farce, a mockery, a distortion, a negation of all that is right. It is a contradiction such, perhaps, as the world had never seen before. The loser of a war in a most unjust cause placed in the same moral category with those who fought for what the world today abhors!

Why? Because the victim, the one over whom the war was fought, was tossed back to the loser eleven years later, for the purpose of restoring national unity, of bringing the whites of the North and those of the South together again.[21]

This injustice becomes all the more glaring since it was the entry of the Negro into the war that really saved the Union. Abraham Lincoln said so no less than nine times most positively—a fact that the white press, North and South, has most religiously ignored.

LINCOLN AND THE NEGRO

In his speeches and debates Lincoln at times went even further than many pro-slavery exponents in preaching opposition to universal human rights. For instance this: "There is a physical difference between the white and black races which, I believe, will forever forbid the races living on terms of social and political equality. And inasmuch as they cannot so live, while they do remain together there must be the position of superior and inferior, and I, as much as any other white man, am in favor of having the superior position assigned to the white race."[22]

Furthermore, in his eulogy to Henry Clay[23] he had blasted the white abolitionists, among whom were such highly honored citizens today as Emerson, Garrison,[24] Wendell Philipps,[25] the two Beechers,[26] and former President John Quincy Adams. He said they deserved "the execration" they were receiving.

He even went so far as to blame Negroes for the war. Summoning a number of Negro leaders to the White House, he told them that without "the colored race as a basis, the war could not have an existence" therefore the Negroes should get out of the United States. To this end he spent a large sum setting up a Negro colony on a most unhealthy island off the coast of Haiti and which proved most disastrous for the Negroes there.[27]

What led Lincoln to say that the Negroes were the balance of power that saved the Union? The North had been suffering demoralizing defeats. It had been very badly beaten at Bull Run. Sir William Howard Russell, correspondent for the London Times, who had seen it all, wrote, "The President and his Ministers, stunned by the tremendous calamity, sat listening in fear and trembling for the sound of the enemy's cannon. . . . Any moment the Confederate columns might be expected in Pennsylvania Avenue. . . . If in the present state of the troops the Confederates were to march on Washington the Capital must fall into their hands. Gen. Winfield Scott[28] (head of the army), is quite overwhelmed by the affair and is unable to stir. The Secretary of War knows not what to do. Mr. Lincoln is equally helpless . . . "

Another defeat at Wilson's Creek,[29] August 10, staggered the North still more. A third defeat at Ball's Bluff,[30] brought tears to Lincoln's eyes. He came out of the telegraph office, tears streaming down and staggered so badly he would have fallen had not the reporters caught him.

General Sherman said, "Nobody, no man can save the country. Our men are not good soldiers. They brag but they don't perform, What is in store for us I don't know."

The end of the Union was in sight. Russell wrote, "So short-lived has been the American Union that men who saw its rise may now see its fall." Lincoln asked for 300,000 men. He got less than 30,000 in five weeks. "Southern independence is no longer a dream but a fact," said Russell.

Lincoln foresaw that also. Here are his own words on the situation; "Midsummer 1862 things had gone from bad to worse until I felt we had reached the end of our rope on the plan of operation we had been pursuing; that we had about played our last card."

He saw a single ray of hope: the help of the 3,500,000 slaves. He would promise them freedom. "I now determined," he said, "upon the adoption of the emancipation policy; and without consultation with or the knowledge of the Cabinet I prepared the original draft of the proclamation and after much anxious thought called a Cabinet meeting upon the subject."

THE EMANCIPATION PROCLAMATION

The Cabinet was shocked at hearing the state to which the Union was reduced. Secretary Seward[31] objected to the official recruiting of Negroes. He said, "It may be viewed as the last measure of an exhausted government, a cry for help; the government stretching forth its hand to Ethiopia instead of Ethiopia stretching forth her hand[32] to the government."

Lincoln said this objection made him delay the proclamation until Pope's disaster at the second battle of Bull Run[33] forced his hand. "Things looked darker than ever," he said. On January 1, 1863, he issued the Emancipation Proclamation. The Proclamation permitted those states, or localities fighting for the Union to keep their slaves. The only clause of real importance in it was the last which read: Negroes "of suitable condition will be received into the armed services of the United States to garrison forts, positions, stations, and to man vessels of all sorts in said service."

Lincoln's appraisal of the services of the Negros can be found in his "Complete Works," and are summarized in the Lincoln Encyclopedia under the heading, "Negro Troops, Importance of," as follows :

"The bare sight of 50,000 armed and drilled black soldiers upon the banks of the Mississippi would end the rebellion at once; and who doubts that we can present this sight if we but take hold in earnest." (To Governor Andrew Johnson, March 1863).

"The Colored population is the great available and yet unavailed force for restoring the Union . . . to now avail ourselves of this element of force is very important, if not indispensable." (To General Banks, March 29, 1863).

"I see the enemy are driving at them (the Negro soldiers) fiercely as to be expected. It is important to the enemy that such a force shall not take shape and grow and thrive in the South, and precisely the same proportion it is important to us that it shall." (To General Hunter, April 1, 1863).

"General Thomas has gone again to Mississippi with the view of raising colored troops . . . I believe it is a resource which if vigorously applied now will soon close the contest." (To General Grant, August 9, 1863).

"The use of colored troops constitutes the heaviest blow yet dealt to the rebellion, and that at least one of these important successes could not have been achieved but for the aid of black soldiers." To J. C. Conklin, August 26, 1863. "Our colored troops . . . unlike white recruits help us where they came from as well as where they go." (To General Sherman, July 18, 1864).

"Abandon all the posts now garrisoned by black men . . . .and we would be compelled to abandon the war in three weeks." (To Governor Randall, August 15, 1864).

"We cannot spare the hundred and forty or hundred and fifty thousand (black troops). . . . Drive back to the support of the rebellion the physical force which the colored people now give and promise us and neither the present, nor any coming administration can save the Union. . . . It is not a question of sentiment or taste but one of physical force which can be measured and estimated as horsepower or steampower are measured and estimated. And by measurement it is more than we can lose and live."

"To lose the help the Negro was giving," he said, "it would be as powerless to save the Union as to do any other impossible thing." (To Chas. D. Robinson, August 17, 1864).

"Keep it (the physical force) and you can save the Union. Throw it away and the Union goes with it." (To Isaac M. Schermerhorn, September 12, 1864).

"I want to take a look at those boys. I read with greatest delight the account of Mr. Dana's despatch[34] of how gallantly they (the colored troops) behaved. He said they took six of the sixteen guns captured that day. I was opposed on nearly every side when I first favored the raising of colored regiments but they have proved their efficiency." (To General Grant, April 1, 1865, after the battle at Petersburg).

Gideon P. Wells, Secretary of the Navy, also said, "There is an unconquerable prejudice on the part of many whites against black soldiers. But all our increased military strength comes from them."

As was said Lincoln was driven by events to make the above admissions. He not only had opposed before the use of colored troops but had ordered back into slavery escaped slaves freed by Generals Hunter, Fremont, and others in the South. However, Union commanders in the South had been using Negroes as soldiers in spite of orders against it.

At the close of the war there were 149 Negro regiments, composed as follows: 120 infantry; 12 heavy artillery; 10 light artillery; and 7 cavalry—a total of 123,156 men. The number that had served were 186,017. But these figures are only for two years, 1863 (when enlistment began) to 1865. Killed in battle, were 36,847. The above figures do not include those who had served under commanders as Butler, Hunter and Phelps in the two years prior to regular enlistment. Regular Negro troops took part in 251 engagements. As for the navy which saved the Union from total defeat in the early part of the war more than a third of its men were Negroes.

Negro soldiers were treated as inferiors especially in the matter of pay. White privates got thirteen dollars a month; white sergeants, twenty-one; white chaplains, a hundred. All Negroes, including chaplains and surgeons, only seven.

But the Negroes distinguished themselves and received highest praise from commanders Grant, Sherman, Slocum,[35] and Lincoln himself. Twenty-one of them won the Congressional medal of Honors, the highest decoration. Thirteen of these were at Chapin's Farm. At New Market Heights,[36] 543 Negro troops were killed outright. Gen. Benjamin Butler, their commander, later told in Congress of that battle.

"There," he said, "in a space not wider than the clerk's desk and 33 yards long lay the dead bodies of 543 of my colored comrades who had laid down their lives to uphold a flag and its honor as a willing sacrifice. And as I rode along, guiding my horse this way and that, lest he should profane with his hoofs what seemed to me the sacred dead, and as I looked at their bronzed faces, upturned in the shining sun as if in mute appeal against the wrongs of the country for which they had given their lives and whose flag had been to them a flag of stripes on which no glory ever shone for them. Feeling I had wronged them in the past and believing what was the future duty of my country to them, I swore a solemn oath, 'May my right hand lose its cunning and my tongue cleave to the roof of my mouth if I ever fail to defend the rights of men who had given their blood for me and my country that day and their race forever.' And God helping me I will keep that oath." (Congressional Record, Jan. 7, 1874, p. 458).

Popular belief is that it was the Emancipation Proclamation that freed the slaves. That document withheld freedom from some slaves, and a Thirteenth Amendment was necessary. As for the Northern army in the South, as Bruce Catton[37] says, it freed the slave, "in precisely the same spirit it had burned barns and shot cattle." It "had nothing in particular against slavery," but had set out to destroy the South as an opponent, tearing up railroads, burning factories, and smashing resources. Since the slave was their most valuable property, he was freed.

What little gratitude there was to the Negro for having restored the Union had almost vanished by 1877. In order to bring North and South together again the Negroes were thrown to the former masters and oppressors. In 1875, the United States Supreme Court declared the Civil Rights Act illegal, thereby virtually nullifying the Fourteenth and Fifteenth Amendments. In 1896 it legalized race discrimination and the jim-crow car, which before the Civil War had existed only in the North. The effect of these were to increase lynchings and riots against Negroes. Anti-lynching bills, introduced in every session of Congress, were defeated. It was not until the first World War when the Negroes were badly needed again that there came some relief.

If Lincoln were correct in saying that without the Negro's help "it would be as powerless to save the Union as to do any other thing," and if it is the restoration of the Union that made possible the America of today what of the evaluation of the Negro and his treatment in the Centennial?

Notes

INTRODUCTION

1. Useful biographical information is also provided in articles by Asukile, Sandoval, Turner, Turner Moore, Calvin, and Gates. See my Works Cited.

FROM SUPERMAN TO MAN

1. For a sense of life as a Pullman porter in Rogers's day, see Larry Tye, *Rising From the Rails: Pullman Porters and the Making of the Black Middle Class* (2004), Beth Tompkins Bates, *Pullman Porters and the Rise of Protest Politics in Black America 1925–1945* (2001), and Jack Santino, *Miles of Smiles, Years of Struggle: Stories of Black Pullman Porters* (1989).

2. Thomas Dixon Jr. was born in Shelby, North Carolina, in 1864. He wrote a popular trilogy of racist novels, *The Leopard's Spots: A Romance of the White Man's Burden. 1865-1900* (1902), *The Clansman: A Historical Romance of the Ku Klux Klan* (1905), and *The Traitor: A Story of the Fall of the Invisible Empire* (1907). The middle book was the source for D. W. Griffith's classic film. *The Birth of a Nation* (1915). Rogers's *From Superman to Man* (1917) was partly a response to Dixon's novel and Griffith's film. Dixon died in Raleigh, North Carolina, in 1946.

3. Jean Finot (1858-1922) wrote *Préjugé des Races* (*Race Prejudice*) in 1905. Although Finot was of French ancestry, he was born in Poland. His book used facts to make the case for racial equality, and was a major source of influence for Rogers.

4. A generic name given to all Black porters, after the Chicago businessman George M. Pullman, who designed and manufactured the train cars.

5. In early editions he is called a Southern state senator; in later editions, he is a senator from Oklahoma.

6. Derogatory term usually for an Italian, but could also be applied to a Spaniard or Portuguese.

7. Rogers did not care for any term defining a person by race, but he generally used the term "Negro," probably the most common usage for people of African descent through the 1950s. See his articles in the Pittsburgh Courier, "We Can Add More Dignity to Our Name by Being Worthy of It" (March 6, 1948) and "Term Negro Should Be Dignified Not Discarded" (December 11, 1948). Over time, he also used black, Afro-American, and Aframerican.

8. The slave trade in the United States was ended in 1808 although some enslaved people continued to be brought illegally.

9. Rogers would also take up the issue of cannibalism in *Africa's Gift to America*.

10. Herodotus was a Greek historian, author of *The Histories* c. 450 B.C.

11. The Scythians were an ancient nomadic people that once inhabited parts of Eurasia from the eighth century BCE through the third century CE.

12. The Issedonians were an ancient people from central Asia.

13. Perhaps Rogers is thinking of the Birhors, a Dravidian people in India.

14. St. Jerome lived c. 342–420 A.D. He was a Christian scholar also known as Jerome of Stridon who translated much of the Bible into Latin.

15. The quotation is from the French philosopher Jean-Jacques Rousseau's *The Social Contract: Or, Principles of Political Rights* (1762).

16. Ira Aldridge was an American-born Black actor who made his living largely on the British stage after 1824, when he was seventeen. He traveled throughout Europe and was well received, particularly in Russia and Poland. He was especially known for his performance as the title character in Shakespeare's *Othello*. Aldridge was planning to return to America in 1867 for a 100-show tour, but unfortunately, died before that could happen. He is included in *Great Men of Color*, vol. II.

17. Abdu'l-Bahá (born Abbás) was the eldest son of Bahá'u'lláh and served as the head of the Baha'i faith from 1892–1921.

18. Karl Liebknecht was a German socialist killed in 1919 while leading the Spartacist uprising with Rosa Luxemburg.

AS NATURE LEADS

1. Hodge Kirnon (1891–1962) was born in Montserrat. He wrote a favorable review of Rogers's first two books in *Negro World* (1922).

2. This is likely Jack Johnson (1878–1946) who became the first African American world heavyweight champion (1908–15). He was a notorious figure, in part because of his relationships with white women. He had three documented marriages, all to whites. He was sentenced to prison for a year and a day in 1913 under the Mann Act (1910) for transporting a white woman across state lines "for immoral purposes" although the alleged actions occurred before the Mann Act took effect. Johnson jumped bail but turned himself in to the United States government in 1920 and served several months in jail. He was posthumously pardoned in 2018.

3. Rogers is probably referring to Benjamin Tillman, who was a fierce segregationist. He had a cranial tumor which necessitated the removal of his left eye when he was sixteen. Tillman was a Democratic governor of South Carolina from 1890–94 and a senator from the state from 1895 until his death in 1918.

4. Joshua 9:21 "Why did you deceive us by telling us you live far away from us, when in fact you live among us? Now therefore you are under a curse and will perpetually serve as woodcutters and water carriers for the House of my God." This was a Biblical justification to explain the menial jobs Blacks were often forced to accept.

5. The quotation is attributed to several people, but the Roman historian Suetonius in his *The Lives of the Twelve Caesars* (121 CE) claimed it was said by Caligula, Emperor of Rome from 37–41 CE.

6. There are mixed opinions on famed journalist and explorer Henry Morton Stanley's views of Africans. He wrote many popular books on his journeys to Africa including *How I Found Livingstone* (1872) and *In Darkest Africa* (1890). In these, he shed both light and darkness on the Continent.

7. The incident is described in Stanley's *Through the Dark Continent* (1878).

8. Chyle is a milky bodily fluid consisting of lymph and emulsified fats, or free fatty acids.

"THE THRILLING STORY OF THE MAROONS"

1. Hubert H. Harrison, from the Danish (later the United States) Virgin Islands, was a political activist and writer. He initially was a socialist before forming the more race-based Liberty League. Rogers wrote on him in *World's Great Men of Color*, vol. II, calling him ""the foremost Afro-American intellect of his time." For more on Harrison, see Jeffrey B. Perry, *Hubert Harrison: The Voice of Harlem Radicalism, 1883–1918* (2008) and *Hubert Harrison: The Struggle for Equality, 1918-1927* (2021). For information on Rogers and Harrison, see Thabiti Aukile "The Harlem Friendship of Joel Augustus Rogers (1880–1966) and Hubert Henry Harrison (1883–1927)" *Afro-Americans in New York Life and History* 34.2 (2010).

2. Cape Francia is an important port city in the north of Haiti. It was later named Cap Haïtien.

3. Bug-Jargal was first written as a short story and then expanded into a novel by French author Victor Hugo in 1826. It is set several weeks before the beginning of the Haitian Revolution. Bug-Jargal is leader of those enslaved and dies heroically while defending some white sympathizers.

4. Coromantee, the English name for enslaved people from the Akan people in the Gold Coast (now Ghana).

5. Short for obeah, a folk religion widely practiced by West Africans and their descendants in the West Indies.

6. This was a peasant rebellion in 1865 led by Paul Bogle and George Gordon who were protesting poverty and poor living conditions for Jamaicans. After twenty-five people were killed Governor Edward John Eyre declared martial law. Some 400 people, many of them innocent. were killed by the authorities, including Bogle and Gordon. Many others were arrested. Bogle and Gordon are now seen as national Jamaican heroes. The harsh actions of Eyre were widely debated in England. For more, see Gad Hueman *"The Killing Time": The Morant Bay Rebellion in Jamaica* (1995) and Mavis Campbell, *The Maroons of Jamaica 1665–1796: A History of Resistance, Collaboration & Betrayal* (1988).

7. The subheading of the article lists one hundred and fifty-one years.

8. St. Juan de Bolas is generally considered the earliest important Maroon leader. He initially supported the Spanish, but later switched allegiance to support the English. His alliance with the English helped to ensure that the Spanish would be vanquished from Jamaica.

9. Clarendon Parish, in the south central part of the island.

10. Cudjoe is often described as the greatest of the Maroon leaders. For more, see Milton McFarlane, *Cudjoe the Maroon* (1977). Rogers included a biography of Cudjoe in *World's Great Men of Color*, vol. II.

11. Jamaican-born British author Robert Charles Dallas wrote *The History of the Maroons, From Their Origin to Their Establishment of Their Chief Tribe in Sierra Leone* (1803).

12. Toussaint Louverture (1743–1803) was a Haitian general who led the rebellion against the French. He was captured by the French and died in prison. Rogers included Toussaint in *The World's Great Men of Color*, Vol. II.

13. The Miskito people, mostly of African and Native Indian mixture, live in Nicaragua and Honduras.

"THE WEST INDIES"

1. The Immigration Act of 1924 established quotas on the number of immigrants not of Northern European descent. It reduced the number of immigrants from Asia by 80%. Countries from Southern and Eastern Europe, particularly Italy and Greece, also saw their quotas slashed to 2% of their group's population as of 1880. Migration from the Caribbean was almost stopped entirely after the Act was passed. The Act stayed in effect until the passage of the Immigration and Nationality Act (also called the McCarran-Walter Act) in 1952, and later the Immigration and Nationality Act (also called the Hart-Celler Act) of 1965, which, especially with its family reunification provision, resulted in the rapid expansion of Caribbean immigration.

2. Rogers vacillates between usage of Barbadoes and Barbados. For the sake of consistency, I have used the latter throughout.

3. Rev. A. A. Barclay would go on to help establish a cooperative of Jamaican Banana growers that challenged the gigantic United Fruit Company.

4. Winston James remarks about this passage that Rogers "was not as accurate as he thought he was, but he was right in regard to *de facto* British rule in the Caribbean at the time." *Holding Aloft the Banner of Ethiopia: Caribbean Radicalism in Early Twentieth-Century America* (1998), 109.

5. Scottish author William Pringle Livingstone wrote *Black Jamaica: A Study in Evolution* in 1899.

6. Ella Wheeler Wilcox, an American poet, wrote *Sailing Sunny Seas*, (1909), a volume of poetry and reflections on her travels through the Caribbean and other regions.

7. Josiah Royce was a leading religious philosopher who taught at Harvard University from 1882 until his death in 1916. He published *Race Questions, Provincialism and Other American Problems* in 1908, containing a controversial essay "Race Questions and Prejudices."

8. W. E. B. Du Bois wrote *The Negro* (1915), which has a chapter on "The West Indies and Latin America." He had vacillating opinions of West Indians in his writings.

9. Robert Russa Moton was the principal of Tuskegee Institute after the death of founder Booker T. Washington. Marcus Garvey attempted but failed to meet with Moton when the latter visited Jamaica in 1916.

10. The term Jim Crow is thought to have originated from a white performer, Thomas Rice, who did a dance "Jump Jim Crow" while in blackface in the 1830s. The term was later applied to state and local laws in the Southern States that allowed racial segregation through the use of "separate but equal" facilities. These laws began in the 1870s and were upheld by the *Plessy v. Ferguson* Supreme Court decision of 1896. Some versions of the law remained in effect until 1964 with the passage of the Civil Rights Act. Rogers would usually not capitalize the term, probably to indicate his objection to the segregationist policies it represented.

11. Bryan Edwards was British-born, but migrated to Jamaica in 1759, when he was sixteen. He inherited several plantations and was a staunch defender of the slave trade. He returned to England and became a leading pro-slavery voice in Parliament, publishing the two-volume *The History, Civil and Commercial, of the British Colonies in the West Indies* (1793).

12. Praedial larceny is the theft of farm produce, livestock, and other property.

13. Many West Indian farmers would disagree with such as assessment. Farming in the islands was often hard work; farmers often were beset by drought, flooding, hur-

ricanes, and insect infestations, leading them in many cases to migrate. For a picture of their struggles see, for example, Eric Walrond's short story collection, *Tropic Death* (1926), especially the opening piece, "Drought."

14. Guineps are olive-sized with a green skin and yellow, sweep pulp. They can be eaten as is or made into a jam or a drink.

15. Pawpaws are similar to but not identical to papayas. A pawpaw has yellow flesh and is slightly larger than a papaya.

16. A cherimoya is a large, green fruit with a creamy white texture, which is why they are sometimes called custard apples.

17. Naseberries, also called sapodillas, are a brownish fruit, the size of a tangerine. They have a sweet, light brown flesh with black seeds.

18. Plums can refer to a wide variety of fruits. These fruits, as well as many others, often go by different names throughout the region.

19. William Ewart Gladstone, Prime Minister of the United Kingdom for twelve years spread over four terms between 1868–94, supported compensation for slaveholders upon Emancipation in the West Indies. His father, John, owned much slave-run property in the area.

20. a tax imposed on the assessed value of an item.

21. Sir David Barbour was a British politician who held several financial positions.

22. Charles Evans Hughes was Secretary of State from 1921–25.

23. Queens Royal College is a secondary school in Trinidad and Tobago, founded in 1859.

24. Mico University College is actually in Kingston, Jamaica. It was founded in 1836 as a Christian, teacher-training college and is still operational. Washington visited Barbados, not Jamaica, in 1751–52. He contracted smallpox while on the island and did not receive any formal schooling there.

25. Harrison is in Bridgetown, the capital. It is a secondary school founded in 1733.

26. Codrington was established in 1745 by the Anglican Church. It is now affiliated with the University of the West Indies in Cave Hill, Barbados.

27. John Brown Russwurm, (1799–1851), was a fervent abolitionist and supporter of Liberian colonization.

28. A dollar in 1920 would be worth about $15 in purchasing power today.

29. The 18th Amendment, enacted into law in 1919, established the prohibition of the manufacturing, transportation, or sale of alcohol. It was repealed by the 21st Amendment in 1933.

30. Evaristo Estenoz led a rebellion of Afro-Cuban peasants against Cuban forces in 1912. US forces were called in to help quell the rebellion. Cuban General Jesus Monteagudo was said to have ordered the killings.

31. The Wandering Jew is a legendary figure who supposedly taunted Christ on his way to the Crucifixion. His punishment was to traverse the earth until the Second Coming of Christ.

BLOOD-MONEY

1. The original text uses "after." Rogers hand wrote the word "fate" in his copy of the story. He made several such hand-written corrections to the printed text. See the copy in his papers at Fisk University.

2. Rogers goes back and forth between calling the family members Parker and Stewart. I have made all references "Parker" to avoid confusion.

3. Leigh is a friend and classmate of Breckenridge.

4. A wicket is a small window through which business is conducted.

THE KU KLUX KLAN

1. The Invisible Empire was a common name for the Ku Klux Klan. Membership in the group reached its peak in the 1920s, having up to an estimated eight million members. They often imbedded themselves in state and local government.

2. Captain John C. Lester and Reverend D. L. Wilson wrote their book *The Ku Klux Klan: Its Origin, Growth and Disbandment* in 1884.

3. The Fort Pillow Massacre took place on April 12, 1864, in Henning, Tennessee. Hundreds of African American Union troops and their white commanders were slaughtered by Confederate Major General Nathan Bedford Forrest as they attempted to surrender. For more, see Andrew Ward, *River Run Red: The Fort Pillow Massacre in the American Civil War* (2005).

4. The much-wounded John Brown Gordon was one of General Lee's favorite generals. He later served as a Democratic senator from Georgia (1873–80) and as governor of the state (1886–90).

5. George Washington Gordon was a Confederate general and one of the initial members of the Ku Klux Klan.

6. Alfred H. Colquitt was a Confederate brigadier general and a Democratic senator (1883–94) and governor (1877–82) from Georgia.

7. The 13th, 14th and 15th Amendments were passed between 1865 and 1870. They established, among other things, the banning of slavery, citizenship for all people born in the United States, and the right of Black men to vote.

"JAZZ AT HOME"

1. Montmârtre is a large hill in Paris's 18th arrondissement that gives its name to the surrounding district, which is the center of the city's cultural life.

2. The *maxime* is an Afro-Brazilian dance popular in European and American café society in the first two decades of the 20th century.

3. *Danse du vêntre*: belly dancing.

4. *Carmagnole*: a popular song during the French Revolution heaping scorn on Marie Antoinette and other members of the aristocracy and their supporters.

5. Bamboula: a drum made by stretching skin over a rum barrel as well as a dance performed to such drums.

6. *Untrodden Fields of Anthropology* was published in 1898 under the pseudonym Dr. Jacobus X. It gave observations on the sexual practices of "semi-civilized peoples" in Asia, Africa, and America.

7. A *ganzá* is a Brazilian percussive instrument made of a metal canister filled with beads or other objects.

8. *Batouala* is a novel by René Maran (1887–1960), born in Martinique. He won the prestigious Goncourt Prize for this 1921 novel which is a harsh attack on colonialism.

9. Box-back coats are jackets with a straight, unfitted back causing it to hang loosely from the shoulders. They were considered more daring than the conventional fitted look.

10. 'patting juba': complex rhythmic foot stomping and slapping the hands, thighs, and knees.

11, William Christopher Handy (1873–1958), composer, musician, bandleader, helped popularize the blues with such hits as the "Memphis Blues" and the "St. Louis Blues."

12. Jasbo Brown (or Jazbo Brown) is a legendary blues musician from the turn of the twentieth century. He is referenced in works by DuBose Heyward, Bessie Smith, and George Gershwin among others.

13. A native of Canada, Brooks (1886–1975) composed such popular songs as "Some of These Days," "Darktown Strutters' Ball," and "Walkin' the Dog."

14. "The Texas Tommy" is thought to be the first swing dance, introduced in San Francisco about 1910.

15. The Furies (also known as the Erinys), are Greek deities from the underworld who personify vengeance.

16. James Reese Europe (1881–1919), while serving in the United States Army during World War one, assembled an outstanding band (the Harlem Hell Fighters of the 369 Regiment), including Noble Sissle. The band was extremely popular in France.

17. Abbie Mitchell was a mixed-race singer and actress as well as the wife of performer Will Marion Cook.

18. Clara Smith was a blues singer with such hits as "Every Woman's Blues" and "Whip it to a Jelly."

19. Mamie Smith had a best-selling record "Crazy Blues" (1920), thought to be the first blues record to be recorded by an African American woman.

20. "Buddy" Gilmore was a jazz drummer and a member of James Reese Europe's Society Orchestra.

21. Will Marion Cook was the author, with Paul Laurence Dunbar, of the musicals *Clorindy, or the Origin of the Cakewalk* (1898) and *In Dahomey* (1903).

22. Paul Whiteman was an American bandleader and composer. Rogers wrote a favorable review of Whiteman's book *Jazz* in *Opportunity* (December 1926) which is included in this anthology.

23. Noble Sissle and Eubie Blake were composers and performers. Together they wrote the music and lyrics for the hit musical *Shuffle Along* (1921). Blake was the subject of the Broadway musical *Eubie!* (1978).

24. Leroy Eliot "Slam" Stewart was an American jazz double bass player. Stewart and Slim Gaillard wrote and performed "Flat Foot Floogle (with a Floy Floy)," a huge jazz hit in 1938.

25. Fletcher Henderson was a pianist, bandleader, and arranger who helped usher in the big band swing sound.

26. Vincent Lopez was a bandleader and pianist popular in the New York jazz scene from the 1920s through the 1940s.

27.The first Clef Club was co-founded by James Europe as a booking/union hall/performance space for Black musicians in Harlem in 1910. Others were soon formed in various locations.

28. William Henry Tyers was a Jamaican-American composer and pianist who wrote "Maori" (1909), "Smyrna" (1910), and "Panama" (1911).

29. Vernon and Irene Castle, a husband-and-wife American ballroom dance team.

30. Serge Koussevitzky was a Russian-born composer and musician who was the musical director of the Boston Symphony Orchestra from 1924 to 1949.

31. Georges Auric was a French composer of music for opera, film, and the stage.

32. Erik Satie was a French avant-garde composer and pianist.

33. Darius Milhaud was a prolific French composer and conductor.

34. Parnassus is a mountain in Greece that was sacred to Apollo. In some myths it was home to the Muses, the goddesses of literature, the arts, and sciences.

35. The popular song "Runnin' Wild" was composed by Joe Grey, Leo Wood, and Arthur Harrington Gibbs in 1922. It was later performed by Marilyn Monroe in the film *Some Like It Hot* (1959).

36. From Lord George Byron's *Don Juan*, Canto xiii, Stanza xi.

"J.A. ROGERS MAKES COMPARISON OF FRENCH AND AMERICAN CUSTOMS"

1. Cracker is a derogatory term used against whites, especially those from the rural South.

2. Habib Benglia (1895–1960), a stage and film performer, was born in Algeria and settled in France.

3. Raymond Poincaré (1860–1934) was prime minister of France three times (1912–13, 1922–24, 1926–29) and president from 1913–20.

4. The Gaumont Palace was a venue for cinema and live performances. The building was situated on the site of the Hippodrome de Montmartre for equestrian events. Leon Gaumont purchased it in 1907 and converted it into a cinema which held over 5,500 people, making it the largest movie theater in Europe. It was reconstructed again in 1930 and operated under the name Gaumont Palace until it was closed in 1972.

5. The Palais du Trocadéro was a concert hall built for the 1878 World's Fair, partially demolished and partly re-created in 1937 to build the Palais de Chaillot.

"'FIRST HAND' IMPRESSION OF 'BLUE BLOOD' BOOSTERS"

1. The revelation was a discussion of the large number of so-called high-ranking Virginians that allegedly had Black blood.

2 The Chicago riot began on the city's South Side on July 27 and ended August 3, 1919. Twenty-three Blacks and fifteen whites were killed. Many others, mostly African Americans, were injured or lost their homes. The riot was initiated when whites began to throw stones at a Black child who had been swimming in an unofficially segregated white area. The child, Eugene Williams, drowned because he was unable to come to shore due to the stone throwing. When Blacks complained about the death, whites attacked them. Violence quickly erupted. The riot is often considered the worst of the many that occurred in the Red Summer of 1919. One result was the formation of an interracial committee: The Chicago Commission on Race Relations. Linda Peters points out that Rogers's pamphlet "The Approaching Storm" was "clearly a response to the race-riot which took place in Chicago in 1919" (13). For more on this, see William Tuttle, *Race-Riot Chicago in the Red Summer of 1919* (1970).

3. Robert Nathaniel Dett (1882–1943) was a Black Canadian-born pianist, composer, and writer, including the essay "The Emancipation of Negro Music" (1918). His most popular piano work was "In the Bottoms" (1913).

4. Garvey was likely not guilty of the charges of mail fraud made against him for allegedly stealing funds intended for the Black Star shipping line; however, he was found

guilty in 1923 and deported in 1927. Rogers felt Garvey's biggest mistake was representing himself at the trial.

5. "forty acres and a mule": Part of the infamous promise Special Field Orders No. 15 (minus the mule) issued by General William T. Sherman on January 16, 1865. President Andrew Johnson annulled the order.

6. Samuel Chapman Armstrong founded the Hampton Normal and Agricultural Institute in 1868. Armstrong, a white man, believed that an industrial training system was the best means of education for Blacks. Booker T. Washington took his schooling there and tried to establish the system throughout the South. The method was widely criticized by many Black leaders, particularly W. E. B. Du Bois. By the 1920s more and more Hampton students adapted Du Bois' position and began to protest conditions at the school leading to a general strike in 1927, when student opposition forced changes to the curriculum.

7. "The Cat Came Back" is a comic song written by Harry S. Miller in 1893.

8. Amalgamation: an archaic term for intermarriage and interbreeding between the races.

"WHAT ARE WE, NEGROES OR AMERICANS?"

1. Portugal did not abolish slavery until 1761 although the practice continued in its African colonies until much later. Portugal's former colony, Brazil, did not abolish slavery until 1888.

2. Madison Grant (1865–1937) was a leading eugenicist, whose use of scientific racism is demonstrated in his book *The Passing of the Great Race* (1916), which preached Nordic superiority and warned of white "race suicide." The book was embraced by Hitler.

3. Lothrop Stoddard (1883–1950) was a white supremacist whose ideas were embraced by the Nazis as well as US President Warren Harding. Stoddard was a member of the Ku Klux Klan, the American Birth Control Society, and the American Eugenics League, and is best known for his book, *The Rising Tide of Color Against White World Superiority* (1920).

4. Lenox Simpson (under the pseudonym B. L. Putnam Weale) wrote several books critical of Chinese including *Indiscrete Letters from Peking* (1906) and *The Fight for the Republic in China* (1918).

5. Robert Wilson Shufeldt (1850-1934) was a scholar of osteology, the study of bones. He was a strong proponent of white supremacy as expressed in his works, *The Negro: A Menace to American Civilization* (1907) and *America's Greatest Problem: The Negro* (1915).

6. Henry Fairfield Osborn (1857-1935) was a paleontologist and long-time president of the Museum of Natural History. He was an advocate of eugenics and a leading supporter of the work of Madison Grant.

7. Frederick Law Olmsted was a famous landscape architect whose achievements include co designing Central Park and Prospect Park in New York City. He also was a reporter and wrote newspaper articles on his travels through the South in the 1850s. Olmsted argued that slavery was harmful to the Southern economy.

8. No added insult in mind: See Randall Kennedy's provocative history *Nigger: The Strange Career of a Troublesome Word* (2003).

9. A Race-man is someone dedicated to and a strong advocate of the causes and rights of Black people.

10. Dred Scott was an enslaved man who pleaded for the freedom of himself and his family since they had lived in Illinois, a free state, for several years. In the Dred Scott v

Sandford Case (1857) it was ruled that no enslaved person could claim to be a citizen of the United States; thus, they could not present a lawsuit in court.

11. Rogers is probably referring to the decision in the case Corrigan v Buckley (1926) in which the Supreme Court ruled that the selling of a house in a "white" neighborhood in the District of Columbia to a Black family was voided. This precedent soon allowed for racially restrictive covenants not only in Washington, but across the country.

12. The Mason-Dixon line is a geographical demarcation determined between 1763 and 1767 between the boundaries of Pennsylvania, Maryland, Delaware, and West Virginia (then part of Virginia). It informally marked the boundary between free and slave states.

13. A news "butcher" is a person who sold newspapers or other goods on a train.

14. This episode is discussed in Mia Bay's *Traveling Black: A Story of Race and Resistance* (2021): 75.

15. pianissimo: to play a musical piece or sing very softly.

16. Rogers would change his unsympathetic position here on the American Indian after learning more about their treatment in the United States. See, for example, his comments in "Race, A Spiritual, not Scientific Question": "The Indian exterminated or herded into cramped corners."

17. Paul Henri Balluet d'Estournelles de Constant de Rebecque was a French politician and diplomat who won the Nobel Peace Prize in 1909.

18. Gilbert Thomas Stephenson wrote *Race Distinctions in American Law* in 1910.

"IS BLACK EVER WHITE?"

1. "One-drop" rule: the principle that any presence of Black heredity in a person made them Black. It was incorporated into the law of numerous Southern states.

2. Scored: criticized severely.

3. Horace Greeley (1811–72) was an American newspaperman and publisher.

4. Mimi Daquin was a mixed-race character in *Flight* who passed for white until realizing the material gain was not worth the loss of her identity.

"TALKS WITH GARVEY IN ATLANTA PRISON"

1. Hiram Wesley Evans was the Imperial Wizard between 1922–39. Evans tried to expand the group to the Midwest from its traditional base in the Southeast, but overall membership in the Klan declined under his leadership.

2. Colin Grant in *Negro with a Hat: The Rise and Fall of Marcus Garvey* (2008), writes that Garvey's job description at the time was as the "'head cleaner'" (396).

3. The reference is to the popular Harlem underground numbers gambling game.

4. *The Philosophy and Opinions of Marcus Garvey, Or Africa for the Africans*, edited by Amy Jacques Garvey, was published in two parts, in 1923 and 1925. The scrapbook is contained in Box 8 of the Marcus Garvey Memorial Collection housed in Fisk University's Library.

5. Doctor Ossian Sweet was, in 1925, charged with murder after defending himself and his home from a white mob in Detroit. His wife and several others who were in the home were also charged. Lawyer Clarence Darrow took the Sweets' case, and the charges were eventually dropped in 1926.

6. The article appeared in the October 30, 1926 issue.

7. Charles D. B. King was President of Liberia from 1920–30.

8. Harvey S. Firestone founded the Firestone Tire and Rubber Company in 1900. Garvey had tried for years to purchase land in Liberia for the African homeland he envisioned. President King of Liberia reneged on his deal with Garvey and in 1926 signed a 99-year lease with Firestone for the land. In 1988 the company was sold to the Japanese Bridgestone Company.

9. Garvey agreed to the terms to have his sentence commuted. In exchange, he was deported from the United States in 1927 and never returned.

10. Garvey married Amy Jacques in 1922. She played a prominent role in his movement. Garvey's first wife was Amy Ashwood. Their divorce in 1922 was extremely bitter, with mutual charges of adultery. See Tony Martin, *Amy Ashwood Garvey* (2007) and Una Y. Taylor, *The Veiled Garvey: The Life & Times of Amy Jacques Garvey* (2002).

11. Rogers and many scholars believe Garvey would have had a better chance of being acquitted if he had hired a lawyer instead of representing himself. Rogers had attended the Garvey trial and written a Writers' Program essay on it (Asukile "Marcus Garvey," 49–55). For more on the trial and Garvey, see Justin Hanford, "Jailing a Rainbow: The Marcus Garvey Case" *Georgetown Journal of Modern Critical Race Perspectives* 2 (2009), Colin Grant, *Negro With a Hat: The Rise and Fall of Marcus Garvey* (2010), Robert A. Hill, ed. *The Marcus Garvey and the Negro Improvement Association Papers*, and Tony Martin *Race First: The Ideological and Organizational Struggles of Marcus Garvey and the Universal Negro Improvement Association* (1986).

["IS THERE SUCH A THING AS NEGRO ART?"]

1. Igor Stravinsky was a Russian-born pianist considered one of the most important modernist composers. Perhaps his best-known work is the ballet "The Rite of Spring" (1913).

2. Purlieus means a surrounding or neighboring area.

3. Aeolian Hall is a music venue near Times Square, New York. On February 12, 1924, Whiteman's orchestra, with George Gershwin on piano, gave the initial performance of Gershwin's concerto "Rhapsody in Blue." The "experimental" concert marked an important milestone in linking jazz with classical music.

4. Walter Damrosch was the long-time director of the New York Symphony Orchestra.

5. Fritz Kreisler was an Austrian-born American violinist and composer.

6. "I Dreamt that I Dwelt in Marble Halls" is also known as "The Gipsy Girl's Dream," and was a popular aria from the 1843 opera *The Bohemian Girl*.

7. From Richard Wagner's opera *Tannhäuser* (1845).

8. "Song of India" is an aria from Nikolai Rimsky-Korsakov's opera *Sadko* (1896). Whiteman adapted it as a foxtrot in 1921.

"J.A. ROGERS DISCUSSES WEST INDIAN WOMEN"

1. Harrison's article "Du Bois a West Indian, Declares Dr. H. H. Harrison," which discuses West Indian immigrants, appeared in the *Courier* January 29, 1927.

2. High yellows (or yellahs) are light-complexioned Black women, often thought to more desirable.

3. Obtain means to take place or occur.

4. Although the Caribbean had some excellent schools, affording them was beyond the means of most people. In the early part of the 20th century, fewer "than 2% of

Jamaican youths received a high school education" ([Samuel] Hurwitz and [Edith] Hurwitz cited in Adler 349). Fortunately, a primary school education often provided the skills needed to succeed.

5. Bert Williams was a Bahamian-born singer known to perform in blackface. He often performed vaudeville with his partner, African-American George Walker. Their most famous shows included *Clorindy* (1898), *In Dahomey* (1903), and *Bandanna Land* (1908). See Eric Ledell Smith, *Bert Williams: A Biography of the Pioneer Black Comedian* (1992) and Louis Chude-Sokei, *The Last 'Darky': Bert Williams, Black-on-Black Minstrelsy, and the African Diaspora* (2006).

6. John Rosamond Johnson was the brother of well-known author and statesman James Weldon Johnson. The two wrote the hymn "Lift Every Voice and Sing" (1900), which is commonly known as "The Negro National Anthem." Rogers's gender bias is evident here. The most significant female he can cite is someone whose importance is for giving birth to two famous sons. He does not even name her: Helen Louise Johnson (nee Dillet). Born in the Bahamas, she was a musician and the first Black female teacher in a Florida grammar school. Helen had passed on her love of literature and music to her well-known sons. Several of the women in the following paragraph are also identified through their connection to their husband rather than through their own often considerable achievements. Amy Jacques Garvey, for example, helped keep the U.N.I.A. operating for many years. For a sampling of her writing, see my *Amy Jacques Garvey: Selected Writings from the Negro World, 1923–1928* (2016).

"WHO IS THE NEW NEGRO, AND WHY?"

1. There has been much debate over the origin of the term "New Negro." Its usage goes back to colonial days. Even its more current usage can be traced much earlier than Locke's anthology, for example the collection *A New Negro for a New Century* (1900), which includes an essay by Booker T. Washington among others. Hubert H. Harrison also used the term as early as 1917. See Wilson Moses *Afrotopia* (pp. 211–12).

2. Hayward Shepard (also spelled Heyward Shepherd) was a freed black man who was the first person killed in 1859 at Harpers Ferry by John Brown and his men. He was trying to defend the arsenal.

3. Denmark Vesey was executed in 1822 for allegedly planning a major slave rebellion in Charleston, South Carolina. He was one of the founders of the African Methodist Episcopal Church in Charleston.

4. The so-called Palestine race riot occurred in 1910 in Slocum, an unincorporated community in East Texas. As many as 200 Blacks may have been killed.

5. The Springfield riot took place in Illinois in 1908.

6. The Longview riot happened from July 10-12, 1919 in Texas, about 125 miles east of Dallas.

7. Coleman Livingston Blease was a Democratic governor of South Carolina 1911–15 and a senator 1925–31. He was a strong supporter of white supremacy.

8. James K. Vardaman was a Democratic governor of Mississippi 1904–8 and a senator 1913–19. He supported maintaining white supremacy by any means including lynching.

9. In Psalms 51:7, it is stated "Purge me with hyssop [a shrub in the mint family], and I shall be clean; wash me and I shall be whiter than snow." There is a hymn "Lord Jesus, I Long to Be Perfectly Whole" with a line "Now wash me and I shall be whiter than snow." It was written by James L. Nicholson in 1872.

10. This quotation has been credited to several people, most commonly Thomas Jefferson and Benjamin Franklin. However, it has never been attributed definitively.

11. Osborn Perry Anderson, John A. Copeland Jr., Shields Green, Lewis Sheridan Leary, and Dangerfield Newby. These were the five slain Blacks who were among the twenty-one men led by John Brown on October 16, 1859.

12. One of Aesop's *Fables*.

"IS THE STAR OF THE FOLLIES-BERGERE REALLY MARRIED?"

1. Spencer Williams was an African American singer, pianist, and composer. He co-authored such hits as "I Ain't Got Nobody," "Basin Street Blues," and "Everybody Loves My Baby."

2. A white marriage (mariage blanc) is a marriage without consummation.

3. Maurice Dekobra, born Ernest-Maurice Kessier, was a well-known French novelist in the 1920s and '30s.

4. Adolphe Menjou was an American actor nominated for an Academy Award in 1931 for *The Front Page*.

5. Myron T. Herrick, a Republican, was United States ambassador to France from 1912–14 and 1921–29. He also served as the governor of Ohio from 1904–6.

6. Harlem theaters that have featured many of the leading Black entertainers including Duke Ellington, Billie Holliday, Pearl Bailey, and Cab Calloway.

"THE NEGRO'S EXPERIENCE OF CHRISTIANITY AND ISLAM"

1. Rogers wrote about the religion, whose message of universal brotherhood appealed to him, in "Rogers Says: Cardinal Principal of the Bahai Faith Is Oneness of Mankind" Pittsburgh *Courier* May 20, 1944, and "The Bahai" Boston *Chronicle* November 24, 1934. He also gave several lectures at the group's center in New York City.

2. From American poet John Greenleaf Whittier's "The Preacher" (1859): "Bade the slave-ship speed from coast to coast / Fanned by the wings of the Holy Ghost." The title character alluded to is the Anglican preacher, George Whitfield.

3. Tertullian was an Early Christian theologian from Carthage. He was a critic of paganism and Gnosticism and is thought to be the author of the *Apologeticus* ca. 197 A.D.

4. Origen of Alexandria was an early Christian scholar who wrote over 2,000 treatises on theological matters, particularly on asceticism.

5. St. Cyprian was born into a Roman African family and became a convert to Christianity, rising to become bishop of Carthage.

6. A person from Numidia, a kingdom in north Africa, parts of which were in what is now Algeria, Tunisia, Morocco, and Libya.

7. Bilal Ibn Rabah was the loyal companion of the prophet Mohammed. He was said to have a dark brown complexion. Rogers includes him in *Great Men of Color*, vol. 1.

8. Simon the Cyrenean was ordered to help Jesus carry his cross to the crucifixion. Cyrene was located in Northern Africa, in what is now Libya.

9. St. Maurice was an Egyptian military leader of the 3rd century A.D. He was martyred in Switzerland for refusing to kill fellow Christians. Rogers writes about St Maurice in "Hitler and the Negro" (*Interracial Review* April 1940), and he is included in *World's Great Men of Color*, Vol. II.

10. Matthias Grünewald was a German Renaissance painter of religious works.

11. Azurara: Gomes Eanes de Zurara, Portuguese chronicler of the 15th century.

12. Born al-Hasan ibn Muhammad al-Wazzan, Leo Africanus was a traveler, scholar, and author, most famous for his *Description of Africa* (1550).

13. Hannibal was a Carthaginian statesman and general who fought against the Roman forces from 183–181 B.C. Rogers writes about him in *Great Men of Color*, vol. 1.

14. Henri Grégoire, a French Catholic priest, who was a strong supporter of racial and religious equality. He wrote *De la Littérature Des Nègres* (1808).

15. Schopenhauer, who built his ideas on those of Immanuel Kant, was a favorite philosopher of Rogers. The concept cited here is from *The World as Will and Representation* (first edition 1818/19; second 1844). Schopenhauer posited that the concept of the individual will is an illusion and that we must suppress this will through asceticism to alleviate suffering. According to Helga Rogers, her husband identified with Schopenhauer's belief that "treating the welfare and rights of others [is] as important as one's own rights" (8).

16. The quotation is from *On the Genealogy of Morality* (1887). The book demonstrates Nietzsche's belief in the innate predatory nature of mankind.

17. Epistle to Philemon 1:10–16.

18. Ephesians 6:5: "Slaves, obey your earthly masters with respect and fear and with sincerity of heart, just as you would obey Christ."

19. Edward Strutt Abdy was an English abolitionist who wrote on racial issues, including the three-volume *Journal of a Residence and Tour of the United States of North America from April, 1833, to October, 1834* (1835).

20. Allen writes of this incident in his *Life, Experience, and Gospel Labours* (1833).

21. The Community Church of New York is still an active Unitarian Universalist church located in Midtown Manhattan.

22. The famous Scopes trial about the teaching of evolution in a Tennessee public school in 1925. William Jennings Bryan was the lawyer for the prosecution and Clarence Darrow represented the defendant, a high school teacher. The teacher was found guilty, but the decision was overturned on a technicality.

23. The expulsion and murder of approximately a million Armenians by Turkey between 1915–16. Turkey still does not recognize its actions as genocide.

24. H. L. Mencken wrote a 1924 piece in the Chicago *Daily Tribune* that "The old game is beginning to play out in the Bible Belt," a very conservative area mostly in the rural south.

25. The riots in East St. Louis in 1917 left up to 150 African Americans and 9 whites dead. During the bloody Red Summer of 1919, numerous race riots took place. The riots were really massacres where rampaging whites entered Black areas killing the residents and destroying the neighborhoods. Among the worst were ones in Washington, D.C. and Chicago.

26. An anti-lynching bill was proposed by Republican Representative, Leonidas C. Dyer of Missouri, in 1918 that would make lynching a federal crime. It was blocked by powerful resistance from Southern senators. Several attempts were made, but the bill never passed. A recent bill (2022) to make lynching a federal crime was finally passed.

27. Probably *From Superman to Man*, which went into a fourth edition in 1924.

28. The one who announces the adhan, the call to Islamic prayer.

29. The guided one, a messianic figure. In most Islamic traditions, he is believed to come to rid the world of evil before Judgment Day.

30.The Shahada, one of the Five Pillars of Islam, and part of the adhan. It is a declaration of faith in Allah.

31. A houri is a woman who will accompany the faithful into paradise.

32. Rogers's statement that there are few Christians in Africa is incorrect. In 2018 599,000,000 Christians lived in Africa, more than on any other Continent. Todd M. Johnson, et al, "Christianity 2018: More African Christians and Counting Martyrs" *International Bulletin of Mission Research* Vol. 42 (2017). Perhaps Rogers is intending Northern Africa, which is largely Islamic.

33. Matthew 25:40: "And the King will reply, 'Truly I tell you, whatever you did for one of the least of these brothers of Mine, you did for Me.'"

34. African explorer and missionary David Livingstone condemned the Islamic slave trade in *Missionary Travels and Researches in South Africa* (1857): "this trade in Hell, this open sore of the world."

35. Domestic slavery was abolished in Sierra Leone in 1928.

"COMMUNISM AND THE NEGRO"

1. Thabiti Asukile posits that "Rogers took a Marxist position on the race problem in America" ("Marcus Garvey" 60). However, while Rogers is critical of capitalism, which he often equates with wage slavery, he also tends to look at Marxism (particularly communism) with suspicion. Most organizations led by whites, he feels, tend to ignore the problems of Blacks. He maintains, as he says in "Who Is the New Negro, and Why?" Blacks "are the only ones that are ever going to speak out frankly and forcefully on [Blacks'] grievances." See also Turner, p. 35.

2. The FBI file is available on-line on FB Eyes: Digital Archives, http://omeka.wustl.edu/omeka/exhibits/show/fbeyes/rogers

3. *The Negro Worker* was the organ of the International Trade Union Committee of Negro Workers of the Red International of Labor Unions and operated from 1928 to 1937. It was titled *The International Negro Workers' Review* from 1928–31.

"AHEAD OF ITS TIME"

1. The William E. Harmon Foundation Award for Distinguished Achievement Among Negroes was given in eight different fields. It was begun in 1926 and ended in 1930. Gold and bronze awards were given, and recipients included writers Countee Cullen, Langston Hughes, Eric Walrond, James Weldon Johnson, musician Nathaniel Dett, and artist Archibald Motley.

2. William Hannibal Thomas was an African American teacher and judge. He gained notoriety for his book *The American Negro* (1901), which attacked many African Americans, particularly women. He favored Black assimilation into white society.

3. See for example "Rogers Visits Claude McKay in Southern France" Pittsburgh Courier June 18, 1927.

4. McKay's novel *Banjo: A Story Without a Plot* (1929) is set among workers on the docks in Marseilles, France. The book was not as commercially successful as *Home to Harlem*.

"THE PARIS PEPPER-POT"

1. Cocoe (coco) refers to starchy root vegetables such as taro or tannia. They are staples in the Caribbean diet and go by many different names in the different islands.

2. Okra is often spelled and pronounced ochroe in Caribbean English.

3. bird-pepper: Cayenne pepper (capsicum annuum). This hot plant goes by different names, and there are different varieties, but in any form it is an essential ingredient in much West Indian cooking.

4. Enfin: in conclusion, finally.

5. Makers and sellers of fashionable dresses and hats.

6. Railroad ham sandwiches were sold on the British rail system until the 1990s. They were often ridiculed for their poor quality. Sandwiches would be prepared with a thin slice of meat cut in half with the top piece arranged diagonally over the bottom piece to make it appear as if there were two slices.

"THE AMERICAN NEGRO IN EUROPE"

1. Henry Louis Mencken (1880–1956) was an essayist and cultural critic. He was editor of the influential journal *The American Mercury* and author of the significant study *The American Language* (1919). For his often conflicted connection to Black writers, see Charles Scruggs *The Sage in Harlem: H. L. Mencken and the Black Writers of the 1920s* (1984).

2. Hofbräuhaus is a well-known Munich tavern.

3. Maximilian Harden, born Felix Ernst Witkowski, was a leading German editor and intellectual writer. He published the journal *Die Zukunft* (*The Future*).

4. The circus was started by Carl Hagenbeck in 1903. It was purchased by Benjamin Wallace in 1907 and became the Hagenbeck-Wallace Circus, which traveled across the United States until folding in 1938.

5. Esther Lee Jones, known as "Baby Esther" or "Little Esther," was a popular singer and dancer in the 1920s and '30s. She is best known for her scat-singing, which was said to have been the inspiration for the voice of cartoon character Betty Boop.

6. Rogers consistently argues for equal treatment of all Blacks, but in particular ones who are to his mind "respectable" in their education and behavior.

7. Roosevelt had dinner at the White House with Booker T. Washington on October 16, 1901. Senators Vardaman and Tillman were among those vigorously protesting the event.

8. British explorer Verney Lovett Cameron was the first European to traverse equatorial Africa from coast to coast in 1875. He wrote about his experiences in *Across Africa* (1877).

9. Paul Belloni Du Chaillu was a mixed-race French-American explorer and anthropologist. He was a popular writer and lecturer on Africa, and is thought to be the first Westerner to see gorillas as well as the Pygmy people. Rogers included him in *Great Men of Color*, vol. II.

10. Joseph Bologne, Chevalier de Saint-Georges, was born in Guadeloupe. He is included in *Great Men of Color*, vol. II.

11. The Peninsular War was a conflict between the Napoleonic French forces against the victorious British, Spanish, and Portuguese armies from 1808–14.

12. The Pyrenees are a mountain range straddling the borders of France and Spain. The Army of the Pyrenees was created in 1792 during the French Revolution.

13. Alfred Amédee Dodds was included in *World's Great Men of Color*, vol. II.

14. The Boxer Rebellion was an anti-foreign attack by Chinese nationalists against American, Austro-Hungarian, British, French, German, Italian, Japanese, and Russian troops between 1899–1901. The coalition forces were victorious, and the Boxers had to pay a stiff indemnity.

15. Verdun was thought to be France's stronghold. It was the site of the longest-lasting battle in World War I. There were huge German and French casualties in the eleven-month battle of attrition in 1916.

16. André Pierre Gabriel Amedeé Tardieu was a right-leaning disciple of former French Prime Minister Raymond Poincaré. Tardieu's cabinet appointments opposed the Radical Socialists. Alcide Delmont, a lawyer, was born in Martinique.

17. Aube: a department in the Grand Est region of north-eastern France.

18. Chocolat was the stage name of the Cuban-born clown whose birth name was Rafael Padilla. He often played the foolish (auguste) clown in comparison to his frequent partner George Foottitt, who played a more sophisticated character performing in whiteface.

19. Joe Alex was a Martiniquan-born singer, dancer, and actor who performed the danse sauvage (savage dance) with Josephine Baker.

20. White actress Mary Blair kissed Paul Robeson's hand in Eugene O'Neill's *All God's Chillun Got Wings* (1924). The controversial scene caused a furor.

21. Bal Blomet is a nightclub located in the Montparnasse section in the south of Paris, in the fifteenth arrondissement. It was a favorite meeting place for numerous artists, writers, and musicians in the 1920s.

22. *maquereau* literally means a mackerel, but it is also a French slang term for a pimp.

23. Alexander von Humboldt was a 19th century Prussian geographer and explorer.

24. Gaspare Spontini was an Italian opera composer and conductor. His best-known work is the musical tragedy, *La Vestale* (1807).

25. Beethoven's 1803 piece for violin and piano, formally known as Violin Sonata No. 9, Op. 47. It was dedicated to violinist Rodolphe Kreutzer, who supposedly hated it.

26. Alexsey Petrovich Yermolov was a 19th century general in the Imperial Russian Army. He fought in the Napoleonic Wars and during the Caucasian War (1817–64).

27. In 1919 there were riots largely over the hiring of white foreign seamen over Black British sailors.

28. *Tit-Bits* was a popular British weekly magazine collecting pieces from a variety of other publications. It ran from 1881 to 1984.

29. Samuel Coleridge-Taylor was a well-known Black British composer and conductor. He is best-known for his three cantatas adapted from American poet Henry Wadsworth Longfellow's *Song of Hiawatha* (1899). He is included in *Great Men of Color*, vol. II.

30. Prince Monolulu was born Peter Carl McKay in St. Croix, part of what was then the Danish West Indies (now the American Virgin islands).

31. Henry Lascelles, 6th Earl of Harewood was a British soldier and peer as well as a son-in-law of King George V and Queen Mary.

32. Hugh Lowther, 5th Lord of Lonsdale was a British sportsman and peer.

33. The orange represented the Protestants of Northern Ireland while the shamrock represented the Catholics of Ireland. The country was partitioned in 1921.

34. Robert Sengstacke Abbott was the publisher and editor of the important Black newspaper, the Chicago *Defender*.

35. Roland Hayes was an African-American lyric tenor and composer.

36. The Indian Home Rule Movement advocated for self-government for colonial India between 1916–18.

37. Turner Layton and Clarence "Tandy" Johnstone formed a popular African American vocal and piano duo in the 1920s and '30s. They also had great success touring Europe.

38. The marriage in 1924 of Leonard "Kip" Rhinelander, son of a millionaire, and Alice Jones, a mixed-race immigrant, became a hot topic of society gossip. When rumor got out that Jones was Black, the Rhinelander family took her to court in 1925 where Jones was forced to expose parts of her body before a judge and jury to determine her race. They decided she was "colored," but would not grant an annulment. In 1929, Jones agreed to a divorce and the marriage was annulled. Jones was given a settlement of $32,500 and $3,600 a year for life. Rogers wrote about the case in *Sex and Race* Vol. II, 346–48.

"THE EMPEROR JONES"

1. Charles Gilpin (1878-1930) was a successful actor, singer, and dancer, best known for his role as Brutus in *The Emperor Jones*.

2. John Louis Spivak was a socialist and later communist investigative reporter. *Georgia Nigger*, a novel about prison camp chain gangs, was published in 1932.

3. Edward Byron Reuter was President of the American Sociological Society in 1933. He published several books including *The Mulatto in the United States* (1918).

4. Thomas Sigismund Stribling won the Pulitzer Prize for his novel *The Store* (1933), However, Rogers would be more interested in his novel *Birthright* (1922), a strong critique of racial prejudice across the United States.

5. *Hallelujah* is a 1929 film starring Donald L. Haynes and Nina Mae McKinney. Although white director King Vidor tried to give a realistic portrayal of the life of a Black sharecropper, the film is now generally seen as helping to perpetuate stereotypes of Blacks.

6. Clarence Muse was an African American actor and screenwriter. He performed in over 150 films, including *Broken Earth* (1936) and *Way Down South* (1939), which he co-authored with Langston Hughes.

7. Nine young African Americans (between twelve and nineteen) were accused of raping two white women in Scottsboro, Alabama in 1931. Despite evidence that the boys were innocent, eight of them were sentenced to the death penalty. There were numerous appeals and the case even got to the Supreme Court. Eventually, charges against four of the defendants were dropped. The others were given a sentence of seventy-five years in jail. One was shot in the leg and permanently disabled. Two escaped and were later sent back to jail. One escaped and was finally pardoned in 1976. The others were pardoned posthumously. The incident gathered an enormous amount of national attention, and is seen as one of the greatest miscarriages of justice in United States history. The case has inspired many poems, plays, films, and novels.

8. A satiric play on the popular marching song, "John Brown's Body," sung by Union troops during the Civil War.

9. This is similar to Du Bois' statement that Black theater should be "by us, for us, about us, and near us" "Krigwa Players' Little Theatre Movement" *Crisis* (July 1926).

100 AMAZING FACTS ABOUT THE NEGRO

1. In a respectful nod to Rogers, Gates has written his own 100 *Amazing Facts About the Negro* (2017).

2. The name formerly given to two human skeletons discovered in Italy in 1901. The skeletons are dated around 26,000 to 22,000 years ago.

3. See Rogers's article "Rogers Says: A Legion in History: Did Negroes Predate Columbus to America?" Pittsburgh *Courier* October 6, 1945. See also Ivan Van Sertima's controversial, *They Came Before Columbus* (1976). Henry Louis Gates, Jr. indicates that Juan Garrido was the first documented Black person in the New World, around 1503 (*100 Amazing Facts About the Negro* 10). He was not a slave but a conquistador.

4. Comte de Volney was a French politician, writer, and abolitionist most famous for *The Ruins; Or, a Survey of the Revolutions of Empires* (1796).

"ITALY OVER ABYSSINIA"

1. For more on these connections, see Mark Christian Thompson *Black Fascisms: Literature and Culture Between the Wars* (2007).

2. Abyssinia is the historical name for the Ethiopian Empire, which comprised the northern half of modern-day Ethiopia and Eritrea. It was founded in 1270 by the Solomonic Dynasty.

3. Gondar (also Gonder) was formerly the capital of the Ethiopian Empire. Gondar was the last part of Ethiopia that Mussolini surrendered in 1941.

4. From December 5–7, 1934, there was a clash at the oasis town of Walwal (also Welwel) where Italians had built a fort on Ethiopian territory. Ethiopia appealed several times to the League of Nations for support, but the League exonerated both sides from blame. Soon after this exoneration, Italy invaded Ethiopia on October 3, 1935.

5. Tripolitania was an Italian colony from 1927–34. It was then combined with Italy's other North African territories, Cyrenaica and Fezzan, in what was known as Italian Libya. Italian Somalia, Italian Eritrea, and the newly conquered Ethiopian Empire formed Italian East Africa from 1936 until 1941 when Italy was defeated by the Allies.

6. Magdala, now called Amba Mariam, is a city in central Ethiopia.

7. Menelik II, baptized as Sahle Maryam, was emperor of Ethiopia from 1889 to 1913. Rogers includes him in *World's Great Men of Color*, vol. 1.

8. Asmara is the capital of present-day Eritrea.

9. Francesco Crispi was an Italian statesman who served as prime minister from 1887–91 and 1893–96. Once seen as a patriot and a founder of the Italian nation, he was driven from power after the Italian defeat in Ethiopia.

10. Oreste Baratieri was governor of Italian Eritrea. After the defeat at Adowa (Adwa), the Italians were forced to sign the Treaty of Addis Ababa in 1896, ensuring Ethiopian sovereignty. Baratieri went into exile in Austria until his death in 1901.

11. Makonnen Wolde Mikael Wolde Melekot (Ras Makonnen) was father of Emperor Haile Selassie and first cousin of Menelik II.

12. Earlier, Rogers had indicated that Baratieri had 25,000 troops.

13. Pierre Laval served as France's prime minister for periods in 1931–33 and 1935–36. His handling of Ethiopia, widely seen as an attempt to appease Mussolini, led to his resignation in 1936.

14. Ramsay MacDonald was prime minister of the United Kingdom from 1929–35.

15. Muhammed Ahmad ibn al Sayyid Abd Allah, known as the Messiah of the Sudan, defeated the British in the 1880s. Rogers wrote about him in *World's Great Men of Color*, vol. 1.

16. Sayid Mohamed Abdullah Hassan waged a twenty-year war against the British, Italians, and Ethiopians in Somalia. He was given his nickname of Mad Mullah by the British.

17. Lidj Yassu (Lij Iyasu) was the designated emperor of Ethiopia from 1913–16 although he was never crowned. He was Menelik II's grandson.

18. The intended marriage between Lij Araya Abeba, nephew of Haile Selassie, and a Japanese woman, Kuroda Masako, was cancelled in 1934 because of political pressure from Italy.

19. The Little Entente was an alliance consisting of Czechoslovakia, Romania, and the Kingdom of Serbs, Croats, and Slovenes (Yugoslavia) formed in 1920–21. It collapsed when Hitler invaded Czechoslovakia in 1938.

20. Muhammad ibn Abd al-Karim al-Khattabi (better known as Abd el-Krim) fought French and Spanish colonization in Morocco, using guerilla tactics to form a separate Republic of the Rif in northern Morocco from 1921–26.

"J. A. ROGERS GETS EXCLUSIVE INTERVIEW WITH EMPEROR"

1. Unfortunately, the Princess died in 1942 when only twenty-two years of age during childbirth. She had married Colonel Abiye Abeba in 1942.

2. Rogers probably intends the Pallazo Venezia in central Rome, which was formerly called the Palace of St. Mark. Mussolini's secret bunker was discovered under the building in 2010.

3. Born as Katherine Lee Yarborough, Jarboro was a Black opera singer. She was the first Black to perform a leading role with a white opera company in America when in 1933 she sang the title role in Verdi's *Aida* at the New York Hippodrome.

4. Located in the eastern part of the country, Dire Dawa is, along with Addis Ababa, the only chartered city in Ethiopia. It was established as a stop along the Addis Ababa-Djibouti railway line in 1902.

5. Masowah (Massawa or Mitsiwa) is a port city on the Red Sea in what is now Eritrea.

6. Ethiopian marathoners are among the best in the world. They first competed at the Olympic Summer games in 1956 and have since won over fifty medals, all in long-distance events.

7. Selassie made seven visits to the United States between 1954 and 1973.

"ROGERS DESCRIBES HIS 'ADVENTURES IN JIM-CROW LAND'"

1. Dickens was horrified over many aspects of American culture, particularly by what he felt were the lack of personal hygiene and the poor public sanitation as reported in his travel work *American Notes* (1842) and the novel *Martin Chuzzlewit* (1842–44).

2. English author Evelyn Beatrice Hall (under the pseudonym S. G. Tallentyre) wrote *The Life of Voltaire* in 1903.

"J. A. ROGERS RIPS 'VEIL OF HYPOCRISY' FROM 'BEST SELLER'"

1. Helper, a Southerner, opposed slavery, but not for humanitarian reasons. His controversial *The Impending Crisis of the South: How to Meet It* (1857) contended that slavery was not beneficial to the white Southern economy because it impeded industrialization. He hoped to have Blacks repatriated to Africa or South America.

2. Northerner Albion W. Tourgée relocated to North Carolina after being wounded in the Civil War. He wrote several novels sympathetic to African Americans, especially *A Fool's Errand, by One of the Fools* (1879), about Reconstruction.

3. Carl Schurz was Secretary of the Interior from 1877–81 and as a Republican senator from Missouri from 1869–75. He was also a Union general in the Civil War.

4. James Gillespie Blaine held several important governmental positions including Secretary of State, Speaker of the House, and Senator from Maine. He may best be known for proposing the Blaine Amendment, which would have prohibited public funds being given to institutions with religious affiliations. It was seen as anti-Catholic in some quarters. In 1875 it passed the House but failed in the Senate.

5. John Roy Lynch was an African American writer, attorney, and Republican politician. He is best known for his book, *The Facts of Reconstruction* (1913).

6. James Holt Clanton served in the Mexican-American War and was a Confederate Brigadier General during the Civil War.

7. Gordon's autobiography was entitled *Reminiscences of the Civil War* (1904).

8. William Hervey Allen wrote the historical novel *Anthony Adverse* in 1933. It was adapted as a popular film in 1936.

"THE SUPPRESSION OF NEGRO HISTORY"

1. Iago says these lines in *Othello* Act 3, Scene 3: "Who steals my purse steals trash; 'tis something, nothing; / 'Twas mine, 'tis his, and has been slave to thousands; / But he that filches from me my good name / Robs me of that which not enriches him, / And makes me poor indeed."

2. DNA studies show that the mixed-race enslaved person Sally Hemings was the mother of six of Thomas Jefferson's children. See Annette Gordon-Reed's *The Hemingses of Monticello: An American Family* (2008).

3. Delphus, the son of Apollo. According to some Greek myths, his mother was Melaina (which means the Black One).

4. There are a number of quotations with cockroaches and roosters. In all of them the rooster comes out on top. Here are two: When a cock invites a cockroach for a birthday party, he has prepared dinner for himself. And: If roosters were judges, cockroaches would be sentenced.

5. Chief Justice John Holt stated in the case of Smith v Brown and Cooper (1701) that "as soon as a negro comes into England, he is free."

6. William K. Gregory wrote *Our Face from Fish to Man: A Portrait Gallery of Our Ancient Ancestors and Kinfolk Together with a Concise History of Our Best Features* (1929). The book shows the evolution of the human anatomy.

7. Rogers speaks of this further in *100 Amazing Facts about the Negro*, pp. 17, 38–39.

8. The well-known English author published his *Outline of History* in 1920. Wells generally was a progressive voice on race throughout his career. In *Outline* he argued against the possibility of racial purity. He says little about Black achievements in the book.

9. Toynbee was one of the most widely recognized scholars of international history in the first half of the twentieth century. The British historian is best known for his twelve-volume *A Study of History* (1934–61). Rogers responded to Toynbee in the Pittsburgh *Courier*: "Rogers Says: Toynbee History Charge is False" October 2, 1954. Du Bois also criticized Toynbee's claims. See Thabiti Asukile, "The Admiration and Complementary Africana Historical Scholarship of W. E. B. Du Bois and Joel Augustus Rogers" *Africology: The Journal of Pan African Studies* (2018). See especially pages 194–205.

10. Sir Arthur Evans was an eminent British archeologist specializing in the Aegean civilization of the Bronze Age.

11. An anthropological period linked with early humans existing 43,000 to 26,000 years ago.

12. Rogers often used "researches" to refer to his work. Though not accepted as correct grammatically, the word is becoming increasingly popular in written and spoken discourse.

13. Marcel-Auguste Dieulafoy was a French archeologist whose work largely focused on Iran.

14. Liudprand was a tenth century northern Italian historian and diplomat as well as being bishop of Cremona.

15. Nicephorus Phocas was a powerful Byzantine emperor who reigned from 963–69. His victories against Moslem Arabs helped revitalize the empire.

16. Rogers also speaks of the Victorian poet in *Sex and Race* (I:204, 216, 299; II: 128) and in *Great Men of Color*, vol. II. Furnivall and Emily Hickey founded the Browning Society in 1881. Both Robert and his wife Elizabeth Barrett had Jamaican ancestry.

17. Frank Morgan. Morgan (born Francis Phillip Wuppermann) is best known for playing the title character in the film *The Wizard of Oz* (1939).

18. Italian author Gabriele D'Annunzio contributed to the screenplay of the silent film *Cabiria* (1914). He was also an Italian nationalist, often seen as having influenced Mussolini.

19. A movement to establish a self-governing nation created from the areas where Blacks were the majority in the Southern states of the Black Belt. The controversial plan was advocated by the Communist Party USA in 1928 and gained support into the '30s.

20. *Plutarch's Lives of the Greeks and Romans* (also called *Parallel Lives*) consisted of pairs of lives (one Greek and one Roman). The work was probably written in the early years of the 2nd century A.D. and was meant to teach moral values.

21. Sergeant George Henry Wanton was awarded the Congressional Medal of Honor for his service with the all-Black 10th Cavalry during the Spanish American War.

22. Shudras are the lowest of the *varnas* (castes) in Indian society, made up of the laboring classes.

23. Antarah ibn Shaddad al-Absi (Antar) was a pre-Islamic Arab poet and warrior. Rogers includes him in *Great Men of Color*, vol. 1.

24. Kafur (Abu al-Misk Kafur) was a Black who rose from slavery to became ruler of Egypt in 946 CE. Rogers includes him in *Great Men of Color*, vol. 1.

25. José Gaspar Rodríguez de Francia was a Paraguayan lawyer and politician. He ruled Paraguay as a dictator (1814–40) after the country gained its independence in 1811.

26. José de San Martín is a national hero in Argentina, Perú, and Chile.

27. Antonio José de Sucre was once president of Bolivia and Perú.

28 The Nicaraguan poet and writer Rubén Dario is often called the father of Modernism.

29. Thomas Babington Macaulay was a British Victorian historian and politician. Macaulay divided the world into two groups: civilized and barbaric nations. His best-known work is the five-volume *History of England from the Accession of James the Second* (1848).

YOUR HISTORY

1. George L. Lee was born in Jamestown, New York, in 1906. He worked for a number of Black periodicals including the Chicago *Defender* and the Pittsburgh *Courier* and did illustrations of many prominent sports figures. He had a series, *Interesting People*, which combined portraits and brief biographical sketches of Blacks.

2. Alfred Samuel Milai, of mixed-race, was born in Washington, D.C. in 1908 and grew up in Locust Dale, Virginia. Milai worked as an illustrator for the Pittsburgh *Courier* for thirty-three years.

SEX AND RACE

"The Black Nun"

1. In *Titus Andonicus*, the Roman Empress, Tamora, has an affair with Aaron the Moor, which results in a mulatto child.

2. G. Lenotre was the pen-name of Louis Léon Théodore Gosselin, a French historian and playwright who lived from 1855-1935.

3. Maria Theresa of Spain married Louis IV of France, her double first cousin, in 1660 in an attempt to bring peace between the two nations. She was largely ignored by Louis after the marriage and died in 1683.

4. The Marquise de Maintenon (born as Françoise d' Aubigné) first met Louis IV while she was the governess of his illegitimate infant son, Louis Auguste. The King rewarded her by giving her the title of marquise. They had an affair and were secretly married after Maria Theresa's death in 1683 although she was never acknowledged as queen. Nevertheless, she exerted much influence over the King.

5. A headdress adorned with a decoration such as an egret's feather or a spray of jewels.

6. A silvery-white earth metalloid substance. In powdered form, it can be used in medicines or cosmetics.

7. Pierre Mignard (1612-95) was known primarily for his court paintings.

8. An official distributer of alms.

9. Louise Marie Thérèse (known as the Black Nun) lived from 1658-1730. Several sources indicate she was the daughter of Maria Theresa, but there is no definitive proof.

10. A dot is a dowry.

11. There are hundreds of these statues and paintings of the Virgin Mary in Western Europe.

"Hannah Elias: The Black Enchantress"

12. Andrew Haswell Green was a lawyer and city planner instrumental in such projects as the New York Public Library, the Bronx Zoo, the Museum of Natural History, and the Metropolitan Museum of Art. He proposed the consolidation of the different boroughs to form New York City in 1898.

13. Harry Kendall Thaw shot and killed architect Stanford White in 1906. Thaw had a long-standing hatred against White for his seduction of the then-sixteen-year-old model/actress Evelyn Nesbit, who would become Thaw's wife in 1905. Thaw had a history of mental illness and was acquitted by reason of insanity in a sensational trial in 1907. William Travers Jerome was the prosecuting attorney against Thaw. For more see Mary Cummings, *Saving Sin City: William Travers Jerome, Stanford White, and the Original Crime of the Century* (2018).

14. This contradicts what was said above that she was "fairly well-educated."

15. "Coon, Coon, Coon" was written by Gene Jefferson and Leo Friedman in 1900.

16. A Newport affair was an expensive, formal dining experience as exhibited in Newport, Rhode Island. It might also be a reference to a scandalous homosexual Newport incident in 1919 involving Navy personnel and civilians.

17. Buck-and-wing dances involved complex dance steps, often done in wooden-soled shoes, with highly animated hopping, energetic movement of the arms, springs into the air, and heel clicking. It combines Irish clogging and African rhythms.

18. There were eight Paris Expositions between 1855 and 1933. The one referred to here was probably the fifth, in 1900.

19. John R. Platt was a retired glass manufacturer when he met Elias, not a senator. There are a number of articles written in the New York *Times* on the case between June 1904 and January 1905.

20. Alfred E. Ommen was a lawyer and city magistrate who died in 1932.

"Remarks on the First Two Volumes of Sex and Race"

21. Francis Galton, the half-cousin of Charles Darwin, was a statistician, using numbers to study human differences. He coined the term eugenics in 1883 in the book *Inquiries into Human Faculty and Its Development.*

22. Rogers would, in fact, declare Lincoln a Negro in his pamphlet *The Five Negro Presidents* (1965). Lincoln is "said to be the illegitimate son of a Negro by Nancy Hanks" (8). After considering the evidence, Rogers writes, "It seems clear that those whites who said Lincoln was a Negro were right" (9).

23. Swedish historian Gunnar Myrdal's highly influential *An American Dilemma: The Negro Problem and Modern Democracy* (1944). Myrdal was specifically chosen because, as a non-American, it was felt he could provide a more objective view on the subject.

24. Rogers also writes about Beethoven in *100 Amazing Facts about the Negro* and in "Additional Great Men of Color" from *Great Men of Color*, vol. II. The question of Beethoven's race still is debated today. See, for example, Nora McGreevy, "Was Beethoven Black? Probably Not, but these Unsung Composers Were" *Smithsonian* June 23, 2020, and Philip Clark, "'Beethoven Was Black': Why the Radical Ideal Still has Power Today" *Guardian* September 7, 2020.

25. Henrique Dias was a 17th century Afro-Brazilian soldier and military leader. He is included in *Great Men of Color*, vol. II.

26. Munchausen syndrome (factitious disorder) is a mental disorder in which a person pretends illness or injury to themselves or others in order to gain attention. It is now called factitious disorder. Munchausen was a fictitious nobleman written about by German author Rudolf Erich Raspe in the novel *Baron Munchausen's Narrative of His Marvelous Travels and Campaigns in Russia* (1785).

27. Preston was an American Shakespearean scholar who wrote *Studies in Shakespeare: A Book of Essays* (1869).

28. Xenophanes was a Greek pre-Socratic poet and philosopher.

29. Strabo was a Greek historian, geographer, and philosopher who is best known for his *Geographica (Geography)* (ca. 7 BCE–23 CE).

30. Ignatius Donnelly was an American politician and amateur scientist whose best-known work is *Atlantis: The Antediluvian World* (1882).

31. Tacitus was a Roman senator and historian (ca. 56 CE–120 CE) best known for his *Histories* (105 CE) and *Annals* (117 CE).

32. Sir Francis Bacon wrote this in his essay "Of Envy" (1625).

33. This is a concept often attributed to Newton, but that does not appear in any of his writings.

"Race, A Spiritual, not a Scientific Problem"

34. The quotation is from a speech by Roosevelt for the Lincoln Dinner on February 13, 1905, at the New York City Republican Club.

35. Willem Adriaan Bonger was a Dutch criminologist who was a Marxist that believed there was a direct correlation between crime and social and economic factors.

36. Aleŝ Hrdlička was a Czech American anthropologist who maintained that mankind originated in Central Europe. His work was often used by supporters of eugenics.

37. Charles Robert Richet was a French physiologist who did pioneering work on immunology and was co-winner of a Nobel Prize in Physiology or Medicine in 1913. He believed in eugenics and the inferiority of Blacks, as expressed in his book *La Sélection Humaine* (1919).

38. *Beyond Good and Evil: Prelude to a Philosophy of the Future* (1886).

39. Grafton Elliott Smith, an Australian-British anatomist, and Egyptologist, particularly of the study of mummies. He believed that ancient Egypt was a major source for the diffusion of civilization.

40. Joseph Arthur de Gobineau was a French aristocrat known for developing the concept of the Aryan master race. He wrote *An Essay on the Inequality of the Human Races* (1853).

41. Frederick Ludwig Hoffman was an American statistician. His book *The Race Traits and Tendencies of the American Negro* (1896) claimed that African Americans were more susceptible to disease, which justified insurance companies charging them higher life insurance premiums.

42. In 1809 Jean-Baptiste Lamarck proposed a theory of evolution (in *Philosophie Zoologique*) stating that acquired traits could be inherited. It remained the prevailing view of evolution into the 1930s.

43. Francis Ashley-Montagu (born Israel Ehrenberg), better known as Ashley

Montagu, was a British-American anthropologist who wrote several works about race. He rejected the idea that one group is superior to another. He may now be best known for his biography *The Elephant Man: A Study in Human Dignity* (1971), which was a source for David Lynch's film in 1980.

44. Otto Kleinberg was a Canadian-American psychologist who examined differences in psychology between African-Americans and Native Americans, concluding that there was no scientific basis for racial superiority. He published *Race and Psychology* (1951).

45. Earnest Hooton was an American anthropologist known for his work on racial classification and on criminality. He wrote the popular *Up from the Ape* (1931).

46. Hermann Joseph Muller was an American geneticist and Nobel Prize winner in Physiology and Medicine (1946). He was particularly interested in the dangers of radiation.

47. Ruth Benedict was a well-known American anthropologist, especially noted for her work on culture and personality. She wrote a pamphlet for US soldiers "The Races of Mankind" (1943) making a scientific case against racism.

48. On January 25, 1942, a Black man, Cleo Wright, was killed by a mob for allegedly breaking into a home and stabbing a white woman in the abdomen. Wright was shot by a policeman and taken to jail because the local hospital would not treat him. A mob then took him, poured gasoline on his body, and he burned to death. None of those in the mob were ever punished.

49. The quotation is one of the founding principles of the Bahá' í faith.

50. Oswald Spengler was a German historian. His two-volume *The Decline of the West* (1918, 1922) posits the idea that modern society mirrors the decline of ancient societies in their death throes.

51. On June 20, 1943, almost 100,000 people, Black and white, engaged in acts of violence in Belle Isle Park in Detroit. 6,000 army troops were sent in to quell the disturbance. When it was over, nine whites and twenty-five Blacks were dead. Over 600 people were injured and damages amounted to two million dollars.

52. John Boyle O'Reilly was an Irish American poet, journalist, novelist, and activist. He was a strong advocate for Irish Home Rule as well as the rights of African Americans and the working class in America. He edited the Boston newspaper, the *Pilot*, for many years.

"Exception Is Taken to Criticism of 'Black Boy'"

1. Theophilus Lewis was a drama critic and writer best known for his reviews in *The Messenger*, where he worked closely with Rogers's friend, George Schuyler. He was a strong proponent that theater could bring about social change and advocated for positive images of African Americans in dramatic work. Lewis also worked for such periodicals as *Opportunity*, the New York *Amsterdam News* and *Commonweal* as well as several Catholic periodicals, including *America*.

2. Marie Bashkirtseff (born Maria Konstantinovna Bashkirtseva) was a Ukrainian/French artist and diarist. Her posthumous journal, begun when she was thirteen years of age, was published in 1887. She died of tuberculosis in 1884, just short of her 26th birthday.

3. To act in a pretentious manner.

4. Theodore G. Bilbo was a Democratic governor (1916–20, 1928–32) and senator

(1935–47) from Mississippi. He was a strong defender of segregation and a member of the Ku Klux Klan. Bilbo worked with members of the Universal Negro Improvement Association in the 1930s on a plan to repatriate African Americans to Liberia.

5. James Oliver Eastland was a senator from Mississippi from 1943–78 who was strongly anti-communist and anti-integration.

WORLD'S GREAT MEN OF COLOR

"How and Why This Book Was Written"

1. Edmund Burke, the Irish statesman and philosopher, made this statement in his *Reflections on the Revolution in France*, Vol. III (1790).

2. Amos 4:11 "'I have overthrown *some* of you, as God overthrew Sodom and Gomorrah, and ye were like a firebrand plucked out of the burning, yet have ye not returned to me,' saith the Lord."

3. According to the Church of Latter Day Saints' (Mormons) beliefs, the Seventies were the disciples mentioned in Luke 10: 1: "After these things the Lord appointed other seventy also, and sent them two and two before his face into every city and place, wither he himself would come." They were seen as special witnesses to God's grace.

4. *Paul et Virginie* is a novel (1788) by Jacques-Henri Bernardin de Saint-Pierre set in the French colony of Mauritius. The novel condemns class divisions and argues for the abolition of slavery. The novel was made into an opera in 1794 and adapted as a silent film in 1910.

5. Antonio Maceo Grajales was a general in the Cuban Army of Independence. He is included in Rogers's *World's Great Men of Color*, Vol. II.

6. Paul Lafargue was a Marxist, and Karl Marx' son-in-law. He was born in Cuba and wrote *The Right to Be Lazy* (1883), which argues for the need of leisure time for laborers.

7. Terence, (born Publius Terentious Afer), was a Roman African writer of comedies. Rogers includes him in *Great Men of Color*, vol. 1.

8. The iconoclastic Schuyler was a journalist and novelist and Rogers's longtime friend. He helped Rogers gain employment at *The Messenger* and *Pittsburgh Courier*, where he held editorial positions, and urged him to collect his short biographical sketches into a book (Schuyler 159). Schuyler wrote several novels in the 1930s that have gained attention in recent years, such as *Black No More* (1931). When he was younger, he supported socialism, racial mixing, and atheism; however, Schuyler became increasingly reactionary in his later years, supporting the Vietnam War, criticizing Martin Luther King Jr. after he won the Nobel Peace Prize in 1964, and joining the anti-Communist John Birch Society. For a sampling of his essays, see Jeffrey B. Leak, ed., *Rac(e)ing to the Right: Selected Essays George S. Schuyler* (2011).

9. *Children of the Sun*, published in 1918 by George Wells Parker, shows the African influence worldwide. Parker was an author much admired by Rogers.

10. *The African Abroad: Or, His Evolution in Western* Civilization is a two-volume set written by William Henry Ferris in 1913. It highlighted the African heritage of many important people including Aesop, Pushkin and Alexander Hamilton. It was a highly influential source for Rogers's works.

11. *Anacalypsis* (1836) is a two-volume work by Godfrey Higgins, a religious historian.

The title comes from a Greek word meaning "discovery" and is the opposite of an apocalypse. The book searches for the origins and development of religion.

12. Gerald Massey, an English poet and Egyptologist, wrote the two-volume *Book of the Beginnings* in 1881. The book expresses Massey's belief that all civilization derived from ancient Egypt. Massey wrote the two-volume *Ancient Egypt, the Light of the World* in 1907. The book discusses the connections between Jesus and the Egyptian god Horus. Massey's work was generally dismissed by academic scholars but was much admired by Rogers.

13. Caesar led two expeditions into Britain, in 55 and 54 BCE. Although Rome wasable to conquer much of the island, fighting continued for some five hundred years. Joseph Conrad in his novella *Heart of Darkness* (1899) considers the similarities of Africans at the end of the nineteenth century to what the Britons were like when Caesar first encountered them.

14. Dom Pedro II, de Alcántara was Emperor of Brazil from 1831-1889. His rule was so favorably seen that his nickname was the "Magnanimous." Rogers included him in *Great Men of Color*, vol. II.

15. Nathan Pinchback Toomer was known for his poetic novel *Cane* (1923), one of the most extraordinary works to emerge from the Harlem Renaissance. Toomer, a light-complexioned man, identified himself as "American" rather than white or Black. He married a white woman, Margery Latimer, in 1931. After her death, Toomer married another white woman, Marjorie Content, in 1934. Rogers wrote an appreciative article on Toomer in the New York *Amsterdam News* (January 2, 1929).

16. António Vieira was a Jesuit priest and writer born in Lisbon in 1608. His fifteen-volume *Sermões* (*Sermons*) was published between 1679–1748. He is included in *World's Great Men of Color*, vol. II.

17. Sir Richard Francis Burton was a 19th century British explorer who wrote of his travels to Asia, Africa, and the Americas.

18. José María de Heredia was a Cuban-born, nineteenth-century French poet.

19. The Forty Members were the members of the Académie Française, established in 1635, who act as the official regulators of the French language,

20. Sidonie-Gabrielle Colette was a French novelist, journalist, and actress. Her best known work is the novella *Gigi* (1944), basis for the film in 1958 and stage production in 1973 of the same name.

21. Francisco García Calderón (1834–1905) was a lawyer and legal analyst of Peruvian descent.

22. The term good neighbor policy goes back to the early twentieth century, but was really implemented during the administration of Franklin D. Roosevelt beginning in 1933. Its main principle was that the United States would not interfere in the domestic affairs of Latin American nations.

23. Lokmon (or Luqman) is thought to have come from Egypt or Nubia. He was known for his great wisdom. He lived around 1100 BCE. Rogers includes him in *Great Men of Color*, vol. I.

24. Ibrahim ibn al-Mahdi was a 9th-century Abbasid prince, poet, and singer. Rogers includes him in *Great Men of Color*, vol. I.

25. Harun al-Rashid was an 8th-century Caliph of the Abbasid dynasty centered in present-day Iraq and Iran. He ruled the Middle East at the height of Islamic world power.

26. The Abbasid dynasty descended from Muhammad's uncle, Abbas ibn Abdul-Muttalib.

27. Al-Ma'Mun was the second son of Harun al-Rashid and succeeded him as Caliph (813–33).

28. Al-Muktafi was Caliph of the Abbasid Caliphate from 902 to 908.

29. Ibn Khallikan was a 13th-century Islamic scholar and jurist. He worked on his important biographical dictionary from 1256 to 1274.

30. Francisco Fernandes was a Spanish physician who brought tobacco to Spain from Mexico in 1558. It was thought to have medicinal value at the time.

31. Jean Nicot was a French diplomat who introduced tobacco to the court in the sixteenth century.

32. Edward Hargraves, along with three other prospectors, is credited with discovering gold in Australia in 1851. He wrote of this in *Australia and Its Goldfields* (1855).

33. In *On Heroes, Hero-Worship, and the Heroic in History* (1841), British writer Thomas Carlyle maintained that "great Men should rule and that others should revere them." It was a belief Rogers generally followed in his historical portraits.

34. From Thomas Gray's "Elegy Written in a County Churchyard" (1751).

35. Nzinga (Ana Zhingha) was Queen of the Ambundu Kingdoms of Ndongo (1624–1663) and Matmaba (1631–1663), located in present-day northern Angola. Rogers includes her in *Great Men of Color*, vol. 1.

36. Rabah Zobeir (also Rabih az-Zubayr) was ruler of Bornu (an ancient sultanate then located on the western shores of Lake Chad, included since 1890 in British Nigeria), was a half-Arab, half-Negro chieftain. Rogers includes him in *Great Men of Color*, vol.1.

37. Shaka was the founder of Southern Africa's Zulu kingdom (1816–28). Rogers includes him in *Great Men of Color*, vol. 1.

38. Jean-Jacques Dessalines was a leader in the Haitian Revolution. In 1802 he became the first ruler of independent Haiti in 1804, leading a bloody reign, killing all the French on the island until he was overthrown and killed by his enemies in 1806.

39. Samori Ture (Samory Touré) resisted French colonial rule in the late nineteenth-century, establishing the Islamic Wassoulou Empire (also known as the Mandinka Empire), which he ruled from 1878–98.

40. English historian and politician John Dalberg-Acton (Lord Acton) stated in a letter to Bishop Mandell Creighton from April 5, 1887, "Power tends to corrupt, and absolute power corrupts absolutely. Great men are almost always bad men even when they exercise influence and not authority."

41. St. Benedict the Moor was an Italian Franciscan friar, later canonized. He was born to African slaves in Sicily in 1526. Rogers includes him in *Great Men of Color*, vol. II.

42. Dr. Albert E. Wiggam was an American psychologist and eugenicist who authored *A New Decalogue of Science* (1923). Rogers would certainly disagree with much of the racist findings in the book.

"Hatshepsut"

43. The Karnak temple complex was built between 2000 BCE and 100 CE. It is in Thebes and remains one of the most visited historical sites in Egypt.

44. The Upper and Lower Egypt, separated by the flow of the Nile River.

45. Horus was an Egyptian deity often depicted as having a falcon head and worshipped as god of kingship and the sky.

46. Nu (also spelled Nun) is the father of the gods and is deified as emerging from the primordial watery abyss.

47. Deir-el-Bahari is a large complex of temples and tombs opposite the city of Luxor.

48. Theodore M. Davis was a lawyer and Egyptologist who participated in many expeditions in the Valley of the Kings between 1902–13.

49. Robert Hichens was an English journalist, novelist, and travel writer. Many of his novels are set in Egypt, and he wrote a popular travel book, *The Spell of Egypt* (1910).

Jan Ernest Matzeliger

50. Turning shoes is a machine process utilizing a lathe to cut the shoe to the proper dimension.

51. Lasting is the process, a mold, that gives the shoe its final shape, holding the shoe in place so the outsole can be permanently attached.

52. Lyman Reed Blake invented a machine to attach the soles of shoes to the uppers in 1858. He sold the patent to Gordon McKay the following year. The two worked together to improve the process.

William Monroe Trotter

53. James Monroe Trotter was actually appointed to be Recorder of Deeds for the District of Columbia by President Grover Cleveland in 1887. The position was traditionally one given to African Americans, starting with Frederick Douglass in 1881.

54. The Niagara Movement was founded in 1905 by a group of African American leaders including Trotter and Du Bois. Trotter left the movement in 1907 after a number of disagreements with Du Bois. In 1911, Du Bois and many of the former members of the Niagara Movement formed the N. A. A. C. P.

55. The National Equal Rights League was formed in 1864 by Frederick Douglass and several other Black leaders. Trotter tried to revive the group, which had been in steady decline, in 1908.The creation of the N. A. A. C. P. drew away most of the League's members and it ceased operations in 1921.

56. In 1914 Trotter challenged Wilson over the segregation of government workers in the White House.

57. In 1917 Black soldiers of the Third Battalion, Twenty-Fourth Infantry, stationed at Camp Logan protested against their treatment, and of other African Americans, by the Houston police. Fifteen white civilians and four Black soldiers were killed by the protestors. Nineteen Black soldiers were executed and sixty-three imprisoned for life.

58. Wilson gave his famous Fourteen Points speech on January 8, 1918. The overall aim of the speech was to make preparations for conditions to end World War 1. African Americans paid particular notice to one point demanding rights, including self-determination for minority groups in foreign countries. Many Blacks felt that this point should apply to racial minorities within the United States, but Wilson never extended it within his own country.

59. It remains unclear whether Trotter's death was accidental or by suicide.

60. *Défi (French) means a* challenge, defiance, resistance.

NATURE KNOWS NO COLOR-LINE

1. The King of France says this to Bertram in Shakespeare's *All's Well That Ends Well* Act 2, Scene 3.

2. Evelyn Baring, 1st Earl of Cromer, was consul general of Egypt from 1883–1907.

3. Paul Topinard (1830–1911) was a French physician and anthropologist who was an advocate of polygenesis, the belief that humanity originated from several sources. He also initially believed cranial size determined mental capacity, with Europeans having the largest skull.

4. *City of God* is a book of Christian philosophy completed by Augustine in 426 A. D. The book contrasts those who indulge in the pleasures of the Earthly City with those who forgo such pleasures in quest of the eternal City of God.

5. Masoretic: the authoritative Hebrew and Aramaic texts of the 24 books of the Hebrew Bible (the Tanakh). It is the textual source for many translations of the Christian Old Testament.

6. The Circassians are an ethnic group native to Circassia in the northern Caucasus, near the Black Sea coast.

7. Mungo Park was an early Scottish explorer who traversed the Niger River in 1796. He led another expedition to the Niger in 1803. Park wrote an influential book on his explorations, *Travels in the Interior Districts of Africa* (1799).

8. Mansfield Parkyns wrote a book on the three years he spent in Abyssinia (1843–46), *Life in Abyssinia*, published in 1853.

AFRICA'S GIFT TO AMERICA

1. John Witherspoon DuBose, a Southern historian and journalist, wrote *The Life and Times of William Lowndes Yancey: A History of Political Parties in the United States from 1834–1864, Especially as to the Origins of the Confederate States* (1892). Yancey was a senator from Alabama from 1862–63, and was a champion of Southern secession.

2. A legation includes a diplomatic minster and their staff. It is below the rank of an embassy.

3. Sydney Smith was an English writer, wit, and Anglican cleric. His *Sermons* were published in two volumes in 1809.

4. James MacSparran was an Irish American clergyman who wrote *America Dissected* (1753).

5. Bayard Taylor was an American author, poet, and diplomat. He may be best known now for his travel writings and his translation of Goethe's *Faust* (1871).

6. Jamestown was settled in 1607, the first successful English settlement in North America; however, it suffered a deadly assault by the Powhatan Indians in 1622.

7. Sir John Hawkins was an English naval commander. In 1562 Hawkins brought 300 enslaved people from Sierra Leone to the Americas and traded them for sugar, hides, and pearls.

SHE WALKS IN BEAUTY

1. Phryne was a beautiful courtesan who was born around 371 B.C. in Boethia but lived most of her life in Athens. According to legend, she was charged with blasphemy,

but when Hyperides disrobed her and exposed her naked body to the judges, they then acquitted her. Many painters and sculptors were inspired by the story.

2. The Eleusinian Mysteries were annual secret initiation rites into the cult of Demeter and Persephone.

3. Epicurus was a Greek philosopher (341–270 B.C.) who maintained that the senses were the most reliable source of knowledge of the world.

4. In 1697 Charles Perrault published several fairy tales in *Histoires ou contes du temps passé, avec des moralités; Contes de ma mère l'Oye.* (*Stories or Tales from Times Past, with Morals: Tales of Mother Goose*). Some of the tales included are "Sleeping Beauty," "Little Red Riding Hood," and "Cinderella."

5. A two pence (tup'ny) coin had little value.

6. The ancient Greeks would insert a hollow tube with mutton fat into a woman's vagina to keep the cervix open, making conception less likely. The sheep's wool was thought to create a physical barrier between the semen and the cervix.

7. There was once a street called Stinking Lane (also called Butcher's Hall Lane) in London, named for the smell from the slaughterhouses located there. It is now called King Edward Street and runs from Newgate Street to Little Britain.

8. Orange girls, often scantily clad, were hired to sell fruits in English theaters, especially after the Restoration in 1660. They were often prostitutes and/or panders between members of the audience and actresses backstage. The most famous orange-girl was Nell Gwyn (1650–87) who started by selling fruits at thirteen before eventually becoming an actress and the long-term mistress of King Charles II.

9. Jean-Honoré Fragonard was an 18th century French painter and printmaker. His works were often thought to be hedonistic and erotic.

10. In Rembrandt's painting from 1643, the naked Bathsheba is being bathed by handmaidens while King David can be seen observing her from a distant tower.

11. A Fleet Marriage took place secretly without banns and away from the partners' home parish. Many such marriages were held at Fleet Prison, but these services were struck down by the Marriage Act of 1753. If Eva and Mr. Pym were to have had a Fleet Marriage, that would not be consistent with the capture of Prince Lucien, which occurred in 1809. See next note. In general, the novel seems to be set during the Napoleonic Wars (1803–15).

12. Lucien Bonaparte was Napoleon's younger brother. The two had quarreled when Lucien questioned his older brother's decision to declare himself Emperor. Lucien also rejected Napoleon's desire to marry him off to a Bourbon Spanish princess. While attempting to flee to the United States, Lucien was captured by the British in 1809. After Napoleon's return to France from exile on the island of Elba in 1815, the two brothers reconciled, but Napoleon was soon defeated at the Battle of Waterloo.

13. Admiral Horatio, Lord Nelson, led the British navy to victory over the French and Spanish fleet at the Battle of Trafalgar on October 21, 1805.

"CIVIL WAR CENTENNIAL, MYTH AND REALITY"

1. The historic Brown v Board of Education of Topeka ruling, desegregating public schools.

2. In 1957, nine teenage Black girls were harassed by a crowd of whites when integrating Central High School in Little Rock.

3. Earl Warren was Chief Justice of the Supreme Court from 1953 to 1969 and the governor of California from 1943–53.

4. June Purcell Guild's *Black Laws of Virginia* was published in 1936. The book presents a chronology and summary of all the laws dealing with Blacks in Virginia. Purcell Guild was a social worker and attorney born in Columbus, Ohio, but lived in Richmond, Virginia for thirty-five years.

5. Hood's Brigade was a Texas infantry brigade active from 1861–65 that was considered one of the elite units in the Confederate army. It was initially commanded by Brigadier General Louis T. Wigfall and then by Colonel John Bell Hood.

6. President Eisenhower.

7. General Ulysses S. Grant III (1881–1968) served in World War I and II as well as other wars. He was chairman of the American Civil War Centennial Commission from 1957–1961.

8. The Military Order of the Loyal Legion of the United States, organized in 1865 by officers of the armed forces that had served for the Union. The organization continues with descendants of the original members and others who share their ideals.

9. The USS Queen of the West was a sidewheel steamer ram boat that greatly aided a Union victory in the Battle of Memphis. It was captured by Southern forces in 1863 and was repaired by the Confederates. It was returned to battle before being sunk by Union forces later that year.

10. Lee wrote this in a letter to General Philip St. George Coke in 1861.

11. Henry uttered these words at the First Continental Congress in Philadelphia in 1774.

12. Sara Agnes Rice Pryor, born in Virginia, moved to New York City after the Civil War. She wrote memoirs, histories, and novels that often dealt with the war. She renounced the Confederacy after moving North.

13. Lee wrote this in a letter to his wife, Mary Randolph Custis Lee, on December 27, 1856.

14. Alexander Stephens, a native of Georgia, said these words in what is known as the Cornerstone Speech delivered at the Athenaeum in Savannah, Georgia, on March 21, 1861.

15. "One may smile and smile and be a villain." Hamlet says this about Claudius in *Hamlet*, Act 1, scene V.

16. Adolf Eichmann was one of the organizers of the Holocaust. He oversaw the deaths of millions of prisoners. After the war, he was captured, but escaped. He was finally captured in Argentina in 1960 and smuggled to Israel where he was tried and hanged in 1962.

17. In February 1861, a group of politicians met in Washington, DC, to try to prevent the secession of those eight southern and border states that had not yet broken with the Union.

18. James Hammond was Senator from South Carolina from 1857–60 and governor from 1842–44.

19. The flag had a single five-pointed star on a dark blue field. It was used to represent several Southern territories and also employed as an unofficial Confederate flag in early 1861. Rogers is probably referring to a marching song from 1861 with this name (also known as "We Are a Band of Brothers").

20. J. Palmer Gaillard was mayor of Charleston, South Carolina, from 1959–75.

21. Rogers is referring to the end of Reconstruction in 1877.

22. Lincoln made these remarks in his first debate with Stephen A. Douglas at Ottawa, Illinois, on August 21, 1858.

23. Henry Clay had a long career as a senator or congressman from Kentucky. Called the Great Compromiser, Clay supported slavery, but his main objective was to preserve the Union. Lincoln gave his eulogy on July 6, 1852.

24. William Lloyd Garrison, leading abolitionist and editor of the *Liberator* newspaper.

25. Wendell Phillips was an abolitionist and supporter of Indian rights.

26. Lyman Beecher, Presbyterian Minister and a leading advocate of Temperance, was the father of writer Harriet Beecher Stowe and Henry Ward Beecher, a clergyman, social reformer, and abolitionist.

27. Lincoln had made several plans to move Blacks out of the United States, possibly to Costa Rica. He also purchased the small uninhabited island of Île à Vache from Haiti in 1862. See Phil Magness' *Colonization after Emancipation* and Eric Foner's *The Fiery Trial*. The talk of repatriation ceased after the Emancipation Proclamation.

28. Winfield Scott was a United States Army General from 1814–61. He was the leading general in the Mexican-American War. Scott was the presidential candidate of the Whig Party in 1852 but lost to Franklin Pierce, the Democratic candidate.

29. Wilson's Creek was an early Confederate victory in a battle fought near Springfield, Missouri, on August 10, 1861.

30. Ball's Bluff was a Union army defeat in a battle in Loudoun County, Virginia, October 21, 1861.

31. William H. Seward was Secretary of State (1861–69) and a senator (1849–61) and governor (1839–42) from New York. He was injured in a separate assassination attempt the night of Lincoln's murder. He may be best known for his purchase of Alaska from Russia in 1867, known at the time as Seward's Folly.

32. Psalms 68: 31: "Princes shall come out of Egypt; Ethiopia shall soon stretch out her hands unto God."

33. In the second battle of Bull Run, Robert E. Lee and Stonewall Jackson led an attack on the Union army commanded by Major General John Pope in 1862. Pope was forced to retreat.

34. Charles A. Dana was a reporter who was made investigating agent of the War Department. Lincoln considered him the eyes of the Administration. He frequently gave reports on the fitness of Union generals and other personnel.

35. Henry Warren Slocum, Sr. was a Union general. He was commander of the left wing of William T. Sherman's army during his March to the Sea.

36. Chapin's Farm, New Market Heights: The Battle at Chaffin's Farm and New Market Heights occurred in Virginia on September 29–30, 1864. Northern forces attempted to cut off the railroad into Petersburg. There were about 5,000 casualties in the fighting, at least 3,300 Union forces. However, the battle forced Lee to draw forces from elsewhere to win the battle, weakening his other forces. African American troops from the 38th Colored Infantry Unit fought in the battle.

37. Bruce Catton was an American historian who is best-known for his writings on the Civil War. He won a Pulitzer Prize for his book, *A Stillness at Appomattox* (1953).

Works Cited

Adichie, Chimamanda Ngozie. "The Danger of a Single Story," TED Global 2009. www.ted.com/talks

Adler, Karen S. "'Always Leading Our Men in Service and Sacrifice': Amy Jacques Garvey, Feminist Black Nationalist." *Gender and Society* 6.3 (1992): 346–75.

Asukile, Thabiti. "J. A. Rogers' "'Jazz at Home': Afro-American Jazz in Paris During the Jazz Age." *Black Scholar* 40.3 (Fall 2010): 22–35.

———. "Joel Augustus Rogers: Black International Journalism, Archival Research, and Black Print Culture." *The Journal of African American History* 95.3–4 (2010): 322–47.

———. "Joel Augustus Rogers' Reflection and End of Life Admiration of Marcus Garvey in New York" *Afro-Americans in New York Life and History* 37.2 (July 2013): 41–79.

———. "J.A. Rogers: The Scholarship of an Organic Intellectual." *Black Scholar* 36. 2–3 (2006): 35–50.

Calvin, Floyd J. "J. A. Rogers Waited 20 Years for His 'Big Moment' in Ethiopia: Calvin Gives Courier Readers 'Intimate Story of Man Who Will Give Them the Truth about War.'" Pittsburgh Courier (November 23, 1935): A1.

———."Rogers Back in U.S. with Startling Facts on Suppressed Race History." Pittsburgh *Courier* (October 31, 1931): 3.

Carroll, Frederick James. "Race News: How Black Reporters and Readers Shaped the Fight for Racial Justice, 1877–1978," PhD diss., William and Mary, 2012.

Claborn, John P. "Ecology of the Color Line: Race and Nature in American Literature, 1895–1941." PhD diss., University of Illinois at Urbana-Champaign, 2012.

Clarke, John Henrik. Ed. and Intro. *World's Great Men of Color*. 2 vols. J. A. Rogers Simon & Schuster, 1972. Vol. 1: ix–xvi.

Drake, St. Clare. *Black Folk Here and There*., Diasporic Africa Press, 2014.

Du Bois, W .E. B. "An Array of Books," Crisis September 1924.

———. *The World and Africa: An Inquiry into the Part Africa Has Played in World History*. Viking Press, 1946.

Fabre, Michel. *From Harlem to Paris: Black American Writers in France, 1840–1980*. U. of Illinois P, 1991.

Gates, Henry Louis, Jr. *100 Amazing Facts About the Negro*. Pantheon, 2017.

Harrison, Hubert. *A Hubert Harrison Reader*. Ed. Jeffrey B. Perry. Wesleyan UP, 2001.

Helga Martha (Rogers) Andrews. "Obituary." www.legarcy.com/obituaries/sptimes/obituary.

Holder, Calvin B. "The Causes and Composition of West Indian Immigration to New York City, 1900–1952." *Afro-Americans in New York Life and History* 11.1 (January 1987): 7–26.

Hutchinson, George. *The Harlem Renaissance in Black and White*. Harvard UP, 1995.

Katz, William Loren. *A Teachers' Guide to American Negro History*. Quadrangle Books, 1968.

Lewis, David Levering, ed. Langston Hughes, "The Negro Artist and the Racial Mountain." In *A Portable Harlem Renaissance Reader*. Penguin, 1995. 91–95.

Logan, Rayford. *The Betrayal of the Negro: From Rutherford Hayes to Woodrow Wilson*. Collier, 1965.
Martin, Tony, ed.. *African Fundamentalism: A Literary and Cultural Anthology of Garvey's Harlem Renaissance* Majority Press, 1991.
Moses, Wilson Jeremiah. *Afrotopia: The Roots of African American Popular History*.Cambridge University Press, 1998.
Owens, Edward Bryan Cooper. "'Know Your History': J. A. Rogers, Vindicationist History and the Use of Black Images." Master's thesis, Clark Atlanta University, 2006.
Parfait, Claire. "'Un-sung Heroes of Afro-American Historiography': The Case of Joel Augustus Rogers" *IdeAs* 16 (2020). https://journals.openedition.org/ideas/9256.
Perry, Jeffrey B. *Hubert Harrison: The Voice of Harlem Radicalism, 1883–1918*. Columbia UP, 2009.
Peters, Linda Ray. "The Life and Works of Joel Augustus Rogers." M.A. Thesis, Northeastern Illinois U, 1978.
Pinckney, Darryl. *Out There: Mavericks of Black Literature*. Civitas Book, 2002.
Rashidi, Runoko. "Life and Legacy of Joel Augustus Rogers: Chronicler of a Glorious African Past." Atlanta *Black Star* (May 9, 2014).
Rogers, Helga M. Biographical Sketch by Helga M. Rogers. 1995. 7–10.
Rogers, Joel Augustus. "Remarks on the First Two Volumes of Sex and Race."*Sex and Race*. Helga M. Rogers, 1944. Vol. III. 1–X.
———. "Young Novelist tells How Pullman Porters Profit During Leisure Moments." Pittsburgh *Courier* (May 10, 1924): 3.
———. "How and Why This Book Was Written." *World's Great Men of Color*: 1946. Simon & Schuster, 1972. Vol. 1: 1–24.
Sandoval, Valerie. "The Bran of History: An Historiographic Account of the Work of J. A. Rogers." *Schomburg Center for Research in Black Culture Journal* 1.4 (Spring 1978): 5–7, 16–19.
"Scholars Mourn Rogers' Death: Split on Works." *Jet* (April 14, 1966): 26–27.
Schuyler, George. *Black and Conservative: The Autobiography of George S. Schuyler*. Arlington House, 1966.
Simba, Malik. "Joel Augustus Rogers: Negro Historian in History, Time, and Space." *Afro-Americans in New York Life and History* 30.2 (July 2006): 47–67.
Sinnette, Elinor Des Verney. *Arthur Alfonso Schomburg: Black Bibliophile & Collector*. New York Public Library & Wayne State University Press, 1989.
Stovall, Tyler. *Paris Noir: African Americans in the City of Lights*. Houghton Mifflin, 1996.
Thorpe, Earl. *Black Historians: A Critique*. William Morrow and Company, Inc. 1971.
Turner Moore, Joyce, with the assistance of W. Burghardt Turner. *Caribbean Crusaders and the Harlem Renaissance*. U. of Illinois Press, 2005.
Turner, W. Burghardt. "J. A. Rogers: Portrait of an Afro-American Historian." *Black Scholar* 6 (January-February 1975): 32–39.
Watson, Traci. "Mummy DNA Unravels Ancient Egyptians' Ancestry." *Nature* 546 (June 1, 2017): 17.
Willis, John Ralph. "World's Great Men of Color." *New York Times* (February 4, 1973): 342.

Index